Producing **BOLLYWOOD**

Producing
BOLLYWOOD

INSIDE THE CONTEMPORARY
HINDI FILM INDUSTRY

Tejaswini Ganti

Duke University Press   Durham and London   2012

Printed in the United States of America on acid-free paper ∞

Designed by Heather Hensley

Typeset in Chaparral Pro by Tseng Information Systems, Inc.

Library of Congress Cataloging-in-Publication Data appear on
the last printed page of this book.

Duke University Press gratefully acknowledges the Humanities
Initiative Grant-in-Aid, New York University, which provided
funds toward the production of this book.

For my hero,
Vipul,

and our two stars,
Saahir and Siddharth

CONTENTS

ACKNOWLEDGMENTS

As in the production of a feature film, there are scores of people who comprise the opening and closing credits of this particular project. Over the numerous years it took for this book to evolve from my dissertation (as I had warned my informants in Bombay, the only thing that perhaps takes longer than making a Hindi film is writing an academic book), I have incurred a number of intellectual, social, and personal debts. It has been a long journey and I have many people to thank for their support, friendship, feedback, advice, wisdom, and insight. I would like to express my deep gratitude to Ken Wissoker of Duke University Press for the tremendous patience and understanding with which he awaited the completion of this manuscript. I thank him for not giving up on me and for his unceasing enthusiasm and excitement about my project over the last decade. My initial fieldwork in Bombay was supported by the American Institute of Indian Studies Junior Fellowship. Subsequent fieldwork in Bombay has been supported by research and travel funds made available by Haverford College, Connecticut College, and New York University. The Humanities Initiative at New York University awarded a Grant-in-Aid to support the production of the book and I thank Terry Harrison and Jane Tylus for their guidance in the application process.

Arjun Appadurai and the late Carol Breckenridge played a key role in transforming my personal passion for Hindi cinema into an academic pursuit. My interactions with Arjun and Carol, when I was a graduate student at the University of Pennsylvania, where I also briefly worked as an editorial assistant at the journal *Public Culture*, opened up new horizons of possibility and avenues of inquiry regarding what constituted appropriate topics of study. If it were not for their interest and encouragement of my interest in Hindi cinema, I may have never embarked on this particular scholarly journey. Lila Abu-Lughod and Barry Dornfeld were instrumental in my decision to focus on producers and the production of Hindi cinema rather than audiences and their consumption practices, at a time when that was the prevailing trend. I thank Lila for her rightful skepticism of my initially proposed research about film audiences in Bombay, which made me reorient my project entirely, and for Barry's insights on how to carry out fieldwork among film producers. Other individuals—from whom I learned a great deal and who were critical in shaping my intellectual outlook and the analytical framework I brought to my research—include Faye Ginsburg, Webb Keane, David Ludden, Owen Lynch, and Toby Miller. Even if not readily transparent, their insights about media, language, history, political economy, cultural policy, social relations, and everyday life have made their way into this book.

There are many people in Bombay I would like to thank for making my research and this book possible. For providing me with my initial home when I first began my fieldwork, I thank my great-uncle and great-aunt, Lakshmanrao and Durga Pappu; I thank Sandra and Sarosh Irani, and Darshana, Ashwini, Alok, and Priyanka Gupta for their hospitality during the later phases of my fieldwork. I am especially grateful to Avantika and Jinx Akerkar, Tanuja Chandra, Anupama Chopra, Ranjan Garg, Sandra and Sarosh Irani, Ajay and the late Kiran Khanna, Sri Prakash Menon, Sylvia and Thelma Pedder, and Sheena Sippy for introducing me to key people within the Hindi film industry, which set the ball rolling for my research. I thank Somi Roy for inviting me to participate in the Mahindra Indo-American Arts Council Film Festival (2009) and Myna Mukherjee for inviting me to be a part of the Engendered I-View Film Festival (2010) programming, which provided me with further opportunities to observe and interact with Hindi filmmakers in New York City.

With respect to members of the Hindi film industry, I would like to thank the following people for their assistance, generosity, hospitality, and kindness—for taking me into their homes and work spaces, for their patience and willingness to put up with my endless questioning, and for the enthusiasm with which they received my research project: Taran Adarsh, Rauf Ahmad, Javed Akhtar, the late Mukul Anand, Shabana Azmi, Amitabh Bachchan, Raj Kumar Bajaj, Rajjat Barjatya, Ritha Bhaduri, Vashu Bhagnani, Ashish Bhatnagar, Mahesh Bhatt, Mukesh Bhatt, Pooja Bhatt, the late Sachin Bhaumick, Kamna Chandra, Aditya Chopra, the late B. R. Chopra, Pamela Chopra, Vicky Chopra, Yash Chopra, Lala Damani, Madhuri Dixit, Nester D'Souza, Sanjay Dutt, Subhash Ghai, Meghna Ghai-Puri, Ravi Gupta, Sutanu Gupta, the late Nazir Husain,

Honey Irani, Rumi Jaffery, Ayesha Jhulka, Dinar Kadam, Rashesh Kanakia, the late Shammi Kapoor, Shashi Kapoor, Aamir Khan, Mansoor Khan, Shah Rukh Khan, Shaukat Khan, Amit Khanna, Punkej Kharabanda, Manisha Koirala, Sameer Malhotra, John Matthew Mathan, R. Mohan, the late Hrishikesh Mukherjee, Firoz Nadiadwala, Komal Nahta, Pritish Nandy, Govind Nihalani, Omar Qureishi, Dinesh Raheja, Rajesh Roshan, Rakesh Roshan, Gyan Sahay, Bharat Shah, Sameer Sharma, Mustaq Sheikh, Manmohan Shetty, Rakesh Shreshta, Shravan Shroff, the late G. P. Sippy, Ramesh Sippy, Rohan Sippy, Sunhil Sippy, Bhawana Somaya, Chitra Subramaniam, Dalip Tahil, and Viveck Vaswani.

Certain individuals, with whom I have remained in contact for over a decade, deserve special mention and my heartfelt appreciation and gratitude for their friendship and the innumerable ways they helped with my research, my stays in Bombay, and the writing of this book: Vikram Bhatt for the openness, trust, and warmth with which he included me in his filmmaking life; Anupama Chopra for being an incredible source of anecdotes, advice, and contacts; Sanjay Jha for his enthusiasm and tireless efforts to facilitate my research; Anjum Rajabali for the most scintillating discussions about filmmaking, filled with wit and insight; Sharmishta Roy for making me feel a part of her family and opening my eyes to the visual, aesthetic, and material dimensions of filmmaking; and Shyam Shroff for his ready willingness to help me in any way big or small, including most recently helping me obtain film stills and providing images of multiplexes for the book. This book would have been a pale shadow of itself if it were not for my interaction, conversations, and friendship with these individuals.

Moving from the process of research to the task of crafting and writing, I have benefited tremendously from several friends and colleagues, near and far. Brian Larkin, Sri Rupa Roy, and Christine Walley deserve special thanks as they have been enthusiastic and supportive of this project since its inception as a dissertation, and I have always been able to rely on them for close and insightful readings of its various iterations. Richard Allen, Janaki Bakhle, Ira Bhaskar, Dipesh Chakrabarty, Lawrence Cohen, Maris Gillette, Lalitha Gopalan, Preminda Jacob, Kajri Jain, Carla Jones, Priya Joshi, Smita Lahiri, Mark Liechty, Rochona Majumdar, Purnima Mankekar, Ranjani Mazumdar, William Mazzarella, Gary McDonogh, Shalini Shankar, Aradhana Sharma, Debra Spitulnik, and Patricia Spyer have all been important interlocutors from whom it has been a pleasure to learn, and with whom to share and discuss my work, formally at conferences and seminars as well as through informal conversations and exchanges.

Members of the two writing groups, which have engaged the most closely with this book—Ayala Fader, Lotti Silber, and Karen Strassler; Sonia Das, Haidy Geismar, Anne Rademacher, and Noelle Stout—not only provided valuable feedback on drafts of chapters, which helped me hone my arguments and clarify my focus, but also created a terrific sense of community and solidarity that helped alleviate the isolation that accompanies intensive writing.

The Department of Anthropology at New York University offers a very collegial and nurturing environment for junior faculty. For someone juggling the demands of teaching, scholarship, and parenting young children, I am very grateful for the way the department protects its junior members from undue administrative work. Through the process of writing this book, my colleagues Bruce Grant, Aisha Khan, David Ludden (in History), Emily Martin, Sally Merry, Fred Myers, Rayna Rapp, and Susan Rogers have been wonderfully supportive and generous in numerous ways—from loaning me books to offering suggestions for further reading, discussing the classics of anthropology, answering my queries about theory, or hearing me think out loud. Two colleagues have had the most sustained involvement with this manuscript: Bambi Schieffelin and Faye Ginsburg, whose office doors and welcoming natures were always open to my requests for advice and feedback. For all queries related to language, I could rely on Bambi to hear me out, offer necessary suggestions, and point me in the right direction. Faye has been an invaluable mentor. From reading drafts of chapters to alleviating some of my teaching burdens to boosting my morale, her guidance, support, good wishes, and immense positive energy have been indispensable in enabling me to finish this book.

I would also like to thank the following individuals, who offered very concrete and specific forms of assistance in the writing of this book: the three anonymous reviewers for Duke University Press, who provided close readings, detailed feedback, and invaluable suggestions about the manuscript; Aliya Curmally and Priyadarshini Shankar, who helped transcribe the bulk of my interviews; Pankaj Rishi Kumar, who took wonderful photographs of key single-screen theaters in Bombay on my request; Neepa Majumdar, who so graciously shared relevant chapters of her in-press manuscript; Anurag Bhargava, for introducing me to the Red Herring reports and always answering my varied questions about finance, stock markets, and corporate dealings; Debraj Ray, for his advice about exchange rates, PPP income, and how to determine the number of cinema halls in India; Omkar Goswami and Vivek Srivastava, for calculating the Purchasing Power Parity rate between the U.S. dollar and the Indian rupee; Jehil Thakkar of KPMG, for sending me the 2009 FICCI/KPMG Report; Kulmeet Makkar of the Film and Television Producers Guild of India, for his help in obtaining film stills; Rohit Sobti and Poonam Surjani of Yash Raj Films, Rajjat Barjatya and P. S. Ramanathan of Rajshri Productions, and Apoorva Mehta and Garima Vohra of Dharma Productions, for their prompt response to my request for film stills; Jennie Tichenor, for her constant administrative support and skillful navigation of NYU bureaucracy, which made it possible for me to employ a research assistant in 2009 while working on the manuscript; Ishita Srivastava, my fabulous research assistant for whom no task was impossible—from trying to track down obscure references to indexing numerous issues of *Film Information*; David Privler and Kathleen Keane, for helping with the crucial tasks of printing, scanning, and mailing the manuscript; Leigh Barnwell at Duke, for her assistance with all of the details in preparing the final, formatted version of the manuscript; and Elaine Kozma for her assistance in preparing the final bibliography.

My entire family—parents, grandparents, brother, aunts, uncles, cousins, and in-laws—has been a bedrock of support and encouragement throughout the long process of writing this book. My earliest memories of the cinema, in fact my early socialization as an avid Hindi film-viewer, are a result of my childhood spent with my maternal grandparents, Subbarao and Venkatalakshmi Pappu, who were keen film-goers. While they witnessed the completion of my dissertation, I wish they were still here to witness its transformation into a book. I regard its publication as a sign of their blessings.

My most sustained period of writing coincided with the birth of my second son, Siddharth, and I could not have finished this book without the nurturing and affectionate childcare provided by Meghan Harrington and Nasim Yaqoob. My older son, Saahir, who has possessed a maturity well beyond his years from the time he could talk, nourishes my soul with the sweetness and purity of his love. His concern for my progress, and selfless emotional investment in the book's completion, are humbling reminders of the world beyond my desk and computer. Siddharth, too young to understand why his Amma spent seven days a week at the office, but old enough to protest it, made coming home from long days of writing joyous with his hugs, smiles, and laughter. Since mere words cannot describe my husband, Vipul Agrawal's indispensable role in this endeavor, and there are not enough words in Telugu, Hindi, and English combined to convey my love and appreciation for him, I take recourse to our other common language, that of Hindi cinema—*baadal bijli, chandan paani, jaisa apna pyaar, lena hoga janam humein kayi kayi baar; itna madhir, itna madhur, tera mera pyaar, lena hoga janam humein kayi kayi baar. . . .*

How the Hindi Film Industry
Became "Bollywood"

"Yeah, I think this question is a little too late now, because it will
change I think, by the time your book comes out."

I was interviewing Shah Rukh Khan—one of the most successful stars of the prolific and box-office–oriented Hindi-language
film industry based in Bombay—for my dissertation research in
1996.[1] We were at Mehboob Studios, located in Bombay's western
suburb of Bandra,[2] where Khan was shooting for the film *Duplicate*; my first question concerned the condescension and distaste
expressed toward popular Hindi cinema by Indian elites and the
English-language media. Khan continued, "I believe this attitude
will change, and I can say that with a lot of conviction, because
I would also blame myself for being in that category say four or
five years ago. I would also think it was not fashionable to like
Hindi films." Little did I realize at the time how prescient his
statements would be. Although my book took much longer than
Khan ever would have anticipated, he was absolutely right in his
predictions about the transformation of attitudes toward popular
Hindi cinema—from contempt to celebration—with Khan himself being an important figure in these changes.[3] Hailed by his
biographer as "the face of a glittering new India" and "a modern-
day god" (Chopra 2007: 11), Khan's celebrity has extended globally across a variety of domains: from the financial—being the
first Indian actor to ring the opening bell of the NASDAQ stock
exchange in February 2010—to the scholarly—being the subject

of an international conference, "Shah Rukh Khan and Global Bollywood," held at the University of Vienna in October 2010.

That Khan represents a "glittering new India" is indicative of the other transformation that has taken place over the course of my research: the change in global representations and perceptions of India—from a "Third World" country to the "next great economic superpower" (Elliott 2006).[4] The Hindi film industry, now better known as "Bollywood," has been an important accoutrement of India's resignification in the global arena, one that is deployed both by the Indian state and the corporate sector in efforts to brand the country as an economic powerhouse in arenas such as the annual World Economic Forum held at Davos, Switzerland. Bollywood is a presence at Davos mainly through its music and its stars; in 2009, Amitabh Bachchan, one of the biggest stars of Indian cinema, was awarded the World Economic Forum's Crystal Award for "outstanding excellence in the field of culture" (Upala 2009). Bachchan reflected about the honor on his blog, "I took pride in the fact that an honor such as the Crystal Award was bestowed on me, an Indian from the world of escapist commercial cinema, a cinema which 50–60 years ago was not such a bright profession to be in. Children from good homes were not encouraged to go anywhere near it: an activity that was considered infra dig.[5] But look how this very escapist cinema had progressed through the years, where today in an International forum of some eminence, I was able to stand and represent my fraternity and my country in a most humbling recognition" (in Lavin 2009).

This book is an examination of the very narrative of progress, respectability, and arrival to which Bachchan alludes in his remarks. It is the story of how the Hindi film industry became "Bollywood": a globally recognized and circulating brand of filmmaking from India, which is often posited by the international media as the only serious contender to Hollywood in terms of global popularity and influence. As an anthropologist, my central focus is on the social world of Hindi filmmakers, their filmmaking practices, and their ideologies of production.[6] I examine the ensuing changes in the field of Hindi film production (Bourdieu 1993), especially those related to the cultural and social status of films and filmmakers—as well as the political economy of filmmaking—and locate them in Hindi filmmakers' own efforts to accrue symbolic capital, social respectability, and professional distinction. These efforts have been enabled by the neoliberal restructuring of the Indian state and economy—intensified from 1991, after the IMF mandated structural adjustment policies—resulting in a dramatically altered media landscape, marked first by the entry of satellite television and then by the emergence of the multiplex theater.[7] I argue that the Hindi film industry's metamorphosis into Bollywood would not have been possible without the rise of neoliberal economic ideals in India. By tracing the transformations of the Hindi film industry for over a decade—one marked by tremendous social and economic change in India—this book provides ethnographic insight into the impact of neoliberalism on cultural production in a postcolonial setting.

When I first began my research about the social world and production practices of the Hindi film industry more than a decade ago, the dominant discourse about mainstream Hindi cinema—generated by Indian political, intellectual, social, and media elites—derided it as an intellectually vacuous, aesthetically deficient, and culturally inauthentic form.[8] Although the images, sounds, and styles of Hindi cinema had been a ubiquitous part of the urban landscape in India for decades (with the exception of the four southern states, which have popular filmmaking traditions in their own respective languages), popular Hindi films were frequently criticized or dismissed as an "escape for the masses"—as in Bachchan's remarks about "escapist commercial cinema"—in the mainstream press, government documents, and well-appointed elite drawing rooms. For example, when I was introduced as someone studying the film industry for my PhD during a dinner party in Bandra hosted by my upstairs neighbor about ten days before my interview with Khan, one of the host's friends launched into a diatribe about the absurdity of Hindi cinema, exclaiming, "What is there to study? All they do is run around trees! I mean how is it possible that such bad films get made? I don't understand how people can stand to watch them, and what does it say about the mentality of the common Indian that he likes such nonsense!" Even those who were more sympathetic to my research, like journalists and others working within the media world of Bombay, expressed their scorn for the film world by asserting that I should only meet the handful of people (according to them) in the industry with the requisite intelligence and education to understand my project, and therefore able to help me.

Now as I write this introduction in 2010, these disdainful attitudes toward my research belong to another era. One of the most notable changes since the onset of the millennium, which Khan had predicted, is the way Hindi cinema, along with the film industry more broadly, has acquired greater cultural legitimacy from the perspective of the state, the English-language media, and English-educated/speaking elites in India. Hindi cinema and Bombay filmmakers are circulating through, and being celebrated in, a variety of sites redolent with cultural and symbolic capital—from prestigious international film festivals like Cannes and Toronto, to elite academic institutions such as Harvard and Cambridge.[9] This enhanced status of Hindi cinema arises from an interconnected set of processes: the increasing academic interest and study of popular Hindi cinema by scholars located or trained in the Anglo-American academy; the avid consumption of these films by the South Asian diaspora; the increasing recognition and celebration of Hindi films in Western cultural spaces; and the emergence of new global markets for Hindi cinema. Underlying these processes is a less explored dimension, however: Hindi filmmakers' own drive for distinction and greater social acceptance, which is the focus of this book.

The rising cultural legitimacy of popular Hindi cinema is a result of what I argue is an ongoing process of the "gentrification" of Hindi cinema and the Hindi film industry. Gentrification, which in its most basic definition means to renovate or convert an area to conform to middle-class taste (OED 2006), is an apt metaphor to describe the changes occurring in the Hindi film industry, which has been concerned with respectability and middle-class acceptance since the 1930s. Conventional accounts of popular Hindi cinema had described it as a cultural form concerned with mass appeal and representing the sensibilities of the slum (Nandy 1998). Despite the close identification on the part of scholars and journalists between Hindi cinema and the working poor, or "masses," of Indian society,[10] what I had observed during a decade of fieldwork, from 1996 to 2006, was that members of the Hindi film industry consistently distanced themselves from such audiences, having identified with and sought acceptance, approval, and respect from more elite segments of Indian society. I characterize this desire for respectability and elite approval as the Hindi film industry's drive to gentrify itself, its audiences, and its film culture. Just as urban gentrification is marked by a vocabulary of progress, renovation, and beautification, which is predicated upon exacerbating social difference through the displacement of poor and working-class residents from urban centers, the gentrification of Hindi cinema is articulated through a discourse of quality, improvement, and innovation that is often based upon the displacement of the poor and working class from the spaces of production and consumption.

The results of this gentrification are evident in three main ways. First, since the mid-1990s, in the films themselves—both in their narrative content and mise-en-scène—there has been a growing concern with wealthy protagonists and the near-complete erasure of the working class, urban poor, and rural dwellers once prominent as protagonists/heroes in Hindi films. When films do focus on non-elites, they still represent an elitist perspective in that the protagonists are frequently rendered as gangsters or as part of some sort of criminal milieu, rather than being the unmarked everyman protagonist of earlier eras of Hindi cinema.[11] Additionally, more and more films are being shot in North America, the United Kingdom, Australia, and Europe rather than in India; thus India itself is increasingly erased from the films.[12] Second, a prominent discourse of respectability, connected to the class and educational background of filmmakers, as well as a newly emergent discourse of corporatization and professional management, serve as further modes of gatekeeping. Additionally, the film industry has become progressively more insular and exclusionary, so that it is very difficult for people without any family or social connections to get a break. Finally, regarding the sites of circulation and exhibition, a new geography of distribution has emerged, one that prizes metropolitan and overseas markets and marginalizes equally populous but provincial markets. Furthermore, the multiplex phenomenon is increasingly transforming cinema-going into an elite pastime within India. My discussion and explanation of these processes are based upon over a decade of ethnographic research, as well as filmmakers' statements and reflections about films and filmmaking over that period, rather than upon in-depth formal or textual analyses of particular films.

The third noticeable transformation of the Hindi film industry, since the late 1990s, has been the efforts by filmmakers and business leaders to rationalize the production, distribution, and exhibition process, most commonly referred to as the "corporatization" of the industry. Historically, filmmaking in India has been very fragmented and decentralized, with hundreds of independent financiers, producers, distributors, and exhibitors, who have never been vertically or horizontally integrated in the manner of the major Hollywood studios or multinational entertainment conglomerates. Although a studio system with contracted actors, writers, and directors existed in the 1920s and 1930s in India, a handful of studios did not monopolize the film business as they had in Hollywood. The majority of Indian studios also did not control distribution and exhibition like their Hollywood counterparts. The lack of integration between production, distribution, and exhibition accounted for the high mortality rate of studios; a series of commercial failures, or even one major disaster, frequently led to bankruptcy. Additionally, film historians attribute the influx of wartime profits during the Second World War as the single most important factor in the rapid decline of studios, with the rise of the independent producer as the characteristic feature of Indian filmmaking (Barnouw and Krishnaswamy 1980; Binford 1989).[13] What is referred to as the "studio era," was actually a short chapter in the history of Indian cinema (Shoesmith 1987).[14] Entities referred to as "studios" in Bombay in the post-Independence period, such as R.K. Studios or Mehboob Studios, were actually production companies set up by prominent stars or directors who turned to producing and procured real estate to create an autonomous production space.[15]

Dramatic changes in the structure of the Hindi film industry have been under way since 2000, when the Indian state recognized filmmaking as a legitimate industrial activity. The entry of the Indian corporate sector into filmmaking—either through the creation of media subsidiaries (Reliance Industries' Big Entertainment), or the transformation of independent production companies into public limited companies (Mukta Arts)—is leading to a greater level of integration between production, distribution, and exhibition than had existed prior to this period. Rationalization is related to the issues of cultural legitimacy and respectability, since much of the discourse around these changes, generated by the general media and the film industry, is articulated through a vocabulary of professionalism and modernization.

I argue that these processes of gentrification and rationalization attempt to resolve the dilemmas posed by the central features of the production culture (Caldwell 2008) of the Hindi film industry: the immense disdain that filmmakers express for both the industry and their audiences, as well as the tremendous uncertainty that characterizes the filmmaking process. This book examines in detail these features of the Hindi film industry's production culture, focusing on filmmakers' quests for social respectability and professional distinction, as well as on their continuous manufacture of knowledge and axioms that try to make sense of the unpredictability of filmmaking. By focusing on the social world of Hindi filmmakers, and their processes of production, I demonstrate how commercially oriented cultural production is a site of social practice and a domain of meaning-making. Through a study of the Hindi film industry's production culture, we gain insights into how the mass media are implicated in the production of social difference, the imagining of the nation, the objectification of culture, and the constitution of modernity in contemporary India.

One of the more unexpected findings of my fieldwork was the frequent criticism voiced by Hindi filmmakers concerning the industry's work culture, production practices, and quality of filmmaking, as well as the disdain with which they viewed audiences. Throughout my fieldwork, I encountered filmmakers criticizing every aspect of the industry—from the working style to the sorts of films being made. For example, producer Firoz Nadiadwala, a third-generation member of the film industry, described Hindi filmmaking as being full of compromises and formulae, and the industry filled with people who were either incompetent or who lacked a proper filmmaking vision. Throughout our interview he periodically punctuated his statements by pronouncing that I would have nothing to write about. At one point, he asserted, "It's such a sorry state of affairs. I don't even think you're going to get anything worthwhile writing this book. *Koi kuch nahi kar raha hai. Kuch nahi kar raha hai.* [No one is doing anything. They're doing nothing.] All they're interested in is, '*Bhai* artist *ko* sign *karo, aur itne mein itne bhej do, aur* picture *mein paisa kamao.*' [Just hire an actor and sell this picture for this much and make money off the whole deal.] There's no quality consciousness, there's no forward thinking, save and except maybe for just three or four people, that's it" (Nadiadwala, interview, October 2000). Criticism of this nature comprises a popular genre of discourse within the film industry and serves as a form of "boundary-work," a concept articulated by Thomas Gieryn (1983) to discuss the ideological efforts by a profession or an occupation to delineate who is and is not a legitimate member. The Hindi film industry for much of its history has been characterized by porous boundaries and very few barriers to entry. Essentially, the "industry" has been a very diffuse site where anyone with large sums of money and the right contacts has been able to make a film. The capacity for complete novices to enter film production has been a characteristic feature of filmmaking in India for decades—one that has been heavily criticized by the state and filmmakers alike (Karanth 1980; Patil 1951). This book examines the boundary-work indulged in by Hindi filmmakers in their efforts to recast filmmaking into the mold of a modern high-status profession.

Not only did I encounter complaints and criticism about films, filmmaking, and the workings of the industry, I discovered an inordinate amount of paternalism and condescension expressed toward audiences, specifically the "masses"—the most common label for poor and working-class audiences—who until the early 2000s were understood to comprise the bulk of the film-viewing audience. For years, in media, state, and scholarly discourses, the masses were posited as the root cause of Hindi cinema's narrative, thematic, and aesthetic deficiencies, and I discovered that the majority of filmmakers I met professed similar views.[16] One of my informants, a screenwriter who was one of the few members of the industry who did not share these views, was often critical of his colleagues' representations of audiences. He related to me the advice he was given when he first began his career—the portions set off in em-dashes are his asides to me:

> I hear people, very, very senior and respected people who have been practitioners for 25 years tell me, "Boss, I will tell you a *guru mantra* (the gospel). You want to write for the Indian audience, you must remember one primary over-riding fact." I say, "What is that?" "That is that the average I.Q. of the Indian audience is not more than that of a 10-year-old. *Yeh, unki,* they are not intelligent. Their I.Q.—I.Q. is one word which they bandy about a lot—is that of a very, very simple child. They are like—somebody has even said this to me—our audience is like monkeys." This is the kind of respect which they have for the audience. (interview 1996)

He went on to recount how filmmakers cited the high rates of illiteracy in India, which indexed a lack of formal education, as the root cause for the stunted intellectual development of the majority of audiences in India.

Such perceptions are rooted in the political discourse produced by the postcolonial Indian state, which has designated the vast majority of the population as "backward" and in need of "upliftment" or "improvement." Thomas Hansen points out that after Independence the national leadership produced a more openly paternalist discourse where the "ignorance and superstition" of the masses were the main obstacles to national development (1999: 47). Therefore the responsibility of reforming social habits, of "civilizing" the Indian masses, and inculcating the values of an Indian modernity became the task of state institutions, the political elite, and the social world of the middle class they represented (Hansen 1999).

The changes in filmmaking and film-viewing that I characterize as gentrification address the roots of these sentiments of disdain in both the production and consumption arenas. According to industry and media discourses, a more educated and socially elite class of people working in filmmaking has led the industry to become more respectable, producing a better caliber of films. These better films are being watched by a superior class of audiences, more commonly referred to as the "classes" or the "gentry" in industry parlance, who are more amenable to experimentation and variety in cinema; therefore, according to industry discourses, elite producers and audiences engender better cinema. The process of rationalization also redresses the problem of disdain because with the entry of the Indian corporate sector and its attendant culture of written contracts, institutional finance, and standardized accounting practices, filmmaking begins to appear and operate more in line with dominant understandings of professional organization and discipline.

UNCERTAINTY

To state that large-scale commercial filmmaking is wracked with uncertainty may appear as an assertion of the obvious; however, how that uncertainty is experienced and managed varies across different film industries. While the "electronically mediated home" is the most economically important site of film consumption for Hollywood (Caldwell 2008: 9), in India the movie theater is the most significant site of film consumption. Domestic theatrical box-office income provides the lion's share of revenues—about 73 percent—in India (KPMG 2009); this is in contrast to Hollywood, where it is less than 15 percent (Caldwell 2008: 9). This reliance on the domestic box-office, however, is represented by the Indian financial sector as a problem that filmmaking in India must overcome in order to reduce the risks for investors (KPMG 2009). Reports by a variety of global consulting firms (Arthur Andersen 2000; KPMG 2009; Pricewaterhouse Coopers 2006a) keep touting the economic potential of alternate and ancillary "revenue streams" such as home video, cable and satellite rights, and mobile telephony.

Although the driving force within the Bombay industry is box-office success, it is a difficult goal, achieved by few and pursued by many; the reported probability of a Hindi film achieving success at the box-office ranges from 10 to 15 percent every year—a figure calculated, for reasons that I explain in chapter five, from the point of view of the distributor and not the producer. One explanation filmmakers offer for this low success rate is that the majority of their audiences possess limited discretionary income and cannot afford to see each and every film in the cinema hall; another, more common, explanation is that such a low success rate is due to the poor quality of filmmaking. Additionally, until the advent of multiplexes, the economics of exhibition worked against films that explicitly catered to niche audiences, since single-screen theaters in India have very large capacities, ranging anywhere from 800 to 2,000 seats.

The process of gentrification, especially the growth of multiplexes, helps to reduce the perception of uncertainty associated with filmmaking by reducing the reliance on mass audiences and single-screen cinemas. Film exhibition practices in India are akin to theatrical or concert performance practices in the United States, with advance reservations, assigned seating, and differential rates of admission connected to seat location, so that most cinemas have two to four classes of ticket prices in ascending order: lower stalls, upper stalls, dress circle, and balcony. The discursive division of the viewing audience is integrally connected to the spatial hierarchies present inside the cinema hall; the "masses" are those who sit in the cheaper seats located in the stalls, while the "classes" occupy the more expensive balcony seats.

Multiplex theaters, the majority of which started being built from 2002 onward, have critically altered the film-viewing experience by charging very high rates of admission.[17] With their high ticket prices, social exclusivity, and material comforts, multiplexes have significantly transformed the economics of filmmaking. Despite constituting a small percentage of theaters in India, multiplexes account for a disproportionate share of reported box-office revenues. The importance of multiplexes within the Hindi film industry was highlighted further in 2009 when a dispute over revenue sharing between Hindi film producers, distributors and multiplex exhibitors resulted in a sixty-day moratorium on Hindi film releases. Although the conflict was with six national multiplex chains, the United Producer Distributors Forum—a coalition of the most powerful producers and distributors in the industry—withheld the release of their films throughout India and the world from April 4 until June 6, 2009, when the disputing parties finally reached a resolution.[18]

Just as multiplexes have been represented within industry discourses as rescuing filmmaking from the poor and unpredictable mass audience, so too have international audiences, specifically within the South Asian diaspora, been touted as a route to rescue the industry from the overall vagaries of the domestic box-office. Since 1998, the international, or "overseas," territory has become one of the most profitable markets for Bombay filmmakers, with certain Hindi films enjoying greater commercial success in Great Britain and the United States than in India. For over a decade Hindi films have been appearing regularly in the United Kingdom's weekly listing of the top-10 highest grossing films and in *Variety*'s weekly listing of the 60 highest grossing films in the United States. The success of Hindi cinema outside of India highlights the significance of the South Asian diaspora as a market for the Bombay film industry, and certain filmmakers have explicitly articulated their desire to cater to diasporic audiences. Diasporic audiences especially in North America and the United Kingdom are perceived as more predictable than domestic audiences and, despite their smaller numbers, are attractive for filmmakers because of the disproportionate revenues generated by the sales of tickets in dollars and pounds.

While gentrification is a manifestation of the film industry's quest to manage unpredictability in the arena of film consumption, the process of rationalization is its counterpart, addressing uncertainty in the production process. For decades, one of the main challenges faced by Hindi filmmakers was the high cost of capital to finance production. Since banks and other financial institutions shied away from funding filmmaking, due to the high-risk nature of the enterprise, capital had to be raised through an established network of financiers, who made money in a variety of other fields, such as construction, jewelry, diamond trading, real estate, or manufacturing. These private financiers charged from 36 to 48 percent interest annually, of which six months' worth had to be paid on receipt of the loan. This funding setup resulted in a financially insecure and fragmented production scenario, in which films began production, but could take years to complete — while producers raised funds — or were sometimes abandoned altogether for lack of funding. There also was significant uncertainty within the production process concerning whether a film, once completed, actually got distributed.

The entry of the Indian corporate sector in the twenty-first century has infused previously unheard of amounts of capital into the Hindi film industry, making available consistent finance, so that the risk of a film not being completed has decreased drastically. Many of the new companies have integrated production and distribution, which reduces the uncertainties around the latter. Measures such as film insurance, coproductions, product placement, and marketing partnerships with high-profile consumer brands have also mitigated some of the financial uncertainties of filmmaking. Despite all of these new methods to rationalize the production process, the overall success-failure ratio of Hindi films at the box-office had not improved by the end of 2010. In fact, based on my analysis of the annual box-office overviews listed in the trade publication *Film Information*, the percentage of hits actually decreased over the fifteen-year period from 1995 to 2010. (See Table 6.) While the film industry has not necessarily improved the hit-flop ratio, it has been successful in terms of attracting new forms of finance capital; this is due to efforts by its members to refashion the industry and filmmaking to target socially elite viewers domestically, and diasporic audiences internationally.

Given the highly unpredictable nature of filmmaking in India—from the uncertainty of audience response to the insecurity of finance for much of its history—the Hindi film industry has developed a variety of practices to manage the risks and uncertainty of filmmaking. Scholars have argued that "audience fictions," generated by producers to manage the inherent unpredictability of audience response, are an integral part of the media production process.[19] I contend that the uncertainty endemic in filmmaking also leads large media industries like the Hindi film industry to generate "production fictions," which are truisms, axioms, and structures of belief about what is necessary for commercial success. This book examines how both production fictions and audience fictions play an integral role in managing the uncertainty of Hindi filmmaking.

FROM HINDI CINEMA TO "BOLLYWOOD"

In May 2007, I was contacted by the assistant managing editor of Southwest Airlines' in-flight magazine, *Spirit*, who asked if I would be interested in being their "expert" and write a brief "Beginner's Guide to Bollywood" for their November issue. "Bollywood"—derived by combining Bombay with Hollywood—was originally a tongue-in-cheek term coined by the English-language press in India to refer to the Hindi film industry.[20] Although dating back to the late 1970s, "Bollywood" gained currency primarily in the late 1990s, with the increased circulation, presence, and recognition of Hindi films in North America, the United Kingdom, and Western Europe, and officially entered the English lexicon in 2001, when the *Oxford English Dictionary* included the term. During my first stint of fieldwork in 1996, the term Bollywood was not a part of the everyday parlance of Hindi filmmakers, having been used mainly by journalists writing for general or trade publications. By the time I carried out my last phase of fieldwork in 2006, however, I felt it was imperative to ask my informants their thoughts about the term, as many prominent stars and directors had publicly expressed their displeasure with it.[21] I encountered a wide spectrum of reactions to the term: acceptance; resignation; indifference; ambivalence; and antipathy.

That Bollywood has become the dominant global term to refer to the Hindi film industry, mainstream Hindi cinema, and even erroneously to all of the diverse filmmaking traditions in India, becomes apparent from the two institutions acknowledged as pioneers in the organization and dissemination of information in our contemporary world: Amazon.com and Google. "Bollywood" as a search term on either site yields four times more results than "Indian cinema" and ten to twenty times more results than "Hindi cinema."[22] The fact that the editorial team of a publication for a regionally focused budget American airline such as Southwest thought an article about "Bollywood" would be interesting and relevant for its passengers, signaled to me that the term had entered the American mainstream.[23]

Bollywood is a contested and controversial term nonetheless, both within the Indian film-studies community and the Hindi film industry. Film scholars are justifiably upset by the indiscriminate use of the term by the media—and even by other scholars—to refer to all filmmaking both past and present within India.[24] An exasperating feature of the global use of the term is the way that Bollywood has become synonymous with any film either produced in India or by diasporic Indians and set in India; Mira Nair's *Monsoon Wedding*, Gurinder Chadha's *Bride and Prejudice*, and Deepa Mehta's *Earth* have all been referred to in this vein. Global media usage of the term "Bollywood" usually demonstrates a complete ignorance that feature films are produced in over twenty languages in India every year and that vibrant and prolific film industries exist in the cities of Hyderabad, Chennai, Bangalore, Trivandrum, and Calcutta.

This ignorance is demonstrated most perceptibly through pronouncements about the sheer size of Bollywood—"largest film industry in the world"—based on the aggregate number of films produced annually in India. While the total number of feature films produced in India is quite high (1,288 in 2009), Hindi films comprise a much smaller proportion— about 20 percent—of that total. The annual film production statistics reflect the total number of films certified for exhibition by the Central Board of Film Certification, which is different from the total number of films actually released theatrically.[25] For example, in 2009, whereas a total of 235 Hindi films were certified, 132 films were released theatrically; out of which even a smaller number could be regarded as "Bollywood" films in terms of their star cast, directors, and narrative/aesthetic style. Neither is Bollywood synonymous with Indian cinema, Hindi cinema, nor with the Indian film industry. In fact, there is no such entity as the "Indian film industry" in terms of nationally integrated structures of financing, production, distribution, and exhibition, even if there is some overlap and circulation of personnel between the six main film industries in India. The "Indian film industry" is a rhetorical trope mostly used in state, media, and corporate discourses to signal the sheer scale of filmmaking in India and demonstrate India's exceptionalism in the global media landscape.

Within the Hindi film industry, while some are indifferent or resigned to the use of the term Bollywood, others are upset by the term because they feel it is essentializing and condescending; represents a kitschy, tacky cinema; or implies that Hindi cinema is a cheap derivative of Hollywood. A comparison to Hollywood is inevitable with a term like Bollywood, which is why many members of the industry profess not to like it. Yet even prior to the coinage of the neologism, comparisons between Hollywood and the Bombay film industry by the Indian press have a long history, dating back to the late 1920s. Neepa Majumdar, in her work on stardom in Indian cinema from the early sound era to the immediate post-Independence era, discusses how the Indian film press created Hollywood epithets for Indian stars, such as "the Indian Douglas Fairbanks" for Master Vithal or "the Indian Mary Pickford" for Ermeline (2009: 54–55). Majumdar points out that such comparisons were also criticized by some explicitly nationalist film magazines and resented by the stars themselves; for example, the star who was referred to as the "Indian Douglas Fairbanks" wrote in a popular film journal that he hated the epithet and that "such names go against our national pride" (in Majumdar 2009: 55).

The Hindi film industry has always defined itself in relation to Hollywood and not any other national cinema. During my fieldwork I observed Hindi filmmakers frequently discussing Hollywood—either by praising it, criticizing it, or comparing themselves to it. Hollywood is a constant symbolic, metaphoric, and narrative presence in the Bombay industry,[26] and since 2006, with its tentative entry into Hindi film production, a material presence as well; therefore, I find Hindi filmmakers' criticisms of the term Bollywood as demeaning or condescending somewhat disingenuous. Furthermore, as evident from Firoz Nadiadwala's comments earlier in the chapter, Hindi filmmakers express a great deal of disdain themselves for their own industry.

I contend that Bollywood does not inherently imply a cheap imitation of Hollywood; if Hollywood is an icon of global popular culture and box-office muscle, "Bollywood" signifies that the Hindi film industry is at the same level—or capable of being at the same level—of global dominance. This is why "-ollywood" has become a very generative and productive morpheme to refer to other centers of media production—such as "Nollywood" for the Nigerian film industry—that index their aspirations for global popularity. The wide use of the term Bollywood by Indian media professionals represents an assertion of sovereignty and cultural autonomy in the global media landscape. Global circulation is not the determining factor, however, in the Hindi film industry's transformation into Bollywood, as Hindi films have had a global market for decades. Since the 1950s, Hindi cinema, along with its stars and music, has been popular in sites as diverse as Nigeria, Greece, Egypt, Indonesia, and the former Soviet Union, but these histories of consumption and circulation precede the coinage and concept of Bollywood. Though some have argued that "Bollywood" is an empty signifier (Prasad 2003), ahistorical and essentializing (Vasudevan 2008), or a culture industry that is distinct from the cinema (Rajadhyaksha 2003), I use the term to index a particular moment in the Hindi film industry's history, a transformation in its filmmaking practices, and a shift in how it imagines its audiences.

The historicity of the term "Bollywood," its indication of a particular style of filmmaking, and its implication in the global circulation of Hindi films, have been addressed by scholars of Indian cinema (Prasad 2003; Rajadhyaksha 2003; Vasudevan 2008). Central to their critical engagements with Bollywood is the figure of the NRI or non-resident Indian, the appellation most commonly used by the Indian state and media to refer to members of the Indian diaspora settled in North America, the United Kingdom, Europe, and Australia.[27] While the growing economic significance of diasporic audiences has been an important feature of the Hindi film industry's makeover into Bollywood, the conscious pursuit of socially elite audiences domestically is also a critical factor in the industry's transformation. Finally, a dimension that has been completely overlooked by an insightful discussion, centering mainly on narrative form, film history, and political theory, is that of filmmakers' own subjectivities and attempts to accrue symbolic capital and cultural legitimacy. I argue that the "Bollywoodization" of Hindi cinema—to use Rajadhyaksha's coinage (2003)—which has been attributed overwhelmingly to diasporic audiences and overseas markets, is also closely tied to Hindi filmmakers' desires to legitimate their filmmaking and their aspirations to be accepted among social and cultural elites.

DEVELOPMENT, NEOLIBERALISM, AND THE POSTCOLONIAL CONDITION

Amitabh Bachchan's statements about how cinema was not regarded as a promising profession in India and that "children from good homes were not encouraged to go anywhere near it" articulates the peculiar sense of social marginality that members of the Hindi film industry have felt over the years. Despite the fact that Bachchan's own social class, family background, and level of education mark him as someone from a "good home"—a phrase that along with its other more common variant, "good family," indexes an amalgam of caste and class status, educational level, occupational identity, and gendered norms of behavioral comportment and propriety—in his remarks we encounter the disdain that filmmakers perceive is directed toward them by those from good homes and good families.[28] In spite of their fame and fortune, I found that Hindi filmmakers were extremely concerned with appearing "respectable," and I examine how this idea is understood, expressed, and enacted within the industry. Beverly Skeggs, in her ethnography about white working-class women in England, points out that "respectability is usually the concern of those who are not seen to have it . . . It is rarely recognized as an issue by those who are positioned with it, who are normalized by it, and who do not have to prove it" (1997: 1). Members of the Hindi film industry have been trying to prove their respectability for decades, and in this book I describe how these efforts are not just about the social backgrounds of filmmakers, but also closely connected to the social class of audiences.

The phenomenon of mainstream Hindi cinema and its makers accruing respectability shares some commonalities with other performance traditions in India that underwent similar social transformations in the colonial era. Scholars have traced the history of how dance forms, such as *Bharatanatyam*, and musical genres of the North (Hindustani) and of the South (Carnatic), earned the exalted status of the "classical" and came to denote a national cultural heritage. These performance traditions acquired prestige and respectability through the efforts of upper-caste, middle-class reformers who criticized the traditional exponents, such as *devadasis* (temple dancers) or *tawa'ifs* (courtesans), for being disreputable and unworthy of these art forms, and encouraged middle-class men and women to learn and perform these traditions (Bakhle 2005; Meduri 1988; Weidman 2006).

The case of filmmaking, however, is also different from classical music and dance in a few important ways: the social class of audiences, nationalist agendas, and cultural politics. The disrepute associated with classical music and dance in the nineteenth century only had to do with the performers and not its patrons, who were traditionally from the aristocracy and nobility. In the case of cinema, though it began as an elite activity in India, it became quickly popular across various social strata by the 1920s, and by the 1940s, film was regarded as a form of mass entertainment.

While music and dance were reformed under the guise of a national tradition at various points of the Indian nationalist movement, film was never accorded any such importance either by leaders of the nationalist struggle or the newly independent Indian nation-state.

Sumita Chakravarty discusses how filmmaking was perceived by the national leadership as having escaped the effects of colonialism, which they felt had marginalized performers and producers of other artistic traditions. She describes the dominant attitudes toward cinema in the aftermath of Independence: "As a decolonizing nation, India now felt threatened from within, victimized by the very forces of modernization it had rushed to embrace. What space would traditional culture (pre-British, premodern) occupy in the new milieu? How could the tide of film mania be stemmed? How could the 'excesses' of the film industry be curbed? Who were the real guardians of the "public interest"? These were some of the questions that were repeatedly raised in official circles, by citizens' groups, by artists, and critics" (1993: 58). Not only was film regarded as a threat to other performance traditions, filmmaking was also not accorded any economic importance by the Nehruvian developmentalist state. Respectability for Hindi filmmakers and cultural legitimacy for commercial filmmaking only became possible when the developmentalist state was reconfigured into a neoliberal one, privileging doctrines of free markets, free trade, and consumerism. Under this new regime, the mass media's significance is gauged by its economic rather than its pedagogical potential, a shift characterized by Ravi Vasudevan as the "displacement of nation as art form by nation as brand" (2008).

Scholars have noted the transformations in the national politico-economic imaginary after the economic liberalization policies instituted by the Indian state in 1991.[29] As Leela Fernandes notes, "while earlier state socialist ideologies tended to depict workers or rural villagers as the archetypical objects of development, such ideologies now compete with mainstream national political discourses that increasingly portray urban middle-class consumers as the representative citizens of liberalizing India" (2006: xv). What I am characterizing as the gentrification of Hindi cinema is part of a broader socio-historical conjuncture where urban middle classes are celebrated in state and media discourses as the main agents, as well as markers of modernity and development in India. Just as the urban middle-class consumer represents the idealized citizen in a neoliberal and globalizing India, the urban middle-class film-viewer represents the ideal audience member for an industry concerned with issues of prestige, respect, and global circulation.

While the impact of neoliberalism has been examined in India primarily with respect to those who have become more insecure or dispossessed by these policies, in this book, I examine a story that goes against the grain, one that may even appear counterintuitive. The growing scholarship about the changes wrought in India by the adoption of neoliberal economic policies frequently asserts, in passing, that elites have benefited, before moving on to a discussion of the social and economic consequences of liberalization on non-elites.[30] In contrast, this book examines the ways that certain sectors of the Hindi film industry have benefited from neoliberal economic policies, which was neither expected nor anticipated by scholars or filmmakers in the mid-1990s. In fact, Hindi filmmakers and scholars have continually predicted the decline of the film industry due to the entrance of technologies such as video, cable, and satellite television, or because of changes in state policy about media imports and foreign investment in media.[31]

This story of "success"—which I qualify with the quotation marks since the idea of success is dependent on particular structural positions within the industry—is of a different nature than that experienced by the Bombay advertising world as examined by William Mazzarella (2003), where the entrance of multinational consumer-goods companies led to new opportunities for Indian advertisers and marketing professionals to position themselves as vital cultural experts and mediators for these global firms. The Hindi film industry has benefited directly from certain changes in state policy, the expansion of the televisual landscape, and the growth of diasporic markets. Globalization—shorthand referring to transnational flows of capital, images, and people (Appadurai 1996)— and neoliberalism—another shorthand to signify the establishment and dismantling of governmental structures to enable those flows (Harvey 2005)—have strengthened the Hindi film industry and made it a more dominant media institution within and outside India. Such a trajectory differs from the standard narratives offered about the impact of globalization and neoliberalism on media industries outside of the United States, which usually equate these processes with the ascendancy of media corporations based or identified with the United States, to the disadvantage of national media institutions.[32]

Another presumed logic that the example of the Hindi film industry disrupts has to do with the nature of capitalism, more specifically "late capitalism" and the regime of flexible accumulation (Harvey 1990). Flexibility, fragmentation, decentralization, and their associated occupational and employment insecurities that are cited as characteristics of a global, late capitalist order, have actually been the defining features of the Hindi film industry since the end of the Second World War. Although Indian and international journalists have relied on the Fordist metaphors of the factory and the assembly line to represent the Hindi film industry, the structure and workings of the industry are the exact opposite: each Hindi film is made by a team of independent contractors or freelancers.[33] The rise of neoliberal policies in India has coincided with—and is contributing to—a greater consolidation and integration of the Hindi film industry, rather than its fragmentation, flexibility, and decentralization. At the same time, the relationship between the film industry and the state has been crucially reconfigured. For decades, the Indian state, operating within a Nehruvian developmentalist paradigm, did not support the Hindi film industry and its forms of filmmaking, which are oriented toward popular entertainment. Instead, state policies treated and taxed commercial filmmaking as something akin to a vice. Since the late 1990s, the Indian state has been lauding the Hindi film industry and appears to be ideologically and materially invested in the project of commercial filmmaking more than ever before.

A discussion of neoliberalism in the Indian context cannot be complete without a discussion of developmentalism. Akhil Gupta argues that development discourse, which locates a particular set of nation-states as temporally "behind" the West, is not just about the economic position of a nation-state relative to others, but more significantly has "created the 'underdeveloped' as a subject and 'underdevelopment' as a form of identity in the postcolonial world" (1998: 11). The postcolonial nature of the Indian state and society allows us to examine the logics of developmentalism and neoliberalism within the same frame. Although the current Indian state replaced a Nehruvian-style development agenda with a neoliberal one—preliminarily in 1985 and more aggressively since 1991—it has not abandoned its obsession with "catching up" with the West. While the methods may have changed, a teleological ideology of modernization still undergirds state economic and social policy. The discussions of filmmaking in India are rife with the allochronism (Fabian 2002)—the false sense of a contemporary society being part of an earlier era—associated with developmentalist logics, whereby the changes besetting the industry, which I have characterized as gentrification, are frequently hailed by commentators in teleological language: "coming of age"; "growing up"; or "maturing." Filmmaking in India is often described globally in a developmentalist idiom as well. For example, American film critics frequently describe contemporary Hindi cinema as akin to older Hollywood films so that a teleological narrative is produced whereby classical Hollywood is Indian cinema's present, while contemporary Hollywood is its future.[34]

During my fieldwork, I observed Hindi filmmakers constantly coming to terms with and contesting the connotations of "backwardness" and inferiority implicit in the label "developing." Rajjat Barjatya, one of the producers of the most successful films in Indian cinema, the 1994 blockbuster *Hum Aapke Hain Koun!*, when discussing the decision to make the film with the latest sound technologies, articulated the introduction of optical and digital sound technologies in India in a very obvious developmentalist narrative: "Revolution is taking place at a very, very fast rate in India: optical stereo in the U.S. was prevalent for almost fifteen years and since the last two years, they have been going ahead with digital, but in India, we introduced optical stereo just one and half years back and already people are switching over to digital. What I'm saying is that maybe we've taken a long time to catch up with the West, but we're almost there. We have caught up with them in a very, very short span of time" (Barjatya, interview, April 1996). In addition to illustrating how the technological properties of cinema become a sign of modernity, Barjatya's statements about "catching up with the West" demonstrate the experience of modernity that Akhil Gupta has termed the "postcolonial condition" (1998). Gupta argues that to be a national subject in a "developing" country like India is to "occupy an overdetermined subject position interpellated by discourses of the nation *and* by the discourses of development to which that nation is subjected" (1998: 41). Although Gupta's research focused on poor farmers in north India, in Barjatya's description of the technological "revolution" taking place in India and his use of the United States as the benchmark of modernity, we see how even urban elites are interpellated by the discourses of nation and development. In this book, I detail how developmentalist logics operate within the field of Hindi film production — with respect to both filmmakers' own subjectivities and representations of the industry and in their representations of audiences and their subjectivities.

PRODUCERS, AUDIENCES, AND THE
SOCIAL LIFE OF TECHNOLOGY

As mentioned earlier, mainstream Hindi cinema had been the object of derision and trenchant criticism for many years, and much of the early writings on Hindi cinema reflected this derision in their dismissive attitude toward mainstream filmmaking.[35] Seminal work on popular Hindi cinema by scholars such as Sumita Chakravarty (1993), Ashish Rajadhyaksha (1986), Rosie Thomas (1985), and Ravi Vasudevan (1989) addressed issues of film history, state policy, genre, aesthetic formations, narrative style, and national identity, establishing the foundation for what has become a highly dynamic field of study. This book joins a growing body of scholarship on Indian cinema that draws upon earlier questions and concerns about history, the nation, genre, representation, and narrative form,[36] but has expanded the focus to include issues of circulation, consumption, exhibition, music, fan cultures, stardom, visual culture, political economy, and globalization.[37]

With a focus on the production culture and social world of the Hindi film industry, this book is also a part of the growing anthropological literature about media forms and practices that seeks to demystify the mass media as it goes beyond the media-text to identify the diverse cultural, social, and historical contexts of media production, circulation, and consumption.[38] An anthropological approach to studying the mass media distinguishes itself from other approaches by its focus on people and their social relations, as opposed to a focus only on media texts or technology (Ginsburg 1994). Anthropologists are centrally concerned with the "making of meaning and the social relations within which this occurs" (Myers 2002: 7). Based on my interest in practice, experience, meaning-making, and social life, I have examined filmmaking and filmmakers in much greater detail than specific films. This focus does not preclude a discussion of specific films; rather than regarding films as texts, however, I regard them as social and discursive objects that come to possess their meaning through practice and social life (Myers 2002), which leads me to concentrate on how filmmakers interpret, discuss, and assign social as well as cultural significance to particular films.

Much of the impetus to study media anthropologically emerged initially from an interest in examining audiences and their consumption of mass media, such as film or television, which expanded and complicated our understandings of the circulation and reception of media forms.[39] An anthropological focus on media production developed somewhat later, although a very robust tradition of studying production cultures in the United States has existed in sociology, communication studies, and media studies for some time.[40] An ethnographic approach to media production is important for deepening our understanding of production and of producers, in this specific case, of Hindi filmmakers who have been either mostly ignored in the scholarship on Indian cinema or have been regarded as isomorphic with the films they produce. In this book, I view

Hindi filmmakers as agents grounded in specific social, historical, and interpretive locations, with their activity of film production as a "social process engaged in the mediation of culture" (Ginsburg 1995: 70). I focus on what Barry Dornfeld, in his work on American public television producers, describes as "the abundance of acts of evaluation and interpretation that cultural producers engage in as a necessary and formative dimension of their productive work and as a self-defining activity in other dimensions of their lives" (1998: 16). This book explores how filmmakers' subjectivities, social relations, and world-views are constituted and mediated by their experiences of filmmaking.

In a site like the Hindi film industry, where negotiations are highly personalized and oral, ethnography grounds the study of media in a specific time and space and offers insights into the processes, possibilities, and constraints of filmmaking that are not apparent from an analysis of the film text. A focus on the process of production allows us to look beyond the instances of "success"—those films that do get completed and distributed in some manner—since many films do not progress beyond a conceptualization stage, and some are abandoned halfway. Such "failures" (Ganti 2002) also add to our knowledge, offering productive insights and possibilities for theorizing about cinema and other media forms. Additionally, in a context of financial secrecy and the willful absence of record keeping, which marked the Hindi film industry for much of its history, ethnography offers insights into the production process that exhortations to simply "follow the money"—to trace the broad contours of capital investment and ownership—could not achieve.[41]

An ethnographic approach to media production is also important, both for understanding how media are produced in different cultural settings, and for countering the ethnocentrism of much of the scholarship on culture industries and mass culture, which are mainly based on the study of North American and Western European media institutions and corporate capitalism. Although the Hindi film industry—like Hollywood—is a commercially driven, blockbuster-oriented industry, its structures of financing and distribution, sites of power, organization of labor, and overall work culture are quite distinct. In contrast to Hollywood, the Hindi film industry is highly decentralized, has been financed primarily by entrepreneurial capital, organized along social and kin networks, and until the early 2000s was governed by oral rather than written contracts.

While this book's focus is on Hindi filmmakers, readers will notice a great emphasis upon "the audience," specifically upon how filmmakers imagine, represent, and discuss film audiences. Not only has scholarship on media production amply demonstrated that audiences are always pre-figured in the production process,[42] a strand of mass communications research has focused on "audience-making," which refers to how media industries actually produce their audiences through a variety of institutional mechanisms (measurement, segmentation, and regulation), so as to reconstitute actual viewers into collectivities that carry economic or social value within a particular media system (Ettema and Whitney 1994). I examine the Hindi film industry's audience-making practices, which are based on the measurement of theatrical commercial outcome interpreted according to the geographic and spatial logics of film distribution and exhibition.

The figure of the audience is central to understanding the nature of Hindi film production. The very label "commercial cinema," which is used to describe the dominant form of filmmaking, has the market, that is, the audience implicated within it. At every level, the scholarly or popular discussion about Hindi cinema is a discussion about the audience explicitly or implicitly; these are broadly of three types: textually based scholarship that chooses to ignore the figure of the audience because it is too problematic, or masks it into the esoteric language of the psychoanalytically imagined "spectator"; ideological analyses, which ostensibly are about films as texts but implicitly construct a figure of the audience, since ideology needs a recipient; or work that justifies the study of commercial cinema by the term "popular," drawing strength from the fact that many people watch these films.

The history of Hindi cinema is frequently represented as a narrative of change mediated through the figure of the audience. Many accounts uncritically espouse the view that Hindi cinema underwent drastic changes aesthetically, thematically, and stylistically because of the changed class composition of audiences.[43] The common narrative found in most general histories of Indian cinema articulates a decline in cinematic standards and quality after the Second World War, usually attributed to the post-war changes in film financing and audience composition. I discuss the narratives of "improvement" regarding cinematic standards and quality that were a dominant feature of the discourse surrounding filmmaking during my fieldwork. These narratives are essentially of gentrification, where cinematic quality and standards are connected to middle-class audiences.

The attitudes toward audiences that I detail in this book offer a different perspective from some anthropological theorizing about media consumption. For example, Dornfeld (1998) argues that a dichotomy between production and reception—or producers and audiences—is untenable, since both partake in processes of production and reception, understood in terms of the generation of interpretations and the engagement in acts of evaluation. Such assertions about the artifice of this divide are based on theorizing from contexts in which producers and audiences are part of the same social and interpretive world (Dornfeld 1998). However, whenever media producers have produced content for large-scale audiences characteristic of American commercial television or Hollywood, there is a strong tendency to deride, stereotype, essentialize, or "paedocratize," because of the fundamental inability to directly observe and know one's audience.[44] Additionally, in cases like the Hindi film industry, the Hindi television industry (Matzner 2010), the Tamil film industry (Dickey 1993), or the Egyptian television industry (Abu-Lughod 2005), where a vast social distance exists between producers and the majority of their audiences, and where producers do not imagine their audiences to be like them at all, then the production/reception divide is an important dichotomy that reveals how social difference is produced, managed, and experienced. This book analyzes how commercial cinema production is based on an articulation of difference, specifically a relationship of "othering," between producers and audiences.

Examining Hindi filmmakers' discussions of their audiences reveals a parallel discourse about the social and aesthetic impact of different media technologies, such as video, satellite television, and the multiplex theater upon cinema in India. Anthropologists have pointed to the importance of examining the distinctive material and sensory properties of media technologies as a necessary component of the ethnography of media (Ginsburg, Abu-Lughod, and Larkin 2002). Ethnographic studies have illustrated how media and communication technologies (and their use) shape and are shaped by the practices of daily life, patterns of social relations, and specific experiences of modernity.[45] Although an in-depth analysis of the physical and sensory properties of video, satellite television, or multiplex theaters is beyond the scope of this book, I discuss these media technologies in terms of the meaning and value invested in them by Hindi filmmakers. I demonstrate how video, satellite television, and multiplexes are differentially implicated in filmmakers' discussions of their own subjectivities and filmmaking practices. In filmmakers' discourses, video is the villain that precipitated the decline in standards and quality, while the multiplex is the hero that has initiated a new era of opportunity and possibility for filmmaking; satellite television occupies a more ambivalent position between the two. The judgmental characterizations of these technologies derive from the metonymic relationship established by filmmakers between the social class of audiences and the specific viewing practices engendered by these technologies. For example, the advent of video is viewed negatively, not only because of issues of piracy and loss of revenue, but also because it represents for filmmakers the retreat of middle-class audiences from the space of the cinema, while the multiplex represents their return. Therefore, a discussion of how new technologies of dissemination and practices of exhibition have reconfigured the relationship between Hindi filmmakers and their audiences demonstrates how media technologies can "impose new social relations" (Ginsburg, Abu-Lughod, and Larkin 2002: 19).

An anthropological emphasis on media technologies also provides a necessary counter to universalist narratives of technological determinism (Larkin 2008; Miller and Horst 2006; Pinney 1997; Pinney and Peterson 2003). The case examined in this book is the multiplex movie theater. While the multiplex in the United States is synonymous with mainstream blockbuster cinema, aggressively oriented toward broad audiences and mass appeal, in India the multiplex signifies exactly the opposite. In India, the multiplex is credited with fomenting and supporting an alternative cinematic practice more akin to art-house cinemas in the United States; accordingly, the multiplex is associated with niche audiences and social exclusivity. The discourse about "multiplex cinema" detailed in this book illustrates the significance of exhibition practices and distribution arrangements to the narrative and aesthetic content of cinema. The narratives of change in filmmaking practice attributed by both filmmakers and the Indian press to technologies such as video, satellite television, and multiplexes demonstrate how cinema must also be analyzed and understood through the technologies of its dissemination.

THE HINDI FILM INDUSTRY AS A RESEARCH SITE

What sort of site is the Hindi film industry for ethnographic research? At one level it seems abstract, diffuse, and unmanageably large in scale, but my focus on those groups with the creative or financial power to make decisions that shape the films—producers, directors, actors and actresses, writers, distributors, exhibitors—and those who shape the discourse about films, filmmaking, and filmmakers—journalists—provided the boundaries for my fieldwork. This fieldwork, carried out in Bombay for twelve months in 1996, with shorter follow-up visits in 2000, 2005, and 2006, was a combination of participant-observation and direct interviews. As a testament to the increasingly globalized nature of the Hindi film industry, the Bombay portion of my fieldwork was supplemented by additional fieldwork in New York, New Jersey, and Pennsylvania in 2001, and intermittently in New York between 2005 and 2009.

The bulk of my time in 1996 was spent observing the production process at various sites in the capacity as a guest, and later as a directorial assistant for two different films (*Dil to Pagal Hai* [The Heart Is Crazy] and *Ghulam* [Slave]), which allowed me to observe the pre-production process as well. In addition to observing how films were produced, I also observed both how "stars" were "produced" by watching elaborate photo sessions orchestrated for the glossy English-language film magazines, and the interactions between film journalists and actors. By attending a number of events (or rituals) of the film industry, such as premieres, *mahurats* (ceremonies which announce the start of a new production), music releases, and award ceremonies like the *Filmfare* Awards, I was able to observe how the industry reinforced, and occasionally celebrated, its discrete identity.

I also carried out formal, taped interviews in English and Hindi with more than a 100 members of the film industry and the film press, from both the trade and gossip magazines. The interviews served as opportunities to clarify and delve further into issues that I had observed at the production sites, and as occasions to gather information about topics that were unobtainable through observation. The interviews also provided the space for industry members to add to and critique the discourse generated by the print media about Hindi cinema and the film industry. My third research strategy involved collecting contemporary written discourse (in Hindi and English) about films and the industry produced by the trade press, mainstream print media, and government institutions, such as the National Film Archive and the National Film Development Corporation, in order to map out the larger discursive terrain about cinema in India.

The expansion of the Internet and electronic communication has enabled me to stay in touch with some of my informants through email and social networking sites such as Facebook. The proliferation of websites having to do with "Bollywood"—Internet news magazines focusing on South Asia, and Hindi producers' own websites—are now another source of discourse about Hindi films and the film industry. Finally, I have kept abreast of the issues and discussions featured in the trade press by subscribing to *Film Information*, a weekly trade magazine published in Bombay since the early 1970s. *Film Information* is one of the oldest of four trade magazines published in English in Bombay that focuses on the business side of the industry: assessing commercial outcome; detailing business deals; providing news of films under production; announcing the release dates of films; and reviewing films with an eye to their commercial prospects.

Focus

Even with a focus on those members with financial or creative decision-making power, the Hindi film industry can still appear as a formidable site for ethnographic research, given the sheer scale of filmmaking in Bombay. If one concentrates on those filmmakers who have the most prestige and command the most financial and symbolic capital within the film industry, however—the "A-list" producers, directors, and actors—then the size of the industry shrinks considerably. Despite hyperbolic media representations about the sheer magnitude of the filmmaking enterprise in Bombay, based on annual production statistics, the proportion of films made by individuals from the A-list has never been more than a third of the total number of films produced and distributed between 1995 and 2006.

Although the A-list comprises a small percentage of the overall Hindi film industry, films from these makers are the ones that tend to generate box-office profits for distributors, which serves as the benchmark for commercial success since distributors have been the main investors in—and bearers of financial risk for—films during most of the industry's history. While a standard criticism within the industry is the oft lamented success-to-failure—or hit-to-flop—ratio, which over the course of my fieldwork peaked as high as 24 percent hits in 1997, and dropped to as low as 7 percent in 2009, the percentage of hits within the A-list is often twice or thrice that of the overall industry—47 percent of the films made by these filmmakers were commercially successful in 1997, compared to 17 percent in 2009.[46] My informants were primarily either from this elite stratum of the film industry or those who were aspiring for that status. My fieldwork was centered on the actors, producers, directors, and writers who possessed various degrees of celebrity within and outside the industry—the very same individuals who were also the focus of journalistic attention.

It is important to convey the absences and limitations of my fieldwork. Certain occupational roles in the film industry are more amenable to the "deep hanging out" that marks the ethnographic enterprise, which played a role in how my research took shape. On a film set, actors, directors, assistant directors, and producers have the most down time, while everyone around them is busy going about their specific duties and tasks. I was the least obtrusive on a set, where I was often the only—or one of a few—women, if I situated myself with the producer, director, or actors, who were often sitting and chatting while waiting for the lighting to be set up. Given that I was in my mid-twenties when I began my fieldwork, I developed a rapport most readily with assistant directors, actors, and young directors, who were around my same age and welcomed me easily into their social world.

Other than my observations of the activities on a film set or film shoot, I did not carry out any research with the vast array of workers— carpenters, camera attendants, light-men, make-up artists, hair-dressers, and sundry others—who in American film parlance are referred to as "below-the-line" and are the vital life-blood of the labor that goes into the production of a film. When taking these categories of film workers into account, the Hindi film industry once again becomes quite vast in size and scale, as there are thousands of such workers in Bombay. My research also did not focus on those members of the industry who are referred to as "technicians" by Hindi filmmakers—cinematographers, editors, choreographers, composers, musicians, sound engineers, art directors[47]—although I had many opportunities to observe these various individuals at work on sets, in editing suites, recording studios, and dubbing studios. There are a multitude of projects to be done about the Hindi film industry from an ethnographic perspective, and recently anthropologists have begun to pay attention to more specific features of Hindi film production, such as costume design (Wilkinson-Weber 2005, 2006) and film music (Booth 2008), adding valuable perspectives on below-the-line workers.

Access

One evening in April 1996, on my way to Filmalaya Studios, where I was going to observe a film shoot, I noticed an unusual sight on the side of S.V. Road in Andheri (a northwestern suburb of Bombay) while sitting in an auto-rickshaw waiting for the red light to turn to green: a white man and a white woman dressed in shorts, T-shirts, sneakers, and carrying large backpacks. Given that this part of suburban Bombay was not a common destination for European or American tourists, the pair stood out among the busy throngs of people going about their evening routines. When I got to the studio, much to my surprise, the backpacker couple was seated comfortably in chairs observing the slightly frenetic proceedings prior to the shoot. The film's producer and executive producer were darting about nervously, for they had invited a number of journalists to witness the shoot that evening; a song that had been billed as "historic" for it featured cameos by a number of yesteryear stars, including the hit star pair of the 1960s, Asha Parekh and Shammi Kapoor, who were sharing the screen after a gap of nearly 30 years. One major point of tension between the two producers was that there were not enough chairs on the set for the actors, distributors, and financiers who would be present.

Meanwhile, the two backpackers, who were occupying valuable real estate in the form of the chairs, were not questioned as to their identity and business on the set. Everyone assumed that they were someone's guests. When the woman backpacker, who was taking photographs, asked me who Asha Parekh was, I finally asked the couple politely who they were. Imagine my surprise when they informed me that they were tourists from Sweden who had come to Bombay on a holiday and did not want to leave Bombay without seeing "Bollywood"! They were no one's guests; neither did they know anyone associated with the film, nor did they know anything about the film. They were basically able to wander on to this set because of the color of their skin. I was incredulous and thought how the reverse could never happen—I would never be able to casually stroll on to a sound stage or studio lot in Los Angeles.

Many months later, in November, when I was observing a different film shoot taking place in a classroom of a local community college in Andheri, two young Indian men who had traveled from Delhi to try to get a glimpse of the glamour of the Bombay film world had wandered onto this set, hoping to meet their favorite star, Aamir Khan. Since I appeared to be involved with the production—sitting next to the director and conversing with other members of the crew—these two men approached me and asked if it would be possible to watch the shoot. By this point in my research I had come to the conclusion that film sets in Bombay were quasi-public spaces, since they were frequently peopled by a myriad of visitors and onlookers, and I told them that if they sat quietly and stayed out of the camera's field, it should be no problem. Unlike the situation with the Swedish tourists, members of this crew did question the two men and commanded them to leave the set.

I relay these anecdotes not only to represent the permeable boundaries of a film set—which enables tourists, curious observers, fans, and anthropologists to wander in—but also to communicate how access to the Hindi film industry is shaped by racial and class privilege. Although being an upper middle-class diasporic South Asian female academic from New York definitely paved my access to the film industry, these social categories were frequently trumped by the privilege of white skin. For example, one afternoon in May 1996, I was waiting to meet a producer in his office. It had taken me several tries to get an appointment. Although the time for my appointment came and went, I waited, aware of the alternative temporality that characterized film business. I looked up from my magazine to see two white European or American individuals being ushered upstairs to the producer's office. When I inquired with the receptionist about why those two had been sent upstairs, reminding her that I had been waiting for a couple of hours, she replied in a matter-of-fact way, "Well, you know those journalists came all the way from Chicago to meet Shiv-*ji*." Thus, within the hierarchy of who is able to gain access to the Bombay film world, being South Asian and from New York defers to being white and from Chicago (or probably anywhere, actually).

Despite being displaced by white journalists, I was on the whole pretty successful in gaining access to the A-list of the film industry. My access to this elite social world was determined by a number of factors: my own social, class, and national location; my occupational trajectory; and my gender. The ease and rapidity with which I was able to gain access to the elite of the Hindi film industry was a result of contacts emerging from my own social networks as a diasporic South Asian living in New York City. I could not have cultivated these particular networks if I had remained in India. Though my own family in India would be identified as solidly middle class, with every member of my parents' generation having attended college and mostly pursuing careers in engineering or medicine, being from the southern state of Andhra Pradesh and residing mainly in the cities of Calcutta and Hyderabad, the chances of me encountering individuals with close contacts to the Bombay film world, who would facilitate this sort of ethnographic research, would have been very remote.

My fieldwork was primarily enabled by two main sets of contacts — one set located in the film industry itself and the other located in the larger social world of filmmakers. My preliminary contacts within the film world were two daughters of a Hindi film screenwriter, both of whom I had met when I was living in Philadelphia as a graduate student at the University of Pennsylvania. The younger of the two was a feature writer for the prominent English-language news magazine *India Today*, who mainly wrote about Hindi films and the film industry. She had a master of journalism degree from Northwestern University, after which she moved to Philadelphia to live with her sister and worked at *Harper's Bazaar* in New York. The older sister was then an aspiring director (she's had several films released since), who had trained at Temple Film School, directing television serials in 1996 and being mentored by a leading Hindi film director. Their mother had been a screenwriter for Hindi films since the mid-'80s. My other main contact was a personal friend from Bombay who I had met in New York, as a result of both of our husbands being faculty in the same department at NYU's Stern School of Business. She had grown up in Bandra, a northwestern suburb of Bombay, with actors, directors, producers, and screenwriters as neighbors, and had gone to school with some actors as well. Her mother-in-law was actually on the Central Board of Film Certification located in Bombay, one of the ten boards that certifies films for exhibition. Her father-in-law had been an accountant and her brother-in-law a travel agent to some filmmakers.

It was really through these two clusters of contacts, which included their families and friends, that I made my way through the film industry. In fact, since I had never been to Bombay before, it was only because of these personal contacts that I was able to start meeting members of the film industry as soon as I arrived in Bombay. What I noticed right away was that social networks and kinship determined entry and access at every stage. Film journalists have frequently gone to high school with certain film stars, which is how they are afforded access, or why a particular journalist deals exclusively with a few stars. Being from Bombay, growing up in certain neighborhoods, going to the same schools, or being part of the same club affords an access to the film industry that is not readily available to most Indians from other parts of the country, unless they are part of the social and kin networks of the industry.

While having my initial contacts paved the way for my research, the key to my sustained and continued access to this world is my position as a scholar in the American academy. During my early fieldwork I was able to meet a large number of people because I was carrying out academic research and receiving a PhD for ostensibly studying about films and filmmakers. People always asked in a slightly incredulous tone: "You mean you can get a PhD in this in America?" For a form of popular culture that had always been criticized as vulgar and low-brow by the English-language press and English-speaking elites, and for a social group whose dominant image was that of being uncouth, uneducated, and unintelligent, being the object of an academic researcher's study granted the cultural legitimacy and symbolic capital craved by many filmmakers. Many people told me the reason they were granting me interviews was because I was writing a thesis—or a book—with academic rather than journalistic intent. I discuss the valorization of formal education in chapter three of this book, which sheds further light on why a twenty-something graduate student in anthropology from New York was able to meet some of the biggest celebrities in India, even the world.

The final factor shaping my fieldwork, particularly regarding access, has to do with being a woman, but not necessarily in the conventional understandings about gender and fieldwork, where women have had more access to women's worlds and men to male spaces and male worlds. The Hindi film industry is extremely patriarchal and male-dominated, and the sites and spaces of production until the early 2000s were highly masculine. Paradoxically, being a woman helped me gain access, as I piqued curiosity and interest, often standing out as being one of the few—and sometimes the only—women on a film set. My curiosity value was enhanced by the fact that I had traveled from New York to study the industry, rather than having tried to join it as an actress. Contrary to common understandings about the gendered dimensions of fieldwork, I actually had a harder time meeting women, specifically the actresses.

While being a woman in this predominantly male world also had its disadvantages, primarily regarding issues of sexual harassment, it afforded me a perspective on the gender politics of the film industry and the concerns around respectability, which are intrinsically gendered. For example, my own ease of mobility through the sites of production and sociality within the industry led to assumptions and speculations by some filmmakers and journalists about my intentions and personal scruples; the fact that I was a married graduate student from the United States did not solve, but actually exacerbated, these judgments. For example, a middle-aged screenwriter called me a "bad penny" when he saw me at an actress's birthday party, while a film journalist present at the same party informed me bluntly that I had come to Bombay to "party rather than do research." A photographer at whose studio I spent many days observing photo shoots for film magazines would continuously chide me, "You're not really married; you're just wearing that *mangalsutra* to fool us."[48] When I expressed my frustration with such comments, attitudes, and unwelcome advances to a young director whom I had befriended, pointing out that I was always very modestly dressed and behaved, he said that no matter how I dressed or behaved, the fact that I had "left my husband for a year to do research of all places among film people" would lead to judgments about my "character." That my behavior did not conform to accepted conventions of how a respectable married woman should behave, sheds light on filmmakers' own perceptions about the film industry as a morally hazardous space.

This book is comprised of nine chapters that detail the production culture of the Hindi film industry, focusing on filmmakers' drive for social distinction and efforts to manage uncertainty, which have contributed to the gentrification of the film industry and Hindi cinema, enabling them to become "Bollywood." These chapters are organized along three main themes: the social status of films and filmmakers; the social and material practices of filmmaking; and the social, material, and discursive practices of audience-making. Chapters one through three establish the wider social and historical context of Hindi filmmaking, dealing explicitly with issues of cultural legitimacy and social respectability connected to the social world of Hindi filmmakers and the politico-historical field of film production. Chapters four through seven address the practices of film production and filmmakers' efforts to make sense of and manage uncertainty. Chapters eight and nine examine the ways that audiences are imagined, discussed, and classified by the Hindi film industry as an essential manifestation of the sentiment of disdain and as an attempt to manage uncertainty.

The Social Status of Films and Filmmakers

Chapter one examines the Indian state's attitudes and policies toward the cinematic medium and its relationship with the Hindi film industry over time, revealing the complicated place of cinema in the politics of national prestige, nation-building, and modernization. This chapter provides the context to understand Bombay filmmakers' own self-positioning and quest for cultural legitimacy, which I discuss in subsequent chapters. It details the shift in official attitudes from a Nehruvian developmentalist paradigm, in which film was solely valued for its pedagogical and communicative potential, to the contemporary neoliberal juncture, where prolific filmmaking traditions are regarded as examples of native ingenuity and a source of economic growth.

By examining filmmakers' narratives about the changes occurring in Hindi cinema and filmmaking from the mid-1990s, in chapter two I identify the sentiment of disdain that permeates the industry's production culture. This chapter focuses on the discourse of progress, most frequently articulated as "coolness," demonstrating the connections between the sentiment of disdain, the category of coolness, the process of gentrification, and the construction of Hindi filmmakers' subjectivities. I argue that filmmaking is an intersubjective enterprise, in which both audiences and technology serve to mediate filmmakers' presentation of their selves.

Chapter three extends an examination of the sentiment of disdain into the social world of filmmakers by focusing on the tremendous concern around the notion of respectability, which has been a longstanding anxiety, dating back to the early days of cinema in India. Here I describe how members of the film industry define, display, and perform respectability, relying primarily upon the trope of the "good family." By examining the gendered dimensions of behavior on film sets, filmmakers' narratives about how they joined the industry, and their valorization of formal, higher education, this chapter reveals the normative power of a particular idea of middle-classness within the social world of the industry.

The Practices and Processes of Production

Chapter four delves into the everyday life of Hindi film production, but it is distinct from the other chapters in terms of style and presentation. It offers a "thick description" of an average day on a Hindi film set and is written in a narrative style, incorporating dialogue and conversations. My goal with such a rendering is twofold: to make the quotidian life of film production palpable for readers, and to convey how one can discern valuable social and cultural insights through participant-observation on a film set. Although written in a narrative and descriptive style, this chapter is no less analytical than the others, for it is governed by specific decisions of what to include and exclude. Each character and conversation has been chosen and constructed to convey specific points about the structure and working style of the film industry. This detailed ethnographic sketch provides the context to understand chapters five through seven. Chapters five and six analyze in-depth key issues raised by the ethnographic material, demonstrating how disdain operates to forge difference. For example, chapter five details the decentralized and fragmented nature of filmmaking, along with the longstanding anxiety about the proliferation of producers in India, which leads Hindi filmmakers to indulge in a particular sort of boundary-work around the figure of the illegitimate producer, most commonly referred to as the "proposal-maker." Chapter five also focuses on the structure, organization, and social relations of the Hindi film industry, revealing the central roles played by distributors, social networks, kinship, and stars in the political economy and production practices of the industry.

Chapter six discusses the work culture of the Hindi film industry, which for decades has been the object of much disparagement, derisive humor, and disdain. It details the informality, orality, flexibility, and thrift that are dominant characteristics of the industry's work culture. Most of the attributes of the Hindi film industry's improvisational and resourceful working style are not valued within filmmakers' discourses and representations, however. Instead, the dominant tone is one of criticism, reproach, and disdain. In addition to describing these sentiments, the chapter discusses filmmakers' efforts to assert their difference from a generic norm—ranging from discourses about behavior to a fetishization of technology.

Chapter seven examines the myriad ways that Hindi filmmakers try to manage the uncertainty endemic to the filmmaking process. Rituals such as *mahurats*, and a reliance on stars and songs, are specific practices that Hindi filmmakers undertake to reduce the risk of commercial failure. Despite their best efforts, commercial success evades filmmakers most of the time, and this chapter discusses how filmmakers make sense of box-office failure by developing "production fictions," explanations that attempt to impose meaning and structure upon the unpredictability of box-office outcomes. A dominant production fiction has been that the industry's commercial fortunes are intimately connected to its structure and work culture, with the implication that if those changed, the industry's overall rates of success would improve; therefore, the chapter describes the structural changes referred to as "corporatization," which ensued in 2003, and the way they interact with the industry's production fictions.

Audience-Making

Chapter eight discusses how Hindi filmmakers imagine and classify their audiences: representations derived from culturalist interpretations of box-office outcome. The binary opposition of the "masses/classes" has been the primary mode for filmmakers to make sense of the vastly diverse audiences for Hindi cinema. The underlying assumption behind this binary is that the masses and classes are fundamentally different, and their tastes and world-views are completely incommensurable. Despite this incommensurability, Hindi filmmakers, for much of the industry's history, strove to make films that would appeal across these divides. Such films are referred to as "universal hits" and this chapter relates the difficulties, articulated by filmmakers, of achieving that form of success.

Chapter nine analyzes the changing status of the universal hit within the Hindi film industry, with the growing significance of overseas markets and the advent of the multiplex movie theater. It describes the transformation in attitudes about the necessity of universal hits and locates them in the changing structures of production, distribution, and exhibition characterizing Hindi filmmaking since 2000. The altered status of the universal hit indexes a shift from the masses to the classes as the imagined target audience for Hindi cinema. This chapter thus reveals how the gentrification of the Hindi film industry is most apparent and visible in the realm of its audience imaginaries and exhibition practices. The valorization of socially elite audiences has less to do with profit and more to do with Hindi filmmakers' concerns about cultural legitimacy and symbolic capital.

NOTES ON PSEUDONYMS, NAMES, FILM TITLES, AND COMMERCIAL CLASSIFICATIONS

Given that Hindi films have highly visible public lives and that many of my informants are well-known celebrities, who are used to having their words and images circulate globally, I have not followed standard anthropological convention of assigning pseudonyms. Instead, I have adopted a mixed approach that is attuned to the specificities of my interactions with filmmakers. I use real names when quoting from formal, tape-recorded interviews, or when relaying observations from public events or public spaces; I use pseudonyms whenever I describe observations, interactions, and conversations where my informants had some reasonable expectation of privacy or when they would not be cognizant that the anthropologist amidst them would treat their statements as a form of data. In certain instances when quoting from a formal interview, I refrain from naming the speaker entirely when he or she has requested that particular statements not be attributed. In such cases, I have identified speakers by the occupational role they perform within the industry. Additionally, certain last names in the Hindi film industry, such as Chopra, Khan, Kapoor, and Khanna, are very common. Unless a kin relationship is indicated, readers should not assume that individuals who share the same last name are related.

Film titles that appear in this book, unless specified, are the titles of actual films. In some instances I have changed a film's title in order to maintain the confidentiality of a speaker when the circumstances required. Hindi film titles mainly appear in the urban landscape and on-screen in their Romanized transliterated form with their own particular orthography, which I have maintained, rather than converting them to the scholarly standards of transliteration with its specific diacritical marks.

Finally, for the sake of consistency I have followed the dominant trade practice of tabulating commercial outcome from the point of view of the distributor, even though I call into question the assumptions that govern the interpretation of commercial outcome. For a host of reasons that are discussed in chapter nine, exact, accurate, or consistent figures and statistics about commercial outcome are notoriously hard to come by in the Hindi film industry. This is a feature of the industry that has been described with some frustration by transnational accounting and consulting firms—like A.T. Kearney, Pricewaterhouse Coopers, KPMG, et al.—which have been preparing hyperbolic annual reports of the potential of the film and entertainment industry in India since 2000. For example, Pricewaterhouse Cooper's 2006 report, *The Indian Entertainment and Media Industry: Unravelling the Potential*, states in its preface that "since much of the industry does not have an organised body, lack of a centralised tracking agency that could provide us with accurate figures was the biggest challenge before us to compile figures and determine the size of each segment. This challenge was exacerbated by the fact that most companies in the industry do not have their financial information in the public domain" (Pricewaterhouse Coopers 2006a).[49] Informants told me that even the trade magazines were, at the most, 80–85 percent accurate in their accounting of box-office outcome. Additionally, the fragmented structure of the industry means that commercial success itself is a relative concept, dependent upon which point in the value chain of filmmaking one occupied—production, distribution, or exhibition. For these reasons, I refrain from circulating numbers related to box-office receipts, for numbers are highly subjective entities in the Hindi film industry.

Part 1

THE SOCIAL STATUS OF FILMS AND FILMMAKERS

CHAPTER 1

From Vice to Virtue

The State and Filmmaking in India

On May 10, 1998, filmmaking in India was accorded the status of an industry by the BJP-led Central government, laying to rest one of the most frequent complaints regarding the state's attitude toward the enterprise of filmmaking—"We're not even recognized as an industry!"—I had heard from Hindi filmmakers during my initial fieldwork in 1996. What was so surprising about the announcement was that none of the filmmakers I had met during my fieldwork ever believed it would happen; they were firm in their views that the "step-motherly" treatment they received from the state, both at the central and regional levels, would continue indefinitely. And yet, two years later at a conference titled "Challenges Before Indian Cinema," the union information and broadcasting minister, Sushma Swaraj, announced industry status for filmmaking.

If the Hindi film industry was not an industry prior to 1998, what was it? What does it mean to be recognized as an "industry" by the Indian state? Why did the state finally recognize it as such? What impact has industry status had on filmmaking in Bombay? That India produces the greatest number of feature films in the world is a fact proudly touted and disseminated by the state in a variety of arenas, and yet for decades the Indian state had officially treated commercial filmmaking as an activity akin to vices like gambling and horseracing. What brought about the change in state attitudes toward filmmaking?

In this chapter, I examine how cinema—its role, significance, effects, and influence—has been imagined and discussed in India by the state primarily at the national level, or what in India is referred to as the "Center" or Central government.[1] Not only does such an examination reveal the complicated place of cinema in the politics of national prestige, nation-building, and development, but it also provides the context to understand Hindi filmmakers' own self-positioning and quest for cultural legitimacy, which I will be discussing in subsequent chapters.

Rather than referring to a monolithic entity, I use the term "state" as a shorthand for an assemblage of practices and institutions that enact governance through a variety of domains under the sign of the Indian state (Gupta and Ferguson 2002; Gupta 1995). Cinema has played a significant role in state discourses about development, nationhood, and modernity in India since Independence in 1947.[2] For over a century, cinema has been woven into the fabric of urban life to such an extent that it seems ubiquitous and, unlike television, was never state-controlled.[3] Though film production primarily has been a private enterprise, it has been an object of state regulation in India since colonial times through censorship, taxation, allocation of raw materials, and control over exhibition through the licensing of theaters. Cinema has also been seen as a "problem," warranting the attention of a number of government commissions, inquiries, and symposia in independent India.[4]

The significance of the granting of industry status, and its radical departure from previous policies, can be understood as a transformation in the regimes of value (Appadurai 1986; Myers 2001)—from modernization to cultural sovereignty—within which cinema has been situated over time in India. I argue that the Indian state's declaration marks a taxonomic shift (Clifford 1988) from a Nehruvian developmentalist paradigm, in which film was solely valued for its pedagogical and communicative potential, to the contemporary neoliberal conjuncture where the existence of multiple, prolific filmmaking traditions are regarded as examples of native ingenuity and a source of economic growth. This shift in attitude has been an important factor in allowing the gentrification of the film industry, especially in terms of its exhibition practices, discussed in this chapter and in chapters two and nine.

My discussion of the discursive field created by the state about filmmaking focuses on the central place of cinema in moral, aesthetic, developmentalist, and modernization discourses about Indian society. I base my analysis on documents and statements from key periods in the history of the Indian state, spanning from the independence movement in the 1930s, the Nehruvian era of the 1950s, the post-Emergency period of the late 1970s and early 1980s, to the era of economic liberalization in the 1990s.[5] Each period has been shaped by the marking of an anniversary connected to the presence and history of cinema in India: in 1938, the Indian Motion Picture Congress commemorated the twenty-fifth anniversary of Indian cinema, marking the date (1913) of the first Indian feature film; in 1956, the Film Federation of India celebrated the twenty-fifth anniversary of Indian cinema by using the first sound feature, produced in 1931, as the benchmark; in 1981, the fiftieth anniversary of talkies was celebrated by the Indian Academy of Motion Pictures Arts and Sciences; in 1995–96, the 100th anniversary of the invention of cinema itself became a cause for commemoration by state institutions such as the National Film Archive and the National Film Development Corporation. The texts and documents accompanying these commemorations are a rich source of information about transformations in attitudes toward, and expectations of, filmmaking in India.

In order to understand the larger ideological context framing state attitudes toward filmmaking in independent India, I first describe how national leaders such as Gandhi and Nehru perceived cinema, laying the foundation for state policies for nearly five decades. Then, I discuss in detail the ambivalence displayed toward films and filmmaking by the "developmentalist state" as manifest in regulations such as taxation and policy prescriptions of the cultural bureaucracy. Finally, I examine the granting of industry status, along with the changing attitudes about cinema in the neoliberal context of the late twentieth century.

1913–1947: CINEMA AND THE INDIAN NATIONAL CONGRESS

Dhundiraj Govind Phalke, who in 1913 made the first feature film in India and later earned the appellation "Father of Indian cinema," was explicitly nationalist in his motivation for making films—he wanted to create Indian images for Indian audiences and establish a completely indigenous or *swadeshi* industry.[6] Yet the Indian National Congress (INC), one of the main organizations fighting against colonial rule, did not accord the medium much importance. Most leaders viewed the cinema as "low" and "vulgar" entertainment, popular with the uneducated "masses" (Kaul 1998). These attitudes are exemplified in the public statements of two of the most prominent leaders of the independence struggle, Mohandas Gandhi and Jawaharlal Nehru. While Gandhi rejected film on the whole as immoral and culturally inauthentic, Nehru viewed film as a dangerous but potentially useful pedagogical medium. Meanwhile, filmmakers at the time responded to their public statements not by countering their criticisms, but by casting film within the terms of discourse set by Gandhi and Nehru.

Gandhi's antipathy toward cinema, which probably stemmed from it being a "foreign" technology, was central to the INC's disregard for film as a potential tool in its mobilizing and organizing efforts. Gandhi declared many times that he had never seen a single film, comparing cinema with other "vices" such as *satta* (betting), gambling, and horseracing (Das Sharma 1993: 136). When the Indian Cinematograph Committee was conducting its exhaustive study of filmmaking and film-viewing in India in 1927, it sent a questionnaire to Gandhi asking him his views about the state of cinema in India. Gandhi returned the questionnaire to the committee with a letter stating that he had no views about the "sinful technology." His letter, dated November 12, 1927, states, "Even if I was so minded, I should be unfit to answer your questionnaire, as I have never been to a cinema. But even to an outsider the evil it has done and is doing is patent. The good, if it has done at all, remains to be proved" (in Kaul 1998: 44). Other examples of Gandhi's disinterest in—and distaste for—cinema included his refusal to send a congratulatory message for the official souvenir being published on the occasion of the twenty-fifth anniversary of Indian cinema, in 1938. His secretary's reply to the request states, "As a rule Gandhi gives messages only on rare occasions, and this is only for a cause whose virtue is ever undoubtful. As for the cinema industry, he has the least interest in it, and one may not expect a word of appreciation from him" (in Kaul 1998: 44). Gandhi emphatically expressed his negativity toward cinema, along with his recognition of its growing popularity, in his paper *Harijan*, in an issue dated May 3, 1942: "If I began to organize picketing in respect of them (the evil of cinema) I should lose my caste, my mahatmaship" (in Kaul 1998: 45).[7]

Gandhi's persistent aversion to cinema did not go unnoticed by Bombay filmmakers. K. Ahmad Abbas, a noted screenwriter, director, journalist, novelist, and short-story writer, who in the late 1930s was working as a publicist for a leading studio, Bombay Talkies, wrote an open letter to Gandhi, which was published in the English-language magazine *Filmindia*, dated October 1939.[8] The tone of the letter is one of filial respect: Abbas addresses Gandhi as "My Dear Bapu" (My Dear Father), wishes him a happy birthday, and "craves his forgiveness" for disturbing him during such a turbulent time (war had just broken out in Europe).[9] He represents himself as a child—a "son of India"—who is rushing to Gandhi, the father of the nation, seeking his approval of the cinema, which he characterizes as the "new toy," for his generation.[10]

Abbas expresses his surprise and "pain" over Gandhi's remarks, reasoning that he would not have been so perturbed by such statements generally—for his own father felt similarly about films, thinking them an "imported vice from the West"—but Gandhi's position as a national and world leader imbued his opinion with much greater significance and consequence. Abbas fears that Gandhi's disapproval would reinforce others' hostility toward the medium, which would prevent cinema, "one of the world's most useful inventions," from achieving its full potential and leave it open to abuse by "unscrupulous people."

Abbas then wonders how it is that Gandhi developed such a poor opinion of the cinema and asks whether he has ever seen a film.[11] He admits that many films are of questionable aesthetic, social, and moral value, and that many producers "exploit the baser passions of man to make money." Abbas also concedes that Gandhi and others of his generation would disapprove of the "playful romanticism" his generation "gloats over" in most films, and that he does not expect Gandhi to see or approve of romantic films. Abbas describes cinema as a neutral medium of expression, which could be "an instrument of much good in this world." He discusses other inventions, such as the radio and the airplane, which have revolutionized and benefited modern life, but should not be condemned because they have also been exploited by "unscrupulous persons," such as Hitler, for undesirable ends.

Abbas speculates that the root of Gandhi's distaste for cinema lay with the fact that most films dealt "exclusively with sex and love themes." In order to counter such an impression of cinema, Abbas elaborates the various pedagogical functions films have fulfilled in other countries. He discusses how documentaries and other types of nonfiction films have been utilized for the purposes of education, news, general knowledge, anti-crime, and political information. He assures Gandhi that the demand for these sorts of "extra-entertainment, non-commercial films" is increasing, and that a considerable portion of the program in cinemas is being devoted to such "useful" films. Abbas also states that, even among entertainment films, "the socially useful and morally uplifting element is steadily on the increase," and then lists twelve such examples, both Indian and American, which he guarantees that if Gandhi were to see, he would have "nothing but praise for them." Among the American films, Abbas lists *Life of Louis Pasteur*, *Life of Emile Zola*, and *Boys' Town*; the Indian examples include films about poet-saints such as *Sant Tukaram* and *Sant Tulsidas*.[12] He points out that each of these films has been very popular with millions of cinemagoers all over the world. Abbas further informs Gandhi that some "patriots" are attempting to "produce a film record of your own inspiring life."

In his closing, Abbas expresses his feeling that the nationalist movement led by Gandhi has "indirectly caused much purification and regeneration" in Indian filmmaking. He attributes Gandhi's leadership as having created an environment conducive for improvements in cinema, resulting in better and "more socially useful films." Abbas presents a narrative of improving standards in cinema connected to the increased interest in the medium by "honest and socially conscious people," and states that a decade earlier, good films were not produced because "educated and 'respectable' folk" viewed films as "evil and loathsome." He asserts that such prejudices are breaking down and argues, "The 'cleansing' of the Indian films will be in direct proportion to the number of honest and responsible people who are able to take the place of ignorant profiteers, who dominated the industry for so many years. We want more decent people to take interest in this industry, so that it becomes an instrument of social good rather than a *tamasha* [spectacle]" (in Bandyopadhyay 1993: 145). Abbas's argument, that cinematic quality is connected to the class position of its producers, is a view still articulated by contemporary filmmakers, a point I elaborate in chapter three. He warns Gandhi that the future of good filmmaking in India is actually in his hands, pleading with him to change his opinion about cinema: "But these people may be discouraged and kept away if you and other great men like you continue to count the cinema among such vices as gambling and drinking. You are a great soul, Bapu. In your heart there is no room for prejudice. Give this little toy of ours, the cinema, which is not so useless as it looks, a little of your attention and bless it with a smile of toleration" (in Bandyopadhyay 1993: 145).

Although he failed to win over Gandhi, Abbas constructs certain dichotomies about the nature of cinema in India that have persisted till the present day. By representing it as a neutral technology that has been abused by individuals who are solely interested in profit, he tries to counter the image of cinema as a vice. He constructs a dichotomy that has to do with the intentionality of filmmakers: those who make films for money contrasted with those who make films for higher artistic and social purposes. The other main dichotomy present in the letter concerns entertainment and its opposites: art, edification, or social reform. Entertainment is defined as the activation of "baser" passions. Love, romance, and sex have nothing to do with art or expression but are the main criteria for designating films as morally and aesthetically deficient. Such "romantic" films are presented as containing very little socially redeeming value. Discussing film in conjunction with religion and patriotism, Abbas elevates the medium from the lowly status assigned to it by Gandhi and others. Rather than trying to argue a case for the importance of entertainment, he goes to great lengths to articulate how film can be something more than "mere" entertainment. In his representation, the main purpose and value of cinema is as a type of moral pedagogy. Abbas predicates his arguments on a future-oriented view of cinema, asking Gandhi to give film a chance because it will become something useful and good.

Unlike Gandhi, Nehru was not averse to the cinema, but was critical of the kind of films being made at the time.[13] In a message to the Indian Motion Picture Congress held in Bombay in 1939, Nehru stated, "I am far from satisfied at the quality of work that has been done. Motion pictures have become an essential part of modern life and they can be used with great advantage for educational purposes. So far, greater stress has been laid on a type of film which presumably is supposed to be entertaining, but the standard or quality of which is not high. I hope that the industry will consider now in terms of meeting the standards and of aiming at producing high-class films which have educational and social values. Such films should receive the help and cooperation of not only the public, but also of the State" (in Kaul 1998: 41). Once again, entertainment is synonymous with poor quality and low standards, and the significance of the medium is articulated in terms of its pedagogical potential. Like Abbas, Nehru assesses the present as deficient and hopes for better films in the future. Other nationalist leaders expressed similar instrumentalist hopes for the medium. In the January 1943 issue of *Filmindia*, Sarojini Naidu, a renowned poet and member of the INC, asserted, "Cinema can do to a whole people what a loving and devoted wife (can) do to an erring husband: to root out superstition; to make people rational and make them better informed; and to give them useful entertainment" (in Kaul 1998: 51).

This view of film—as a tool for modernization—crucially shaped state policy and rhetoric toward cinema in independent India. During and after Nehru's tenure as prime minister, a number of institutions and policies were established to promote "high-class" filmmaking. While the Nehruvian perspective on cinema has been the dominant one, noticeably in the creation and maintenance of a cultural and cinematic bureaucracy to counter commercial cinema, Gandhi's moralism, and his view of cinema as corrupting, has also lingered in prohibitive policies such as censorship and taxation. Additionally, both the critique of the present state of cinema and the simultaneous valorization of the future encountered in Abbas's and Nehru's statements have been a consistent feature of the discourse surrounding cinema in postcolonial India.

1947–1997: CINEMA AND THE DEVELOPMENTALIST STATE
Ideologies of Development and Modernization

> Films are too important to be left to filmmakers alone.
> —H. Y. Sharada Prasad, Director, Indian Institute of Mass Communication

The above statement, made during Prasad's speech of welcome at the 1979 Symposium on Cinema in Developing Countries held in Delhi, best encapsulates official attitudes toward the medium of cinema for much of India's post-Independence period. Cinema has been a consistent feature in discussions about development and modernization in India, and Hindi filmmakers have been interpellated as partners in these projects for decades. Much of the discourse about film in India communicates that it is a very powerful tool that can either be used for the greater good, or be very dangerous if in the wrong hands. It then becomes the state's responsibility to ensure the production of films that engender positive or beneficial effects, as well as prohibiting those that can be damaging. Examples of the state's prescriptive role include the system of national awards for films instituted in 1954, while its proscriptive role is primarily enacted through the institution of film censorship, which has been carried over from the colonial period.[14]

As a result of the high rates of illiteracy and the unparalleled popularity of films and film stars in India, the state has viewed film as a pedagogical tool in its modernization agenda. Illiteracy, or the lack of a formal education, signals to government functionaries that vast portions of the populace, who are referred to as the "masses," are easily influenced—or incited by—onscreen images. Since the masses are perceived as very malleable—and in need of proper molding—elected officials and bureaucrats throughout the decades have been exhorting filmmakers to make "socially relevant" films to "uplift" the masses. For example, in the Silver Jubilee Souvenir Program, published by the Film Federation of India on the occasion of the twenty-fifth anniversary of Indian sound films in 1956, a section titled "Blessings and Greetings" contains statements made by a variety of state leaders on the role of cinema in Indian society. The Chief Minister of Bombay[15] asserted, "A film, as we know, is the most powerful medium of our age, which not only influences but moulds the cultural outlook of the people. The film industry, therefore, can play an important role in carrying the message of peace and progress to the masses. I am glad to see that some producers have realized this, but it is necessary for the industry as a whole to come forward and help the people and the State in this matter" (FFI 1956: v). The Chief Minister of Uttar Pradesh[16] described in greater detail the possibilities and problems of film in India, "Films not only provide the most popular form of entertainment in modern times but they are proving also a most powerful and effective medium of education and cultural advancement. They have immense possibilities of doing good as well as harm to Society . . . The responsibility for reforming the public taste is of the producers and is a public duty which carries its own reward. Pandering to what is vulgar in human nature will degrade all of us" (FFI 1956: vi). Both leaders echo earlier statements by Nehru and Naidu where entertainment is subservient to education, and filmmakers bear the burden of some manner of social reform. The Indian state's concern with socially relevant cinema is connected to its "hypodermic-needle" understanding of media effects and influence.[17] In this simplistic top-down causal view of media influence, cinema—and audio-visual media in general—can directly influence behavior and shape attitudes and subjectivities.[18] The Supreme Court of India, in a 1989 judgment about film censorship, asserted this point of view unequivocally, "A film motivates thought and action and assures a high degree of attention and retention as compared to the printed word. The combination of act and speech, sight and sound, in semi darkness of the theatre, with elimination of all distracting ideas, will have a strong impact on the minds of the viewers and can affect emotions; therefore, it has as much potential for evil as it has for good and has an equal potential to instill or cultivate violent or good behavior. It cannot be equated with other modes of communication. Censorship by prior restraint is, therefore, not only desirable but also necessary";[19] therefore, a film is judged according to the perceived positive or negative effects its main theme may precipitate in viewers, and thus in society. This perspective provides the continued justification for film censorship as well as institutions such as the Films Division—the state-funded documentary filmmaking institution.

Thus, a striking characteristic of the state-generated discourse about cinema is the intense ambivalence—a complex mixture of pride, disdain, hope, and fear—expressed toward films and filmmaking, which arises from the multivalent nature of the medium: film is a product of science and technology, a mode of communication, an art form, a source of entertainment, and a commercial activity. This ambivalence is a result of the postcolonial nature of the Indian state and its particular relationship to modernity—a relationship that has been defined primarily by the apparatus and discourse of development, which has positioned "Third World" nation-states like India as "behind" the West (Gupta 1998: 10).

Itty Abraham, in his work on India's nuclear program, describes the postcolonial condition as marked by a specific experience of time, which he characterizes as "time-in-waiting." This condition is one in which the future can be seen in the present, through the examples of advanced industrialized nation-states, combined with a simultaneous awareness of one's own lagging development. Consequently, postcolonial time "drives state action in an endless search for 'modernization' and 'development,' which leads to an anxiety about world rankings and never 'catching up' while constantly projecting the moment when it may happen" (Abraham 1998: 19).

This obsession with rankings, superlatives, and coeval temporality has also been a feature of the state-generated discourse about cinema. Since the motion picture is a technology, "a true product of the modern age" (Chhabria 1996: 1), two features about cinema in India are used to represent the modern nature of the Indian nation-state: first, the sheer volume of films produced yearly affords India the distinction of being the "world's largest" producer, surpassing even that preeminent example of modernity, the United States; second, the history of cinema in India as contemporaneous with the history of cinema in the world—"India is among the earliest countries in the world to have adopted cinema" (Karanth 1980: 1)—counters connotations of technological incompetence, cultural domination, and backwardness that saddle terms, such as "Third World," or "developing," which historically located India in the international political and economic order. The date of the first screening of motion pictures in India, July 7, 1896, becomes an important signifier of India's participation in the modern world, since "Indian audiences had their introduction to projected motion pictures in the same year as British, Russian, and American audiences, barely six months after the first 'Cinematographe' show at the Grand Café in Paris" (Karanth 1980: 1).

While both the simultaneity of the filmic experience and the existence of large-scale film industries have been represented as an index of modernity and cultural sovereignty, over the years the dominant tone about the

Hindi film industry and filmmaking has been that most films produced in India are escapist, frivolous, formulaic, for "mere entertainment": not sufficiently "meaningful" or "artistic." For example, in 1998, at the International Film Festival of India (IFFI), the minister of information and broadcasting, S. Jaipal Reddy, stated that while India is the largest film-producing country in the world, filmmakers should focus more on quality than quantity. He expressed his hope that interacting with the best filmmakers from all over the world, at venues such as the IFFI, "would help us to make better films" (Gupta 1998). Since Nehru, what has been operating in state discourses toward cinema, especially with respect to the relationship between entertainment and quality, is the "logic of deferrence" (Krishna 1999), where entertainment has been viewed as something that a postcolonial, "developing," nation-state like India cannot afford.[20]

In an attempt to foster "good" cinema and counter the dominant mode of filmmaking—as represented by the Bombay industry—in 1960 the state established the Film Finance Corporation, which became (in 1980) the National Film Development Corporation (NFDC). These state institutions were responsible for financing films of "high artistic content" (Dayal 1983) and "serious" filmmakers, defined primarily by their rejection of the aesthetic, generic, and production conventions of Bombay cinema, becoming known as the "New Indian" cinema.[21] Films falling under this category—also referred to as "parallel" or "art" cinema—were characterized by their social realist aesthetic, smaller budgets, location shooting, absence of song and dance sequences, use of lesser-known actors, and a naturalistic style of acting (against the big budgets, elaborate sets, songs, superstars, and melodramatics of mainstream Hindi cinema).[22]

The state's constant criticism and efforts to promote an alternative cinematic form have resulted in a dismissive and disparaging attitude on the part of filmmakers. In 1996, during my first phase of fieldwork, the most common characterization made by filmmakers of the state's attitude toward the film industry was the term "step-motherly," with its connotations of abuse and neglect. Veteran producer B. R. Chopra described the relationship between the film industry and the state as one-sided, opportunistic, and extractive: "You find that the government is interfering with us quite a bit, putting restrictions on us, and taking away the biggest slice of our earnings. The whole picture industry, whatever they've done, they've done all by themselves, without the aid of the government. According to me the film industry has not been able to get the favor of the government, except when it serves the government's purpose . . . The only thing they've done is to develop the parallel cinema and to help it.

That's all, but they've not done anything for the common man's cinema" (B. R. Chopra, interview, 14 August 1996). Chopra is referring to the most common rhetorical division of the film-going audience in India—as posed by members of the film industry, journalists, bureaucrats, and intellectuals—that the "common man," also referred to as the "masses," watches commercial films, while the elite audiences of the "classes" watch the art or parallel films. I will be discussing how the audience is imagined within this masses-classes binary in greater detail in chapter eight.

Subhash Ghai, one of the top producer/directors of the Bombay industry spoke with me at length about the relationship between the state and the film industry. He characterized the state's attitude toward the industry as a combination of fascination and distance, with leaders who are aware of the popularity of films and their influence over people's lives, but are unwilling to learn about the particularities of the industry. The reason that the state has not attempted to know or study the industry, according to Ghai, is because of the general distaste for cinema. He described the condescension that state officials have toward cinema, which he felt was based on their age and class: "They're all senior people who think that film or entertainment is not a serious man's business. All these *buddas* [old fogies], politicians, government officials, they think 'Cinema—ha ha ha—my servant goes, but I stop him from going to the cinema.'"

Ghai asserted that politicians articulate the importance of cinema periodically during election campaigns because they realize the "pull" of cinema and its ability to "mobilize voters." He also claimed that political leaders were aware of the key cultural and nation-building role played by films, "When they think about national integration, when they get their calls from Indian embassies from all over the world, that cinema is holding our culture over there. Cinema is a representative of Indian culture abroad." According to Ghai, however, once in power, officials put aside the film industry's concerns, "They are again back to their normal, 'Oh, cinema is not a serious man's business.'"

Criticizing the Indian state's attitudes toward filmmaking as short-sighted, Ghai brought up the United States as a counterexample where the state has encouraged and recognized the value of entertainment as an industry. He argued that American films have enabled the United States to dominate the world culturally, even leading to the dissolution of the Soviet Union. "They're totally ignorant about the problems of the film industry, not realizing that [in] America, [the] entertainment industry is the second biggest industry after aerospace industry, exporting $600 bil-

lion, right? America became Big Brother because of the entertainment industry . . . because they've patronized the entertainment industry, so the
best of talent from Europe and everywhere came to America and made
America, and America fascinated every country and now it broke Russia.
I would say Michael Jackson and Robert De Niro—they broke Russia. It is
a threat to France; it is a threat to Japan; what is the threat? Bill Clinton?
No: movies. Movies have such an impact on other nations, because children grow up with movies. Children grow with three things: with their
school; with their parents; and . . . movies" (Ghai, interview, 10 December 1996). According to Ghai, the reason that the Indian state has not
realized the potential of filmmaking as an industry, economic activity,
and global cultural and ideological force is because, "these oldies never
saw cinema; they were never in touch with cinema" (Ghai, interview,
10 December 1996). Despite his flippant tone, Ghai's comments about
political leaders' antipathy toward cinema correspond with the history
of statements about the medium. Gandhi apparently saw only one film
in his life (Jeffrey 2006; Kaul 1998).

Cinema as Vice

While some of Ghai's statements are hyperbolic, his assessment of the
Indian state's lack of interest in the film industry as an economic enterprise is accurate. Unlike the U.S. government, which from the early part
of the twentieth century treated filmmaking as a business and helped
Hollywood to distribute its films globally (Miller 1998), the Indian state
did not accord filmmaking much economic significance, even though
shortly after Independence India became the second largest film producing country in the world. Despite filmmaking being the second largest
"industry" in India in terms of capital investment—and the fifth largest
in the number of people employed (Ray 1956: 32)—the developmentalist
economic ideology of the newly independent nation-state constructed a
hierarchy of needs in which filmmaking was not considered an essential
or important sphere of economic activity. Entertainment was not viewed
as a necessity in a country that at the time of Independence had a literacy rate of 18 percent, had an average life expectancy of 26 years, was suf-
fering from a food crisis, and had over one million refugees to resettle.
Instead, rapid industrialization, infrastructural development, and food
self-sufficiency were the main priorities of national economic policy.

Certain policies imposed immediately after Independence had long-
lasting repercussions for filmmaking. For example, a moratorium on
"non-essential building," due to the shortage of cement and building ma-

TABLE 1 TAXES LEVIED ON CINEMA

	Central Government	State Government	Local Government
Producer	Import duty Excise duty Censor-certification fee		
Distributor	Excise duty		
Exhibitor	News reel hire	Electricity tariff License fee Entertainment tax Publicity tax	Show tax House and water tax

Source: Based on Mittal (1995).

terials, meant that most states imposed a ban on theater construction. As a result, India has an extremely low number of movie screens—ranging from approximately 13,000 in the 1990s (the number varies because it includes mobile cinemas) to about 11,000 in the early 2000s—given the size of its annual theater attendance, which is approximately 3 billion (FICCI 2006).[23] In fact, despite being the world's largest film-producing country, India has one of the lowest ratio of screens to population: 12 screens per million people; in comparison, the United States has 117 screens per million people (Dua 2006). Most state governments also stipulated that movie theaters could not be constructed near schools, colleges, places of worship, residential areas, and government offices.

Economic policies have treated cinema as a source of tax revenue rather than as an engine of growth. Taxes levied on cinema are akin to those levied on "vices" such as gambling and horseracing (see Table 1 for a list of taxes levied upon cinema at the various levels of the state). The main bulk of taxation is collected by individual state governments through the entertainment tax, which is a sales tax imposed on box-office receipts, ranging in rates from 20 to 75 percent. While the British colonial government instituted the entertainment tax in 1922, in independent India it was continued and augmented by other forms of taxation. Most state governments increased entertainment tax rates soon after Independence. For instance, the tax rate was 12.5 percent before the Second World War in most provinces, with temporary wartime increases, but by 1949 rates ranged from 25 to 75 percent across the country, with an average of 33.5 percent. Municipalities also began to levy both entertainment taxes and duties on the transport of films from one place to another. Producers sending films out of the country discovered that they had to pay an exorbitant import duty to the Indian government in order to bring their own film prints back into the country. Additionally, there were sales taxes, other import duties, internal customs duties, income taxes, show taxes, and charges for censorship. By mid-1949, film industry organizations estimated that 60 percent of all box-office revenues were being taken by the state in the form of taxes (Barnouw and Krishnaswamy 1980: 138–39).

Of all of the various taxes filmmaking is subject to, entertainment tax has been the most contentious issue between filmmakers and the state at the regional level. For decades filmmakers have been requesting the Central government to either reduce, standardize (the tax varies from state to state), or abolish the tax altogether, but to no avail. For example, in 1955 at the "Future of Indian Films" seminar initiated by the *Sangeet Natak* Akademi (The National Academy of Music, Dance, and Theater), a number of filmmakers asserted, in their presentations, that the entertainment tax was a significant obstacle to the growth and improvement of filmmaking. S. S. Vasan, president of the Film Federation of India, declared, "It is this entertainment tax which has been the bane of the industry. The incidence of this tax, being so high, more than even the betting tax, has not only discouraged people from getting entertained, but has also adversely affected film production in this country" (in Ray 1956: 37). Nehru who was present for the inaugural session of the seminar, categorically dismissed such concerns in his address, stating bluntly, "I am not convinced by Vasan's argument . . . I do not see at all, broadly speaking why entertainment should not be taxed" (in Ray 1956: 11).

By the 1990s, filmmakers' arguments against the entertainment tax ranged from the issue of equity—that television, cable, and satellite are not subject to entertainment tax—to the moral/philosophical: that they are providing a great service to the nation by entertaining people, so why should the government tax entertainment? During our interview, producer G. P. Sippy asserted, "For entertaining people, you should get some reward from the government. What is a movie? It brings a smile on your face. If we make even one face smile, that's the biggest social service which a person does; instead they [the government] will say, 'Oh you are exposing the bodies!'" (G. P. Sippy, interview, 22 September 1996). As apparent from the discussion of state attitudes thus far, entertainment, however, is considered the very antithesis of social service: it is considered a luxury that a developing nation cannot afford.

Cinema as Cultural Problem

While state policies of taxation and licensing accorded films the status of a vice, state cultural policies treated mainstream films as a threat to other art forms. Even as a British colony, India was the world's third largest producer of films; therefore, from the point of view of the national leadership after Independence, filmmaking was seen as having escaped the effects of colonialism, unlike other artistic and performance traditions that had suffered greatly. In fact, the popularity of films and their music was viewed as a threat to novelists, painters, classical singers and dancers, and folk performers. A myriad of ministries, academies, and institutes, dealing with the visual, performing, and literary arts, were established shortly after Independence.[24] The Indian state, in an effort to revive and support the "traditional arts" and "high culture," excluded cinema from these categories and placed it under the purview of the Ministry of Information and Broadcasting, rather than the Ministry of Cultural Affairs.

The cultural bureaucracy consistently viewed cinema as a "problem" that warranted the attention of a number of government commissions, inquiries, and symposia in independent India. In such inquiries, filmmakers time and again singled out state policies as the source of problems besetting filmmaking, while bureaucrats and state functionaries blamed more intangible factors, such as audience taste. One such instance of this tension is apparent in the *Report of the Working Group on National Film Policy* (henceforth referred to as "the Working Group"), which provides a detailed look at the perception of Indian cinema as articulated by a branch of the state's cultural bureaucracy.

The Working Group, comprised of filmmakers and bureaucrats, was appointed by the Ministry of Information and Broadcasting in 1979; their task was to study the state of the film industry in areas such as production, technology, distribution, exhibition, financing, export and import, censorship, and taxation, and from this to suggest a national film policy. In 1980, after eight months of study, the Working Group submitted a 153-page report that outlined many policy recommendations—none of which were implemented—including a comprehensive film policy as well as suggestions on labor legislation and training facilities.

One area in which the Working Group was to concentrate their inquiry—and formulate policy recommendations—was the status of cinema as an art form and an instrument for social change. The report argued that the main factor impeding the growth of cinema as an art form in India was the government's indifference toward the health of cinema, as evidenced by many of its policies: taxation, customs and excise duties, as well as regulations governing the construction of theaters. The Group claimed that "the role of the Government in the promotion of good cinema, particularly in the context of a developing society, has not been sufficiently recognized in India" (1980: 9).

The consequence of governmental apathy was that despite the artistic achievements of Indian cinema (mainly measured by the awards won at international film festivals), much of it was characterized by "culturally vacuous films, which are exclusively designed for making money through audience manipulation" (Karanth 1980: 9). Expressing anxieties about the market and easily manipulated audiences, the Working Group called on the government to "provide a national platform for good cinema, to positively encourage the production of good films, to take such films to the largest number of people, and to initiate the audience in the appreciation of good cinema" (1980: 10).

In accordance with such goals, the Working Group recommended the establishment of an academy, the *Chalachitra* Akademi,[25] with the design of promoting cinema as an art form, on the same lines as the *Sangeet Natak* (Music-Dance-Drama), *Sahitya* (Literature), and *Lalit Kala* (Visual Arts) academies. Acknowledging that its list of fifteen broad functions, which ranged from maintaining a national film archive to operating a children's film center, would be an expensive venture, the Working Group argued that such an investment in "the propagation of film culture and the changing of audience taste" should be viewed as an investment in education and culture. Otherwise, "it is futile to expect that audiences can be converted to good cinema," and without proper audience support, "good cinema" would largely remain superfluous to the lives of most people (Karanth 1980: 15). The Group concluded this section of the report by stating that the establishment of the *Chalachitra* Akademi, with the objective of "promoting cinema as an art form and as a medium of culture, is absolutely necessary" (1980: 15).

According to some members of the cultural bureaucracy, however, the acknowledged failure of cinema to become a full-fledged art form in India was the result of it being a non-Indian, technological, mass-produced form. The Working Group asked a former chairwoman of the *Sangeet Natak* Akademi, Kamala Chattopadhyay, her views about the status of cinema as an art form. Referring to the enormous volume of films produced in India, she argued that creative art forms could not be undertaken on a mass scale. Comparing cinema to Indian drama, Chattopadhyay argued that traditional dramatic performances attained a reasonably high level of quality because they were expressions of the people's traditional consciousness, whereas cinema in India was "a form superimposed with a lot of appendages of mechanical and technological character. It is not a spontaneous instrument, springing from the soil and the people; therefore, except where there have been creative persons, and these necessarily have been few, the result has not taken on any worthwhile aesthetic value" (in Karanth 1980: 113).

The main conclusion that one draws from examining the report of the Working Group—along with other examples of official discourse—is that cinema in India constitutes a social problem of significant proportion, but that it also contains a tremendous potential to reshape society. The concerted efforts to formulate a national film policy and develop cinema into an Indian art form show the state as being centrally involved in the creation of a modern "Indian" culture; such efforts span a history, from the specifically cultural articulations of nationalism in the late nineteenth and early twentieth centuries (Chatterjee 1993), to Nehru's post-Independence initiatives, which established the vast cultural bureaucracy still in place today. The expectations of and claims made upon the state, as expressed in the *Report*—to homogenize a field as diverse as Indian cinema, change audiences' tastes in film, and use film to advance national interests—all point to the significance of cinema in constructing a certain state-sponsored modernity.

Since Independence, cinema has had multiple significations, representing varying regimes of value within state discourses: as vice; as art form; as tool for development; and as index of modernity. The 1950s witnessed debates centered around whether film could ever be an authentic indigenous cultural form (Chakravarty 1993), which were attitudes still expressed in the 1980s, as evident from the *Working Group Report*. The primary regime of value for cinema was developmentalist, until the time of my initial fieldwork in the mid-1990s, when new regimes of value began to be articulated around cinema, namely those of cultural heritage and economic ascendancy. In the next section, I detail the shift in attitudes toward mainstream cinema and filmmaking, from being a heavily criticized and maligned form of media, to one which the state actually celebrated, touting as an example of India's success in the international arena. This transformation is located in the altered media landscape produced by economic liberalization and the subsequent cultural nationalism engendered by these processes.

Cinema as National Heritage

The sheer volume of film production and the history of cinema in India, especially its contemporaneity with the West, is represented in state publications as a sign of the nation-state's modernity. On July 7, 1896, a representative of the Lumière Brothers, traveling from Paris en route to Australia, screened the first motion pictures in India, in Bombay's Watsons Hotel—six months after its originary screening in Paris on December 28, 1895. This history became a cause for celebration, evident by the state's investment at both the central and regional levels in commemorating the centenary of cinema, in 1995 and 1996. The Ministry of Information and Broadcasting (MIB) created a National Committee for the Celebration of the Cinema Centenary, which organized a series of countrywide commemorations. Though the first screening of motion pictures in India did not take place until July 1896, the commemorations were kicked off with the 26th International Film Festival of India (IFFI), held in Bombay in January 1995.

The concern with temporality, or what Abraham terms "postcolonial time" (1998), is apparent in the reasons offered for initiating the celebrations even before the actual anniversary of the first film screenings in India (or in Paris for that matter). At the inauguration ceremony for the IFFI, in Bombay on January 10, 1995, the union minister for information and broadcasting, K. P. Singh Deo, remarked, "It is fitting that the first international film festival in this centenary year of world cinema is being held in India, the most prolific film producer in the world, and in Bombay, the birthplace and capital of Indian cinema" ("International film festival opened" 1995). The English-language booklet, "A Hundred Years of Cinema in India: A Conspectus," produced by the MIB's publications division, raises the issue of the discrepancy between the arrival of motion pictures in India and celebrations having begun in 1995. It also points out that the first short film made by an Indian was not until 1899, and thus "One may therefore wonder that our country should legitimately be observing the cinema centenary between 1996 and 1999" (Rangoonwalla 1995a: 1). The booklet resolves this issue by explaining, "Yet, our keeping pace with the rest of the world, which is celebrating the centenary of cinema in 1995, has been justified by a pioneering experiment in 1894–95 to make the image move. This was *Shambarik Karolika* (Magic Lantern) a show by Mahadeo Patwardhan and his two sons, where three slide projectors throwing double colour plates created an illusion of movement.

Since it also told a story with the external aids of narration and music, this could be taken as India's first exploration of the moving image" (Rangoonwalla 1995a: 1). The Hindi version of this booklet produced a few months later, in July 1995, asserts more definitively India's right to celebrate the centenary of cinema in 1995: "We regard the birth of cinema in India to be the invention of the Magic Lantern, by Mahadeo Patwardhan and his two sons in 1894–95, and from this perspective, we are also celebrating the centenary of cinema with the rest of the world in 1995" (Rangoonwalla 1995b: 2).

In contrast to Chattopadhyay's statements about cinema as an alien cultural form, these booklets, produced by the MIB fifteen years later, provide indigenous antecedents and firmly locate cinema as a part of Indian aesthetic and performative traditions. All of the debates about the foreignness of the medium, which were articulated as late as 1980 in the *Working Group Report*, have been effectively displaced by descriptions of the cultural rootedness of early cinema in India. The Hindi booklet declares that "in the silent era, films were made on all topics related to Indian traditions and sensibilities" (Rangoonwalla 1995b: 9). Cinema is linked to indigenous cultural traditions through content from the early filming of theatrical performances and via stories from Hindu epics serving as the inspiration for the first features.

In addition to proclaiming the cultural authenticity of cinema and India's coeval participation in the global technological order, the centenary commemorations initiated in 1995 also laid claim to the site of the first Lumière screenings in Paris as part of a common heritage. During the IFFI, the National Film Development Corporation (NFDC) commissioned an art director from the Hindi film industry to recreate the original venue of the Lumière Brothers' first screenings at the Nehru Centre.[26] "Thanks to NFDC and the genius of art director Nitin Desai, cinegoers can now walk down the historical Paris boulevard where cinema was born," stated a newspaper article about the recreation of the site of the original Lumière Brothers' screening. The article described how Nitin Desai, a noted art director of the Bombay film industry, spent close to a million rupees and took six weeks to transform the portico of the Nehru Centre into a replica of Paris's Rue Scribe, the street on which the Grand Café—the site of the original screening of the Lumière Brothers' cinematographe—was located. The nineteenth-century Parisian ambiance was heightened with shop fronts, and both a horse carriage and a vintage car were parked on the "street," while during the inaugural ceremony NFDC employees sported bicornes (the two-cornered hat worn by Napoleon) and bore posters titled "Cinematographe Lumière." The exhibition space was converted into the Grand Café, decorated with a wooden model of the cinematographe and a plaster of Paris statue of Auguste Lumière. During the inaugural function, which was attended by the French ambassador and some members of the Hindi film industry, the ten early Lumière shorts were screened in what one newspaper report described as a "dutiful repetition of the past" ("NFDC's tribute to first film venue" 1995).

The commemoration of the past was not solely a European one; as a tribute to a century of Indian cinema the NFDC also organized a temporary film museum, with items from landmark Hindi films, and produced a stage show, "Cinema Cinema 100," in collaboration with the Hindi film industry. The stage show, which was televised live nationally on *Doordarshan*, the state broadcaster, was a combination of speeches, tributes, song and dance performances, and edited sequences of the landmarks of Indian cinema, organized chronologically into four main eras.

During my fieldwork I was able to attend the final commemorative event, which was the Indian Cinema Centenary Celebration, organized by the National Film Archives in conjunction with the Department of Cultural Affairs of the Government of Maharashtra, on July 7, 1996. The event was a combination of public and semi-public rituals inscribing the history of cinema in India onto the urban landscape of Bombay.[27] The key attraction was a procession of members of the Hindi and Marathi film industries to the site of the Watsons Hotel, where the Chief Minister of Maharashtra unveiled a plaque affixed to the building proclaiming its historical importance.[28] The plaque simply stated, "Lumière Brothers' 'Cinematographe' was first screened here on 7th July, 1896, at the erstwhile Watsons Hotel, thus sowing the seed of one of the most popular of the art forms of this century, cinema in India."

After the parade and unveiling of the plaque, the proceedings shifted to the nearby Y. B. Chavan auditorium for the final ceremonies of the day, which involved inaugurations of the weeklong film festival and an exhibition of photographs documenting the 100 years of Indian cinema. Sixteen people—a combination of government officials and film personalities—sat on stage against a graphic of a motion picture camera and the words, "100 Years of Indian Cinema," emblazoned in Marathi on a backdrop of marigolds.[29]

Various government officials made short speeches about the historic importance of the occasion and on the significance of cinema in India. The minister for cultural affairs, Pramod Navalkar, declared that "this is an industry where there are no divisions based on caste, language, religion, or region." The director of the National Film Archives, Suresh Chhabria, asserted, "It is really the public of India that has taken cinema to their hearts and minds. Nowhere in the world has a public taken to cinema as much as has the public of India. It is really them we have to thank." Once the speeches were done, the same Lumière films that were screened a hundred years before—*Arrival of a Train*, *Workers Leaving a Factory*, *By the Seaside*, and *Baby's Dinner*—were screened in the auditorium. After the screenings, most people trooped upstairs to the exhibition of film stills, posters, and photographs organized by the National Film Archives to represent a visual history of the hundred years of Indian cinema.

What was striking about these rituals of commemoration was the extent of the state's involvement. While the state had been involved in the regulation, documentation, disciplining, and discussion of filmmaking since colonial times, its role in commemoration and celebration—other than the annual ritual of national awards, begun in 1954—had been minimal. Various filmmaking organizations, such as the Film Federation of India and the Indian Academy of Motion Picture Arts and Sciences, held events and produced publications—in 1956 and 1981, respectively—commemorating the twenty-fifth and fiftieth anniversaries of Indian sound films.[30] These earlier commemorations were initiated and organized by filmmakers, with bureaucrats and government officials providing felicitations and commentary, while the centenary celebrations were initiated and organized by state institutions, with filmmakers playing a small role.

Whereas the earlier state-generated discourse was filled with prescriptive statements directed at the Bombay film industry to create "socially relevant" films to "uplift" the masses, statements from the various events and texts associated with the centennial commemorations were light on criticism of popular cinema. Instead, they detailed the prolific nature of film production in India, emphasizing India's lead over the rest of the world, reiterated that the history of cinema in India was as old as the history of the medium itself, and asserted the popularity of domestic films within India. The centenary commemorations demonstrated the transformed symbolic significance accorded to the institution of cinema by the state, at both the national and regional levels, by the mid-1990s.

I attribute the growth of this symbolic significance to the changes in the media landscape engendered by the processes of economic liberalization. After the advent of satellite television in 1992, dubbed by the press and some commentators as an "invasion," the mass media became the locus of public debates, controversies, and anxiety around questions of Indian nationhood, cultural sovereignty, authenticity, tradition, and identity.[31] During this period, the state's policy rhetoric regarding media was focused more on safeguarding national sovereignty and "Indian values" than "uplifting the masses" (Mankekar 1999). In addition to satellite television, the other noticeable feature of the transformed media landscape was the increased presence of Hollywood films, both in their original English and dubbed versions. With the appearance of American content on television and in theaters, Hindi films took on the value of cultural authenticity and Indian-ness vis-à-vis Hollywood films. It was not simply in their identity as indigenously produced films, however, but also in their very objectified and elaborated representations of Indian-ness, discussed in the next chapter, that films from the mid-1990s operated as signs of the nation.

Cinema as Economic Enterprise

The Central government's announcement giving industry status to filmmaking actually took place at a conference in Bombay, titled "National Conference on Challenges Before Indian Cinema," organized by the Federation of Indian Chambers of Commerce (FICCI) and the Film Federation of India (FFI), which are both private trade and industry organizations.[32] The conference was held at the plush five-star hotel Leela Kempinski and attended by representatives of the two organizations, as well as state officials and members of the Hindi film industry.[33] The proceedings were structured in such a manner that filmmakers presented papers in sessions chaired by government ministers—from the Information and Broadcasting Ministry, the Department of Education, the Department of Revenue, and the Reserve Bank of India—who then provided the concluding remarks for each session.

The dominant tone of the presentations was of crisis and appeal: that filmmaking in India was undergoing a series of crises due to mounting costs, exorbitant taxation, rampant piracy, and a lack of regularized finance; an appeal was made to the Central government to take the lead in ameliorating these conditions. Nearly every presentation discussed how the state had been negligent toward cinema for decades, so that any achievement on the part of filmmakers thus far had been entirely on their own.[34] Amit Khanna, a longstanding member of the Bombay industry who has occupied a myriad of roles from writer to producer, asserted in his presentation that "successive governments have done precious little for this business, and if the Industry has survived for so many decades it is not with the Government's help, but in spite [of] it" (Khanna 1998: 6).[35]

Veteran producer/director J. Om Prakash, in his presentation about the necessity for institutional finance, listed nine achievements on the part of filmmakers and then pointed to the potential of Indian films in the global market, akin to the Indian information technology industry. "Imagine if the industry could reach such great heights without the support of the Government [or] institutional finance, then imagine what the industry could achieve for the nation? If proper incentives and infrastructure facilities are provided, the country can compete with Hollywood initially in a small way, but later on, once the industry gains momentum, then the country can give competition to Hollywood. See the growth of [the] high-tech computer software industry. Who would have thought that India would compete with developed nations in such sophisticated area? . . . We can produce world class international films and compete with 20th Century Fox" (Prakash 1998: 15). Prakash's statements contain the allochronism and telos intrinsic to development discourse (Gupta 1998) regarding the unexpected global success of the Indian software industry as well as the desire to overcome the constraints of postcolonial time (Abraham 1998) in terms of the film industry. A key difference in his remarks from those presented in previous sections, however, is their external address. Rather than helping to transform Indian society, film becomes a means to compete in the global economic order, thereby accruing prestige unto the nation on the world stage.

The common appeal across all of the presentations was that the Central government needed to grant industry status to filmmaking, make available institutional finance, and bring policies regarding filmmaking under the purview of the Central government, rather than the various state governments. Although all of the presentations were critical of government policy, the overall tone was polite, respectful, and patient— similar to Abbas's letter to Gandhi discussed earlier—and many speakers took care to end their presentations with a declaration of how filmmakers were good citizens who always provided service to the nation. Producer/ director Yash Chopra ended his presentation, "It may be added with all humility that the Indian film industry has always been in the forefront— be it war or earthquake or any calamity—and in every aspect of life shall be able to contribute much more towards the national integration and towards the government exchequer, and will feel rightfully proud as a responsible community of this great country. *Jai Hind* [Long Live India]" (Chopra 1998: 28).

Given the history of state attitudes toward filmmaking and the unfulfilled promises regarding policies and regulations governing cinema, apparent from filmmakers' statements presented earlier in this chapter, it came as quite a surprise when Sushma Swaraj, the union minister of information and broadcasting, announced industry status for filmmaking in her remarks at the end of the conference. Various news media reported on filmmakers' reactions to the announcement. English-language news-magazine *India Today* described the scene, "The Applause was thunderous. Bollywood bigwigs, including Yash Chopra and Subhash Ghai, were among those on their feet clapping jubilantly. Union Information and Broadcasting Minister Sushma Swaraj had just announced 'industry status' for the Indian film industry" (Aiyar and Chopra 1998). The national daily *Indian Express*, in an article titled "Bollywood celebrates 'Independence Day,'" quoted producer J. Om Prakash stating, "Swaraj has exceeded 90 percent of our long overdue demands" and FFI president Sultan Ahmad saying that "it was more than what we'd asked for" (Desai 1998).

The state's most immediate reason for granting industry status had to do with trying to "rescue" the Hindi film industry from the "clutches of the underworld," or organized crime, and weaning it from its dependence on "black money" or unaccounted and untaxed cash income.[36] The finance capital for filmmaking in India has been connected to the vast unofficial—or "black"—economy, which some scholars estimate is nearly half the size of the official economy (Kumar 2005). One of the results of the high rates of taxation in India has been the creation of a parallel economy with high amounts of unregulated economic activity—mainly cash transactions—and large sums of unreported (thus untaxed) income, commonly referred to as "black money."[37] The Hindi film industry has been one of the main places to invest unreported income in India. The nature of finance meant that the majority of financial transactions and business dealings in the film industry have been in cash, where the accounting is highly secretive and most contracts have been oral.

Both the *Indian Express* and *The Times of India* had lengthy editorials the next day, endorsing the move and arguing that it was long overdue. *The Times* stated,

> With its newfound status as an industry, Indian cinema finally gets the long overdue official recognition it deserves. Sooner or later the government had to shed its blinkered vision, which consistently denied a reality that was an intrinsic part of the Indian lifestyle, that had shaped Indian attitudes, fantasies, and fashions over several generations. If movie icons have influenced social behavior, films for their

part, have been the most conspicuous unifying factor, by consistently addressing a multi-cultural, multi-lingual, multi-religious audience in a pan-Indian voice. It was incumbent on the government to recognize the importance of a medium which literally translates the concept of "unity in diversity," especially given the increasingly fractured nature of the country's socio-political ethos. ("Boost for Bollywood" 1998)

Common to both editorials was the perception of the dominance of organized crime—"the underworld," in Indian parlance—in filmmaking, and that industry status would "exorcise the spectre of the underworld, which reportedly finances one-third of all Bombay films" ("Boost for Bollywood" 1998). The *Express* asserted that although the film industry called itself an industry for decades: "Behind that dignifying epithet lurked a shadowy business that could be hardly termed respectable . . . With the recognition of the film industry, its dependence on dubious sources of funding will hopefully end" ("Finally an Industry" 1998). While criminal activity has always played some financial role in filmmaking—profits from the Second World War black-marketeering were invested in the Hindi film industry—in 1997, a few high-profile murders of filmmakers, attributed to gangsters, brought the connections between organized crime and the Bombay film industry into the national and international media spotlight.[38]

While the declaration of industry status took place on May 10, 1998, and Swaraj promised that the "modalities would be worked out soon" ("Boost for Bollywood" 1998), the more concrete assertion of industry status did not occur until October 19, 2000, when filmmaking or the "entertainment industry" was recognized as an "approved activity under 'industrial concerns,'" according to the Industrial Development Bank of India Act of 1964. Being designated an industry communicates that filmmaking is part of the organized industrial sector. It was this recognition that paved the way for financing from banks and other financial institutions, since prior to this announcement, banks chose not to extend loans for filmmaking, due to its high-risk nature. Govind Nihalani, a longstanding and critically acclaimed director, explained the impact of industry status to me: "It created a confidence among the financing community, that after all, this is not such a speculative business, that it's possible to treat this industry as a proper business and if controlled well, and here—it's very simple—you control your budget, bring in the right inputs, and then it is a viable industry" (Nihalani, interview, May 2006). Since 2000, industry status has introduced a greater variety of financing for filmmaking. Both the banking and corporate sectors have begun to invest in filmmaking, either by providing loans or by creating production companies. Some of the largest Indian industrial houses and corporations have created media subsidiaries that have entered television and film production. Another source of finance is the stock market, and some film production companies and exhibition companies have become public limited companies, with their stock listed and traded on the Bombay Stock Exchange. Industry status by the Central government also set the tone for state governments to rethink their policies toward filmmaking; although entertainment tax is still a source of contention between filmmakers and the government, some states offer tax breaks for films shot in their territory, while others have enabled the current boom in multiplex construction all across India by offering tax holidays to exhibitors and real estate developers.

While the initial declaration of industry status was explained in the familiar mode of the state's role in trying to improve cinema and film-making—that cinematic quality was related to sources of finance, and the state needed to play its part in cleaning up filmmaking by helping filmmakers escape from the clutches of dubious finance—subsequent discourse has focused on the economic potential of filmmaking. Rather than perceiving it as a vice or as a problem as it had in the past, since 2000 the Indian state has perceived commercial filmmaking as a viable, important, and legitimate economic activity that should be nurtured and supported. Government agencies, in partnership with film trade organizations, promote the export of Indian films at markets held during major film festivals such as Cannes. Regulations regarding foreign investment within the media sector have been relaxed, so that up to 100 percent foreign direct investment (FDI) is allowed in any aspect of filmmaking: financing, production, distribution, exhibition, or marketing. At various international fora, government officials court foreign investment by representing entertainment media as a high-growth industry in India. For example, at the World Economic Forum held in Davos, Switzerland, in 2006, the India Brand Equity Foundation—a public-private partnership between the Ministry of Commerce and Industry and the Confederation of Indian Industry (CII)—distributed a report, "Entertainment and Media," which provided an overview of the various media forms and their economic potential in India. After stating that "India today is a major emerging global market," the report asserts, "The Indian Entertainment and Media Industry has out-performed the Indian economy and is one of the fastest growing sectors in India" (Pricewaterhouse Coopers 2006b: 1). The report concludes, "With a host of factors contributing to the double-digit growth of the industry and an added easing of the foreign investment norms, the E&M Industry in India thus is a sunrise opportunity that presents significant avenues for investment" (Pricewaterhouse Coopers 2006b: 20).

To fully comprehend the dramatic shift in attitudes toward cinema—from a tool for social change to an engine of economic growth—it is illustrative to compare the following two statements made by state officials separated by a span of twenty years. The first statement was made by the Chief Minister of Maharashtra, A. M. Antulay, in 1981, on the occasion of the fiftieth anniversary celebrations of Indian sound films. He wrote, "The film being the most effective medium of communication, its potential, besides providing wholesome entertainment to the masses, lies in its tremendous capacity to create social consciousness among the people about all evils, and this must be harnessed to the maximum benefit of society at large. I am glad that the film industry as a whole is helping every national cause in its own way" (in Ramachandran 1981: 8). The second statement was made in 2000, by Arun Jaitley, minister of information and broadcasting, during a conference held by FICCI titled "The Indian Entertainment Industry: Strategy and Vision." He stated, "The entertainment industry, along with the IT industry, have become the buzz words globally. It is being widely recognized and accepted that together these two sectors will increasingly dominate the world economic landscape. Recognizing the importance of this industry, the budget for this year has given major concessions to this segment, which will pave the way for its rapid growth. It is expected that, taking advantage of these measures by the Government, the Indian entertainment industry would take the initiative in multiplying manifold its revenues, contribution to the exchequer, employment potential, and foreign exchange earnings" (Arthur Andersen 2000). Although both ministers expect filmmakers to serve the nation—either socially or economically—film for the former is a medium of communication and means for social transformation, while for the latter it is a vehicle for economic ascendancy. Jaitley's remarks also acknowledge that state economic policies are key for the success and growth of filmmaking—a point that filmmakers had been arguing since the 1950s, but went unheeded for decades.

Along with a change in the language used to discuss cinema—from "film" to "entertainment industry," from "social consciousness" to "contribution to the exchequer," there has also been a significant change in the nature of reports and publications generated about filmmaking. For more than four decades, the various inquiry committees, symposia, and conferences were initiated by the state, mainly via the Ministry of Information and Broadcasting, to study the problem of cinema primarily both as an art form and as a tool for development in India. Since 1998, FICCI, rather than the MIB, has been the main organization sponsoring conferences and discussions about filmmaking in India—as part of the larger category of the entertainment industry—primarily through its annual convention, "FRAMES: Global Convention on the Business of Entertainment." As apparent from the title, the focus is on the commercial aspect of cinema—the film industry is analyzed with respect to its projected turnover, export earnings, and tax revenues; rather than via the state bureaucracy, these reports and financial analyses of filmmaking are produced by multinational accounting and consulting firms such as Arthur Andersen, Pricewaterhouse Coopers, KPMG, and A. T. Kearney, along with Indian firms such as Yes Bank.

Although filmmakers who spoke at the 1998 conference presented industry status as crucial to the health and success of filmmaking, in my later visits to Bombay, members of the industry I spoke to were less sanguine about the impact of industry status. Many felt that other than granting industry status, the state had not done much to address the issues facing filmmaking, specifically the problems of piracy, high taxation, and unreasonable export and import regulations. Shravan Shroff, a member of the board of directors of the Shringar Group—an integrated distribution and exhibition company—and the director of their exhibition division, Fame Cinemas, shared his views about the role of the government in filmmaking: "I think the role of the government is pretty non-existent. They don't do anything. They granted the industry status so there is funding from IDBI [Industrial Development Bank of India] but proactively, are they working with industry bodies, like how the U.S. government works with the MPAA to look at piracy issues? Not really" (Shravan Shroff, interview, May 2006).

While many filmmakers were subsequently dismissive about the impact of industry status, I contend that the symbolic significance of the declaration was tremendous. It was only after gaining industry status that top industrial houses and corporations, such as the Birla Group, Tata Group, Sahara, Reliance, and others began their forays into film production. FICCI created its Entertainment Committee in 1998; prior to this, there were no formal or institutional partnerships between the world of Indian business and the world of filmmaking. There were no laws or regulations preventing Indian corporations from entering film production, distribution, or exhibition.[39] The dominant image of the film business, as a disorganized money-laundering operation, populated with unseemly characters, made it difficult for publicly traded companies to venture into this domain. Industry status granted legitimacy to filmmaking, within the larger financial and corporate community, that had not existed previously.

Chitra Subramaniam, who at the time of our meeting was an executive producer with Percept Picture Company—a production and distribution company created in 2002 by Percept Holdings, a media and communications conglomerate—explained the impact of industry status within the corporate world: "There was a certain amount of respectability. What does that mean? That means you can have different sources of financing, which therefore makes it respectable; that makes it something that corporates decided to get into it because—even if they wanted to get into entertainment—it was a field that nobody knew how it was run. You know it was a typical Mom and Pop shop kind of thing" (Subramaniam, interview, May 2006). "Respectability" has been a longstanding concern of Hindi filmmakers and in chapter three I discuss other avenues of achieving and displaying respectability on the part of the film industry. Subramaniam's characterization of filmmaking as a "Mom and Pop shop" is a reference to the centrality of kinship networks within the Hindi film industry. She continued by pointing to why corporations are entering filmmaking, "Companies like ours are companies that have gotten in because they feel that this is a good business to get into . . . I think the corporates are here to stay. I think that a lot of companies will get into it: new sources of financing which are accountable; revenue streams are improving; distribution channels are improving; you know . . . all these things are coming in, so people are seeing it as a business opportunity of basically creating content and finding ways of revenue streams to get that content across" (Subramaniam, interview, May 2006). Longstanding industry members hail these developments as positive steps toward bringing greater discipline, efficiency, and financial transparency to filmmaking. "Corporatization" is the favorite term bandied about by Hindi filmmakers and the Indian press, which is used to describe the efforts of the Bombay film industry to become more organized. In chapter seven, I discuss the multivalent nature of the terms "corporate" and "corporatization," and the way they articulate with the film industry's own practices of creating distinction.

In addition to new modes of financing and producing films, the other concrete impact of industry status has been in the exhibition sector, most visibly manifest by the boom in multiplex construction. From the late 1990s, news of ventures and agreements to construct multiplex cinemas in India kept surfacing periodically in the media, since the exhibition sector was regarded as severely underdeveloped, with theaters in short supply for such a vast film-going public. India has one of the lowest ratios of screens to population in the world. Although the first multiplex theater in India opened in New Delhi in 1997, there were no others until after 2000, when the Central government's granting of industry status to filmmaking, in 1998, was actually operationalized into more specific policy. In 2001, with the professed aim of promoting tourism, several state governments announced tax incentives, such as the complete or partial waiver of entertainment tax for a prescribed period, in order to spur new investments in the exhibition sector.[40] The first four-screen multiplex in Bombay was inaugurated on October 25, 2001, taking advantage of new tax benefits granted under the state of Maharashtra's newly formulated multiplex policy, which granted a complete exemption from entertainment tax for any theater with a minimum of four screens totaling at least 1,250 seats in its first three years of operation, and then a 75 percent exemption for the next two years (Shringar Red Herring Prospectus 2005).[41] The pace of multiplex construction in India has been quite rapid: from 80 multiplex screens in 2002 to about 900 screens by 2009 (Mukherjee 2009). Six national chains account for more than 80 percent of the multiplex theaters in India, representing a significant consolidation of the exhibition business, while the single-screen sector remains relatively fragmented in terms of ownership, operation, and branding.[42]

However, rather than increasing, the total number of screens in India appears to be declining, as it has been for a number of years.[43] According to statistics compiled by the Government of India's Ministry of Statistics, the number of permanent cinema halls in India decreased approximately 27 percent between 1999 and 2009, from 9,095 to 6,607.[44] Of these, about 300 are multiplexes with a total of 900 screens, which leads to an estimated total of 7,207 screens for all of India in 2009—a 20 percent decrease in the number of screens from the previous decade. Therefore, the expansion of multiplexes thus far appears to not have actually increased the overall number of screens in India, despite the main argument advanced by members of the industry most involved with the development and expansion of multiplexes: that India is severely "under screened," hence their ventures are necessary to rectify that situation. The reason is that while multiplexes are mushrooming throughout the urban centers of India, the large single-screen theaters that have been the mainstay of the theatrical exhibition sector for cinema have been slowly closing down. Since the 1980s with the advent of video and the expansion of television, movie theaters have faced a variety of challenges due to high taxation, video piracy, competition from other modes of entertainment, and capricious audience behavior. As mentioned earlier, entertainment tax has been one of the most contentious issues between filmmakers—especially exhibitors who bear the brunt of the tax most directly—and the state at the regional level, resulting in periodic strikes on the part of theaters as a way of protesting heavy taxation. For example, in a span of less than one year, approximately one thousand single-screen theaters in Maharashtra went on strike three times—refusing to screen films from periods of a few days in May and October 2003, to three weeks from March to April 2004—to protest the state's entertainment tax rates and multiplex incentives.[45]

Although exhibitors I met in 1996 discussed the difficulties facing the theatrical sector, they were generally optimistic about the future. By 2006, however, with the spread of multiplexes throughout Bombay, the owners and managers of single-screen theaters I met were much less optimistic about the future. Rajkumar Bajaj, who controlled some landmark single-screen theaters in downtown Bombay, and at one time was referred to as the "South Bombay King," asserted, "multiplexes are definitely killing the single-screen cinemas."[46] He explained that most single-screen theaters were going out of business, as they were unable to earn the revenues necessary to pay salaries or even electricity bills. Although one of Bajaj's theaters, Eros Cinema, was still doing reasonably well, according to him, because of its location and well-maintained interior, his overall demeanor during our interview was one of resigned acceptance of the changes at hand, stating at one point, "It's nobody's fault; it's only our bad luck."

While Bajaj appeared resigned, Nester D'Souza—manager of the erstwhile Metro Cinema and former president of the Cinematograph Exhibitors Association of India (CEAI), which spearheaded the theater strikes in 2003 and 2004—offered a variety of social, economic, and political explanations for the troubles of single-screen cinemas. As we sat in his office, surrounded by the sights and sounds of construction—since the Metro was being converted to a multiplex in 2006—D'Souza castigated state policy, specifically the tax holidays offered for multiplex construction.[47] Arguing that it was not "fair to the mass of the people," D'Souza objected to the standard reasons explaining the benefits offered for multiplexes. "Come on, what do you mean he [the multiplex operator] has put up a new project, therefore it [a tax holiday] has to be given? When I put up a new project, did you give me a tax benefit? So why are you differentiating with him?" D'Souza challenged the right or claim of multiplexes to any sort of government benefit, asserting, "From 1936, I [referring to Metro and not himself personally] have been paying the government, you [the multiplex operators] did nothing. His [the multiplex operator's] argument is, 'you recovered your investment.' So I say, you too will recover your investment just like we did, even with 75 percent tax rates." Regarding the oft-cited claim that multiplexes were equipped with far superior amenities and state-of-the-art sound and projection facilities, D'Souza asserted that his theater was not inferior: "Dolby, DTS? I have that; I have a bigger screen. What else does he have? Cleanliness; toilets? That we all have to have." He posited that rather than a blanket policy that favored multiplexes over single-screen theaters, the state should establish a set of standards for service and quality as the basis for extending tax benefits, regardless of screen numbers. Thus, older single-screen theaters would also have an incentive to upgrade their facilities, and those whose facilities were on par with the multiplexes, like the Metro, would not be unduly disadvantaged.

D'Souza chafed at what he felt were the state's unduly unequal policies favoring multiplexes over single-screens, "Today all the cinemas have died, and I am not saying it's only because of multiplexes; but, you know, you have really created an uneven field. You are giving him tax breaks, but not giving me any tax breaks. You bend backwards or even change the rules for him. We are all supposed to close down at one o'clock [1:00 a.m.]. How come he can close down after? Now why am I, why was I not allowed to do that? Now that has nothing to do with the quality difference between a multiplex and a single-screen" (D'Souza, interview, May 2006). State policies favoring multiplexes, which cater to high-income individuals, over single-screen theaters, which draw viewers from a broad socioeconomic spectrum, are a powerful manifestation of what Leela Fernandes has described as the "politics of forgetting," which is a "political discursive process" whereby an assertive middle-class identity works to displace the poor and working classes from public space and national political discourse (2004).

This chapter has detailed how—after years of disapproval, disdain, criticism, and neglect—the Indian state changed its attitudes and policies toward commercial filmmaking. From being regarded as a locus of "sinful technology" (Gandhi) in the 1920s, and a producer of "culturally vacuous films exclusively designed for making money through audience manipulation" in the 1980s (Working Group), filmmaking became a "serious business" that has to be "tuned to the demands of today's competitive business economy" (FICCI 2003).[48] The intersection of neoliberal economic rhetoric with the rise of cultural nationalist politics signified by the Hindu nationalist and pro-business Bharatiya Janata Party (BJP) were important factors in the shifting attitudes toward filmmaking and the Hindi film industry. It was no accident that a BJP-led government granted industry status to filmmaking, since its support base is heavily drawn from the small business owner and entrepreneurial class who also comprise the vast distribution, exhibition, and finance apparatus for Hindi filmmaking. Additionally, as I will discuss in the next chapter, Hindi films from the mid- to late 1990s—emptied of all poverty and class conflict and populated with wealthy families, Hindu rituals, and elaborate weddings—presented a nostalgic vision of Indian culture and "family values" that frequently corresponded with, or did not pose a challenge to, the BJP's own cultural rhetoric.

The granting of industry status fits in with the new economic imaginary (Wyatt 2005) articulated by the Indian state since the advent of neoliberal reforms. Satish Deshpande (1993, 2003) discusses how the Nehruvian era emphasized the centrality of production, symbolized by key heavy industries—steel, power, mining—as the path toward a modern and successful national economy, which served as a metonym for a modern and successful nation. He points out how Nehru, in his statements and policies, was consistently forging connections between production and patriotism. Deshpande argues that the contemporary Indian state's economic imaginary, with its emphasis on consumption, represents a significant departure from the Nehruvian one; when production is valued, it is that which serves the needs of global markets rather than those of the nation (2003: 73).

These changing regimes of value within the economic imaginary—from production to consumption, from domestic needs to global markets—help to account for the altered status of filmmaking, from an extravagant expenditure of scarce capital and resources to an engine of economic growth. Software is not the only commodity to displace steel in the national economic imaginary (Wyatt 2005); as apparent from Arun Jaitley's statements, films also occupy an important position in that imaginary. Film exports—India has been exporting films since 1950s, and systematically since the 1970s—are now seen as a potential gold mine of foreign exchange earnings. Cinema's significance in a neoliberal economic imaginary arises, however, from its ability to circulate in a variety of global markets, which becomes a cause for nationalist celebration. With cinema occupying an important position in the national economic imaginary, the circulation of Hindi films in places like the United States, United Kingdom, or Germany represents the success of the Indian nation on the global stage. That the Hindi film industry is the only other dominant globally circulating film industry, and that Hindi films are registering equal or higher box-office grosses than Hollywood films in advanced industrialized countries such as the United States, Japan, or Britain, are facts interpreted by the Indian state, press, and filmmakers through a matrix of national pride and distinction. The steady stream of European, Australian, Canadian, and American representatives of tourist boards and film councils to Bombay, meeting Hindi filmmakers and offering incentives to shoot in their countries—with the hopes of increasing tourism from India—demonstrates how filmmaking can operate as a medium for reversing the typical economic relationship of the First to the Third World, which had defined India's status in the world system since Independence.

In an era dominated by neoliberal discourses of market forces and free trade and the dismantling of state supports and the public sector, the growth and survival of the Hindi film industry, despite official neglect, has been recast by the Indian state, corporate sector, and media as a symbol of native ingenuity and success.[49] This resignification of the film industry is an important dimension in its gentrification, as it has accorded filmmaking a level of legitimacy and respectability that had not existed in earlier periods. The next two chapters examine how this resignification interacts with the film industry's longstanding concern with cultural legitimacy and social respectability.

CHAPTER 2

From Slumdogs to Millionaires

The Gentrification of Hindi Cinema

"With the multiplexes, seeing a movie has become an elite affair." In December 2005 I was standing in the Soho branch of Chanel with Asha Mehta, a Hindi film actress who was visiting New York City with her boyfriend, director Tarun Kumar, whom I had known since 1996.[1] The three of us had met for lunch nearby and were strolling through the neighborhood when Mehta spotted the Chanel store and decided to check out their handbags. While Kumar was paying for the purchase, a purse with a price tag greater than my monthly rent, Mehta was discussing what she felt was a drastic change in the social status of Hindi cinema: "Before, the elite didn't watch, or they said they didn't watch, even if they did, because they looked down upon it. But now Hindi movies are stylish and cool; Bollywood is everywhere—even in the discos."

Over the years, I had been hearing some variation of Mehta's assertion—that Hindi films had become "cool"—from a number of people associated with the Bombay film industry. During my first stint of fieldwork in 1996, when I interviewed Bhawana Somaya, the editor of *G*—a glossy, English-language film magazine—she related how her teenage nieces had informed her, "By the way, Hindi film is in now; it was out earlier." In 2006, during my last research trip to Bombay, Shravan Shroff, the thirty-something CEO of a national chain of multiplex theaters, asserted during our interview, "I think Hindi films are very cool now," while Nester D'Souza, the manager of the erstwhile Metro Cinema declared, "It's no longer uncool to be seeing a Hindi film."

Implicit in the deployment of cool as a category is its opposite or other—a period when such a desired status for Hindi films had not been achieved—as Shroff elaborated upon in his assertion, "Earlier it used to be uncool to see Hindi movies. During my school days, when I had to tell somebody that my father has something to do with the film industry, I couldn't say it because people thought that it was really stupid. How can you have anything to do with the Indian film industry? And we guys grew up on Hollywood films and aping films like *Top Gun*, etc." By stating that he grew up with Hollywood films, Shroff indirectly communicated his elite class position, since the circulation and presence of such films prior to the mid-1990s was very limited in India.[2] Additionally, India is one of the few countries in the world where locally produced content is predominant: even with the greater presence of Hollywood films, foreign content comprises only about 5 percent of total screen time (Kheterpal 2005). Despite being the third generation of his family to be involved with the business side of filmmaking, Shroff's earlier disavowal of Hindi films and filmmaking positions him within a very specific and circumscribed class fragment of Indian society—the elite who, according to Mehta, looked down upon Hindi cinema.[3] The present for Shroff is marked not by shame and repudiation, however, but by pride and acceptance, which he attributes to the improved quality of films:

> I think the kids today ape Shah Rukh Khan and Saif Ali Khan and I think it's really cool to be associated with Indian films. And the quality of Indian films has gone through the roof, so today, you know, I have no qualms in admitting to the world that I work in the Indian film industry. I think it's really cool because people look up to it and say, "Wow, that's such a fantastic job." You know, twenty years back when I was in school, people used to snigger and I used to feel really foolish telling people that my father has something to do with the Indian film industry. So it's been a total change. (Shravan Shroff, interview, May 2006)

Not only do Shroff's statements represent the disdain that Hindi filmmakers have historically expressed toward their own practice, but they also reveal the tremendous concern for acceptance by individuals who filmmakers regard as their social peers, but not as their typical audience. Shroff's allusion to the "kids today" who "ape" leading actors Shah Rukh Khan and Saif Ali Khan is not a comment about the newfound popularity of Hindi film stars (who have always commanded tremendous fan followings), but about the popularity of such stars among a small social fraction who, from Shroff's perspective, would have never been fans during his youth.

Thus, from the perspective of the Hindi film industry, "cool" is an attribute that includes films, filmmakers, and audiences. When used as an adjective to describe Hindi films, cool signifies a general state of improvement marked by higher production values as well as a visual style and narrative content that is coded as modern and sophisticated. From Mehta's statements, it is apparent that cool also refers to the open and acknowledged consumption of Hindi films by socially elite audiences and to the circulation of these films in spaces marked as upscale. Finally, as apparent from Shroff's remarks, cool denotes a self-confidence among filmmakers where they are not embarrassed or apologetic about filmmaking and the film industry; therefore, "cool" is a polysemic category that encompasses aesthetics, affect, social class, identity, and subjectivity.[4]

In this chapter, I examine the film industry's discourses of quality and change—indexed by such declarations of Hindi films' newfound coolness—in order to illustrate the connections between the sentiment of disdain, the category of coolness, the process of gentrification, and the construction of Hindi filmmakers' subjectivities, specifically their sense of self and relationship to the larger world (Holland and Leander 2004). Hindi cinema's social transformation or path to "coolness," often lauded by filmmakers and journalists, began in the mid-1990s with the erasure of the signs and symbols of poverty, labor, and rural life from films, and with the decline in plots that focused on class conflict, social injustice, and youthful rebellion. While journalists, filmmakers, and scholars attribute the narrative and aesthetic changes that I label as gentrification to changes in audience demographics (Deshpande 2005; Inden 1999; Joseph 2000b), I argue that filmmakers' own subjectivities, generational status, and class backgrounds play an important role in these transformations. Filmmakers' explanations for the aesthetic qualities of mainstream Hindi cinema and their narratives of change and progress display concerns about social status, cultural identity, and modernity.

Nonetheless, filmmakers' characterizations also reveal how audiences are centrally implicated in their evaluative discourses about Hindi cinema, as commercial filmmaking is a complex intersubjective enterprise, where audiences comprise the "significant others" (Mead 1934) who help to define filmmakers' subjectivities as cultural producers.[5] While the constitution of the subjectivity of a self-identified commercial filmmaker—one

who makes films for audiences who number in the millions (or billions) —
like other instances of self-making, is dialogical, social, and dependent
upon the interactions with others (Kondo 1990; Mead 1934; Taylor 1992),
these others — in the case of Hindi filmmakers — are not actually observable people, but imagined interlocutors (McQuail 1997: 112). All of the
remarks at the opening of this chapter demonstrate the existence of
imagined interlocutors — and arbiters of taste — whose consumption of
Hindi films have accorded them an upgraded status. If certain imagined
audiences have elevated the reputation of Hindi cinema, others are held
responsible for the opposite, and this chapter explores the discourse of
quality, mediated through the figure of the audience. The final significant element in the discussion about cinematic quality and filmmaker
subjectivity is the role of technology, specifically the agentive character
attributed to video, satellite, and the multiplex theater for precipitating
changes in films, audiences, and filmmakers; therefore, in filmmakers'
discourses, both audiences and technology operate as significant agents
in the transformations of Hindi cinema; I illustrate how they both serve
to mediate filmmakers' presentation and representation of their selves.

This chapter is organized into three main sections, corresponding to
filmmakers' narratives of change and temporality regarding the quality
and status of Hindi cinema. I begin with filmmakers' criticisms of filmmaking in the 1980s — a decade that was emblematic of Hindi cinema's
uncool past. While filmmakers cite the arrival of video as the catalyst for
the decline in cinematic quality, I reveal how such evaluations of quality
are connected to the imagined audience for Hindi cinema in the 1980s.
I discuss filmmakers' ambivalence toward these audiences and the manner in which they distanced themselves from them as a self-defining activity. In the second section, I detail the discourse of improvement that
begins in the mid-1990s, which is mostly pegged to the arrival of satellite
television and the changing class composition of film audiences. I outline the significance of certain features of the social world of filmmakers,
however — specifically generational identity, class background, and personal taste — in order to understand the changes that enabled Hindi films
to be considered cool a decade later. Finally, I discuss the impact of the
multiplex theater and its role in producing a new generic category in relation to cinema and a social category with respect to audiences. Additionally, I address how this particular technological innovation is invested
with tremendous liberatory and artistic potential by filmmakers, which
enables them at last to make the films that they want.

THE ANTITHESIS OF COOL, AKA THE '80S
The Era of Video and Trashy Cinema

During many of my conversations and interviews with filmmakers, the 1980s emerged as a particularly dreadful period of filmmaking, in contrast with both earlier and later periods of Hindi cinema. Aamir Khan—one of the most successful actors in the industry who produced the internationally celebrated *Lagaan* (Land Tax) in 2001, and then made his directorial debut with the critically acclaimed *Taare Zameen Par* (Stars on this Earth) in 2007—asserted vociferously, "[the] '80s, I believe, was the worst period of Indian cinema. The number of films which were trashy were unbelievable, and I as an audience was, you know, really shocked!" He related that, as a teenager watching films, during this period he was extremely disappointed by the kind of films being made, which he described as "horrible." When I asked him what was horrible about the films, he exclaimed, "What was not horrible? That would be easy to answer. They didn't have good stories; they didn't have good music; they didn't have good lyrics; the performances were loud; and the scenes were horrible; and nothing was nice about them! They were just trashy—the right word for them is trashy. Ridiculous films were being made. Very few of them were nice. You could really count the number of films in the year, which were decent and, you know, worthy of viewing, and that also reflected in the [box-office] collections because the collections started dropping" (Aamir Khan, interview, March 1996). Other filmmakers mentioned clichéd plots and dialogues, excessive violence, garish sets, and vulgar choreography as further illustrations of the decline in cinematic quality by the mid- to late 1980s. One of the most successful and influential producer/directors in the contemporary industry, Karan Johar, attributed the degeneration in filmmaking to the general social malaise of the decade where, in his words, "nothing happened either in society or in politics." Johar's comments were made to a group of NYU faculty (including me) and graduate students who had the opportunity to visit his film shoot in Sleepy Hollow, New York, in November 2005.[6] He continued by asserting that "kitsch" did not exist in "Bollywood" until the "South Indian invasion" during the 1980s "when everyone was dancing on pots, pans, utensils, and suddenly, hundreds of dancers are dancing behind the main pair."[7]

What Johar was referring to was a phase in the Bombay industry, starting in 1983, when a number of Hindi films were produced and directed by filmmakers from the Telugu and Tamil-language film industries, most frequently starring the southern actresses, Sri Devi or Jaya Prada, with the Bombay star, Jeetendra.[8] These films exhibited a style of choreography that was frequently derided by the press at the time as calisthenics, and a visual style described as kitschy. During my fieldwork in 1996, I encountered a curious ambivalence among Hindi filmmakers regarding the southern Indian film industries: while the Telugu and Tamil film industries were often described as more efficient, disciplined, and organized than the Bombay industry, and certain directors, actors, and technicians were held in highest regard, lauded as innovative path breakers,[9] the overall characterization of South Indian cinema (referred to as a collective rather than by the individual language cinemas) was not very flattering. Everything was described as more excessive than in Hindi films: the visual style more garish, the women heavier-set, the humor cruder, and the drama louder.[10]

The dominant explanation for the "horrible" '80s had less to do with the influence of South Indian cinema, however, and more to do with the introduction of videocassette technology and its concomitant problems of video piracy and changes in the patterns of film consumption. Home videocassette recorders began to be imported into India in 1982, when the Indian government relaxed import restrictions for VCRs and color television sets for a short period before the ASIAD games, which took place in New Delhi in November of that year.[11] An estimated one million color television sets were imported as a result of this policy change, with the total number of sets in India increasing from five thousand to five million in less than two years (Pendakur 1989). While the number of videocassette recorders imported was lower, the impact on the Hindi film industry was noticeable by the fact that references to the "video menace" started appearing in the film trade press by early 1982. For example, the trade magazine *Film Information*, dated April 10, 1982, reported that at least a thousand pirated videos of the film *Desh Premee* were circulating in Bombay prior to the film's release on April 23, thereby cutting into the film's potential business ("The Real Stab" 2007 [1982]: 23).

Initially, filmmakers only sold video rights for overseas distribution and did not entertain the option of domestic video rights, in a futile attempt to stave off competition from the new medium.[12] Videos of Hindi films were openly screened in a variety of public venues, however, such as hotels, restaurants, cafés, and long-distance buses. Emerging in 1983 and spreading rapidly throughout India, the video parlor (or video theater) was the one institution that caused the greatest anxiety for the film industry: it was a simple hall with a television and a VCR, seating anywhere from 50 to 100 people (Pendakur 1989), who could watch several films on video at a fraction of the cost of movie theaters. Producers and distributors did not realize any revenues from these screenings and kept pressing lawmakers to crack down on them. Trade magazines like *Film Information*, in the period from 1982 to 1984, were filled with filmmakers' outrage about the open sale, circulation, and screening of Hindi films on video, reminding readers that such circulations were illegal.

Social Class and Cinematic Quality

While the economic impact of video on the theatrical exhibition sector is evident, how did the advent of video result in a decline in cinematic standards or in Khan's words, "trashy" films? What was it about video that engendered poor filmmaking? It is in this realm of explanation where the discussion of cinematic quality really becomes a discourse about audiences and a commentary on class, and the trashy "'80s" actually span a period from about 1985 to 1994. Filmmakers and the English-language press in India laid the blame squarely on the changing class composition of audiences frequenting theaters.[13] In response to my question about the changes that he had witnessed over time in filmmaking, Ramesh Sippy—the director of *Sholay* (Flames, 1975), one of the most successful and iconic Indian films of all time—presented a narrative of decline mediated through technology and class. Speaking about the impact of VCR technology, Sippy said, "Besides losing revenue, the type of audiences began to change very drastically. The upper classes completely skipped cinema, and as television sets became cheaper, and video came in more, you found the middle classes disappearing. So what you had left was the common man from the lower classes." With the VCR leading to an upper- and middle-class "flight" from movie theaters, leaving only the lower classes as the ticket-buying public, the quality of filmmaking began to suffer, according to Sippy, "So it was a vicious circle. Films started to deteriorate in their content because they had to appeal to the lowest denominator, which meant much more basic kind of films—crude films, action, thrills, a crude kind of romance—which drove even the occasional viewer from the other classes further away. If he wanted to think once in a while to go and see a film, then he went and saw it and considered it all crap and just couldn't go back" (Ramesh Sippy, interview, 25 April 1996). In Sippy's remarks, we see the connections asserted between audiences, their class position, and cinematic quality. His assertion that lower class taste in cinema was abhorrent to viewers from more elite backgrounds has been a longstanding feature of the discourse about audiences, social class, and taste generated by the film industry and English-language media in India.

In fact, even prior to my fieldwork I had encountered Sippy's narrative in articles appearing in prominent nationally circulated English-language news magazines. For example, *India Today*'s cover story, "Cinema Turns Sexy: Films become increasingly raunchy, ribald and explicit," from November 15, 1991, begins by quoting various members of the Hindi film industry expressing their displeasure with the state of filmmaking, and then offers its explanation: "Cinema is the moving mirror of the times, and they have changed. The biggest shift has been in the composition of the audience in cinema halls. The frontbenchers—those who go to whistle and leer at double entendres and bare skins—now extend to the dress gallery [the most expensive seats in a movie theater], while the more genteel folk stay home and watch video . . . the halls are now overflowing with young men who want something new, exciting, and fast-paced" (Jain 1991: 28–29). "Front-bencher" is a specific audience category used by the film industry and the press to describe viewers who sit in the cheapest seats, which happen to be in the very front of a movie theater. As a short-hand reference to poor male viewers, the category is highly pejorative and, apparent from the above description, suffused with assumptions about the links between class, gender, age, and taste in films and behavior in theaters. Filmmakers and journalists perceive and represent poor young men as having the most prurient tastes in cinema—in complete opposition—and the most distasteful—to elite audiences.

The idea that the movie theaters were filled with "front-benchers," whose tastes are diametrically opposed to "more genteel" audiences, was the subject of the cover story, "The goonda as hero," for the February 16, 1992, issue of *Sunday* which had as its subheading, "Hindi films move away from middle-class values and cater to front-benchers" (Khanna and Dutt 1992: 63). The authors argued that since middle-class audiences stopped patronizing movie theaters, fewer films were being made that targeted their tastes and sensibilities. Producer and lyricist Amit Khanna explains: "Audiences in movie halls comprise urban lumpen youth. Since the returns from video and cable are not commensurate with the returns from the box-office, today's films are by and large being made for the front-bencher—the guy who lives in Dharavi and is only too aware of the breakdown of the system" (Khanna and Dutt 1992: 64).

The article also featured an extended discussion about the box-office failure of *Lamhe* (Moments) that further illuminated perceptions in the film industry about audience expectations and taste being based on class

FIGURE 1 Anil Kapoor and Sri Devi in *Lamhe*. Courtesy and copyright of Yash Raj Films, www.yashrajfilms.com.

distinctions (Figure 1). *Lamhe* was released in November 1991 and continued to have a rich discursive presence over the course of my field-work—from five to fifteen years after its release. The film represented a love triangle of sorts—spanning two generations and two continents—set amidst an extremely elite social world where the protagonists lived in palatial homes both in Rajasthan and England. It was a highly anticipated film by producer/director Yash Chopra, whose previous film had been a huge commercial success, so its disappointing performance at the box-office was described as "one of the biggest shocks of recent times."[14] Rauf Ahmed, the editor of *Filmfare*, a leading English-language film maga-zine, offered an explanation for *Lamhe*'s failure, "Everyone in *Lamhe* just talks and talks and talks. The front-benchers, who are the only people in the cinema halls today, don't have the patience for so much dialogue" (Khanna and Dutt 1992: 68). Though categorized as a flop at the box-office, *Lamhe* was considered a major hit on the video circuit, but according to the article, "Since the major profits still flow in from box-office returns, filmmakers such as Chopra are now finding out that they will have to cater to the front-benchers, or else face financial ruin" (Khanna and Dutt 1992: 69).

As apparent from the remarks above, this perceived need to cater to poor and working-class audiences, though represented as a commercial imperative, was suffused with normative value judgments and disdain, where such audiences were castigated for their alleged tastes in cinema. The direct effect of such bad taste upon cinematic quality was elaborated by Sippy, who was honest about his own filmmaking, acknowledging that he did not do his best work during the late 1980s and early 1990s. Although Sippy asserted that a good director should not make excuses for his mistakes, his explanations for his filmmaking in this period relied heavily on the degeneration narrative. Discussing a few films of his that were both box-office and critical failures, Sippy attributed their lack of success to the general commercial scenario of the time: "These films were made in a period where the video invasion had begun, so we were losing a lot of the discerning audiences. Actually during that entire period we will not find very many great box-office successes, whatever kind of film you made. The standards fell all around—no excuses meant here—but when the returns are not there at the box-office you do get disturbed. After all you owe responsibility to the distributors and financiers to bring out a product that makes money. So you had to start curbing your budgets, because the returns were not really there at the box-office." Sippy's distress at the poor box-office outcome of his films and his subsequent measures to ameliorate the situation is not presented as a simple commercial decision, but one that crucially reshaped his filmmaking practice: "You start curbing budgets; somewhere you start restricting your area of thinking; because before, my way of thinking always was, 'Don't talk to me about budgets, I just want to make the film that's got to be made.' After that I started to think that the budget is important, and it's got to be kept in mind. So maybe I started mentally, sort of, drifting into that trap, and probably at the same time subjects that were picked on were not as nice . . . so everything seemed to be working the wrong way around" (Ramesh Sippy, interview, 8 July 1996). Sippy's reflexivity about this period, along with his own representation of his internalization of the constraints imposed by the changing technological and economic landscape for filmmaking, is an example of how the subjectivity of a commercial filmmaker is forged in concert with figures of the imagined audience, mediated through box-office returns and new technologies of distribution such as video.

Although the above discussion of the deterioration of cinema thus far hinges centrally on an interpretation of commercial outcome, box-office collections in India are not the objective, transparent indices of audience demographics or behavior that they are purported to be. Given the absence of empirical data and the lack of verifiable systems for collecting information about the demographics of film viewership, filmmakers' and journalists' pronouncements about certain categories of audiences and cinematic standards should not be taken as statements of some empirically observable reality; instead, they throw into relief attitudes held by media practitioners (film and print) about age, gender, class, and the public consumption of films. A dominant assumption of this discussion is that sex and violence are synonymous with lower standards and poorer quality. This discourse sets up opposing categories of "middle classes" and "masses/front-benchers," which have different values arising from differing material conditions, resulting in differing aesthetic standards and cinematic tastes. The much-maligned front-benchers are young, poor males who see movies in theaters and are represented in this discourse as vulgar, prurient, violent, and profane. They are this way because the movies they allegedly enjoy watching repeatedly—making them box-office hits—are characterized as having the same qualities. Due to the sheer numbers of front-benchers, filmmakers have no choice but to cater to their degenerate taste, thus positing the "masses" as the root of the "decline" in Hindi cinema.

In this schema, the middle classes—"genteel" and watching films on video in the privacy of their homes—due to their different morals and values, have distinct cinematic preferences and aesthetic standards, characterized by their dislike of the films that front-benchers enjoy. The depiction of the increasingly mass nature of film as an adulteration of a middle-class standard is present even in academic treatments of Indian film history. Scholars present a narrative where, since Independence in 1947, the Hindi film industry, which had grown and changed in response to an influx of illegal profits from the Second World War, extended beyond its educated middle-class audience of prewar days to a new mass audience of uprooted peasants "confronting the unsettling realities of urban and industrial life" (Binford 1989: 80). The growth of this audience in the urban landscape precipitated what Ashis Nandy characterized as "the expansion of low-brow mass culture" (Nandy 1987). The movie theater can be said to have become a primary locus of this "low-brow" culture, as the middle classes did not frequent it anymore.

Common and Unfashionable Entertainment

I contend that the dominant association between mainstream Hindi cinema and the masses—firmly established by film scholars, filmmakers, and the English-language press—was the root cause for Hindi films not being considered cool or fashionable for such a long period. Shah Rukh Khan mentioned during our interview how he too at one time did not consider it "fashionable" to like mainstream Hindi films, instead preferring Hollywood films, which were considered more fashionable. Describing Hindi cinema as "pure, *masala* entertainment," "a modern form of *nautanki*," and a "modern form of street theater," Khan explained that the main audiences for Hindi films were those that, because of their limited economic means, had no other options for entertainment.[15] Although he did not use the terms "masses," or the "common man," his description of the target audience for Hindi cinema alludes to these concepts.

Khan's explanation for why Hindi films were an object of distaste and condescension by social elites is remarkably evocative of Bourdieu's arguments about class, taste, and the practice of distinction (1984). He surmised that expressing a distaste for Hindi cinema was a way to communicate one's class position and cultural capital.

> The people who perhaps condescend or look down upon, of course, one way of looking at it is that it makes them feel superior if they look down upon Hindi films. It makes them feel a little more educated, I guess. It makes them feel a little more media literate, because they know that blood is not blood when it is shown in films. A song is not really sung by us, and they are also the same people who, I guess, have some other mode of entertainment available to them, because of being a little better off economically also—and having access to foreign films and entertainment via video, laser discs, and travels abroad. (Shah Rukh Khan, interview, 15 March 1996)

Khan also articulated that Hindi films did not possess much symbolic capital: "It does not make a good conversation piece to come back home and tell that I saw x-y-z Hindi film. It makes more of a conversation piece to like *Phantom of the Opera* than some Hindi movie." When I asked him why that was the case, he explained: "Because it's a common mode of entertainment. It's not a specialized mode of entertainment. It's not skiing, high up in the Alps. It's not shooting some pool. It's not playing bridge with a beer in your hand. It's not going to a discotheque, in mini skirts. Whenever things are more inaccessible or more special, they become more important to people. This is common entertainment. For me to say that I saw x-y-z Hindi film—because even the *rikshaw-wallah* [rickshaw driver] has seen the film—it doesn't make it special at all" (Shah Rukh Khan, interview, 15 March 1996). After communicating this tremendous consciousness and awareness about the low cultural status of Hindi cinema and its audiences, Khan characterized his involvement in a somewhat populist vein, "I for one would say, very frankly, that I make films for that person who has no other mode of entertainment, and my job is just to entertain them, and I am very happy, and I'm very proud I can do that. I don't give a damn for people who don't think it's special." However, Khan admitted his initial ambivalence about working in Hindi cinema: "Five, six years ago, because of my education perhaps—being from St. Columba's School in Delhi—and then doing my graduation and master's and stuff, I may have also thought I wanted to make films always, but always thought that I'll make films which are different. There is no different thing. They are all the same films. Finally, it is just which one entertains you. And I have come to grips with that" (Shah Rukh Khan, interview, 15 March 1996). Despite the populist undertones of his assertions, by mentioning his elite high school, college education, and graduate degree, Khan locates himself within a social world that would normally not be associated with Hindi cinema.

His ambivalence about the form of popular cinema and the link he posited between the films and the socioeconomic status of their audiences came up later in our interview as well. We were discussing the global circulation of Hindi films, and Khan expressed his surprise at some of their unexpected peregrinations: "Even in Switzerland I saw some houses playing the films we've done, which is strange, because Switzerland is a very high per-capita kind of place, where I didn't think Hindi films would reach." He marveled that "foreigners" actually liked Hindi films: "We just need to make them a little less tacky, and I'm sure we can reach the international market" (Shah Rukh Khan, interview, 21 March 1996). Not only do Khan's statements reveal his underlying disdain for the mainstream cinema, they also illustrate the underlying developmentalist attitudes that accompany a discussion of Hindi cinema and its audiences. Given his characterizations of Hindi cinema as a medium produced explicitly for the Indian masses, it was surprising to Khan that Hindi films actually circulated in a "developed" country like Switzerland—as signified by its high per-capita income—and that foreigners, by which he most probably meant white Europeans, would like them.[16] As Hindi films have been circulating internationally since the 1950s, Khan's idea of "the international market" is obviously a very circumscribed one—representing the industrialized North.

All of the statements presented thus far illustrate how commercial filmmaking is predicated on a sharp dichotomy between filmmakers and audiences, through which filmmakers also constitute their identities as sophisticated social elites. The primary audiences for Hindi cinema in the 1980s and early 1990s are represented as a distinct class from filmmakers. Although filmmakers allude to the existence of more elite viewers, their presumed absence in the cinema hall renders them as if non-existent. The sentiment of disdain, which I argue is an integral part of the production culture of the Hindi film industry, is apparent in the discussion of frontbenchers and declining standards of Hindi cinema. However, just about four years after the articles discussed above proclaimed that filmmakers had to "cater to front-benchers or face ruin," Khan was predicting that attitudes toward Hindi cinema were changing for the better. In the following section, I discuss the changes in films, filmmakers, and audiences that occurred in the industry and filmmaking from 1994 to 2002 that made it possible for films to be considered "cool" a decade later.

THE PREHISTORY OF COOL: 1994–2002

Box-Office Bonanza

In January 1996, when I arrived in Bombay to start my fieldwork, the dominant mood within the film industry was of optimism: that audiences were "coming back" to theaters because the quality of films and of movie theaters was improving immensely. The optimism was connected to the unanticipated and astounding box-office success of two films, *Hum Aapke Hain Koun!* (HAHK; What Do I Mean to You!) and *Dilwale Dulhaniya Le Jayenge* (DDLJ; The Braveheart Will Take the Bride). When HAHK was released in 1994, the Hindi film industry was absolutely stunned by its phenomenal success, for it had been written off after preview screenings as one of the biggest flops waiting to happen. It was initially dismissed by the industry as a long, boring "wedding video," due to its 14 songs, 195-minute running time—lengthy even by Indian standards[17]—elaborate depictions of North Indian Hindu wedding rituals, and the absence of a villain or violence[18] (Figures 2–3). With its portrayal of excessively wealthy but harmonious families, traditionally dressed heroines,

FIGURE 2 Scene from *Hum Aapke Hain Koun!* Courtesy and copyright of Rajshri Productions.

FIGURE 3 Madhuri Dixit and Salman Khan in *Hum Aapke Hain Koun!* Courtesy and copyright of Rajshri Productions.

FIGURE 4 Shah Rukh Khan and Kajol in *Dilwale Dulhaniya Le Jayenge*. Courtesy and copyright of Yash Raj Films, www.yashrajfilms.com.

and young lovers who were willing to sacrifice their love out of a sense of duty to their families, the film challenged the dominant norms of film-making at the time. Its relatively linear and episodic narrative structure, very minimal plot, and lack of a villain were also not typical of main-stream Hindi films at the time.

The industry was again taken by surprise the following year with the release of DDLJ, a love story involving two Indians born and raised in Britain, which appeared as if it would surpass HAHK's box-office suc-cess (Figure 4). While DDLJ had a more familiar theme of young lovers who have to battle against parental opposition to their union (an un-yielding father), its most unusual element—widely commented upon by the press—was that the young couple chose not to elope. In earlier love stories, youthful rebellion was the norm, and young lovers ran away together in order to make a new life for themselves despite parental opposition. DDLJ presented a different male protagonist, one who ap-peared almost passive in contrast to earlier heroes. In DDLJ, even though the heroine's mother encourages the young couple to elope—this in itself an unusual portrayal—the hero refuses to do so and works very hard to win over the heroine's father, to gain his permission for their marriage, despite the fact that the heroine's marriage had already been arranged by her father to his best friend's son. DDLJ has earned the title of the longest running Indian film of all time, having completed 800 weeks in Bombay's Maratha Mandir theater as of February 18, 2011. Both films, due to their tremendous success in India and in diasporic markets, had an enormous impact on filmmaking—in terms of themes, long titles, visual style, music, and marketing—for the next decade. They ushered in an era of what the industry termed "family entertainers"—love stories filled with songs, dances, and cultural spectacle like weddings, set against the backdrop of extremely wealthy, extended, and frequently transnational, families.

The extent of HAHK's and DDLJ's success was beyond the industry's expectations because of the altered media landscape that Hindi filmmakers were operating in by the mid-1990s, which included the presence of satellite television. Both films were also touted as initiating a resurgence in theater going, which was remarked upon by the English-language press in articles like "Goodbye to Formula?" (Chandra 1995) and "Back to the Movies: In the Age of TV, Audiences Flock Back to Movie Halls" (Chatterjee 1996). The tone of these articles was in stark contrast to the scenario presented a mere four years earlier. Whereas earlier articles had been overly pessimistic in their assessment of the state of filmmaking and the health of the Hindi film industry, this later batch was filled with statements about the magic of cinema and the new wave of innovation sweeping through the industry. For example, "Goodbye to Formula" asserted, "Business is booming, but clichés are passé . . . The box office is lapping up un-Bollywood films, leaving traditional wisdom stumped. Even the money men are now looking beyond the twin peaks of violence and vulgarity" (Chandra 1995: 120). These sentiments were a strong contrast to the industry's own previous articulations of gloom and, as well as scholarly accounts that, focusing on earlier periods of the Hindi film industry, continually predicted its decline due to the entrance of technologies such as video and cable television (see Chakravarty 1993; Pendakur 1989; Vasudevan 1990).

The commercial performance of HAHK and DDLJ demonstrated to the film industry that in the age of satellite, cable, video piracy, and increased competition for audiences, it was still possible to generate astronomical profits at the box-office. Taran Adarsh, the editor of *Trade Guide*, a weekly trade magazine, characterized to me the impact of HAHK on the industry:

One *Hum Aapke Hain Koun*, and the economics of the Hindi film industry has gone haywire I would say, because in today's times when we have cable, we have video, we have television, we have video piracy, we have a lot of factors which oppose the big-screen entertainment, yet to have a film doing a business of 200 crores[19] [2 billion rupees] in the first year is a very difficult task. If someone would have told me that it's going to do 200 crores, I would have laughed it off, but it's a fact! So, when a film did 200 crores, people realized, "Oh, that means there is business. We have to make good products." (Adarsh, interview, September 1996)

Shyam Shroff, the head of the distribution company Shringar Films, and the father of Shravan Shroff, explained that the increased business potential that these two films signified was connected to their quality. "In a gap of one year, you have two major blockbusters like never ever have happened in the film industry. You have that kind of business waiting for you; the point is now you have to have a picture to collect that kind of audience, that kind of money. If you make a bad movie, you don't expect people to go and pay you" (Shyam Shroff, interview, April 1996). Shroff and Adarsh both expressed a tautology that I heard frequently during my fieldwork: audiences will only come to see a good film, and the way to know if a film is "good" is when audiences come to see it. Of course, their statements linking commercial success with cinematic quality is in direct contrast to the arguments presented in the previous section, especially in relation to the discussion about *Lamhe*—an acknowledged "good" film that performed poorly at the box-office. In the discussion about the 1980s, the dominant view presented by the press and filmmakers was that "bad," "trashy," or "vulgar" films were the ones that did well at the box-office and that good films like *Lamhe* did not have much commercial scope. The unanticipated success of HAHK and DDLJ therefore necessitated a major re-envisioning of the industry's axioms about filmmaking and audiences. Similar to filmmakers' discourses about the '80s, however, cinematic quality in the '90s was linked to the advent of new technologies and the social class of audiences.

The Era of Satellite and Returning Middle-Class Audiences

The attitudes toward new media technologies underwent a remarkable transformation between the two periods. Whereas video was posited as the reason for the degeneration of Hindi cinema in the 1980s, the presence of satellite television was cited as a factor for the improved production values of Hindi films in the 1990s. If video made filmmakers take shortcuts, satellite made them try harder. There were two strands to this argument—enticement and education—each addressing the distinctly imagined class-based identities of the audience. One explanation, based on middle-class ideals of domestic comfort and privatized leisure, centered on trying to entice assumedly elite viewers away from their television sets. Filmmakers argued that since they faced increased competition from satellite television, they had to spend lavishly to project a cinematic experience unavailable at home. Rajjat Barjatya, the director of marketing for Rajshri Films, explained their decision to make *Hum Aapke Hain Koun!* with optical stereo sound as a way to deal with the challenges posed by satellite television: "That is the only way we can combat video and satellite TV, which is penetrating almost every home today . . . When you sit at home you have 50 channels, and at least 45 to 50 films are being screened every day if you include the TV and cable channels. Why [would] a person come to a cinema? The film has to be extraordinary; the cinema has to be extraordinary; the entire experience has to be extraordinary, only then will he come" (Barjatya, interview, April 1996).

The other explanation had to do with the reforming tastes of the implied mass audience. Filmmakers argued that with audiences being exposed to the "best" in the world, or to "international" standards, they demanded no less from Hindi films. DDLJ's director, Aditya Chopra, explained that audiences were becoming better judges of quality and more discerning in their tastes, which he attributed to satellite television and its plethora of channels: "Mainly due to satellite, they see so much international stuff that when they come and see a Hindi film . . . I've seen [the] audience talk today about camerawork, about sound, about effect, which was unheard of! A common man saying, '*arre kya* light *kiya* shot *ko!*' [Look how well he lit that shot!]. You know, they [didn't used to] talk like that! But nowadays they do, so it's a positive step" (Aditya Chopra, interview, April 1996). According to Chopra, the consequence of audiences becoming more cinematically literate is that they patronize better quality films, enabling the box-office to be a truly accurate and transparent signifier of cinematic quality: "At least earlier, even bad films used to run. Now, thankfully, no bad film does well, which actually harms us more; if a bad film does well, it harms us more, even when a good film does not do well. When a bad film does well, you suddenly get shaken *ki* [that] 'Oh God! It's going to take a lot of time for them to actually understand that [on the one hand] this is not good, [and on the other] this is good'" (Aditya Chopra, interview, April 1996). Chopra's comments about "bad films" running at an earlier time are an allusion to the trashy '80s and indicate the impact of audience taste upon filmmakers; he represents audiences' poor choice in films as undermining his aesthetic sensibilities. The implication here, consistent with the audience-based narratives of cinematic quality presented in the previous section, is that more discerning audiences will lead to better filmmaking.

The other feature of the '90s media landscape was the regular presence of dubbed Hollywood films. Rather than expressing anxiety about competition from Hollywood films, filmmakers were quite confident in Hollywood's inability to appeal to the vast majority of Indian audiences. In fact, some filmmakers welcomed their presence as a sort of pedagogical tool for audiences, which would enable Hindi filmmakers to improve their own filmmaking. Screenwriter Honey Irani—who wrote *Lamhe*—predicted, "The audience which is watching will also improve. They'll accept new things from us. When they've seen, they've opened their eyes to see, '*arre, arre, yeh bhi ho raha hai, yeh ho raha hai*' [Oh, this is also happening; this is happening], so when we do some experiment, they will accept it, instead of rejecting it. So definitely it will help them to grow and help us to grow" (Irani, interview, May 1996). Once again an intrinsic connection is asserted between audiences and filmmakers—whereby the evolution or maturation of audience taste has a positive impact upon filmmakers' own identities as creative individuals and artists.

If the altered media landscape of the '90s fostered cinematic quality by helping the "masses" or the "common man" to become more discerning viewers, the other feature of the discourse of improvement was the celebrated "return" of middle-class audiences to the cinemas. Producer/director Rakesh Roshan was blunt in connecting quality to the composition of the audience, asserting, "First we were stuck with front-benchers, but now directors have a choice" (in Chandra 1995: 122). Komal Nahta, the editor of the trade magazine *Film Information*, stated that wealthier people were patronizing Hindi films again, evident by the "hi-fi people of Bombay" arriving at the movie theaters in the posh areas of downtown Bombay via their latest imported cars. He also mentioned that college students, who were once dismissive and contemptuous of Hindi films, had started watching them because films like HAHK, DDLJ, and others appealed to their sensibilities. More than the content of films, however, Nahta emphasized the material conditions of film-viewing as the main impetus for elites to return to cinema halls.

For these last six or seven years, the ultra-rich people—from Malabar Hill in Bombay, Nepeansea Road—they had stopped going to the cine-

mas [for] two reasons: first, they saw all of the films on the videos; second, the cinemas were in a pathetic state. Now videos are not there[20]
and cinemas . . . [have] the air conditioner [that] is always on. They've
got the best sound system. They've got lovely seats. They've got different classes where the highest classes are so high-priced that they are
assured that these *jhopad-patti wallahs* [slum-dwellers] will not come
and sit next to them, and with the air conditioning on and all, they've
realized *ki* [that] film-going is a pleasure. (Nahta, interview, September 1996)

Differential pricing of tickets, based on seat location, meant that class
hierarchy and separation had always been maintained inside the cinema
hall. Nahta's observation that the most expensive seats in the theater
were priced so high that wealthier viewers were assured that slum-
dwellers would not be sitting next to them, however, demonstrates that
the narrative of improvement in the mid-'90s was less about the quality
of cinema, than about the *quality of the viewing experience* for middle and
upper classes, who were seeing all of the films on video anyway. With the
steep increase in ticket rates, the "front-benchers"—who according to
the press were "extending to the dress-gallery" (Jain 1991: 28–29) by the
early '90s—had been priced out of these areas and put firmly back in their
place in the cinema hall; therefore, the celebrated "return" of audiences
to theaters in the mid-1990s was really about reinforcing social hierarchies and re-inscribing social distance into spatial distance within the
public space of the cinema hall. The advent of multiplexes several years
later, with their extremely high ticket rates, means that elite viewers do
not even have to acknowledge the existence of poorer viewers, as they are
simply priced out of the movie theater; thus, with respect to theatrical
exhibition, a literal process of gentrification has been taking place.

Gentrified Films

If the return of middle-class audiences to the theaters was interpreted
and explained as a sign of cinematic progress, what were the features of
this new and improved cinema? Many scholars have discussed how films
from this time period were very different from anything that had come
before.[21] Aesthetically, films in this period exhibited vastly improved production values that included digital sound, foreign locations, extravagant
song sequences, and lavish sets. Much greater attention and emphasis
began to be paid to the clothing, styling, and physique of stars, as well as
the overall production design of films. Narratively and thematically, the

most noticeable differences had to do with the representations of class, youthful romance, and the Indian diaspora.[22]

A very visible contrast between the successful films from the mid- to late 1990s and earlier Hindi films, focusing on families and romance, was the nearly complete erasure of class difference and the tremendous focus on wealth. All signs of poverty, economic hardship, and struggle were completely eliminated from these films, and the protagonists, rather than being working class or lower middle class as they were in earlier films, were incredibly rich—usually the sons and daughters of millionaires. Sachin Bhaumick, one of the most prolific and successful screenwriters, who began his career in the Hindi film industry in 1956, commented on what he found peculiar about HAHK: "India is such a poor country, but the picture, *mein koi* economic crisis *nahi hain* [there isn't any economic crisis in the film]. Not a single character is poor. All of them are happy, and all of them are rich, and all of them have no monetary, economic problem" (Bhaumick, interview, October 1996). Not only was there an absence of poverty, the moral valence about wealth had also shifted within these films. Sharmishta Roy, the art director for some of the biggest hits of the late 1990s and early 2000s, who played a key role in defining a new visual style that became identified as the hip and cool new Bollywood, discussed how the representations of the wealthy had changed in Hindi cinema: "People we show as rich now . . . we don't show them as flashing their money. You see when we used to have *zamindars* [wealthy rural landlords] in our films, they were very rich and they were flashy. Or they were autocratic and feudalist in their attitudes. It's not so now. The rich are rich, but they are not bad. The whole concept has changed. Previously, rich was bad and poor was good, right? Rich is not bad anymore, and that's not how they're going to be portrayed either" (Roy, interview, October 2000). Roy's statement about the moral values associated with wealth and poverty is a reference to earlier eras of Hindi cinema, where the main villains in films were frequently moneylenders, rural landlords, and wealthy businessmen, while peasants, workers, or others of modest economic means were the heroes. Whereas wealthy businessmen were frequently the symbols of exploitation, injustice, and even criminality in Hindi films from the 1950s through the 1980s, by the mid-1990s they were more commonly depicted as benign, loving, and indulgent fathers.

The narrative focus and valorization of wealth was also explained in terms of the aesthetics of production design. During my interview with screenwriter Anjum Rajabali in 2000, he narrated an anecdote in response to my observation that all signs and references to poor people had disappeared from contemporary films. He told me that he had come up with an idea for a script with the mill closures in Bombay as the backdrop—he thought he could base the protagonist in one of the *bastis* (slums), trying to fight the mills being shut down. He convinced a director with his idea, and so he and the director went to a producer to pitch the story. The producer was absolutely aghast and exclaimed, "But we can't make a film like this! We can't have such poor people. They're so poor—it won't look nice!" Then the producer asked, "What will Ajay Devgan [the star that they had in mind for the role] wear?" When Rajabali responded, "I don't know, jeans, a kurta, and *chappals* [sandals]," the producer was horrified and exclaimed, "Ajay Devgan can't wear chappals! What if we set it in Canada? Then everyone can look nice." Rajabali complained, "No one in the industry wants to show a slum anymore." He told me that in his previous screenplay, *Ghulam*, when the producer asked him if it was set in a slum or a lower middle-class colony, he answered "lower middle-class colony," for the sake of expedience since, "slum has become a really bad word."

With Rajabali's story in mind, I asked Roy her thoughts about why most contemporary Hindi films did not depict slums or working-class milieus as they had in the past. She surmised that the directors she worked with had grown up in a very privileged setting and were basically interested in replicating or improving upon that world. She explained that they would not have much interaction with, or desire to represent, people of lower class backgrounds because it would contradict the directors' aesthetic sensibilities: "Okay, if there has to be an interaction between someone from the *basti* [slum] and someone from an upper-class society, there will still be a slight amount of crudeness to it, because people who come from a *basti* will not have the same sophistication as someone from the upper society. I don't think they ever want to get into that, everything has to be very, very classy" (Roy, interview, October 2000). Roy's statements illustrate how the discussion about quality and aesthetics in cinema is imbued with judgments about social class.

With the erasure of poor and working-class protagonists from filmic narratives, love stories from the mid-1990s were also quite different from earlier eras, which frequently had class difference as the source of parental disapproval, which therefore played the central conflict in films. With protagonists of the same class background, the source of dramatic tension and narrative conflict in films from the mid-'90s was internalized and centered on the conflict between individual desire and duty to one's family. The plot manifestations of this conflict either involved a love triangle or strict parents who eventually yielded to their child's choice of partner. In both types of stories, the character was torn between someone he or she loved and someone he or she was obligated to marry. Roy explained, "That kind of feudalism is not there in our films any more. It's more about people from equal societies falling in love, and then there's probably a triangle now. I think that's what most of the themes are there today, it's not so much rich versus poor and opposition, it's more about a triangle, all from the same society" (Roy, interview, October 2000). With her choice of the term "feudal" to describe the plots and themes that focused on class conflict, Roy implicitly positions the '90s films, with their emphasis on elite social worlds, as a more modern and desirable state of affairs in filmmaking.

Although Hindi films have had a long history of depicting youthful rebellion, especially against strict fathers,[23] after HAHK and DDLJ, the theme of compliant lovers, willing to sacrifice their love for the sake of family honor and harmony, became the dominant norm. The hero and heroine's passivity—and obeisance to patriarchal norms of honor and notions of filial duty—illustrated the essentially conservative outlook of these Hindi films, regardless of their cosmopolitan and MTV-inspired visual style. These family entertainers presented a commodified Indian identity arising from a specific North Indian Hindu cultural milieu, based on stereotypes about the "joint family," the Indian English phrase to denote a multi-generational, patrilocal household. Thus, the success of such films was interpreted by the media and the state as a celebration of "family values" and an affirmation of "Indian tradition" in an increasingly globalized world. Discussing the part of the plot in HAHK where the female protagonist decides to sacrifice her love out of her sense of duty to the family, Bhaumick declared, "Madhuri, anytime could have spoken out, 'I'm not going to marry my brother-in-law, because I'm in love with Salman Khan,' but there is a tradition: the girl should not talk before the elders, and they kept it up, and this clicked now in the '90s. Very fantastic thing. That shows in our heart; we have maintained our values" (Bhaumick, interview, October 1996).

The emphasis on family values and Indian tradition extended to the cinematic depiction of diasporic Indians as well, which was a significant transformation ushered in by this period of Hindi filmmaking. Since the mid-1990s, Hindi films have frequently represented Indians living abroad as more traditional and culturally authentic than their counterparts in India. While earlier Hindi films used characters of Indians living abroad for comic relief or as villains, many Hindi films after DDLJ have diasporic Indians as their protagonists and are set almost entirely in countries like Australia, Canada, England, or the United States. Thus an authentic "Indian" identity—represented by religious ritual, elaborate weddings, large extended families, respect for parental authority, adherence to norms of female modesty, injunctions against premarital sex, and intense pride and love for India—is mobile and not tied to geography. One can be as "Indian" in New York, London, or Sydney as in Bombay, Calcutta, or Delhi.

Through their valorization of patriarchy, the Hindu joint family, filial duty, feminine sexual modesty, and upper class privilege, the family films of the mid- to late 1990s were much more conservative than films from earlier eras; however, their visual, narrative, and performative style made them appear modern and "cool." Shah Rukh Khan, the male lead of DDLJ, characterized it as a very "modern" film, asserting that all of the analyses about its success being based on a celebration of traditional values had missed the point: "I think people have pinpointed the wrong reason for its success. They talk about its values, they talk about going back to the old values like respecting parents." Rather than being rooted in tradition, Khan argued that his character was actually very savvy, a welcome change from the standard depictions of young romantic heroes in Hindi films:

> I think it's a very yuppie character actually. I think it is completely illogical, stupid, and childish, the way our hero behaves otherwise in films—where he runs away with the girl. I was asking a writer, he said, "Okay you run away," and I asked, "Where do you run away?" Finally where do you run away? You can't run away from the earth, so it's a futile thing. You lose out on a job; you lose out on money; you lose out on credibility; your parents don't like you; you're fighting against the world; you meet rapists on the way; you're traveling on trucks; it's like, "Why lose out on all that?" Get your way done, in a little more, management-like way, like the yuppie of *Dilwale Dulhaniya* did . . . he got his way done; he got married to the girl, and it didn't pass him any hardships. (Shah Rukh Khan, interview, 20 March 1996)

Khan's criticism of plots featuring youthful rebellion as illogical and futile—and his characterization of DDLJ's lack of defiance and unwillingness to challenge patriarchal authority as modern—is a response to the routinized representation of young romance in Hindi cinema; essentially, what is socially radical—romantic love across social divides—in the context of a highly stratified society, where the majority of marriages are arranged and endogamous, appears cinematically clichéd. Within the context of the history of this particular genre in Hindi cinema, DDLJ's intrinsic social conservatism appears radically different. Khan's representation of his character's complicity with, rather than resistance to, dominant social norms as comprising a more rational approach to life—akin to a yuppie manager—reframes traditional notions of filial duty as a modern practice.

Khan continued with his observations about how DDLJ reflected a modern outlook and represented the values of a younger generation, which he described as less interested in codes of propriety and honorable conduct than with favorable outcomes:

> There's more of a younger generation feel today, which is more competitive, more intelligently competitive. It's . . . no longer for your honor or my honor. I don't give a damn for your honor or my honor, as long as the thing is done. So the films are becoming modern, but because old ideas and values are so deeply imbibed, people like to hold on to them. So, on the face of it they would like to still believe what they've always believed, but somewhere, subconsciously, a film like *Dilwale* works for me mainly because it's a modern film, and maybe that is why it is becoming more fashionable to like Hindi films. (Shah Rukh Khan, interview, 20 March 1996)

The increasing modernization of Hindi cinema was not only leading to its improved status within elite social spheres, but also among the second generation within the film industry, according to Khan. Predating Shravan Shroff's statements, cited at the beginning of the chapter, by a decade, Khan asserted that, since Hindi films were "not as silly as they used to be, say twenty years ago," he believed that the children of filmmakers, who "I'm sure didn't think much of the films," were also changing their attitudes and becoming less embarrassed about working in the industry. From Khan's perspective, this younger generation of filmmakers was further responsible for "modernizing" Hindi cinema, described in terms of a "reduction in melodrama and larger-than-life performances," thereby enabling Hindi films to begin to be regarded as fashionable or cool. A different perspective about such changes was offered by producer/director Govind Nihalani: "There is no anger anymore" (Nihalani, interview, May 2006), alluding to the absence of plots and narratives focusing on issues of social justice and equity, which have had a long history of representation in mainstream Hindi cinema.

Generation Bollywood

By 2000, the dominance of films focusing on the love lives and dilemmas of wealthy protagonists, often located in the diaspora, was commented upon by the English-language press. *Outlook* magazine's article, "Riverdale Sonata," with the subheading, "*Desi* is out. As target audiences change, Hindi cinema gets itself a designer Archie-comics look," pointed out, "there are no subaltern angry young men any longer; new Bollywood speaks the language of an affluent, growing middle-class" (Joseph 2000b). Similar to earlier discussions about the economic centrality of front-benchers in the 1980s, the rationale offered for the changes in cinema was attributed to audiences, specifically the emergence of diasporic audiences as a very lucrative market for Hindi filmmakers. The article argued that the "vastly attractive, but demanding overseas market has forced Hindi films to become hip and sophisticated" (Joseph 2000b).

While audiences, specifically imagined target audiences, are central to a discussion of commercial filmmaking, I contend that some of the most apparent changes in Hindi cinema in the mid-'90s—in terms of mise-en-scène, themes, and protagonists—which have been too readily attributed to overseas markets, also have to do with filmmakers' own personal tastes, privileged social backgrounds, generational identity, and desire to counter the condescension expressed toward commercial Hindi filmmaking. In fact, these filmmakers initially made films that appealed to their own sensibilities, which happened to work in certain markets, rather than doing any sort of a priori quasi-market research about diasporic or elite audiences in urban India. For example, producer/director Karan Johar, a second-generation member of the film industry, whose films have been extremely successful in overseas markets, exemplifying the gentrified narratives and aesthetic discussed earlier, was asked in an interview for the English-language weekly *Tehelka* about his "obsession with perfect colors, perfect figures, and saturated opulence." Johar replied, "I think it comes from my need for beauty and good looks, which all through my childhood I didn't have" (Chaudhury 2007). Describing his films as portraying a very aspirational lifestyle, Johar also explained his cinematic choices in terms of his personal history and social background: "People ask me why there's no poverty in my films—but I've lived a very, very sheltered life. The only trauma I had to deal with was being fat, so my films were about the things I knew about. My first film had to be about heartbreak and first love" (Chaudhury 2007).

Johar's first film, *Kuch Kuch Hota Hai* (KKHH; Something Happens, 1998), was a love triangle peopled with wealthy, stylish protagonists, decked out in designer brands (Figure 5). The film's narrative, which unfolds in flashback, spans a decade where the protagonists are substantively introduced during their final year in college. Sharmishta Roy, who has been the art director for all of Johar's films, discussed the criticisms leveled against the production design for the film, specifically the college portions:

> *Kuch Kuch Hota Hai* to a lot of people it looked like a comic strip. It was meant to be an Archie comic. It was meant to be Riverdale High . . . We achieved what we were setting out to do, because that was my briefing. I was told, "It's Riverdale High." It's not any ordinary college. It's not a college that you see in Bombay, because that's no fun . . . you can see that on television every single day. What we're trying to do is give the people a feeling that they've come to college, which is really great; it's great fun, and this is where they meet and life was so beautiful. (Roy, interview, October 2000)

She attributed the aesthetics and styling of contemporary films as a generational phenomenon, "Our films today are being made by younger directors who are very, very Western in their outlook. Their exposure to Western society is more than to our villages in India." Speaking about another portion of KKHH, which is set in a children's summer camp, Roy admitted that such a concept was alien in India, but praised directors like Johar for introducing such novelty into their films.

> We don't know of summer camps over here . . . when I was talking about the upbringing of the directors today, they're not absolutely Indian. I mean, they know of summer camps and they've probably been to them also, so that's what they're bringing into our Indian society, and our Indian society is lapping it up because it's such great fun. We have heard over and over again we are a poor country, and no one wants to see that thrown in your face all the time. You go into a theater and you want to escape all that, and that's what these guys are doing; they're just packaging things so well that it's entertaining; it's touching; and it's visually pleasant. (Roy, interview, October 2000)

The notion of entertainment as a form of escape is a common feature of the discourse surrounding mainstream cinema. Whereas the more conventional understanding of Hindi cinema is as a form of fantasy, and thereby a brief respite or escape for low-income viewers from their daily

FIGURE 5 Shah Rukh Khan and Kajol in *Kuch Kuch Hota Hai*. Courtesy and copyright of Dharma Productions.

struggles, Roy's comments here present a different sense of escape, that from the perspective of socially elite viewers who are tired of being reminded that they are from a "poor" country. By presenting a picturesque, glamorous, manicured world erased of all signs of poverty, Hindi films like KKHH offer a chance to escape the signs of other peoples' harsh lives. Such gentrified films allow wealthier audiences, including filmmakers, to briefly escape the "postcolonial condition"—the reminder of being national subjects in a poor or "developing" country like India (Gupta 1998). Unlike dominant explanations offered by journalists and scholars, which centered solely on audiences, Johar's and Roy's statements also remind us of the relevance of the social world and personal background of filmmakers for the form and content of Hindi filmmaking.

While Roy foregrounded the presumed "Western-ness" of certain filmmakers' social and cultural backgrounds, other prominent filmmakers associated with this period articulate the importance of kinship and cultural traditions in shaping their cinematic practice. Sooraj Barjatya, the director of HAHK, stated on the Rajshri Productions website, "I make films with the family at its centre, and for the family, because I've been brought up in an environment where the family mattered more than anything else. So it is but natural that my films reflect this point of view. My upbringing, though not totally conservative, has been very traditional, and it is this traditionalism you see reflected in the film."[24] In the rest of his remarks, Barjatya mentions how he "subconsciously imbibed" the images of family weddings, which led to their incorporation in HAHK.

The highly affective portrayals of "Indian-ness," found in films like HAHK and DDLJ, coincided with the influx of American programming on satellite television in India. Such films represented a response to the altered media landscape within India by a generation of filmmakers who were in their early twenties when satellite broadcasts began in the country. Aditya Chopra, the director of DDLJ, which was heralded as starting the trend of films focusing on the diaspora, spoke at great length with me about satellite television and how it clarified his sense of cultural identity and crystallized his goals as a filmmaker:

> There is some stuff shown on satellite which you might not agree with ethically or morally or whatever, and you want to show to them that listen it's cool—it's good you watch all this—but don't forget we're Indians and we can still entertain, and we can still have fun with our own culture. You don't have to take your clothes off and dance! And dance to a music which actually doesn't make sense. You can listen to a folk kind of a song and have the same fun. So that's what I think cable and TV helps you, it sets up your goals more clearly. This is what we're up against and this is also what we should be able to do. (Aditya Chopra, interview, April 1996)

Chopra's remarks present a strong sense of national identity, and anxiety over the impact of satellite television on ideas about entertainment and sentiments of cultural belonging. His proprietary attitude about culture and sense of purpose as a filmmaker was to counter satellite television's potential role as an agent of cultural imperialism. Speaking about the younger generation, Chopra posited his mission: "The basic attitude of the youth is that whatever you see that is foreign is cool, so you need to actually shake them up and say, 'It's cool to be Indian!'" (Aditya Chopra, interview, April 1996). In Chopra's statements, the meaning of "cool" extends beyond its connotations of approval and desirability to include cultural sovereignty and national pride. The connection between coolness and cultural pride was referenced a decade later by Shravan Shroff, who asserted that Hollywood would not be able to wipe out filmmaking in India, like it had in other parts of the world because "Indians just love their own films and I think it's really cool" (Shravan Shroff, interview, May 2006).

Chopra's cultural pride came across strongly when recounting his inspiration for making DDLJ. He stated that he had initially wanted to make an international film that would showcase to the world—by which he really meant Western audiences—through a love story, the essence of Indian culture, in terms of emotions, sociality, and kinship behavior:

> I feel that the West can learn a lot from just the fact as to how we, our culture—the way we think, the way we react, the way we love, is . . . so wonderful, which is somewhere or the other missing in the West. They are a little held back in their emotions; we are not; we give; we really react! I feel it's so wonderful that we can be so passionate about life. I feel we can share that with them, because they have this image which is "Oh there's this poor country, which is struggling all the time, which is the world of snake-charmers," or something like that, and you need to change that. "Okay, forget all that and see we've come a long way. Besides that, even with our progress, we've not forgotten our roots." (Aditya Chopra, interview, April 1996)

The essentialist dichotomy Chopra poses, between India and an undefined "West," has a long history, dating back to the colonial era. India's affective and emotional superiority is akin to the material/spiritual dichotomy constructed by nationalist leaders in the nineteenth century, as is the idea of a cultural bedrock that cannot be dislodged with material change (Chatterjee 1993). Like Roy, Chopra also exhibited a concern about dominant representations of India as a "poor country," and was eager to alter global perceptions.

His decision to base his characters in England was in order to highlight their cultural identity. Talking about the main father character, Chopra explained, "I wanted to exaggerate being Indian, so to put a man in India and be Indian is nothing; you throw a man out for twenty years and he's still stuck to it, that shows you: it brings the Indian-ness [out] more. So that gave me a very big advantage for my characters and my plot, so that's why I placed them, so that's why he became an NRI [non-resident Indian]" (Aditya Chopra, interview, April 1996). As he continued to develop the idea for the film, Chopra realized that it would also be very relevant within India, because with the onset of satellite, he felt, "We were going a little away from the roots." According to Chopra, while he did not have a "higher" motive, other than making a good film that would be commercially successful, he stated he was "trying to make a film that would somewhere make you pause and think, and somewhere make you react, and make you feel nice about what you are—about being Indian. That was at the back of my mind, but not the main motive" (Aditya Chopra, interview, April 1996). Chopra's insistence that his main motive was to make a widely appealing film, but that he still had something larger he wanted to communicate, is an example of the negotiation involved in making what gets designated as "commercial cinema," that is, films aimed at wide audiences. Throughout his interview, he articulated a tension between making the film he would like to make versus what he believed others would like to see.

Whether discussing Indian youth seduced by foreign media, Westerners who need to be educated about India, or audiences who could feel nice about being Indian, Chopra's remarks are replete with references to imaginary interlocutors who motivate his filmmaking practice. Another instance where an imaginary interlocutor occupies a significant presence is in filmmakers' discussions of the condescension expressed toward mainstream Hindi films. Like Shravan Shroff, many of the filmmakers most associated with "Bollywood" are second- and third-generation members of the film industry, who related the impact of criticism by their social peers outside the film industry. Chopra, whose father, Yash, began his directorial career in the late 1950s, recollected that when he was a child, he could "stand up" for Hindi films against the condescension of his peers, but he admitted, "I mean obviously you do get affected—say your dad makes a film and someone says something—that happens quite often—'Oh that film was bad.' So, it hurts you; you feel bad, because we have a tendency to believe that our identification is our film, so it's like actually saying something against my dad" (Aditya Chopra, interview, April 1996). He asserted that a motivating factor behind his filmmaking was to counter the criticism leveled against mainstream Hindi cinema: "You know, my target is not to get a pat on my back by my parents or friends who are close to me, who are going to like, in any case, whatever I do. No, that's not the point. The point is, okay, there is this guy who keeps talking shit about films: I need to convince him. I need to give him something so good that he will also—[so] he just can't help but like it" (Aditya Chopra, interview, April 1996). It is this desire for acceptance and approval that is a significant driving logic behind the gentrification of Hindi cinema and the transformation of the industry into Bollywood.

Thus far I have been discussing a younger generation of filmmakers who began their careers in the late 1980s (Barjatya), or mid- to late 1990s (Roy, Chopra, Johar), and whose fathers or grandfathers were also filmmakers. The changes in filmmaking initiated by these makers had an impact on films produced by older filmmakers as well. One notable example is Subhash Ghai, the producer/director who began his career in the late 1970s and was quite commercially successful in the 1980s—the very period that was derided as trashy and vulgar by the press and other filmmakers. His films from 1997 onward have been markedly gentrified in terms of protagonists, production design, conflicts, and narratives. Since 1999, his films have enjoyed greater commercial success outside of, rather than within, India. Speaking in Bombay in 2000, Ghai related how filmmakers needed to think about the "global Indian" and their problems, which he felt made for "more effective cinema" than films focused on issues of class exploitation. He referred to films revolving around personal relationships and generational conflict as "international," and described *Yaadein* (Memories) the film that he was currently working on: "I am making a movie of a British Indian who has been living there for the last twenty-five, thirty years, and his three daughters have been brought up there. He . . . is very orthodox, very conservative. The daughters are not, so the conflict of values—what happens and how he handles his three daughters, and how the three daughters handle him—is the theme of *Yaadein*" (Ghai, interview, October 2000). Ghai felt that the issue of generational conflict transcended the limitations of culture and nation, reasoning that the film would appeal to people living in Britain and in India, unlike films focusing on farmers or *zamindars* (rural landlords)—issues he felt were specific to India.

Expressing his relief that he was not limited to making films about "U.P., Bihar, or Punjab," Ghai asserted that films about personal relationships enabled him to grow as a filmmaker. He implicated changes in audiences as allowing him to finally break free from restrictive mindsets and realize his full potential as a filmmaker:

> I am completing my twenty-five years as a director now. In 1991 I started feeling that I am jogging in the same place, because as a director, and as a visionary, and as a person I have grown, but I had to make those films only—rural films—all the time. I was now allowed to try other parameters, which is happy news for a progressive filmmaker like me—that you can go ahead, think something new, innovate something; then people are going to accept that. That's why I could go for *Taal*, otherwise I would have made a very sentimental, highly melodramatic film, which I used to make—like *Ram Lakhan* or *Karma*—in the '80s. So, the evolvement and development you see in my cinema, it is thankfully [due] to the growth of the audience also. (Ghai, interview, October 2000)

Ghai's presentation of self is mediated through the choice of narrative focus and the figure of the audience. Ghai portrays certain topics as more reflective of his cosmopolitan outlook—which is what I think he means by "progressive"—and credits audiences for enabling him to realize his potential as a filmmaker. Like Ramesh Sippy, Ghai represents his evolution as a filmmaker as an intersubjective experience where (imagined) audiences play a significant role in fashioning his filmmaking practice.

This section has delved into some detail about how the social world of filmmakers, changes in the media landscape, and trends in Hindi filmmaking from the mid-'90s resulted in a gentrified cinema, in terms of both the content and style of films. This gentrified—or in the words of the filmmakers above, more "modern," less "feudal," not as "silly," more "international"—cinema is the starting point for Hindi films to be regarded as "cool." However, what truly enables Hindi films to arrive socially, and what allows filmmakers to make the films they really want, hinted at by Ghai above, is the arrival of the multiplex.[25]

THE ARRIVAL OF COOL: THE MULTIPLEX

"What I think is the best thing that has happened to the Indian film industry in the last five years are multiplexes," declared Meghna Ghai-Puri, Subhash Ghai's daughter and the president of Whistling Woods International—a film school started by her father in 2006. We were sitting in her office at Whistling Woods, located in Film City, a sprawling state-owned film and television production facility in Goregaon East, a northern suburb of Bombay. It was May 2006, and we were discussing the changes that had taken place in filmmaking since the turn of the millennium. Continuing with her praise of the multiplex, which centered on the smaller seating capacities of the theaters, Ghai-Puri asserted that multiplexes were "encouraging a young breed of filmmakers to make interesting, intellectual films, which were capturing a certain audience," who were "more sophisticated" than before (Ghai-Puri, interview, May 2006). Akin to the advent of video and satellite television in earlier periods, the arrival and expansion of multiplex theaters have generated considerable discourse by the Hindi film industry, as well as the print and broadcast media, about audiences, aesthetic standards, and cinematic idioms. Much of this discourse is marked by a strong rhetoric of change, progress, and modernization, whether it is addressing the materiality and phenomenology of cinema-going or the symbolic and aesthetic dimensions of film production. Similar to the discussions about video and satellite, the one about multiplexes also serves as a commentary about class, taste, consumption, and filmmaker subjectivity.

While multiplexes have transformed the material conditions and experience of seeing a movie in a theater in India and produced new audience imaginaries within the Hindi film industry, the feature most commented upon by journalists and filmmakers has to do with the engendering of a new type of cinema. Around 2003, the English-language press in India started to discuss the emergence and economic viability of what was initially termed "niche cinema," which soon got labeled "multiplex cinema," and attributed a causal relationship between the sites of film exhibition and cinematic practice. Initially used to describe films made with smaller budgets and lesser-known actors, about themes that were characterized as "off-beat" and "different" from a purported Bollywood norm, understood to appeal only to English-educated, affluent, urban audiences, the definitions and descriptions of "multiplex cinema" have been as much about audiences and viewing practices as they have been about aesthetic properties and narrative content.

In the early days of the multiplex in India, they were lauded for their implicit pedagogical function—frequently characterized in a developmentalist vein—of improving the cinematic tastes of the Indian viewer. By offering a range of non-mainstream cinematic choices, multiplexes were cited as the catalyst for reforming the average Indian taste in film, which had been stunted for so long by the formulaic fare produced by the Bombay film industry. For example, in the article, "The Multiplex Effect," which appeared in the *Indian Express*, the director of the first multiplex in the northern Indian city of Kanpur, Shailesh Gupta, discussed how, when his theater first opened, "Hindi had a virtual monopoly on the minds of the audience," and that there was little interest in any other cinema, even big-budget Hollywood films. Eight months later, however, due to his programming decisions to screen a variety of films, patronage of an English-language film like *Bend It Like Beckham* brought in decent business. Gupta was willing to experiment with his programming, even if it did not garner huge returns, for he assigned himself the responsibility of inculcating more sophisticated tastes for his patrons: "I am keen to help in the maturing process of the Kanpur film-goer" ("The Multiplex Effect" 2003).

Similar to the discussion about video, front-benchers, and the trashy '80s, the idea of multiplex cinema is premised on the correlation between content, audience, and conditions of viewing. Multiplexes, with their smaller seating capacities and much higher ticket prices—which translates into more elite audiences—were hailed by a number of filmmakers, associated with the parallel cinema movement of the 1970s and '80s, as making cinematic risk-taking commercially viable. In the above-mentioned article, veteran filmmaker Adoor Gopalakrishnan, whose films are in Malayalam and are consistently categorized as "art" or non-commercial, asserted, "Audiences and exhibitors are now looking for a different kind of cinema. The advent of multiplexes has also encouraged this change in mindset. If you have a film that might not necessarily run house-full in a 1,000-seat hall, you now have the option of showing it in, say, a 200-seat auditorium, where it might very well draw a full house" ("The Multiplex Effect" 2003). The November 2007 issue of the English-language film magazine *Filmfare* featured an interview with the veteran actress Shabana Azmi: "What the multiplex has done today is release the producer from having to cater to the lowest common denominator. The multiplex has demonstrated that Indian audiences are not [a] monolith, and it is possible to make niche films that can become successful" (Ghelani 2007: 130). In November 2009, at a panel discussion titled "Re-Framing Indian Cinema," held at New York University in conjunction with the Mahindra Indo-American Arts Council Annual Film Festival, director Shyam Benegal spoke of the impact of multiplexes as thoroughly groundbreaking for Indian cinema. He reflected on how, until the advent of multiplexes, every film that was released needed to be able to fill at least 80 percent of the capacity of single-screen theaters in order for the distributors to break even: "For years and years this was an enormous problem. We always used to say, 'Why are we having these huge cinemas? Why does it have to be like this? Why is it that only big pictures can be made, big block-busters?' . . . So you couldn't possibly make films of a smaller kind; it had become almost impossible. It's really when the multiplexes started that everything started to change. You didn't have to look at the audience as one big grey mass" (MIACC 2009b). Contrary to the above statements, I discuss in chapter eight how mainstream Hindi filmmakers conceive of their audiences as comprised of diverse constituencies, whose varying tastes need to be addressed or transcended, not a monolithic "grey mass."

A couple of years earlier, for a special feature about multiplexes in *The Indian Express*, Benegal narrated a familiar history of cinematic decline connected to the advent of technology and class composition of audiences in the cinema hall. Rather than satellite television, however, multiplexes were the technological catalyst for improved cinema. Discussing the 1980s, Benegal wrote, "TV took away the urban middle-class audiences and cinema came to be patronised by the working classes alone— or those who could not afford a TV set at home and those who didn't have access to TV. At this time, film had to rely on an entertainment concept that would gather the largest possible audience—a common denominator sufficiently lowered and spread thin. A kind of dumbing-down was taking place" (Benegal 2007). While mainstream Hindi film-makers castigated video and working-class audiences for the poor quality of filmmaking generally, Benegal focused his comments on the impact of television and working-class audiences on non-mainstream forms of filmmaking. Describing the emergence of an "alternative cinema move-ment" in the 1970s, which targeted "the professional middle-classes and educated audiences," he declared that with the spread of television and the retreat of middle-class audiences from theaters, alternative cinema was "wiped out." With the advent of multiplexes, the possibility for an alternative cinematic practice was revived once more: "The opportunity created in the '70s and then lost in the '80s came back with the multiplex in the late-'90s" (Benegal 2007). For Benegal and his peers, the structures of production, distribution, and exhibition, which depended on pleasing large numbers of people, were viewed as inimical to quality cinema. Quan-tity—either in terms of seats in a cinema or the number of viewers—is seen as incapable of producing quality. The equation of poor quality and poor taste with large numbers has a long history that is not unique to the Indian context (Williams 1983: 192–97). As with many Hindi filmmakers, cinematic quality is also integrally connected to the presence of middle-class audiences in theaters.

The very attribute that Gopalakrishnan, Benegal, and Azmi lauded about multiplexes—that they provided a space for films of ostensibly limited appeal—was also a criticism leveled against them initially. For example, an article about the impact of multiplex films on mainstream Hindi films appearing in the November 2007 issue of the English-language film magazine *Filmfare*, asserted, "Till two years ago, 'multiplex films' was a euphemism for films that were looked upon as too niche, experimental, and commercially nonviable. If and when such films got made, their business was restricted to a few screenings at the still na-scent multiplexes in select cities" (Amin 2007: 69). The overall tone of the article was overwhelmingly positive, however, claiming that 2007 was a "watershed year for the non-mainstream Indian film industry." It char-acterized the impact of multiplex cinema as "a wind of change taking the Indian film industry by storm," where "the boundaries between main-stream and offbeat are blurring" (Amin 2007: 69). The reasons offered had to do with the unanticipated commercial success of certain smaller budget, less conventional films, which communicated to filmmakers that audiences were open to new subject matter. The willingness of top stars to work on projects by directors regarded as "niche" was also cited as a sign of changing times.

During fieldwork in Bombay in 2005 and 2006, I encountered many comments about the paradigmatic effect of multiplexes on Hindi filmmaking. The main thrust of those comments had to do with how certain films would have never been made, or if made never released, prior to the advent of multiplexes. Elaborating upon her point about the revolutionary impact of multiplexes, Meghna Ghai-Puri stated, "A good thing that it's done is that a film like *Iqbal* can actually see a 75- to 80-print release in India, which couldn't have happened earlier. A film like *The Little Terrorist*, which is a documentary film, actually got a release in the theaters. Again, something that would have never happened earlier" (Ghai-Puri, interview, May 2006). Ghai-Puri's comment about *Iqbal* was echoed by many others; *Iqbal* and *Page 3*, both released in 2005, were the two most talked about examples of unconventional films that had reasonably successful runs in multiplexes during that time. The films were very different from each other in terms of theme, plot, protagonists, and visual style: while *Iqbal* was a sweet, touching tale about a deaf and mute Muslim teenager's dream to play on the national cricket team, *Page 3* was an acerbic and cynical journey into the immoral and decadent world of celebrities in Bombay, as observed by a journalist who writes for the society/gossip pages of a newspaper.

What both films had in common were the absence of major stars, major directors, diegetic song sequences, or expectations for success. While both films were touted by their makers and the press as "hits," setting into motion pronouncements about audiences, changing tastes, and changing cinema, the determination of commercial success is nonetheless relative, an issue I examine further in chapters five, eight, and nine. *Iqbal* and *Page 3* did reasonably well in Bombay, but not in other parts of India; the trade press, which assesses commercial outcome from the point of view of the distributor, classified both films as "coverage to commission-earners," indicating that distributors recovered their investment, but did not necessarily earn a profit. The point to be noted here is the simple fact of not losing money was interpreted as a sign of success. Talking about the impact of multiplexes on filmmaking, producer/director Vikram Bhatt cited *Page 3* and *Iqbal*: "These kinds of films would have been washed out before" (Vikram Bhatt, interview, January 2006). Bhatt's declaration was related to the star cast of both films and based on the dominant industry credo that major male stars are necessary to draw crowds to theaters, hence necessary for commercial success. Like HAHK and DDLJ a decade earlier, *Iqbal* and *Page 3* defied the film industry's expectations and contravened its production fictions; while the former films proved that unparalleled commercial success was possible in a competitive media landscape, the latter demonstrated that audiences existed for films that strayed from mainstream conventions. If HAHK and DDLJ, by virtue of their stupendous business, were "good" films from the perspective of the industry, *Iqbal* and *Page 3* were "good enough" films in terms of their business. In both decades, the return of middle-class and more elite audiences to the cinema hall was cited as the determining factor for these films' successful commercial outcome.

The commercial viability of limited or narrow appeal was represented by filmmakers as truly enabling, revealing the way multiplexes articulated with filmmakers' subjectivities in a manner similar to discussions about video and satellite in earlier periods. Vikram Bhatt reflected upon the effect of multiplexes upon his filmmaking: "Even my film, *Ankahi*, maybe, I would not have made it three years back, four years back, because I don't know if, if it's going to really involve the masses though it's a very simple tale. It's a tale of adultery, so that appeals to all kinds of classes and masses, but even then I feel somewhere the audience would be—it would be a more multiplex film" (Vikram Bhatt, interview, January 2006). At a panel discussion about multiplexes held in Bombay in September 2009, reported in the *Indian Express*, documentary-turned-feature filmmaker Kabir Khan asserted, "Thanks to multiplexes, we're now making films we couldn't possibly have made earlier" (Pillai 2009).[26] An important reason, according to director Sujoy Ghosh, was because "A multiplex audience is usually more accepting of different kinds of films and is more aware of trends in global cinema" (Pillai 2009). For all of the filmmakers quoted here, the multiplex serves as a metonym for a certain type of film, as well as a certain type of audience, which poses far fewer creative constraints on filmmakers than audiences who frequent the traditional single-screen theaters.

The audiences frequenting multiplexes are the arbiters of taste, critical to a determination of Hindi films as cool. When asked if it was the people making films or the people watching them that accorded Hindi films their improved status, Vikram Bhatt replied, "It's because the people who are watching the films that is allowing them to be cool" (Vikram Bhatt, interview, January 2006). Ghai-Puri elaborated that the "youth" demographic—in the Indian context most commonly used to refer to teenagers, college students, and people in their early twenties—was most responsible for Hindi cinema's improved status. She explained that the lavish material experience that multiplexes offer has made cinema-going among youth very attractive, hence, cool: "I think that multiplex culture has really brought in that coolness to Hindi movies. I think the coolness factor really comes from the teenagers, school-going, college kids—they always went to the cinema, but I think its becoming cooler now to go to the cinema because of the whole experience they're getting when they go" (Ghai-Puri, interview, May 2006).

Bhatt elaborated that with the multiplexes and their particular audience profiles, the form and idioms of mainstream cinema were undergoing a transformation. Like Shah Rukh Khan, Bhatt described Indian cinema as a *nautanki* art form replete with melodrama and passion, "You know there was melodrama and there was screaming and 'Gabbar Singh! *Main aa raha hoon!*' [Gabbar Singh, I'm coming!] That kind of idiom was there, which is now finished; the audience laughs at that. So the audience wants more subtle, near-natural performances" (Vikram Bhatt, interview, January 2006). Bhatt asserted that if filmmakers wanted to target younger audiences, then films had to appear "cool" since such audiences "don't want to see 'uncool' things; they don't want to see over-the-top drama; they don't want to see the heroines cry; they want more subtle— the whole audience starts to get very edgy and shifty the minute that they know a very emotional scene is going to happen now. Somebody's dead and the heroine is going to cry—they don't want to see it. They're like 'Okay, just skip this; we understand her pain; let's get on with it.' So I think that's the way it's changing" (Vikram Bhatt, interview, January 2006). While a decade earlier Shah Rukh Khan credited a younger generation of filmmakers with reforming Hindi cinema from its melodramatic excesses, Bhatt here credits a younger generation of viewers for the same feat. Common to both perspectives is the function of affect and emotion in characterizing Hindi cinema as something either cringe-worthy or praise-worthy and the role of youth in bringing about cinematic change.

"Multiplex cinema" is, however, an ambiguous category in terms of form and content, since during my research I encountered notions of the multiplex film that were at variance with the characterizations presented above. The day I went to visit Tarun Kumar during his film shoot at Kamalistan Studios in January 2005, he was quite anxious, since his latest film, *Awaaz* (Sound), was about to release, and he was nervous about its box-office prospects since it did not boast a hugely popular cast of stars, though it was produced at a high budget.[27] During lunch in his trailer, Kumar brought up the topic of his upcoming release and was particularly annoyed by the fact that another action film was opening on the same

Friday as his; then he reasoned, "Well, you know there are two different audiences actually for these films, *Awaaz* is really a multiplex film, while the other one is more a single-screen film." Perplexed by his characterization, since *Awaaz* did not appear outside the conventions of mainstream Hindi cinema—it was a fast-paced thriller, about a man's quest to capture a dreaded criminal, replete with songs and action sequences shot extensively in European locations—I said, "But I thought multiplex films were films like *Jhankaar Beats* and *Mumbai Matinee*"—films that focused on the various emotional and relationship dilemmas of upper middle-class Bombayites. Kumar responded patiently, "No, those are crossover films.[28] Multiplex films are those [that] are more elite. Single-screen films are more massy." Kumar's statements revealed the symbolic capital carried by multiplexes within the film industry, mainly due to their association with elite audiences. By asserting that his film was a multiplex film, Kumar was signaling a host of associations that would accord his film status and prestige—the main being that urbane, educated, sophisticated audiences would want to see his film, which implied that his film was urbane, sophisticated, and cool.

FROM UNCOOL TO COOL

An interest in filmmaker subjectivity led me to focus on the notion of coolness that has been so prominent during my fieldwork. This chapter has demonstrated how the discourse about coolness within the Hindi film industry is a discussion about cinematic quality, filmmaker subjectivity, and the social status of audiences. By examining Hindi filmmakers' discourses of quality and change, this chapter explored how commercial filmmaking is a complex intersubjective endeavor, where audiences comprise the imagined interlocutors with whom filmmakers are in constant dialogue. It illustrated how a driving logic behind the oft-remarked transformation of Hindi filmmaking in the mid- to late 1990s was filmmakers' desire for legitimation by social elites or individuals who were not regarded as the traditional audiences of Hindi cinema. Filmmakers' narratives of change also reveal the significance of technologies of distribution, such as video, satellite television, and the multiplex theater, in mediating their subjectivities as cultural producers.

A prominent feature of the discussion about cinematic quality is the sentiment of disdain expressed toward certain films and certain audiences. Although, as "commercial" cultural producers, Hindi filmmakers are frequently identified with their audiences in media and scholarly discourses, what this chapter has shown is how filmmakers strive to distance themselves from the bulk of the viewing audience. For many years, a central tension for Hindi filmmakers was the disjuncture between their actual audience and their desired audience, a tension that appears to have been resolved with the arrival of the multiplex theater. Poor, working-class, or other socially marginal audiences have been consistently scapegoated by filmmakers, both mainstream and alternative, as the root cause for bad cinema and substandard filmmaking. By contrast, middle-class and more socially elite audiences are represented as the catalyst for quality, since they enable, according to filmmakers, the pursuit of high standards and the realization of creative potential. Therefore, just as the urban middle class is represented as instrumental for a globalizing, "shining," "new" India in state discourses (Fernandes 2006), middle-class audiences are represented as responsible for a modern, fashionable, new cinema in industry discourses. The correspondence between middle-class identity and high quality is not merely relegated to a discussion of film form and content, but also to the social world of the Hindi film industry. The next chapter examines the significance of the middle-class as a normative social category in the film industry's concern with respectability.

CHAPTER 3

Casting Respectability

For a few days in March 2005, the Bombay film industry was embroiled in what became known as the "casting couch" scandal. India TV, a private television network and a recent entrant on the burgeoning Indian televisual landscape, aired footage one Sunday morning of a Hindi film actor, Shakti Kapoor, soliciting sex from a reporter, who was posing as an aspiring actress, in exchange for helping her to get her first break.[1] The goal of this undercover "sting" operation—as it was referred to by India TV— was to expose the "casting couch" syndrome within the Bombay film industry and perform a crucial social service: according to the head of the network, "Parents of girls coming in from small towns to Mumbai can now tell their girls to be more careful" (Pherwani 2005).

What was interesting about this whole episode was the contrast between the media's discussion of it and the film industry's reaction to it. The press overwhelmingly described the manner in which the whole operation was conducted as entrapment, and the Indian media was dominated by criticism of India TV's methods and goals, as well as discussions about journalistic ethics, right to privacy, and the boundaries between public and private.[2] While much of the public response was a type of cynical amusement, the film community's response bordered on the hysterical. The uproar within the film industry was not caused by Kapoor's attempts to exchange roles for sex, but that in his efforts to persuade the reporter/actress to have sex with him, Kapoor named three of the top actresses of the film industry and asserted—on national television—that they had sex with top producers and directors, whom he also named, in exchange for roles.[3]

The reaction of the industry was swift: the very next day, the Film and TV Producers Guild, an association of the most powerful producers in the industry, called for a ban against Kapoor, and condemned the "slanderous, mischievous, and unsubstantiated aspersions" cast by the actor against leading film personalities, advising its members not to hire Kapoor for any of their productions. In a statement to the press, the Guild also asserted, "The Guild would like to clarify to all concerned that all of its members who represent the cream of the entertainment industry have always stood for the highest moral, ethical, and professional values and have been the fountainhead of the growth of this vibrant industry" ("Call for Ban Against Shakti Kapoor" 2005). Although offering a public apology to all of those he had named, Kapoor maintained in interview after interview that the television channel had framed him. Producers, directors, and actors who were not a part of the Guild came out in support of Kapoor, expressing their solidarity at news conferences. By the end of the week, the Guild had lifted its ban on the actor as well.

That the Hindi film industry was in an uproar over this particular representation of itself as a lewd, lecherous, and hyper-sexualized space yields insights about the type of image that the industry has been trying to cultivate for decades: one that valorizes Indian middle-class norms of respectability and morality, explicitly linking the moral and social status of cinema with the class backgrounds of film personnel and film audiences. Reactions to Kapoor's statements ranged from "He is maligning the industry and spoiling its name. I think everyone should take action against him for talking about respected people like this," and "Our film industry is full of professionals who belong to respectable, cultured families," to "It's ridiculous to even point a finger at such respectable people. The Johars [the last name of one of the producers named by Kapoor] are the most decent and cultured people I've worked with" (Upala and Khan 2005).

In this chapter, I examine the anxiety and desire around the concept of respectability, which manifests itself not only during scandals like the Kapoor's casting couch one, but in a myriad of everyday ways in the Hindi film industry. As apparent from K. Ahmad Abbas's letter to Gandhi discussed in chapter one, Hindi filmmakers have been concerned with their social and moral reputations and garnering approval from social, cultural, and political elites for quite some time. When I first arrived in Bombay in 1996—nearly a decade prior to the Kapoor scandal—I encountered many declarations on how filmmaking was becoming a respectable profession as a result of the changing social and class backgrounds of recent entrants. This view was frequently expressed in a tautology: "The film industry is becoming a more respectable place because girls and boys from good families are now joining the industry; because the film industry has become more respectable, girls and boys from good families are now joining it." The frequent pronouncements of respectability emphasized the industry's tenuous claims to it, as the above scandal demonstrates.

This concern with respectability, which can be traced back to the early days of cinema in India, is a facet of the framework of disdain that characterizes the film industry's production culture. The roots of moral and social stigma for the Hindi film industry are located across three main sites: the origins of its finance; the social origins of its members; and the class location of its audiences. As I discussed briefly in chapter one, the illicit nature of some of the sources of film financing as well as the film industry's connections to the "black" economy and organized crime has been the object of censure by the state and the media for many decades. Parallel to the state's anxiety over "black" money was the anxiety expressed by members of the film industry concerning "tainted" women—those from courtesan backgrounds—who became actresses in the earlier eras of cinema in India. Film journals in the 1930s acknowledged the moral stigma associated with cinema, positing that the involvement of women from educated upper-class backgrounds was the key to improving both the cinema and its reputation (Majumdar 2009). Finally, as chapter two's discussion of trashy films and front-benchers demonstrated, the gender and class composition of its audiences also imparted an aura of disrepute to the film industry. The Hindi film industry has been involved in "stigma management" (Goffman 1963) across all three domains for quite some time.[4] While official industry status resolved the stigma connected to finance, the multiplex resolves the stigma associated with audiences. Here, I examine how filmmakers deploy the concept of respectability to manage the stigma associated with working in the industry.

Within the film industry, respectability is primarily articulated through the trope of the good family, which has its roots in the emergence of a middle class in nineteenth-century colonial India (Chatterjee 1993; Joshi 2001). Good families are defined by their upper-caste status, middle-class to upper-class position, high levels of formal education, practice of modern professional occupations (medicine, engineering, law, journalism, civil service, teaching), and gendered norms of sexual modesty. Since actresses have historically borne the burden of the film industry's moral reputation (Majumdar 2009), respectability also serves as a discursive framework for discussing women's sexual behavior. Scholars tracing the history of the emergence of social groups identified as the middle class in Europe and South Asia or examining the contemporary formations of middle-class identity in both regions have demonstrated how the ideal of respectability is a defining feature in the self-constitution of a middle class.[5] Although the elite members of the Hindi film industry occupy an economic position much higher than the "middle" of Indian society, their explicit concerns about respectability reveal the normative power and value of middle-classness within their social world. Thus, for Hindi filmmakers, the disjuncture between class position and social status (Weber 1947: 428) results in efforts to reconcile the two through the display and performance of respectability.

I focus on these displays and performances of respectability, which operate as practices of "face-work" (Goffman 1955) by members of the Hindi film industry.[6] The ideas of "face" and "face-work" serve as useful frameworks with which to understand filmmakers' concerns over and expressions of respectability. Goffman defines face as an "image of self delineated in terms of approved social attributes" (1955: 213), and face-work as the actions that are necessary to appear consistent with this image. He points out that particular groups can have a characteristic repertoire of face-saving practices that structures the performance of face-work. Hindi filmmakers, in their efforts to appear respectable, draw on a set of practices, discourses, and tropes that moves their claims to this identity forward. For the remainder of the chapter, I detail the face-work practices of filmmakers. I first briefly relay the history of women's participation in the film industry, since they have been at the center of the industry's anxieties around respectability. Then, I describe the gendered dimensions of behavior on film sets and other spaces of production that reveal different norms of comportment and mobility for men and women. Finally, I examine the discursive sites of face-work: filmmakers' narratives of how they entered the profession; their definitions and valorization of middle-class identity; and their value for formal higher education. While the neoliberal transformations of state and society in India are charged with reorienting the emphasis of middle-class identity (Deshpande 2003; Fernandes 2006; Mazzarella 2003), members of the film industry articulate a notion of respectability that draws on older understandings about middle-class behavior and practice.

"Excuse me, this is the first time I've worked with this unit, so I don't know people, what is your name?"

I was standing on the side of the set waiting for instructions and was startled when one of the stars of the film, Madhuri Dixit, asked my name. I was working as an assistant for the film *Dil to Pagal Hai* (The Heart Is Crazy) at the time (August 1996), and though this was the film's second shooting schedule, it was Dixit's first—the previous schedule in June did not require her presence.[7] After seven months of fieldwork in Bombay, visiting and observing film shoots, I was aware of the intricate norms of hierarchy which governed the patterns of interaction on a film set, and it normally would never involve a star of Dixit's stature—the highest paid actress in the Hindi film industry at the time—expressing curiosity about, much less starting a conversation with, an assistant. My task of keeping costume continuity involved silently observing actors and noting everything they wore for a particular scene in order to avoid any lapses in continuity over the course of the shooting schedule. As the fifth assistant to the director, the maximum interaction I would have with such a star as Dixit should have been knocking on her dressing room door to inform her that a shot was ready, so what sparked Dixit's curiosity enough that she approached me? I speculated that, as a woman working as an assistant, I was quite an anomaly on a film set. Three months later, when I had a chance to interview Dixit during another shooting schedule for the same film, she confirmed my hunch when she remarked that I had been, "the first woman assistant that I ever saw on a set; otherwise I've never met anyone."

During the course of my fieldwork in 1996, I too never met any other women working as assistants on the direction side, and seldom on the production side; if actresses or dancers were not required for a particular shoot, I was frequently the only woman on the set. My continuous presence on sets, studios, and offices often perplexed those who were unaware of my research project, leading to frequent speculations about who I was, since I did not seem to fit into any of the expected roles for women—actress, dancer, journalist, hair dresser, costume designer, or choreographer—visible at various production sites. Some people thought I was someone's wife; others thought I was a girlfriend; perhaps the most inventive speculation was that I was actually an actress who had devised an ingenious method of trying to get my first break—"doing research."

The reasons for the marginal presence of women have to do with the dominant image of the Hindi film industry. Due to its historical connections to courtesan culture, organized crime, "black money," and as noted in the Shakti Kapoor scandal, stereotypes about the "casting couch," the film industry has long been viewed as an unsavory place, especially for women. In the very early days of cinema in India, women were not willing to act due to the stigma attached to public performance.[8] Acting, singing, or dancing for an audience was associated with prostitutes and courtesans, and thus regarded as outside the boundaries of decent society. The public nature of the filmic image appeared to violate the dominant norms of feminine modesty. Even prostitutes were unwilling to act in films, since that would appear as a public disclosure of their occupation, so in the first Indian feature film, *Raja Harischandra*, the role of the queen was played by a young man.[9] When women began to act in films by the 1920s, many were from mixed British or European and Indian parentage, frequently of Christian or Jewish backgrounds, and commonly referred to as Anglo-Indians. These women, due to their hybrid ethnic and cultural heritage, were already deemed outside of normal society and thus less bound to social conventions concerning respectability.

With the introduction of sound, filmmakers needed actors and actresses who could speak the vernacular and sing well, which meant that the Anglo-Indian women (and the wrestlers) who had dominated early cinema were no longer viable. One source of talent, specifically in dance and music, came from the male and female descendants of the *tawai'f* (courtesan) tradition in India. Courtesans had existed for centuries in the subcontinent and were traditionally the exponents of high culture in the courts, performing classical music and dance in their salons for royal patrons.[10] The British (Oldenburg 1991) and the newly constituted Indian middle class of northern India (Joshi 2001) played an instrumental role in the decline of courtesan culture in nineteenth-century India, and even though courtesans continued their establishments in more attenuated circumstances even after Indian independence, they had lost their main source of patronage with the end of monarchy.[11] Their association with classical dance and music was also a source of unease for the political and cultural leadership, which had internalized the colonial Victorian criticisms of the courtesan institution as depraved, decadent, and immoral, and so went to great pains fashioning a sanitized classical tradition that could be deemed respectable and legitimate (Bakhle 2005; Meduri 1988; Weidman 2006).

Thus, in the early days of cinema in India, the trope of the good family is situated in opposition to the courtesan tradition. Due to the hereditary nature of all performance traditions—including that of the courtesan—stating that an actress was from a "good family" communicated that she was not from a courtesan lineage, along with several other things: class, caste status, and level of formal education. Even if not hailing from a courtesan lineage, many of the early actresses came from economically marginal backgrounds and were the main financial support for their natal families. Such families, having urged their young teenaged daughters to act in films, would also be regarded as the obverse of the good family. Memoirs, biographies, and film periodicals from the 1930s and 1940s display a tremendous concern about actresses' social background.[12] For example, in her autobiography, Durga Khote—an actress who began her career in 1930—recounted that producers were on the lookout for educated women from good families because "in those days women from good families and films did not go together" (Khote 2006: 33). Khote, a college-educated woman from an upper-caste and upper-class Maharashtrian family,[13] described how the producers of her first film, in which she had a very minor role, used her family background as a marketing tool, "The film advertisements had started appearing two months earlier. Mr. Bhavnani—shrewd businessman that he was—took full advantage of my name: that is, the name of both my families. The Lauds and Khote were highly esteemed families of the time, and Mr. Bhavnani used that fact. Newspapers carried huge advertisements headlined, 'Introducing the daughter of the famous solicitor Mr. Laud and the daughter-in-law of the well-known Khote family" (Khote 2006: 35).[14] The film, according to Khote, turned out to be "the very dregs, worthless in content and in production values," and she described how she became the object of a great deal of vicious criticism from the Maharashtrian community and the press. She recounts that it became difficult for her to venture outside her home and go anywhere in the neighborhood because of the constant gossip, and that both her natal and conjugal families were tremendously upset with her, for in their opinion she had "brought shame to the good names of the families."[15]

Two letters published within a couple of months of one another in the English-language film magazine *Filmland*, in 1931, further illustrate the concerns around acting and respectability. The first letter, published in September, "Should Respectable Ladies Join the Films," written by an actress who chose to remain anonymous—simply listed as "a lady artiste"—argued against film acting as an honest means of livelihood for women from educated and cultured backgrounds. The problem was not with acting per se, but with the people that one came into contact with in the studios.

> It would require a high moral courage and character to withstand the scandal that accompanies the actress in and out of the studio. The actresses [who] are usually found to support a film career come from houses of ill-fame [and] have already thrown their morals to the airs, [finding] the filmland as a proper scope for their enjoyment. It is but horrible for any society girl to work in such disreputable surroundings. These actresses are naturally very free in their behavior and are easily accessible for corruption. Such being the condition, it is but natural for the people connected with the film industry, irrespective of their position, to be morally loose. If any society girl—out of sheer necessity—has to take up this career as an honest means of livelihood, she cannot expect any better treatment from the hands of those persons who are accustomed and habituated to low morals. (In Bandyopadhyay 1993: 109)

The actresses from the "houses of ill-fame" were most likely women who came from—or were thought to come from—courtesan backgrounds. The writer also presented studios as sites of debauchery and sexual harassment, where innocent women were lured with the promises of a bright future, but "any one who does not respond to the desires and wishes of the producers and the directors is doomed and is thrown out in the long run or is treated in a most cruel manner" (in Bandyopadhyay 1993: 110). She ended the letter by asserting that her "educated and cultured sisters" should not join films until the low morals of the studios and associated personnel improved. She also pointed out that education and culture were not necessary for acting; therefore the energy with which some filmmakers were advocating that college-educated women join the film world could be better directed to improving the moral standards of studio life.

In November of the same year, a rejoinder to this letter was published in *Filmland*, titled "Why Shouldn't Respectable Ladies Join the Films," by the actress Sabita Devi—whose real name was Iris Gasper. Devi asserted that her experiences as an actress were completely unlike that of the "lady artiste." She insisted that she was always treated with utmost respect and courtesy, and all of the men she had worked with were "thorough gentlemen" who "still hold on to the traditions of the East in respect of their attitude towards women" (in Bandyopadhyay 1993: 111). She acknowledged that because of the shortage of respectable actresses, women had been recruited from the "lowest strata" of society, but that these "unfortunate" women were frequently very reserved on the set and did not behave in the manner described in the previous letter. In fact, Devi went on to assert that women were equally responsible for any type of harassment they encountered and that "the attitude a man takes towards a woman is governed by the latter's own integrity of character, by her actions, her words and her manner; if she be true, womanly, and modest, no man can approach her in any other spirit than that of the deepest reverence and respect, and in my opinion no man is so bereft of these instincts, which help in recognizing true womanhood, than to dare approach her in any but the manner I have described above" (in Bandyopadhyay 1993: 113). She stated that any woman with talent, courage, and a chaperone could work hard and achieve success honorably. The letter ended with Devi's invitation to the "lady artiste" to visit her studio, where she would be happy to show that it was not the corrupt or licentious site described in the previous letter: "the actors and principals are gentlemen of the East in the truest sense of the word, and that actresses have not flung 'their morals to the airs'" (in Bandyopadhyay 1993: 113). The themes of Devi's remarks have been remarkably persistent features of the film industry's discourse about respectability over time. The tautology—that respectable women behave respectably—surfaces in later actresses' characterizations of the film industry and is a mainstay in discussions about the issue. Devi's reference to the "gentlemen of the East," and her general defense of the reputation of the film profession, is also similar to assertions ("they are the most decent, cultured people I know") defending the reputation of contemporary Hindi filmmakers presented in the opening of this chapter.

The concern with respectability and actresses' social backgrounds continued to be a source of discussion in the national media after Independence. Waheeda Rehman, who debuted in Hindi films in 1956 and was a leading actress from the late 1950s and 1960s, described in an interview in the national English-language magazine *Illustrated Weekly of India* that cinema and the film industry had achieved respectability by the time she began her career.

> Before the '50s there was a social stigma attaching to the cinema, which was, by and large, condemned as not fit for even boys from good families, leave alone girls, though a Devika Rani or a Leela Chitnis may have been an exception to the rule. But when I entered the field, the industry had already gained respectability. I was lucky to have been given the opportunity to build up an image of "dignity." It is up to the

star to make what she will of her image. In an industry where it's all show, naturally you cannot give an inch without their [*sic*] extracting a yard. As long as it's your talent they are drawing on you have nothing to lose. (In Garga 1996: 165)

Like Devi, Rehman emphasizes the actress's agency in determining her reputation, but such agency appears only possible for women who are already marked as respectable by virtue of being from "good families." In this manner, both Devi's and Rehman's remarks evoke ideologies of the new *bhadramahila*: the respectable woman as constituted by middle-class nationalists in nineteenth-century Bengal and examined by Partha Chatterjee (1989). Chatterjee discusses how such women, educated and hailing from middle-class homes, were able to venture out into public spaces without fear of censure or disrepute because their social demeanor, styles of dress, eating habits, and religiosity marked them as separate and superior, both to westernized women and to working-class women. Just as her "culturally visible spiritual qualities" shielded the new respectable woman from any moral hazards associated with venturing outside the home (Chatterjee 1989: 629), the respectable actress from a good family possessed the qualities to ward off the unscrupulous and licentious men prowling the studios.

While actresses like Rehman, who obviously had a vested interest in the idea, insisted that the film industry had become respectable by the 1950s, some form of stigma was still attached to women acting: this is apparent not only by the fact of such assertions as Rehman's, but also in the practices of social reproduction carried out by filmmakers themselves who did not allow their daughters or daughters-in-law to act. Raj Kapoor—a hugely successful and popular star, director, and producer—insisted that his daughters-in-law, both leading actresses in their time, quit acting after they married his sons (both actors) because "the Kapoor family women do not act." Kapoor's father, Prithviraj, had begun what became the most well-known acting dynasty within the Hindi film industry. Raj's sons also became actors, while none of his daughters did. When Kapoor's granddaughter Karisma decided to pursue acting after his death, it created quite a stir in the film industry and was heavily commented upon by the Indian film press, especially because, unlike "star sons"— a term used by film journalists to refer to the sons of former actors— who are "launched" with much fanfare and have their debut films lavishly produced by their fathers, Karisma's debut film was not produced by her family and was regarded by the industry as a B-grade venture. In fact, while the sons of actors, producers, directors, and writers have been entering the film industry as actors since the early 1970s, it is only from the mid-1990s that "star daughters" have had a presence in the industry.[16] Nonetheless, actresses from film families still comprise a smaller proportion than actors from film family backgrounds. Many prominent film families whose sons became actors did not follow the same pattern with their daughters: the most that one would hear about them in the press was in relation to their weddings.[17]

Even in the late 1990s I encountered statements indicating that the stigma attached to working in films still endured, and that women continued to bear the burden of the film industry's reputation. Ayesha Jhulka—an actress who grew up in Delhi and in her own words came from a "very disciplined family," as her father had been in the air force—relayed the main perceptions that her friends and family had of the Hindi film industry: "They feel that the industry is a very bad place, and they feel that it's a dirty place and no respected family's daughter should be doing that. *Acche ghar ke ladkiyan filmon mein nahi jaati hai* [Girls from good homes do not join films] and all that stuff. I also have faced a lot of opposition from my relatives" (Jhulka, interview, 28 May 1996). Jhulka landed her first role as a result of winning a beauty pageant in Mussoorie in 1988; it was sponsored by Weston Cassettes, an audio company that had ventured into film production.[18] The reward for winning the pageant was the lead role in a Hindi film.[19] She explained that she was able to become an actress due to the support from her grandparents and parents, despite opposition from her larger extended family. Rather than offering the more common explanation, locating the stigma of acting within the public nature of the filmic image, Jhulka speculated that the reason for the bad reputation of the film industry had to do with the openness with which actresses enjoyed their social and sexual freedom. The visibility of an actress's mobility and autonomy—that her various relationships and liaisons were always in the public eye—was what led to her tarnished reputation.

> When articles are written and when people are talking about films and affairs and things like that, it's very open you know? Everywhere it happens, but the film industry is so open, people can see it happening, so they visualize it to be a very bad thing. Like today they'll see one girl with one man; tomorrow they'll see her with another man . . . you know after a few years, she'll be with another man; she'll get married to the fourth person, which is a very normal thing in any human

being's life. It happens in high societies. It happens even in lowest of societies, but they don't want to accept it. (Jhulka, interview, 28 May 1996)

Even though Jhulka surmised that a scenario where a woman had multiple relationships prior to marriage was a social norm rather than an aberration, she was quick to point out that "we have girls coming from very, very good families here, and it's not a bad place you know once you are here." She also believed that people living in Bombay were less judgmental of actresses, since they have more exposure to—and awareness about—the film industry. Echoing Devi and Rehman from earlier eras, however, Jhulka indirectly acknowledged the potential problems of sexual harassment that women could face, asserting that it was up to women to manage this issue: "You should just know how to handle the wrong people."

What becomes apparent from examining the pronouncements about respectability within the Hindi film industry, through the various decades, is that it is always in a state of becoming: it is a process that has been initiated, but not fully achieved; for if the industry had completely achieved respectability, members would not have to keep announcing its attainment or its temporal dimension, whereby the past of disrepute is contrasted with the present of respectability, evident also in Amitabh Bachchan's remarks in the introduction of this book.

Although the pronouncements of the industry as a more respectable place were circulating during my initial fieldwork, most of the discussion centered on actresses. Because of the nature of the industry's work culture, very few women were involved in the area of film production at that time. Assistants who normally begin in their teenage years work long irregular hours, frequently into the night, and are at the beck and call of their bosses. Even when a shoot is not going on, assistants are expected to be constant companions to either the producer or the director; such a working scenario is perceived by many families as having the potential for sexual harassment or exploitation. The site of my fieldwork caused a great deal of consternation among my own extended family, which kept warning me to be "extra careful" while I was in Bombay.

When I returned to Bombay in 2000, I was pleased to see women working as assistants to directors, producers, and production designers. With each subsequent trip I have noticed the greater presence of women in film production. In my conversations with some of these young women, who were English-educated and came from middle-class backgrounds, they remarked that their families were more amenable to their working in the film industry because it was becoming more organized, professional, and respectable. Sharmishta Roy, the art director introduced in the previous chapter, whose father was also an art director, recounted how her family was initially opposed to her working in the industry, but that the stigma did not exist any more. Like other women she also euphemistically acknowledged that "problems" could arise for women, but it was up to them to "deal with" them. "See, my family, my father, was very reluctant to let me get into the film industry. There was a certain stigma attached to women working in the industry. That is not there any more, right? I think we are all very respected. You could work anywhere in the world, and you'd probably encounter the same problems. It depends entirely on how you deal with it. And what kind of responses you evoke from other people" (Roy, interview, October 2000).

Roy surmised that the change in the film industry's image had to do with the greater job security it offered compared to previous times, although she thought for recent entrants it could still be very unreliable. She also felt that the change had to do with an increasing number of middle-class men and women entering the field. Roy described how she was careful to learn about the family backgrounds of people she was hiring as assistants: "You see, before I take in my assistants I interview them, and I make sure I know what kind of family background they have. So initially they [the parents] are hesitant to let their daughter come in, because, film industry, you know? And once they have met me, and they've discovered that I am like most people, it's easier for them to send their daughters" (Roy, interview, October 2000). Roy's statement that she was "like most people" indexed a normative middle-class social world and habitus shared between herself and her potential assistants: in her domestic arrangements—she lived in a joint/extended family household (her parents, younger brother, and his wife) in a three-bedroom flat in a high-rise building in Bandra; in her personal comportment—modestly and simply dressed, wearing little to no makeup; in her personal habits—she did not smoke or drink; in her work ethic—hardworking, focused, and the recipient of multiple awards for her art direction; and in her family background—her mother was a housewife, and her sisters were college-educated and settled in North America, while her brother worked in the computer animation industry.

The increased presence of women across the various sites of production was touted by members of the industry and the media as yet another

FIGURE 6 Box-Office, Fame Adlabs, Andheri (western suburb of Bombay), 2006. Photo by the author.

sign of the growing respectability and professionalization of the film industry that had been set into motion from the beginning of the millennium. Respectability became indexed in interesting ways. For example, during fieldwork in 2006, the owner of a chain of multiplex theaters in Bombay proudly showed me the young women sitting behind the ticket windows at one of the theaters and mentioned that they were the first cinema halls to have "girls" selling tickets (Figure 6). The fact that women were comfortable enough to work in such a capacity at his theater signaled the intrinsic high quality and respectability of his establishment. He also asserted that women working in the box-office signaled the improvement that cinema and cinema-going had undergone in the last few years.

While the involvement of educated women from middle-class and upper-class backgrounds was cited as necessary for the moral and aesthetic improvement of cinema and the film industry in its early years in India (Majumdar 2009), by the late 1990s the participation of women from such backgrounds in filmmaking indexed the overall respectability of the Hindi film industry. Talking about the growing presence of filmmakers' children in the industry, Pamela Chopra, the wife of noted producer/director Yash Chopra, used the example of Karisma Kapoor to communicate the tremendous shift in perceptions that had taken place: "Can you just imagine Raj Kapoor's daughter saying, 'I want to become a heroine'? Oh my God no! And yet, when Daboo's daughter [Karisma; Daboo was the nickname for Raj Kapoor's son, Randhir] decided she wanted to become a heroine, Daboo couldn't say no. Because the industry had changed by that time" (Pamela Chopra, interview, 26 March 1996). The status and condition of women as a social, cultural, and moral index of a community, society, or nation, has a long history dating back to the colonial project in South Asia and elsewhere.[20] The presence of middle- and upper-class women both on-screen and off-screen has mutually indexed respectability within the industry: actresses from "good families" signal that the industry is a respectable place to work, enabling the entry of women from similar social backgrounds to work behind the scenes in the industry; with greater numbers of women working in production, acting starts to lose some of its stigma as well.

As I have already noted, however, when I first began my fieldwork there were few women working behind the scenes and the set was an extremely masculinized space. In such a scenario, how was respectability discussed and enacted? In the next section, I examine the gendered dimension of behavior on sets and other sites of production.

PERFORMING RESPECTABILITY

One evening, while I was waiting to carry out an interview with an editor of a trade magazine at his apartment, a young woman and her mother came to seek advice about getting a break in the industry from the journalist's friend, Imran, who presented himself as an industry insider and expert.[21] The woman and her mother sat down next to me on the sofa. From their conversation with Imran, which was in Hindi, I gathered that this was not their first time meeting him for advice on this matter.

They mentioned meeting a producer, whose name I did not recognize, and Imran asked how the meeting went. The mother said unhappily, "You know he wanted her not to sign any films for a year and a half, until the release of his film." Imran responded, "I checked this guy out. I asked around and this guy, he's a small-time producer, and he doesn't have a very good reputation. He's more like a 'Casanova' [he used the English word]. He likes to keep seeing new girls and boys and then tries to bind them to some type of contract where they can't sign any other film, and so I don't think you should take the offer."

The mother agreed, "Exactly, what if some big break comes along and she's bound because of this other film?"

Imran then warned the mother, "You know you should not be visiting producers like this with your daughter. This is not the right way to try and break your daughter into the industry. It is not right to take a girl around like this. It will give producers the wrong ideas. You should hire a secretary—a good secretary—who knows the industry, and the secretary can go around to producers with the portfolio and get the contacts. A secretary will be able to do a lot more than you as a mother can."

The above anecdote communicates the very stereotypes of the industry as an unsavory and hyper-sexualized space that many of its members have been trying to counter for years. Imran's reprimand to the mother reveals how actively soliciting producers for roles can be interpreted by them as an excessive willingness or desperation, a situation ripe for sexual harassment and exploitation. The fact that Imran advised the mother to hire an agent for her daughter, one who would use photographs to mediate the interaction with producers, underscores that such a practice was not necessarily the norm within the Hindi film industry.[22] The avenues for a novice actor to get noticed—without any prior kin or social connections to the film industry—are constrained in gender-specific ways.

Male actors hoping for their first big break often visited sets, hoping to catch the eye of a producer or a director, or to develop an on-set social relationship so that they may build up a network of contacts. For example, one day in April 1996, while I was observing a film shoot, I finally asked one of the assistant directors about a tall, broad twenty-something who had been attending the shoot regularly. I was curious as to who he was, for he came to the set every day and simply sat to one side without ever speaking to anyone. No one ever seemed to pay him any attention. The assistant director replied to my query with a nonchalant, "Oh, him? He's the struggler." "Struggler" is a common term for actors without any kin or social connections who are trying to get a break in the film industry. I started noticing the steady stream of "strugglers" who visited the various film sets that I was observing. While the process could be quite boring, uncomfortable, or humiliating, I noticed that the men who were "struggling" to get into the industry did not seem to be struggling for a living: they could afford to spend their days on film sets and not at work. Some of them worked on television as a way of earning an income and then spent the rest of their time on film sets.

Roaming film sets, however, was a very gendered practice, restricted to men. If actresses did the same, they would be communicating that they were willing to go to any lengths to get a role, and would be vulnerable to harassment and exploitation. While men can actively seek work, women require someone to advocate for them. The most common route for unconnected women to garner leading roles was to be "discovered," implying their passivity in the process. The news of producers' discoveries is a recurrent feature of film journalism in India, and such discoveries are disproportionately of women. Winning beauty pageants such as Miss India, Miss World, and Miss Universe—after which individuals are commonly offered leading roles in films if they desire to pursue an acting career—is another method for women to become actresses. In these various instances, being sought after by filmmakers, rather than seeking them out, is an important dimension of displaying respectability, based on archetypical gender binaries: men are active and struggling; women are passive and waiting to be discovered; men are public, women private.

Not only did I notice different norms for entering and navigating the industry, I also observed how everyday life on sets was distinctly gendered. At film shoots, actresses frequently had a parent, family member, close friend, or personal staff member present at all times. Part of this extensive retinue has to do with the fact that many actresses start their careers in the film industry when they are about fifteen or sixteen years old; this contrasts with men, who are in their early twenties. Even unmarried women in their late twenties had a parent or a friend present on the set during film shoots, however. For instance, Madhuri Dixit, who was at the peak of her acting career and was almost thirty years old at the time of my initial research, frequently had her father present on the set of *Dil to Pagal Hai*. He paid little attention to the shoot, and sat quietly reading a book. While actresses frequently had to wear sexy, revealing clothing in certain sequences, once they were off camera their body language changed, going to great pains to cover themselves and create a zone of modesty and privacy in the very male and very public space of the set.[23] For example, I observed actresses covering their thighs with a towel or their torso with a shawl if the clothing they wore was leaving those areas exposed. Whenever possible, actresses retreated to their makeup rooms or trailers in between shots, while actors frequently stayed present on the set, if the time in between takes was short. All of these practices reinforce that the film industry is perceived as a morally hazardous space for women and illustrate that the very fact of being an actress brings a woman's sexuality into the foreground, marking her as an openly sexual being, in a manner not experienced by actors.

However, being regarded as an object of male desire is necessary for an actress's standing and success within the industry. Rani Mukherji, who began her career in 1997, spoke to a group of us from NYU in 2005, when she was shooting for *Kabhi Alvida Na Kehna* (Never Say Good-bye) in the New York area. In response to a question about the "male gaze" posed by a graduate student, Mukherji said she never felt uncomfortable on a film set, but she did wonder at times about the reactions in a movie theater. Mentioning that in her earlier years she had gone to see her films in theaters, protected by the anonymity of a Muslim woman's *burqa*, she commented about the whistling and clapping that occurred in theaters during songs or other erotically charged moments in films: "You think, 'Wait a minute, is that okay?' But if it wasn't there, it would also be worrisome."[24] Actresses are thus constantly negotiating between the onscreen requirement of physical desirability and the off-screen demand for social respectability. While the former is necessary for professional success, the latter is important for high social status.

This negotiation was apparent during a photo shoot involving Aishwarya Rai I observed in 1996. Rai, currently one of the most well-known Indian actresses globally, was a former model and Miss World 1994, and was just beginning her career in Hindi films during my first stint of fieldwork.[25] One part of Rai's photo shoot took place on a fishing boat anchored in the Arabian Sea adjoining Versova, a northwestern suburb of Bombay (Figure 7).[26] Since the only women on the boat besides me were Rai and her hairdresser, I was drafted to help out in small ways, like holding up a sheet so that Rai could change her clothes. During one part of the shoot, Rai posed in a modest, one-piece bathing suit with a knee-length sarong wrapped around her waist, which covered her thighs. She perched on the stern of the boat while the photographer stood in front of her clicking away, and his assistant crouched down behind him and took his own photographs of Rai. After the shoot, Rai complained to me about the assistant, specifically the angle from which he was taking photographs of her. She was worried about his intentions and kept asking me if I knew anything about him and whether he was a "decent" guy. She was also concerned about her outfit being too revealing and said, "In my modeling days, I was always very fussy and particular about what I wore, so I don't want people to think I've changed now." The "now" indexed not only Rai's transformation from being a model to an actress, but also a movement across vastly disparate moral worlds—from the high status and respectable world of modeling and advertising to the more ambiguously positioned and morally questionable film industry. Rai's anxieties about the assistant's photographs and her clothing arose directly as a result of the

FIGURE 7 Aishwarya Rai's photo shoot by Rakesh Shreshtha, Versova (western suburb of Bombay), 1996. Photo by the author.

aura of ill repute that inhered in the film industry when she began her career.

Respectability was not only an embodied practice, but also a fertile subject of discourse within the film industry. In the following section, I focus on the three main topics that emerged from my interviews, through which respectability was explicitly indexed: origin stories; discussions of middle-classness; and the value attributed to formal higher education. Each topic generated a specific trope that underlies the varied statements of diverse filmmakers: the "accidental" nature of becoming a part of the industry; the binary of *filmi* vs. middle class; and the generational clash over education.

DISCOURSES OF RESPECTABILITY

Just by Chance

The majority of people I met during my fieldwork represented their involvement or entry into the film industry as a complete accident—something that they had never anticipated, desired, or planned for when younger. For example, Madhuri Dixit responded to my question of whether she had always wanted to be an actress: "Actually no, I never thought I'd be an actress someday. I didn't have any intentions and I was not really interested. With me, it just happened. I think that's where destiny comes in. I was offered a film and I took up the offer, and that's where the bug bit me actually: when I did my first film, then I got interested" (Dixit, interview, 25 November 1996). When I asked Manisha Koirala, an actress who hailed from a politically elite family in Nepal—her grandfather and two great uncles were prime ministers at various points in the country's history—whether she had planned on being an actress, she replied, "No it was out of the blue. I was always interested in theater, but I never thought of films as a professional career. I was thinking of becoming a doctor in fact, and out of the blue I just wanted to have—I just wanted to earn—some pocket money during my vacation, and so I just got into films. Then it grew serious with me. Initially I had not taken it seriously" (Koirala, interview, 23 May 1996). Even the beauty pageant winner, Ayesha Jhulka, stated that she was never interested in acting, and that her foray into beauty pageants was just for "fun"; she initially rejected the film offered to her because she was studying to be a fashion designer and did not want to leave her course of study. She then had second thoughts and decided to give acting a chance: "I thought, if these people have offered me [a role], why not try?" All three women presented their initial foray into acting as completely fortuitous or frivolous, rather than their life's goal, plan, or dream.

I contend that the explicit disavowal of any prior desire or ambition to be a part of the film industry, along with the reliance on the trope of chance or destiny, is a form of "face-work" performed especially by actresses, which is closely connected to the moral stigma historically associated with women working in the film industry. In the case of Koirala, her explanation was a particularly palpable instance of face-work: a few months later when I was interviewing Meena Iyer, a journalist who wrote for the English-language film magazine *Filmfare*, she informed me that Koirala was her "discovery." According to Iyer, she had met Koirala at a party in Delhi, through a mutual acquaintance who had informed each of the other's presence at his home that evening. "Apparently she came because she got to know that I was a film journalist and she thought that she'd get me to introduce her to people in Bombay," Iyer recalled. "You're so pretty, why don't you join the movies?" Iyer had told the aspiring actress, so the next day Koirala and her mother met the film journalist at the airport as she was returning to Bombay. Iyer remembered Koirala's mother mentioning to her that her "daughter is keen" and asking whether she remembered the conversation the two had had the previous evening: "Did you mean that?" Iyer responded affirmatively and told them to come to Bombay; both mother and daughter arrived in the city a couple of weeks later. Iyer introduced them to some of the top producers in the industry with a very positive outcome: "Wherever I went she was signed immediately. It was because she was so pretty. That was the basic qualification, nothing else" (Iyer, interview, August 1996).

The issues of working style, hierarchies of access, and structural organization also raised by this example are discussed in chapters five and six. The point here is less about the veracity of either Koirala's or Iyer's statements, and more about how in her interview with me, Koirala completely erased any agency on her part in getting her first break as an actress. When I asked her to elaborate on how she got her first role, which was the female lead in a big-budget multi-generational drama produced and directed by Subhash Ghai, one of the top filmmakers of the industry, she merely stated that Ghai had given her a screen test. When I asked her how she met Ghai, she informed me that Iyer had introduced them to each other. The difference between Koirala and the mother-daughter pair discussed in the previous section is that Koirala's interest in becoming an actress was mediated by Iyer, who facilitated meetings with some of the most successful and prestigious producers in the film industry.

For women to express an intentional, willful desire to be a part of the film world, with its attendant scandal and morally questionable characters, would imply some sort of affinity with this social world, which occupies the opposite moral pole from that of the good family. Chatterjee argues that public visibility and mobility was possible for the respectable middle-class woman because of her embodiment and internalization of all of the qualities associated with the domestic private realm he terms the "spiritual" sphere of everyday life (1989). Actively aiming at becoming a film actress, whose visibility and availability for male fantasy constitutes her as an object of desire, directly counters the qualities associated with the respectable woman. Koirala, Dixit, and Jhulka all came from upper-middle-class and upper-caste backgrounds, and as we saw in Jhulka's earlier statements, a family's resistance to its daughter, granddaughter, or niece becoming an actress is a visible marker of its respectability.[27] Good families are those who object to or discourage their female kin from becoming actresses; the trope of family resistance has been a common feature in many actresses' entry narratives over the decades.

The accidental entry trope was articulated not only by women, however, but also by men. In this instance, the trope served as a form of face-work that was less about managing the moral stigma of working in the industry than managing the intellectual and social disdain expressed toward popular cinema by social and cultural elites. Amit Khanna started his career in the film industry as a writer. At the time of our initial meeting, in 1996, he was the CEO of the newly formed Plus Channel India, Ltd.—an integrated audio/television/film production company that was dissolved in 2000—and currently is the chairman of Reliance Big Entertainment. He related his entry into the film industry as a series of fortuitous circumstances. After regaling me first with his knowledge of early anthropology, specifically James Frazer's *The Golden Bough*, Khanna described his entry into the world of filmmaking in the early 1970s as "exceptional," mainly because he came from a background that would normally not have anything to do with Hindi cinema. Asserting that he was one of the few young men at his college in Delhi who was familiar with Hindi films, he nevertheless claimed that, "It was obviously not the kind of career option which a person with my background looked at. I would have probably gone on to study [journalism, joining] the Civil Services or [going] abroad to graduate school" (Khanna, interview, June 1996). After communicating that he was of a highly educated literate background, Khanna described how he ended up in the Hindi film industry: "So the decision to come to films was a quirk of circumstances. There was a friend of mine who was with me in college: he owned a cinema theater in Delhi, and his father fell sick and [he] and his brother both had gone off to the U.S. for their [undergraduate education] and they just asked me if I could help them with their theater. That was my first contact with the intricacies of Hindi cinema, and by that time I knew Dev Anand [a famous actor, producer, and director] well and I decided to come to Bombay" (Khanna, interview, June 1996).

Khanna spent a great deal of time detailing how his presence in the world of filmmaking was unanticipated and—as with the story of his friend's theater—more the result of his helpful nature than any focused intentionality. With his statements about his background and his lack of explanation about how he had gotten to know Dev Anand, with whom he began his career in the film industry, Khanna went to great lengths to portray himself as a cultured, educated, literate individual who countered the dominant stereotypes of the film industry. He was the president of the Film and TV Producers Guild that briefly banned Shakti Kapoor during the casting couch scandal; he also has been centrally involved with efforts to represent and recast the industry into a more professional and corporate entity, which I discuss in chapter seven.

The trope of accidental entry was mostly deployed by individuals who were first-generation members of the film industry. This trope operated to display their respectability mainly through a disavowal of any agency regarding becoming a part of the morally questionable and intellectually bereft world of the Hindi film industry. Emphasizing the fortuitous nature of involvement was another way to index their belonging to "good families." The good family was often synonymous with a middle-class family, and in the following section, I examine how the category of middle class was discussed and indexed within the film industry.

"Filmi" versus Middle Class

In an interview with the Internet newsmagazine *rediff.com* in February 2007, Shah Rukh Khan was asked about the contrast between his own middle-class upbringing and that of his two children, and whether he worried about the potential negative impact of his wealth and stardom on their lives. In his response, Khan launched into a lengthy discussion where he used the term "middle class" numerous times to indicate that despite his fame and wealth, he was essentially "a middle-class boy" from Delhi, concerned about instilling the right values in his children, which included a respect for education. Acknowledging that it was "strange" to be identifying as middle class when "you have a BMW outside your house, which is one acre big," Khan nevertheless described himself and his wife as "very middle-class as far as how we deal with things is concerned: how we talk in the house; we don't have a lavish lifestyle beyond the fact that the peripherals [like his car and home] that come with my filmmaking or film stardom" (Someshwar and Sivaswamy 2007). Stating that he took a strong personal interest in his children's education, Khan likened his involvement with his children to that of his own father: "I do what my father used to do with me. He was an educated middle-class man of good nature, and polite, so I try and be all that. The only difference is there are too many hoardings [billboards] of mine in the city. That's the only difference between my father and me" (Someshwar and Sivaswamy 2007).

That one of the biggest movie stars in the world, let alone India, represented himself as middle class, suggests the value of this category within the Hindi film industry. In this particular context, middle class denotes social status rather than economic position. The precise power of the category derives from its ability to signal a whole host of associations that are regarded as the antithesis of the social world of the film industry. While scholars have noted other Indian contexts where the category of middle class is an object of censure or criticism (Mazzarella 2005), in the Hindi film industry, this category is a desired and celebrated one, both in terms of audiences and the family histories of filmmakers. For example, Shashi Kapoor, an actor and producer popular from the 1960s to the 1980s and the younger brother of Raj Kapoor, described how his father—who was a popular star—raised him and his siblings in an atmosphere that he referred to as middle class: "He was from a generation where even if you were a film star, even if you were earning well, at that time according to those days, you preferred to have a middle-class atmosphere, middle-class family; so, when we kids were brought up, we were brought up . . . very middle class, not the sons of the stars . . . you see nowadays: there was no car given to us; we went to a middle-class school— Don Bosco High School—and in our street, even though there were lots of film people, there were lots of other people—literary people, business people, professional people, service people, army people. But we were all middle class" (Shashi Kapoor, interview, 8 August 1996). Kapoor represents a middle-class atmosphere by a lack of ostentatious display, minimal consumption, an English-language education, and his membership in a diverse social group and community larger than the film industry.

Kapoor's statements also present a middle-class social world as the desired norm. Another manifestation of the valorization of middle-classness that I encountered during my fieldwork was its juxtaposition with the term "*filmi*." For example, Madhuri Dixit deployed this binary when discussing her decision to act in a film, "It was a very difficult decision for me to make because we're not from a *filmi* background . . . my parents, my relatives—nobody has anything to do with films—and I come from a very middle-class kind of background, so my parents weren't sure whether they'd like to see me acting in films" (Dixit, interview, 25 November 1996). "*Filmi*" is an Indian English term used pejoratively to describe behavior, fashion, and lifestyles that appear to be overly influenced by, or evocative of, popular Hindi cinema or the film industry. *Filmi* also implies ostentation, flamboyance, crudeness, immorality or amorality, and a disregard for formal education. "Middle class" represents a social or behavioral norm that is *filmi*'s opposite, marked by modesty, thrift, propriety, morality, and a value for education.

The binary opposition of *filmi* and middle class was not only utilized by individuals like Dixit, who strongly identified with being from a middle-class family, but also by second-generation members of the film industry who did not identify with the class position essentially, but with its normative moral authority. While first-generation members of the film industry, who hailed from middle-class backgrounds, had their specific family histories to index their own respectability, filmmakers who grew up within the film industry—as members of its second, third, or fourth generations—often discursively distanced themselves from the social world of the industry, signified by the term *filmi*, and represented their childhood and formative years as essentially middle class. For example, the producer/director Aditya Chopra, whose father and late uncle were also prominent producers and directors,[28] responded to my question about what it was like to grow up within the industry:

> In spite of me being . . . an insider, as you call it, we were brought up very differently. We were not brought up with such a *filmi* background as such, so my basic perception of the industry for a long time was as an outsider . . . it was just that the atmosphere, the way my parents are, the kind of people they are, they didn't socialize so much; their friends' circle was a little more away from the industry. Not consciously so, but it just happened that way, even my friends at the school I went to . . . were a bunch of people who were from middle-class homes who were normal people. (Aditya Chopra, interview, April 1996)

Chopra's remarks represent a form of face-work in that he distances his parents and himself from the social world of the film industry. By asserting that his upbringing was different, his parents did not socialize with other filmmakers, and that his friends were "normal people," Chopra constructs *filmi* as an undesirable state and represents his "outsider" status as a marker of respectability.

Akin to the trope of accidental entry expressed by first-generation filmmakers, many individuals whose parents were filmmakers explained to me that their parents had consciously kept them away from the film world. For example, actor/producer/director Aamir Khan asserted, "My father has been a producer and my uncle has been a director/producer for the last thirty years, and so in that sense it's true that we have been born into a film family and been involved with films, but our parents kept us away really from the film line so I didn't really attend shootings and I didn't really experience much of the film line as a child. Even at home, the way our family has brought us up, they kept us away from the film line and we really didn't know that our parents were involved with films [or that] films were anything special or anything different" (Aamir Khan, interview, March 1996). Khan not only distanced himself from the film industry, but also from the films themselves by relating how his parents restricted his film-viewing when he was a child: "I wasn't allowed to watch films . . . till the age of about fifteen, I had barely watched any films at all" (Aamir Khan, interview, March 1996). Such assertions appear as examples of face-work, however, since Khan, as a child, played a small role in his uncle's 1973 film *Yaadon ki Baraat* (The Procession of Memories), and in later parts of our interview he reminisced about childhood memories of film composers and writers working at his home: "Music directors used to come home and to my uncle's house or my father's house and they used to have the music sittings at home, and the story sittings at home. So I used to love to sit with my folks and hear the stories that they were listening to. The scripts they were working on, and the music sessions they would have; it used to be fun to watch the music director composing and singing a tune" (Aamir Khan, interview, March 1996). As I discuss in chapter six, filmmakers' homes are important sites of production, and members of the film industry, including Khan, specifically attribute an advantage to those who have grown up within the industry.

It was really in response to my opening question about growing up within the film industry that members of the second generation, like Aditya Chopra and Aamir Khan, articulated the most distance from its social world. In contrast to my other questions about films and filmmaking, this one in particular appeared to touch on deep-rooted anxieties about the moral and social stigma attached to the Hindi film industry, which derived from its history of connections with the—also stigmatized—hereditary performance traditions. Representing one's childhood as distant from the socially aberrant world of the film industry by virtue of judicious parents, who essentially embodied middle-class values and took care to shield their children from the implicitly corrupt world of the industry, established filmmakers' own families as good ones. If first-generation filmmakers disavowed their active agency in initiating their film career as a way to showcase their respectability, second- and third-generation filmmakers did so by disavowing any active interest or participation in the social world of the film industry.

A further instance of this disavowal was the ambivalence first-generation filmmakers expressed toward their profession, along with their efforts to provide their children with the means to pursue an alternate career, which mostly took the form of valorizing formal higher education. In the next section, I address how formal higher education operates as an important measure and index of respectability for the Hindi film industry.

The Importance of Education

Given the multiple avenues for entering the film industry, members of the industry represent a wide range of schooling and educational backgrounds—from obtaining master's degrees to not even finishing high school. Since the two years after tenth grade, which in other parts of India would be regarded as high school, is institutionally separate and termed "college" in Bombay, many filmmakers talk about going to "college," which actually translates into being educated through the twelfth grade. The distinction to be noted is the term "graduation," which communicates that an individual has gone to college in a more American sense of the term and received a bachelor's degree. While there is no educational norm, higher education is definitely valorized and respected within the industry, and those who have college degrees tend to foreground this aspect of their background. For example, during our interview, Shah Rukh Khan made it known that he had gone to an elite private high school in Delhi, had "done his graduation," that is, earned a bachelor's degree. He also mentioned a master's degree. At the *mahurat* (a ritual undertaken by a producer to mark the start of a new film project) of the film *Prem Aggan* (Love's Fire), actor/producer/director Sanjay Khan informed the gathered audience that his nephew Fardeen, who was being introduced in the film, and had graduated from the University of Massachusetts. "Fardeen could have gotten a good, well-paying job—earning 50 to 60 *lakhs* [5–6 million rupees] a year—with a multinational corporation, but he opted instead to express himself onscreen."

Khan's announcement of his nephew's American college degree and the subsequent representation of his decision to pursue acting as one choice out of many possible corporate career options is another example of face-work in practice, since the dominant stereotype of actors, especially of "star sons," is that they are poorly educated and by implication, not very intelligent. For example, a producer described the majority of actors as "illiterate" or "semi-literate" and responded to my question about the changes he had observed in the industry: "We haven't really moved from Meena Kumari to Manisha Koirala. Meena Kumari was an illiterate, so is Manisha Koirala. Except Manisha Koirala speaks better. Madhubala dropped out and never went to college—nor did Madhuri Dixit. So what has changed? Akshay Kumar, Saif Ali Khan, Anil Kapoor: nobody has changed." Screenwriter Sachin Bhaumick continuously punctuated his comments about various members of the film industry by listing their educational qualifications. He was critical of filmmakers who did not try to educate their children, characterizing stars' sons as taking the easy route to money and fame: "This is the one industry [in which] you don't need very much education to earn a lot of money" (Bhaumick, interview, October 1996).

Sanjay Dutt, in his recollections of how he became an actor, reinforces

Bhaumick's point about the insignificance of formal education. Dutt, whose parents, Nargis and Sunil Dutt, were very highly esteemed actors in the 1950s and 1960s, stated that his parents always wanted him to study and "go through college as a normal child," even offering to send him to the United States. Dutt characterized himself as a "big fool" for not taking them up on their offer: "I'm not the studying type, so that's the reason I came into films. I said, 'I don't want to study.' I told my father, 'Please, you're wasting your money, your time. I don't study. I can't study.' So he says, 'What do you want to do then?' I said, 'I want to be an actor.' So they got angry and upset about it, but eventually when they thought about it: it made sense, so then he started putting me into training and I started getting into it slowly" (Dutt, interview, May 1996).[29] While Dutt pointed to his disinterest in academic pursuit as a precipitating factor in his film career, Manisha Koirala cited achievement in the academic realm as an explicit reason for why she did *not* want her younger brother, Siddharth, to become an actor: "I never studied in a great school. He studied in one of the best schools in India . . . and I was thinking, if he goes to Oxford or to Cambridge, he can get into something more serious. I'm not saying filmmaking is not serious, but it's not a great profession for life, not in India . . . and especially an actor's job" (Koirala, interview, 23 May 1996). In each of these comments a college education is intrinsically valued, despite its lack of relevance for a successful career in acting. Rather than questioning the necessity of formal higher education for acting, filmmakers devalue and denigrate acting because it does not require a college degree. That fame and wealth is possible without the middle-class accoutrement of a college education is more a source of anxiety and stigma for filmmakers than it is a basis of liberation from dominant social norms about education.

This anxiety was most marked among film families, and many second-generation filmmakers described how their parents were ambivalent about them entering the industry and insistent on them pursuing higher education. Dutt's recounting of his parents' initial disappointment over his career choice was echoed by many other second-generation filmmakers. Producer/director Rakesh Roshan, whose father was a prominent music director (composer) in the 1950s and 1960s related: "I knew as a child that I always wanted to become an actor, and my father was very against it. He wanted me to study first" (Roshan, interview, May 1996). Roshan described how he used to skip school to go see movies and that when his father came to learn of his truancy, he was packed off to boarding school. Aamir Khan recalled his family's opposition when he expressed an interest in becoming an actor: "My parents were very against it. They didn't want me to be in the films. Their reason was that they felt it's a line with no stability, and they didn't want me to go into something unstable, where one day you're successful and the other day you're not . . . so they were worried about my future in that sense. They would [have preferred] that I worked hard at my studies . . . and probably become a doctor or an engineer—something more stable" (Aamir Khan, interview, March 1996). According to Khan, when he chose not to pursue a college education, his family and friends were shocked, since "it was a very big deal, if you're not a graduate." He stated that everyone in his social world pressured him to go to college, for otherwise he would appear to be "un-educated." Aditya Chopra asserted, "I wanted to make films, but my mom said, 'No, you have to finish your B.Com. [bachelor of commerce]. You have that degree.' It [didn't] make sense to me till now, why I've got that degree. But I did five years of college from Sydenham, which is the best commerce college we have in Bombay" (Aditya Chopra, interview, April 1996). This valorization of formal higher education by first-generation members of the film industry, who did not have many years of formal schooling, can be understood as a response to the dominant stereotypes of Hindi filmmakers—as uneducated, uncouth, and unrefined—that appeared in a variety of discourses generated by the state, English-language press, middle-class audiences, and other filmmakers. The ambivalence about filmmaking as a career and the great regard expressed for higher education is another manner in which Hindi filmmakers assert their respectability in line with dominant middle-class norms about education and occupation.

Although Aditya Chopra felt his college degree was irrelevant to his goals of becoming a filmmaker, his mother (Pamela) explained at great length the role of formal education in improving the quality of filmmaking and raising the social status of the film industry. During our interview, she declared that a "more educated group of people" were working in the industry and compared it to the past: "Let's face it. Maybe, thirty–forty years ago, the people who were acting—or even the music directors, or even the other technicians—they were not educated people. They were people who learnt on the job. It was like learning a trade . . . and some of them came from quite dubious backgrounds. A lot of the heroines—some of the heroes—they were not very comfortable in polite society . . . They didn't have anything to say for themselves. They could not express their feelings or their achievements or their aspirations or their aims . . . They were not trained to do that" (Pamela Chopra, 26 March 1996). In Chopra's statements, education is defined only in terms of formal schooling and is opposed to the experiential, practical learning characterizing work in the film industry. The lack of formal education coupled with the disreputable social backgrounds of actors and actresses, alluded to by Chopra, resulted in an industry characterized by inarticulate and by implication, unintelligent, individuals. This scenario was changing for the better, according to her, and the key was a more formal professionalized training: "There are people who are actually trained for it. People who've *had*, who've either been to the Film Institute, or who have studied filmmaking and now; they treat it like a career. So as that has changed, a better class of people has come into the industry, so naturally the perception of the industry has also changed, among those people who don't belong to it" (Pamela Chopra, interview, 26 March 1996). Interestingly when Chopra made these remarks in 1996, there were not that many individuals who were formally trained in filmmaking working in the industry, and the most common method of training was—and continues to be—either apprenticeship or growing up within the industry. What is important in Chopra's statements is the connection made between formal training, the social class of filmmakers, and the improved status of the film industry. Formal education—either second-generation filmmakers attending college or filmmaking institutionalized as a type of objectified, codified knowledge—is regarded as the route to social respectability and by implication, cinematic quality.

Although a detailed discussion of the formalization of training in filmmaking is beyond the scope of this book, I want to mention briefly efforts by producer/director Subhash Ghai to transform filmmaking from an apprenticeship-based trade into a formally trained profession. A graduate of the state-funded and state-run Film and Television Institute of India, Ghai embarked on an ambitious project in 2000: to create a private film school that would better serve the needs of the Hindi film industry in terms of talent and training. He represented this project as his contribution back to the industry and to ameliorate the situation where a person like him, without kin and social connections, who would normally find it difficult or nearly impossible to gain access to the industry, could be trained and pursue a career in filmmaking. "I had a vision somewhere to institutionalize the industry, and I myself am a self-made man. I came alone in this industry and I didn't have a family background. Other people made movies for their families and they died. Everybody talked about cinema, but they never gave back anything" (Ghai, interview, October 2000).

Ghai's vision, Whistling Woods International: Institute for Film, Television and Media Arts, opened its doors to its first entering class in July 2006. Its informational catalog opens with "A Note from Subhash Ghai," where in seven paragraphs he lays out his motivation for creating the school. One reason given is the improvement of the quality of cinema in India, which can only be had with proper training: "India needs a world-class cinema and therefore a world-class media school. In Mumbai, thousands of aspirants come from all over India and even from abroad to join the film industry, but they don't have the guidance or a platform from which they can realize their potential. These aspirants need structured education and a space especially designed to develop their skills in aesthetics and technique" (Whistling Woods International Prospectus 2006–7: 5). Another part of the note emphasizes how filmmaking is a profession that requires a proper formal education, like other more valued and respected professions in India: "I must add that in this fast-growing industry and an ever-changing world, parents or guardians of talented youth must realize that education in this field is as important as it is in medicine or engineering or any other profession. Aspiring filmmakers must get professional training, and Whistling Woods International, after meticulous research and development, has designed every course to maximize the artistic, technical and professional development of its students, to give them the best skills possible in building a career in film" (Whistling Woods International Prospectus 2006–7: 5).

When viewed against the broader concerns about respectability, an institution such as Whistling Woods represents not just the formalization and professionalization of training in filmmaking, but also a catalyst for bringing about respectability to filmmaking and the Hindi film industry in general.[30] Requiring that its applicants be both proficient in English and have at least twelve years of formal schooling situates Whistling Woods within the broader post-secondary educational landscape in India. By providing people without any social or family connections a systematic avenue, through training, internships, and career fairs, to enter the film industry, Whistling Woods implicitly addresses the potential for exploitation faced by unconnected individuals, who may fall prey to the "casting couch." Of course the costs of attending this institution, coupled with the English and educational requirements, means that this sort of training and access is restricted to individuals from upper-middle-class or even more socially elite backgrounds.[31] Sridhar Kumar, a struggling director from a small town in India, was skeptical of Whistling Woods's impact in terms of providing access to the industry.[32] Looking through its catalog after I had returned from my visit and tour of the institute, Kumar pointed out that the brochure was intimidating—with its stock photographs of boardrooms and classrooms peopled with an array of non–South Asian individuals. He conjectured that the costs and the emphasis on English as a medium of instruction would make the institution appear completely inaccessible to someone from a small town or nonmetropolitan area in India. Shaking his head, Kumar said dismissively, "This is just a place for rich kids." Thus institutions such as Whistling Woods are also centrally involved in the gentrification of the Hindi film industry.

RESPECTABILITY, ANXIETY, AND HIGHER EDUCATION

This chapter has focused on Hindi filmmakers' anxieties around respectability, which have been expressed primarily through concerns about the social origins of its members—mostly actresses—the practices of female modesty, the disavowal of interest in or connection to the film industry, and the valorization of formal higher education. In filmmakers' discussions, the middle class emerges as a normative social category and the arbiter of respectability, against which the film industry is measured. Although Hindi filmmakers' concern with respectability has been a longstanding one, the conditions of its possibility can only be achieved with the shift from a developmentalist to a neoliberal paradigm. With its commercial and entertainment orientation, the Hindi film industry always fell short of the goals of social uplift and modernization outlined by the Nehruvian developmentalist state. In chapter one I discussed how the neoliberal transformation of the Indian political economy reconfigured the value and status of filmmaking. What the present chapter has demonstrated is that despite the reconstitution of middle-class identities in India under neoliberalism discussed by scholars (Dwyer 2000, Fernandes 2006, Mazzarella 2003), the film industry is a site for the continued presence and valorization of older definitions of middle-classness, based on qualities of modesty, self-restraint, and self-discipline. The significance attributed to the notion of respectability is the most telling example of filmmakers' sense of its tenuous presence within the industry.

In fact, the continued relevance of the concept of respectability corresponds to the new structures of financing and production that have come about for Hindi filmmaking since 2000. With the increasing presence of the Indian corporate sector, traditional members of the film industry are concerned with demonstrating their ability to fit into this other social world. Chapter seven focuses on how Hindi filmmakers try to recast film-making into a modern, high-status profession. In order to make sense of those efforts, however, it is first necessary to understand the general working style, production practices, and overall structure of the Hindi film industry, which I turn to in the following three chapters.

Part 2

THE PRACTICES AND PROCESSES OF FILM PRODUCTION

CHAPTER 4

A Day in the Life of a Hindi Film Set

When family members visited me in Bombay during my field-work in 1996, they were curious and excited to see a film shoot, or "shooting," as it is more commonly referred to in India. After-ward, they invariably complained about the repetition, tedium, and boredom they experienced while observing the shoot. They asked, "How do you do this every day? Don't you get bored?" I was also asked some variant of these questions by a number of people in Bombay who had had the opportunity to observe film shoots in the city.[1] Given that my dissertation was to be an ethnogra-phy of film production, film shoots were the most logical sites to begin my research. As my research progressed, I realized that film shoots not only yielded information about specific produc-tion practices, but also many insights into the structure, orga-nization, and social relations of the film industry itself. In this chapter, I present a detailed sketch of a typical day on a Hindi film set in order to impart the spirit and essence of the working style of Hindi filmmakers as well as to bring to light prominent charac-teristics of the industry's structure and organization.[2] This typi-cal day is a composite drawn from my observations of a variety of film shoots. Although the sketch is written in the present tense, it is not a timeless ethnographic present, but represents Hindi filmmaking of the late 1990s and the early 2000s. The sketch also provides the foundation for understanding the prominent dis-courses of change and progress that are addressed in chapter seven, as well as how audiences are represented and discussed, examined in chapter eight.

The sketch illustrates some of the main features of the work culture of the film industry: the prevalence of face-to-face interactions; the significance of kinship as a source of talent; the set as a meeting space; the highly oral style of working; and the very visible manifestations of hierarchy. It also puts forth the flexibility—by which I mean the ability to make impromptu decisions, the capacity to adapt to uncertainty, and a willingness to change the course of action—that is characteristic of Hindi filmmaking. Additionally, it portrays conversations about audiences, commercial outcome, and Hollywood that are significant components of the industry's production-talk, which provides insights into the prevailing ideologies of production and self-representations of the industry. Finally, it depicts the presence of Hindu rituals, which have become incorporated into production routines, as well as the tremendous diversity—regional, linguistic, and religious—of members of the film industry.[3]

A Hindi film set is a very multi-lingual environment, with a fair amount of English spoken by principal decision makers, as well as code-switching between Hindi and English. For the sake of readability, however, I have presented all of the conversations in English and indicate with italics those sentences that originally occurred in Hindi, indicating with roman type those words that remain in English even when the conversation is in Hindi. In keeping with the idioms of Indian English, I maintain the use of Hindi honorific suffixes such as *ji* (sir/madam) and *saab* (sir), as well as words and phrases like *haan* (yes), *accha* (good, okay), and *theek hai* (okay, alright), because these are commonly employed in everyday speech. Since the terms used for the various crew positions and tasks on a film set in India differ from those used in the United States, I use local terminology and provide definitions when necessary.[4] The two chapters following this sketch analyze in depth the issues raised by the ethnographic material.

AMBA FILM'S PRODUCTION NO. 39: *MERA DIL*
AAPKE KADMON MEIN HAI (MDAKMH; MY HEART
IS AT YOUR FEET), DAY 1

It is the first day of the first shooting schedule of MDAKMH, produced by M. K. Malhotra, written and directed by Rakesh Chadda, and starring Vijay Khanna, the currently reigning matinee idol, and Sulekha, a recent Miss India pageant winner from southern India, who is being introduced in this film. During this schedule, a song and dance sequence celebrating

FIGURE 8 Shooting floor, Film City, Goregaon (northwestern suburb of Bombay), 2005. Photo by the author.

Diwali will be shot in eight-hour shifts, over the span of two and a half weeks.[5] An elaborate set depicting the courtyard of a two-story *haveli*, a traditional Indian mansion, has been erected at Filmistan—a studio located in the northwestern suburb of Goregaon—inside one of their larger sound stages, which are called "shooting floors" in Bombay.[6] Consisting of an enormous free-standing concrete structure with no sound-proofing, air conditioning, or toilets, this particular shooting floor stands 95 feet high, 150 feet long, and 120 feet wide (Figure 8).

While the shift begins at 9:00 a.m., the art director, Shantanu Sen, arrives with his assistants by 7:30, in order to put the finishing touches on the set: decorating the arches around the courtyard with garlands of fresh marigolds, placing *diyas*—the small clay oil lamps traditionally used to illuminate homes during *Diwali*—in the numerous alcoves along the wall, and painting *rangolis*—colorful patterns used to decorate homes during festivals—on the floor. Around 8:30 a truck arrives with all of the lights, and workers start unloading the equipment, bringing it onto the set. Another van arrives with the camera and its attendants. The cinematographer, Satish Menon, reaches the set shortly thereafter with his assistants and begins the task of lighting the set. Workers place lights on stands in various corners of the set and overhead on the catwalk, while one of Menon's assistants starts to take light readings. Meanwhile, the sound recordist sets up his equipment—a reel-to-reel tape player, a large speaker, and headphones—in one corner of the set.

By 9:00 a.m. the director, Rakesh Chadda, and the dance director, Tanaaz Khan, arrive with their respective assistants.[7] Two spot boys—men who do all forms of miscellaneous work on a film set—immediately bring chairs for Chadda and Khan, who nonetheless remain standing. Chadda says, "*Hey man, get me some tea: it will wake me up*," Menon walks over to Chadda and starts discussing where he wants to place the camera for the first shot.

Khan interrupts, "Rikki, all of the background dancers are here today so we really should do that overhead crane shot first with everyone in the frame."

"I didn't hire the crane for today," Menon interjects, "because I didn't think we needed it today. I thought we were doing the tracking shots."

Chadda asks, "Do you think we can get the crane for tomorrow?"

"I'll have to check that it's not already booked by another unit," Menon replies. "You know there's only one crane of that height in Bombay."

"In that case," Khan says, "let's do the first *antara* [stanza] today. We can use all of the dancers today." Then she turns to her two assistants, "Kabir, Sania, go get the dancers and start showing them the steps."

While Khan's assistants summon the background dancers, who have been lounging outside the set, an assistant director (AD) goes to the makeup rooms to inquire whether Sulekha has arrived and if she is getting ready. The actress is present, along with her mother and sister, and is having her hair and makeup done, but is also waiting for her designer to arrive with her outfits for the song. Another AD calls Vijay Khanna on his cell phone to find out if he is on his way to the set; he is informed by Khanna's man-Friday that "*saab*" (sir) is still sleeping, as he was shooting for another film until 2:00 a.m.

While he waits for the actors to get ready, Chadda keeps himself busy with his cell phone—sending text messages to his friends and playing games. A man in his early thirties, with a thick manila file folder in his hand, approaches him tentatively.

"Rakesh-*ji*?"

Chadda, without looking up from his phone replies, "*Haan*? [yes]"

The man clears his throat and introduces himself, "*Sir, I'm Alok Sharma, I am Mrs. Mishra's—Mrs. Mishra, your neighbor, they live on the same floor as you—I'm her nephew. I spoke to you on the phone concerning my script.*"

Chadda looks up, staring at the man for a moment. "Yes, of course, please sit." Realizing there's no chair next to him, Chadda turns around and yells, "*Hey spot boy! Bring a chair here!*"

Sharma sits down and takes out a large sheaf of paper held together with staples and hands it to Chadda. "*Sir, I've written this screenplay, if you would read it . . .*"

Chadda interrupts, "Tell me the story in one line."

Sharma clears his throat again, "It is about a woman's struggle against the society."

Chadda interjects, "*Oh no, that is really clichéd! What's new about that?*"

Sharma protests, "But sir, I haven't finished: the woman is a journalist who goes to a village in Rajasthan to expose child marriage."

Chadda retorts, "Is this a film or a documentary? How is this commercial?"

Sharma continues, "She falls in love with the local schoolteacher who is also trying to stop the practice."

Chadda sighs and asks, "So the schoolteacher is the hero? Who do you have in mind for that role?"

"I was thinking that Vijay-*ji* . . ."

"You want Vijay-*ji* to do a heroine-oriented film?" Chadda interrupts. "You think the top star of the country will agree to play second lead to a heroine?"

"*That is why I thought, it will be out of the ordinary. Audience will see him in a new role,*" responds Sharma.

"Have you spoken with him?"

"*Ji nahin* [no sir]," Sharma answers. "I was hoping that after you read the script that you could speak to Vijay-*ji* about it, and if he likes it then he could speak with Malhotra-*saab*."

Seeing the film's producer, M. K. Malhotra, arrive, Chadda stands up, cutting short his conversation with Sharma, "*Theek hai,* [okay] I'll have a look and get back to you." The writer looks crestfallen and calls after him, "Thank you; my mobile number is on the title page of the script!"

"Duffer," Chadda mutters to himself as he walks toward Malhotra and his two tall and lanky sons. "*Hello, Malhotra-saab, how are you?*" he asks, to which the producer replies, "*You tell me, Rikki, is everything alright?*"

Chadda answers, "*Absolutely fine, how do you like the set, it's quite grand isn't it?*"

"*The amount of money you made me spend on it, it should be,*" Malhotra retorts.

"*What to do, Malhotra-saab,*" Chadda rejoins. "*You know for our art director only the best materials will do!*"

While Malhotra and Chadda are conversing, spot boys place chairs behind them and rush off to bring another round of tea. Sitting down and taking a sip from his tea, Malhotra speaks to Chadda.

"*Rikki, meet my sons—the older one is Vikky, short for Vikram—he's twenty-one years old—and the younger one is Lucky, short for Lakshman: he's eighteen years old. Put them to work; make them your* assistants."

Chadda responds, "*Of course, but both of them have so much presence, why don't you have them become* actors? *I'll direct that* picture. *I already have three assistants.*"

"*Yes, yes, I will do that, but right now they are young and immature, first they should learn a little bit about this field, if they're not able to become* stars, *at least they can get into* direction."

Without registering any emotion at Malhotra's characterization of direction, Chadda shouts out for his chief assistant, "Sanjeev! Sanjeev! Where's Sanjeev?"

Arif, another one of his assistants, rushes to Chadda's side, "I think he's outside, sir."

"Well, go and tell him to come inside," Chadda says firmly.

Arif dashes outside the set to find Sanjeev smoking a cigarette and texting on his cell phone. "*Sanjeev! Rakesh-ji is looking for you. He seems a little angry.*"

Sanjeev quickly stubs out his cigarette on the ground and hurries inside to where Chadda is sitting with Malhotra, "Yes, Rakesh-*ji*?" "*Saala!* [idiot] When I call for you—you need to be within hearing range, got that?"

"*Ji* [yes]," murmurs Sanjeev.

Chadda says slowly, "Anyway, this is Vikky and Lucky, Malhotra-*saab*'s sons, who are joining the direction team from today—why don't you show them around the set, fill them in on the details, and catch them up with what needs to be done around here."

Sanjeev, who had been assisting Chadda for the past four years, understanding his boss's demeanor of resigned frustration, adds, "How about if they are in charge of costume continuity? We don't have anyone doing that yet."

Chadda turns to Malhotra and asks, "*Theek hai* [Okay]?"

Malhotra responds, "*Badiya* [excellent]."

Sanjeev turns to Lucky and Vikky and says, "Come with me, I'll show you the set and get you the costume continuity notebook. We have to go upstairs."

As they walk toward the staircase on the left side of the set, Lucky remarks, "I didn't know that the balcony and stairs were real. I just thought it was all for show."

Sanjeev responds, "It had to be real and sturdy because, in the opening of the song, all of the girl dancers will be at the balcony with Sulekha and then will follow her down the stairs."

Once they're upstairs, Lucky surveys the set below and exclaims, "Wow yaar [dude]! It looks really good from here! *Hai na*, [isn't that so] Vikky?"

Vikky nods, "Yeah, Dad always demands the best."

Sanjeev adds, "Our art director, Shantanu-*da*, is very good. So, you two are interested in going into direction?"

Vikky replies, "Not really, I actually want to be an actor, but Dad thinks that I need to be a little older before he launches me, so I'm just preparing now — you know, taking some acting classes with Namit Kishore, learning diction, training at the gym. Dad thinks that spending some time as an assistant will also be useful experience . . ."

Lucky interrupts, "I definitely want to be a director! Hopefully, I'll get my chance to direct a film soon after Vikky *bhaiyya*'s [brother] launch, and then we can be a complete team — Dad as producer, me as director, and *bhaiyya* as star!"

From his vantage point, Sanjeev notices the Hindu priest entering the set. He tells Vikky and Lucky, "Let's go down; *Punditji* has come."

As the three walk back downstairs, Keshav, Chadda's third assistant, comes up to Chadda and Malhotra and says, "*The priest has come for the prayer ceremony.*"

Chadda tells Keshav to fetch Sulekha from her makeup room. She appears, wearing a robe and large curlers in her hair, accompanied by her mother. Sulekha, her mother, Malhotra, Chadda, Khan, Menon, and all of their respective assistants gather in a corner of the set where the priest performs a Ganesh *puja* for the production to commence auspiciously.

During the *puja*, a short, balding middle-aged man with a paunch enters the set quietly. Malhotra's production manager, Iqbal, notices him and motions to Malhotra. Malhotra turns and nods to the man and dispatches Iqbal to find a spot boy to fetch a chair and water for the visitor. Once the *puja* is over, Malhotra gets up off the floor and walks over to the visitor who has been quietly observing all of the activity on the set.

"*Agrawal-saab, what a surprise, what a surprise! How are you? When did you arrive from Delhi? Will you have tea, or a soft drink?*"

The visitor, Prakash Agrawal, a distributor from Delhi, is considering

buying the distribution rights of the film for the Delhi-U.P. territory.[8]
"Tea without sugar; I came the night before last. So, the shooting *hasn't begun
yet? Where are the* actors?"

Malhotra replies, *"They're getting ready. Today they are shooting a big
song, which I guarantee will top the music* countdown shows *as soon as the*
album *releases. See how grand the* set *looks!"*[9]

Agrawal retorts, *"Yes, the* set *is nice, but does the film have a strong story*?
Audiences *don't come to the* theater *to see sets, they come for good stories."*

"Of course, this picture *has a great story! It has great songs, big* stars, *and
it will be shot in beautiful foreign* locations—*one* outdoor schedule *will be
in Lick*—" Malhotra turns to his production manager, *"Hey, Iqbal, what is
the name of that tiny* European *country?"*

Iqbal answers, "Lich-ten-stein."

Malhotra continues, *"Aah yes*, Lickenstein. *Another* schedule *will be in*
Cro . . ."

Even before he has a chance to turn and ask, Iqbal pipes up, "Cro-a-
tia."

Without skipping a beat, Malhotra resumes, *"Yes, Croshia—no one in
India has ever shot at these locations before—it will be a completely new experience for the* audience—*to see such* fresh locations! *After all how often
can you keep seeing the same* Switzerland, England, Australia, America,
you know?"

Agrawal continues, *"The price you're asking for Delhi-U.P. seems a bit high
for an untested combination like Vijay and Sulekha. Also Rakesh Chadda's last
couple of* pictures *were* flops."

Unfazed by Agrawal's skepticism, Malhotra persists, *"The combination
of a* superstar *like Vijay Khanna and a new girl like Sulekha will set the screen
ablaze I am telling you! And Rikki's last two films? I didn't produce them, but
the problem was that those films were not promoted properly. Other producers
don't understand the importance of* marketing. *Those films were treated like
stepchildren. I treat every film I produce as my own flesh and blood. Rikki is
like my own son. All of his films with me have been* hits. *I have so much faith
in this* project *that I am not even selling* [the rights for] *Bombay* [territory].
I will be distributing *the film myself in Bombay."*

Agrawal responds with, *"The heyday of the* love story *is gone.* Audiences
have gotten bored with romance. *Nowadays, they want* action *and* comedy.
All of the hit *films last year were either* action *films or* comedy *films."*

Malhotra exclaims, *"But this film is much more than a* love story! *It has
everything—*romance, drama, emotions, comedy, action. *Just you wait and*

see! It will appeal to everyone from six to sixty, from the front-benchers *to the* families!"

"*Malhotra-saab, last year I had to bear so many losses and the* market *is tight nowadays, but our relationship goes back for many years which is why I have come to you today. Otherwise,* distributors *do not even want to offer an* MG *anymore and would rather distribute the film on a* commission *basis*," counters Agrawal.[10]

Malhotra responds, "*Oh, Agrawal-saab, have you ever suffered a loss with any of my pictures? For a picture that will be released next year, the price is not high at all, in fact, when you take* delivery, *you will think it's fifty or sixty lakhs less than what it should be!*"

Agrawal and Malhotra continue their negotiations over the sale of the film's distribution rights for a few more minutes until finally they both stand up, shake both hands, and Agrawal leaves the set. Malhotra looks very pleased and calls out after him, "*I will definitely let you know when the first* trial [screening] *is of the film. You must come!*"

By this time it is noon, and the star, Khanna, has still not arrived; Malhotra is becoming angry. "*Rikki, where is that idiot? Who does he think he is? Just because a few of his films have become* super hits, *does it mean he can do whatever he wants? If this picture* flops, *will he return my money?*

Chadda tries to placate him, "*Malhotra-saab, he just called a little while ago; he is very sorry; he will be here very soon.*" Chadda looks at his watch and tells one of his assistants to announce to the crew to break for lunch. He turns to Malhotra, "*Please come and have lunch with me, I have home-cooked food.*" While the workers, dancers, and assistants eat lunch outdoors seated on the ground, Chadda, Menon, Khan, Malhotra and his sons retreat to a large air-conditioned room in a building adjacent to the shooting floor, where lunch has been laid out on a table. One of the spot boys serves lunch to everyone and leaves the room.

As Chadda is about to start his lunch, his cell phone rings. Looking at the caller ID, he announces to everyone in the room, "*It's Sunil calling about Vijay's new* release."

Sunil Taneja was the editor of one of the industry trade magazines that collected information about the box-office performance of films, and he had called Chadda to inform him of the first day box-office report of Vijay Khanna's latest film.

Answering the phone, Chadda says, "*Haan,* Sunil, tell me, what are the reports? *Accha,* Bombay is bumper? How about Delhi-U.P.? I see. *Theek hai,* keep me posted. Thanks, bye." Chadda closes his phone with a slightly troubled expression, "Vijay's film, *Pyaari Batein*, is carrying mixed reports. It had a bumper opening in Bombay and Delhi City, but not so good in U.P., Bihar, or C.P.-C.I." Turning to Malhotra, he asks, "Malhotra-saab, are all territories closed for our film?"

"*Not yet, C.P.-C.I. is still* open. *Don't worry Rikki, I'll have buyers lining up for the film. Pyaari Batein is not a* universal subject; *there's nothing in it for the* masses *or the* interiors. *I'm not surprised that it didn't get a good* opening all-India."

Menon adds, "I heard *Pyaari Batein* was too much like *Mohabbat Masti*. That film was a flop. There's no action in either film and you know action is always a safe bet in smaller centers."

Chadda concurs, "*Haan*, that's true, but Vijay doesn't have the image of an action hero. The problem with *Mohabbat Masti* was that the romance angle between the hero and heroine was too different. People have to remember that this is *Hindi* cinema we are making and our audiences don't accept everything. This isn't Hollywood!"

Lucky, Malhotra's younger son, adds, "My friend Jai went to see *Pyaari Batein* yesterday—first day, first show—and he said it was mind-blowing! It was too good!"

"Nowadays, Vijay's films are doing much better in the overseas and the metros. Somehow, the interiors are not connecting with his films," Chadda reflects.

Malhotra retorts, "*That's because the Singhanias* [the film's producers] *only make films for those* territories. *Rikki, not to worry, our film has universal appeal. Just you wait and see,* all-India *and* overseas, masses-classes, *everyone will love it!*"

Khan, who has been flipping through a film magazine during this exchange, pipes up, "Hey look here are photos of the *mahurat* of *Awaaz*—it was quite a fabulous evening! Jawahar Singh spared no expense after all he was launching his son, Rohit. I wonder how the film is going? You know the Singhs: they don't talk about their films or show them to anyone from outside. You would think they were protecting the Kohinoor diamond!"

Vikky, Malhotra's older son, answers, "I work out in the same gym where Rohit's co-star, Amar Kohli, does, and seems that Rohit's dad is not happy at all with the way the film is turning out. He's thinking about getting rid of Suresh Gupta and directing it himself!"

"No way!" Khan exclaims.

"Wow! Poor Suresh," Chadda chimes in.

The visibly surprised group is about to discuss this tidbit of gossip, when someone knocks on the door. Lucky opens the door and a short, slight man enters the room, followed by a tall, muscular man in his mid-twenties. Chadda recognizes the first man and exclaims, "Jignesh-*bhai*, *what's up? Why are you here?*

Jignesh replies, "Rakesh-*ji*, I have brought someone to meet you and Malhotra-*saab*, allow me to introduce Tanuj Singh. He has come here from London, where he was studying acting."

Singh steps forward and does an exaggerated *namaste* to everyone in the room — holding his palms together very straight and bowing his head slightly. Chadda and Khan appear amused by his gesture. Malhotra concentrates on his lunch. Chadda asks Singh, "*So you've come here from London to work in Hindi films, why?*"

Singh replies, "*I've been a big fan of Hindi films since I was a child . . .*"

Khan exclaims, "Oh so sweet, his Hindi has a British accent on it!"

Singh responds, "Actually I'm not from London. I studied acting at the Royal Academy in London."

Chadda asks, "So now, do you know how to act?"

Singh replies, "I think so."

Chadda retorts, "Either you know it or don't know it."

Singh hurriedly responds, "I do know how to act: I've done street theater; plays in college; worked with Alyque Padamsee; did Shakespeare in London."

Chadda asks, "Do you want to work in films or in television?"

"Definitely films! My dream has always been to be on the big screen," says Singh.

"Have you done any films yet or signed any?" asks Chadda.

"No, not yet," replies Singh.

Chadda offers, "Word of advice — even if you haven't signed any films, you need to talk about possibilities in a big way."

Singh adds, "Actually, I have talked to some people about doing a role in Sunil Mehra's next film."

Malhotra finally looks up from his plate, and says to Chadda, "*Rikki, how long has that Mehra been planning his next film? It seems like he makes a film every ten years!*"

Jignesh pipes up, "*Accha, Rakesh-ji, Malhotra-saab, we'll make a move. Tanuj has an appointment in town — since we were in the area I thought why not have him meet you?*"

Singh does another *namaste*, "Thank you for your time and it was very nice meeting you."

Once they both leave, Malhotra turns to Chadda and says with a chuckle, "*Rikki, he seems more suitable for a* villain *than a* hero."

Khan protests, "No Malhotra-*saab*, he was cute—in an ugly-ish sort of way!"

Khan then turns to Chadda and asks, "*Accha* Rikky, when you went to U.S. a few months ago, what movies did you see? Anything good?"

Chadda responds, "I saw *A.I.*, which was very interesting—very different than the typical Spielberg film, you know? I also saw *Memento*, which was great, but you know that kind of film would never work here. Our audiences would get thoroughly confused. I bought a lot of DVDs. I spend so much money when I go to the U.S.!"

Lucky asks, "What did you buy?"

Chadda replies, "So many I can't even remember! I bought a lot of classic films to add to my collection that I didn't have before, like the *Godfather* trilogy that got reissued with all of the special features. I bought *Jurassic Park, Independence Day, Twister . . .*"

Vikky interrupts, "Oh man, the special effects in Hollywood are mindblowing! They are so realistic! We could never do that here!"

Malhotra interjects, "*They don't think of stories anymore in Hollywood, they just think of sequences of special effects and put some story on top.*"

"There are good special effects in India, like in *Hindustani* and *Kaalapani*—those were so real, they looked like English films," asserts Menon.

Malhotra concurs, "*Just imagine, those were* South Indian *films—so much money was spent. The* South *is leading us in* technicians *and* music. *They are very* dedicated. *They take more* risks *and when they spend money, they do it with conviction. Look at the* track record *of the* director *who made Hindustani! What a* track record! *Gentleman, Kaadalan,* and *Hindustani— all* super hits! *Just amazing!*"

Just then the door opens and a short portly man wearing glasses walks in. Malhotra cuts short his comments and exclaims, "*Debu-da! How are you? Where have you been all these days? I was trying to reach you but something is wrong with your* mobile!"

Debojit Das, a veteran screenwriter, settles himself down on an empty chair and says, "*I had gone to Kolkatta for my niece's wedding and you know how it is in a house where a wedding is taking place—absolute chaos! Hello, Rikki, Tanaaz; how is everybody?*"

Everyone nods and reciprocates Das's greeting. Chadda smiles and says warmly, "*So Debu-da, from the twinkle in your eye, I can tell that you have something good for us.*"

Das chuckles and says, "*Ah Rikki, your father used to say the same thing to me. What a great* director *he was. If he were here today, he would have been very proud of you!*"

Malhotra chimes in, "*A great director and a great friend! I remember when we both came to Bombay together from Delhi—what days those were—sharing a room in Prabhadevi . . .*"

Before Malhotra can continue with his reminiscing, Chadda cuts him off, "Debu-*da*, do you have something to narrate for us?"

Das says, "Of course, I have a subject for a light romantic comedy" and launches into his story: "See, the hero is a total debauched guy—drinking, womanizing—and his girlfriend is this tart. His parents are dead, but he lives with his grandparents—who are millionaires—and they won't give him any of his inheritance until he marries a respectable girl. So he and his tarty girlfriend find some girl who dances in a bar and hire her to play the part of his wife, but that girl is smart also; she doesn't just want a lump sum, but a percentage of the inheritance. He and the dancer show up at his grandparents' place pretending to be married. When he asks for his money, the grandparents say not until the firstborn—now they have to fake a pregnancy also!" At this twist in the story, the room bursts into laughter.

Pleased with the reaction, Das continues, "When the girlfriend is getting worried about the hero getting too involved with the dancer girl, he reassures her that he'll get the money and just dump her. Now the dancer overhears this and decides to teach him a lesson. She takes grandpa to a restaurant to show how the hero is hanging out with the tart girlfriend rather than being at home with her. So the grandparents kick the hero out and transfer the property to the dancer and fictitious child. That is the basic story."

Everyone starts laughing and praising Das. Khan exclaims, "Mindblowing Debu-*da*! It's been so long since such a light, fun film has been made, right Rikki?"

Chadda reflects, "Yes, for a film like this casting is really important because there has to be really good chemistry between the hero and the heroine . . ."

Malhotra interjects, "*Debu-da you've done it again! What a great story! Music should be by Amar-Prem and lyrics by Saahil-saab. You know who'll be perfect for the part of the boy? My nephew* [sister's son] *Rajiv—he's ready, and we were just waiting for the right* subject *for his debut. Can you* narrate *to him tomorrow?*"

Das replies, "*Of course; I have time tomorrow.*"

Malhotra turns to his younger son, "*Lucky, dial Micky's number, let's see if he's free. He should be—he's done with* college, *so nowadays he only goes to the* gym *all the time.*"

Lucky dials the number and speaks to his cousin first, "Hello, Micky-*bhaiyya*? It's Lucky. Yah, I'm at Filmistan with Papa and he wants to talk to you."

Malhotra takes the phone and says, "*Hello, Micky-beta* [son], *how are you? . . . I'm here with Debojit Das . . . Yes, the writer. He just narrated to us a brilliant* subject *and you're perfect for it. Do you have time for a* narration *tomorrow? . . . Perfect! Come over at eleven o'clock . . . Yes, at home. Accha, beta. Give my regards to your parents . . . Bye.*"

Hanging up the phone, Malhotra turns to Das and says, "*Excellent, Debu-da. We'll meet tomorrow at home.*"

A beaming Das stands up and says, "*Okay, Malhotra-saab, we'll meet tomorrow. Bye Rikki, say hello to your mother. Bye-bye everybody.*" Everyone in the room responds, "Bye Debu-*da!*"

While Malhotra, Chadda, and others are finishing their lunch, Khanna arrives—followed by his man Friday, Raju, who is carrying his clothes—and without a word goes directly toward his makeup room, where a journalist from the new film magazine *Filmi Duniya* had been waiting outside since ten o'clock to conduct an interview.

The journalist stands up and tries to approach Khanna, "Vijay-*ji*, I'm from *Filmi . . .*" but Raju stops her.

"*Sir is busy, he has to get ready for the shoot.*" After a few minutes, Khanna's personal makeup man enters the room, followed by Raju.

As soon as the break is over at one o'clock, Khanna emerges from the makeup room, dressed in a cream-colored silk brocade kurta, and goes to the set. He is followed by the makeup man, Raju, and the journalist. There, Khan begins to demonstrate the choreography for the song. She first shows Khanna his part without music, counting out the steps, "Okay, Vijay—see here, you come forward—one, two, three, four—and then sideways—five, six, seven, eight—got it? Let's try with the music." Khan picks up a microphone to communicate with the sound recordist, who is out of view behind a screen on the opposite end of the set, "Bharat-*ji*, start the music—*pehle antarey se* [from the first stanza]—give me a few beats lead." When the music begins, she performs the steps alongside Khanna. They go through this routine a few more times, and then Khan looks around, "Where's Sulekha? She's not ready yet?" Khan sends one of the ADs to inquire about how much longer Sulekha will take to get ready. She tells Khanna, "Vijay, let's run through this a couple of times. I'll do Sulekha's steps now and you practice yours." After a few more rehearsals, Khan tells Khanna, "*Theek hai* [That's fine]; take a break. We need Sulekha to continue."

Khanna sits down and motions to Raju, who has been standing in the background watching his boss the entire time. *"Raju, give me the phone and matches."* Raju immediately hands over Khanna's cell phone and holds out a pack of Marlboro Lights with one cigarette pulled out slightly for his boss to remove. Khanna takes the cigarette and holds it out in his left hand for Raju to light, meanwhile he sends a text message on his phone with his right.

Raju clears his throat and says, *"Sir, that woman from the magazine is still here."*

Khanna looks up from his phone, *"Kahaan [where]?"* He then notices the journalist standing to the left of him in one of the arches framing the courtyard. He tells Raju, *"Oh, I forgot! Bring her here."*

Raju walks over to the journalist and says, *"Sir is calling you."*

When she reaches Khanna at his spot near the center of the set, he apologizes, "I am so sorry to keep you waiting. Please sit. It is always so busy on the first day of a schedule! What's your name?"

"Malini."

Before she can say anything further, Khanna flashes his famous smile and says, "Ah, lovely name! Tell me Malini will you have some tea or a Pepsi? It's quite hot, cold is better, no?" Turning to Raju who was waiting attentively nearby, he orders, *"Bring a Pepsi for the lady."* Turning back to Malini, he asks, "Now tell me, which magazine are you from?"

With this barrage of attention from one of India's top film stars, Malini's frustration at waiting for five hours in the heat dissipates rapidly, *"Filmi Duniya* [Film World] — it's a new magazine started by Sunita Tandon, who used to be the editor of *Starz*. We would like to feature you on our inaugural cover. I think Sunita-*ji* had called and spoken to you about it?"

"Of course, of course, Sunita is a dear friend. Anything for her," responds Khanna.

Malini continues, "I'd like to take your interview for the cover story . . ." Khanna cuts her off.

"Of course, of course, definitely. We can do it right now. Go ahead, ask me."

As Malini takes her notebook out and starts fishing for a pen in her bag, Khanna exclaims, *"It's about time!"*

Malini looks up. "Sorry?"

Khanna gestures toward the entrance of the set. Sulekha has just walked into the set with her mother, sister, and dress designer, Rita Chandra, in tow. They walk directly to where Chadda, Khan, and Menon are seated, in front of a video monitor near the camera. Chandra starts apologizing profusely, "So, so sorry to keep you all waiting Rakesh-*ji*, my tailor master fell ill and then I had to special order the silk for the *ghagra* [long full skirt] from Italy, you know, because you cannot find this shade of blue in India, so everything took much longer than planned!"

Chadda shrugs her off and tells Sulekha, "We're shooting the *pehla antara* [first verse] first, okay?" He calls out to Vijay who is seated farther away, "*Accha* [okay], Vijay, ready?"

Khanna who was speaking to the journalist, stands up and says, "We'll continue after I give this shot, okay?" and walks toward the group. Khan takes them both to a less crowded area of the set so that she can supervise their rehearsal. Khanna and Sulekha rehearse their dance steps together a few times. As a trained *Bharatanatyam* dancer, Sulekha picks up the routine quickly.

Chadda asks Khan, "*Okay, shall we do a* take?"

Khan nods her approval, "*Haan* [yes], let's do it." She calls out to her assistants who are standing right behind her, "Kabir, Sania, get the dancers in position."

Chadda tells his assistants to inform Menon that they are ready. Arif rushes to Menon, while Sanjeev starts announcing loudly, "Quiet! Quiet, please!"

The actors and dancers get into position; the lights are switched on; Chadda and Khan take their seats in front of the video monitor; and Menon sits behind the camera, which is placed on a trolley. Sanjeev roars once more, "QUIET! TAKING!"

Khan speaks into the microphone, "Start sound! Roll camera!"

Keshav holds up the clapboard in front of the camera, quickly says, "*Mera Dil Aapke Kadmon Mein Hai* song three, shot one, take one," and then sounds the clap.

When Khan says, "Action!" Menon's assistants on either side of him slowly push the camera on a track toward the background dancers arrayed in the center of the courtyard. As the music swells, the group parts in the middle, revealing Khanna and Sulekha dancing side by side.

After two measures of music, Khan, with her eye on the monitor shouts, "Cut it! Good job!" She turns to Chadda, who had been watching the whole sequence along with her on the monitor, "Rikki, what do you think, good, no?"

Chadda answers, "Mind-blowing! Print this one." Behind one of the arches, a spot boy breaks a coconut to celebrate the first shot of the day and pieces are distributed to everyone on the set.

Malhotra, who watched the shot seated under an archway to the right of the camera, takes a piece of coconut, looks at his watch, and mutters to Iqbal, *"Wow, they took the first shot so quickly? It's only about to be three o'clock. If they keep going at this rate, my grandchildren will be able to come to the premiere!"*

Munching on the coconut, Khan tells Chadda, *"Let's take one more as a safety."*

Chadda responds, "Okay, but not too many extra takes, you know how Malhotra is *kanjoos* [miserly] about spending money on [raw] stock. Who would think on such a big film that we have to measure our stock?"

After one more take of the same sequence, the camera and lights have to be positioned differently for the next shot, and it is time to give the workers their tea break, so Khanna and Sulekha decide to retreat to their respective makeup rooms, which are air-conditioned, unlike the set. The dancers, who don't have makeup rooms, step outside the set for their break, as it is close to 100 degrees Fahrenheit inside when the lights are on. Khanna asks Malini, the journalist, to accompany him to his makeup room so that they can finish the interview. As he is exiting the set, he encounters Malhotra who is on his way out as well.

"Hello Malhotra-saab, did you see the shot?"

Malhotra replies, *"It was absolutely great! The two of you will be an amazing pair onscreen! Okay, Vijay, I'm off, come home sometime, Mrs. Malhotra keeps asking about you."*

During the tea break, another producer, Vinod Lakhani, arrives at the set with his assistant in order to speak to Khanna about acting in a film that he is producing. Discovering that Khanna is in his makeup room, Lakhani decides to wait for him. He tells a spot boy to bring a couple of chairs outside the set and waits there for Khanna. After the tea break, Arif is dispatched to the makeup rooms to inform the actors that they are needed on set. He knocks on Sulekha's door first, "Ma'am, shot is ready," and then on Khanna's door, "Sir, shot is ready." Sulekha walks out of her room first with her mother and sister. Khanna leaves his room a little later, along with a couple of his friends who dropped by to visit with him.

As Khanna walks toward the entrance of the set, Lakhani approaches and greets him, *"Namaste Vijay-ji."*

Khanna replies, *"Lakhani-saab, how are you? I have to give this shot; I'll be just a minute. Are you fine here or you can also sit inside. Will you have tea or a soft drink?"*

Lakhani answers, *"I'm fine right here. I don't want anything. Thank you."*

Despite his answer, once inside, Khanna still dispatches a spot boy to serve tea to Lakhani and his assistant, who drink it readily. He also makes a spot boy bring chairs and tea for his friends.

Keshav asks Arif, "*Who is that with Vijay-ji? Someone important?*"

Arif replies, "*No man, they're his hangers-on/sidekicks, but even a star's hangers-on start taking on the airs of a star.*"

The second shot is of a close-up of Khanna singing the first line of the *antara*. After a couple of rehearsals, they decide to shoot. The music begins, and the camera with a zoom lens slowly tracks toward Khanna, who lip-synchs, "*Amavas mein chaand nikla mere dil mein jalaya diya* [The moon (a reference to his love) has appeared on this dark night, lighting the lamp in my heart]."

"Cut!" shouts Khan. Turning to Chadda, she says, "What do you think?"

He nods and says, "*Accha hai.* [It's good.] Let's print it."

The third shot is an extreme close-up reaction shot of Sulekha responding to Khanna's declaration. Her line, "*Meri rooh ki gheraiyon mein teri awaaz goonjey* [Your voice echoes in the depths of my soul]," proves difficult for her to lip-synch, as she barely speaks Hindi. After several rehearsals, Khan and Chadda decide to film. During the filming, Sulekha stumbles over the word *gheraiyon* (depths). They try again and then she fumbles over the word *goonjey* (echoes).

After ten takes, Khan says to Chadda, "*Rikki, we have to do something else. How much longer can we keep doing this? It's a simple line, but she doesn't know Hindi. If this is the case today, then what will we do for the rest of the shoot?*"

Chadda responds, "*Haan, she needs a lot of coaching. We'll put Arif on it. Anyway, we will* dub *her voice for sure* — obviously *we won't* use *her voice.* We can't change the lyrics at this point after the song is already recorded. Why don't we pull back from the extreme close-up and shoot her through a row of *diyas* [clay oil lamps] to get a diffuse effect, and then we won't notice her mouth movements so much?"

Khan says, "But all of the *diyas* are on the wall; how would we do that?"

Chadda thinks some more, walking around the courtyard. "What about if she has a *diya* in her hand? The part of the line that she has trouble with — we shoot the *diya* and then zoom out to a medium close-up of her singing the rest of the line, you know, like that song in *Devdas?*"[11]

Khan says, "That would work, then we would have to make sure that she can hold that *diya jagah jagah* [everywhere] for the rest of the *antara*."

Chadda chuckles, "*Whenever she can't get a line, we'll take a close-up of the lamp.*"

Khan bursts into laughter. "You're too much!"

Chadda walks over to Menon to inform him of the changes. Menon says, "If you want me to shoot a *diya* then I'll have to change the lighting set-up."

Looking at his watch, Chadda says, "Change the lighting set-up quickly; the shift is almost over."

Meanwhile, Khanna has stepped outside the set to meet with Lakhani. As there are only two chairs, Lakhani's assistant stands up so that Khanna may sit.

Khanna asks, *"So Lakhani-saab, what brings you here?"*

Lakhani responds, *"I've got an excellent story and you are perfect in it."*

Khanna inquires, *"Do you have the* script? *I don't have time to hear a narration right now. After this shoot, I have to go to Aradhana* [name of a recording/dubbing studio] *to* dub *for a film."*

Lakhani responds, *"If you like the idea, then I'll get the script written!"*

Khanna retorts, *"Oh Lakhani-saab, those days are over! Nowadays I don't agree to do a film that doesn't have a* bound script."

Lakhani replies, *"If you want a script, remember that* English [language] *picture, Notting Hill? It's something like that."*

Khanna stifles a groan, *"Now I'd like to do roles that are slightly different from my usual ones."*

Lakhani persists, *"Please think about it—the money is good—there are some* NRI *investors from the U.S. and Canada. You can get a lot more than your standard remuneration."*

"How much more?" asks Khanna.

"Currently you get 30 million, right? You can easily get 40 or 50 million."

Khanna says, *"Okay, I'll think about it. When are you thinking about beginning production?"*

Lakhani answers, "July *ya* [or] August."

Khanna does a double-take, *"What, that quickly! How is that possible! It's already February! Anyway, I don't have any* dates *for the next two years; I'm doing four movies."*

Lakhani says, *"It will get made very quickly; everything will get completed in one or two* schedules! *The entire shoot will take place abroad and will be in* synch-sound *so it's just a matter of 30 or 40 days. Think about it; you can spend the monsoons in Canada and the U.S. with your family, maybe do some stage-shows; think of it as a vacation on our expense."*

Khanna stands up and says, *"Okay, I'll see what I can do, I'll have my* secretary *try to juggle my* dates *around, and I'll give you a reply in a few days. Very well, goodbye."*

Lakhani stands up and folds his hands in departing. While Khanna walks toward the set, Lakhani and his assistant leave the studio. As he enters the set, Khanna hears Chadda say on the microphone, "*Accha* [okay] everybody, pack up!" Khanna turns around and walks toward his makeup room to change; he then leaves for the dubbing studio where he has to dub his dialogues for a different film.

At the end of the shift, all of the workers who receive a daily wage, such as spot boys, background dancers, lighting assistants, and various others line up outside the shooting floor, where Malhotra's production manager, Iqbal, and an assistant have set up a table with a ledger. Iqbal's assistant hands each worker his or her daily wage along with conveyance—money for transportation costs—in cash that Iqbal dispenses from his briefcase. Each worker then signs the ledger to record the receipt of payment. Chadda and his assistants pile into his car to go to the music studio, where the last song of the film will be recorded later that night. Khan and her assistants take off to another film shoot that Khan is choreographing. After Iqbal finishes paying all of the daily workers, he and his assistant take the magazine of exposed film to the lab for processing. The camera is packed up by its attendants and taken back to the offices of Sai Arts—the production company that rented it out for the shoot. After everyone leaves, one of the studio guards locks the entrance to the set.

CHAPTER 5

The Structure, Organization, and Social Relations of the Hindi Film Industry

On November 14, 2009, a panel discussion titled "East and West: A New Co-Dependency" was held at HBO headquarters in New York City as part of the day-long "Film India: The MIAAC-09 Industry Panels." This event had been planned to occur in conjunction with the Mahindra Indo-American Arts Council Ninth Annual Indian Film Festival. Filmmaker Sri Rao was conversing with his agents from William Morris Endeavor Entertainment, who asked him to relate his experience of working on the Bollywood film *New York* with Yashraj Films. Rao and his production company associates were the local line producers for the Hindi film, which was shot extensively on location in New York and Philadelphia during the summer of 2008. Speaking about his experiences working with the team at Yashraj Films, Rao related that while the Bombay film industry exhibited a high level of production expertise, "It's sort of like we both do the same thing, you know us here in Hollywood and them there in Bollywood, but it's like we speak different languages." Asked to elaborate, Rao described how the first two weeks of the shoot were "chaos," because of what he characterized as "cultural differences" between the working styles of the American and Indian crews. "They have grips and gaffers, and we have grips and gaffers, but the expectations about what their grips and gaffers do is very different from what our grips and gaffers do."

Despite Rao's acknowledgment of the differences, his use of

occupational terms, like grips and gaffers, which are not part of the working parlance of the Hindi film industry, his assertion that both Hollywood and Bollywood "do the same thing," and his attribution of conflict to epiphenomenal representations of language and culture, reveal an underlying assumption that the material practices of filmmaking are somehow universal, outside the realms of social relations and cultural context. Throughout the course of my research I have encountered assumptions and questions generated by the conventions, norms, and practices particular to Hollywood, but assumed to be applicable to the structure and workings of the Hindi film industry.[1] Although the main imaginary for feature film production in much of the world is derived from Hollywood,[2] in the next two chapters I aim to denaturalize and de-westernize conventional understandings of mainstream film production and dislodge Hollywood from its default position. Although both Hollywood and "Bollywood" are commercially driven film industries, they are not organized similarly, nor do they operate in the same way. The commercial nature of a media institution does not necessarily render its structure, organization, or working style transparent or universal. Whereas this chapter examines the structure, organization, and social relations of the Hindi film industry, the next one focuses on the work culture of the industry.

While my point of departure is the ethnographic material presented in the previous chapter's portrayal of life on a Hindi film set, I first outline the decentralized and fragmented nature of filmmaking in India to establish the ease with which individuals with access to capital can become filmmakers. Following this, I detail the basic political economy of the Hindi film industry, describing particularly the significance of the film distributor. After that, I illustrate the importance of personal relationships and social networks, which can have the effect of both granting an immediacy to interactions and serving as a form of gatekeeping. I then discuss the significance of kinship, a prominent reason for the industry's personalized nature, as a relation of production and reproduction. Finally, I explain how the industry's hierarchy is made manifest in sites of production by examining in greater depth the centrality of male stars to the production process.

THE "INDEPENDENT" FILM INDUSTRY

During a symposium on Indian and Egyptian musical films held at New York University in January 1999, Gerard Hooper, an American cinematographer who worked on the Hindi film *Satya* (Truth), was asked the main differences between working on an American film compared to an Indian film, as it was his first experience with Hindi filmmaking. Hooper replied that he liked the set-up in Bombay because it was like the independent film world in the United States. I smiled at the delicious irony of applying a label like "independent," with its connotations of being alternative, unconstrained, and oppositional, to the dominant mode of filmmaking in India—the mode most commonly referred to as "commercial."

What Hooper was actually commenting upon was the extremely decentralized, flexible, and freelance nature of the Hindi film industry, characteristics that are belied by the Fordist metaphors of factories and assembly lines used so frequently by Western and Indian journalists to describe it: "Bollywood's dream factories churn out hundreds of films a year" (Bajaj 2011; Dey 2004). While there have been instances of integration throughout the history of the Hindi film industry—producers who venture into distribution, distributors who venture into exhibition, or exhibitors who venture into production—to date it has not resulted in a consolidation of the industry, nor has it precluded others from entering the business. Essentially, the "industry" has been a very diffuse and chaotic place where anyone with large sums of money and the right contacts has been able to make a film. A case in point is the late G. P. Sippy, the producer of *Sholay*, who came to Bombay from Karachi after the Partition of British India in 1947 and made his foray into filmmaking via the construction business. During our interview, Sippy explained that in the process of building apartments in Bombay, he met members of the film world who convinced him to "migrate from the world of real estate to the world of illusion called films" (G. P. Sippy, interview, 22 September 1996).[3]

The potential for complete novices to enter film production has been a characteristic feature of filmmaking in India for decades, and it has been commented upon and criticized in government reports about the state of cinema in India. The 1951 *Report of the Film Enquiry Committee* is a valuable source of information about filmmaking in India during the late 1930s and 1940s. It details the fragmentation of production, remarking that India had a "plethora of producers" compared to Hollywood of the time (Patil 1951: 64). For example, in 1947, 214 producers made a total of 283 films in India, with the highest number of films produced by any single producer being 7; in 1948, 211 producers made 264 films, and the highest number of films produced by any single producer was only 6. Among these producers, a large number—nearly 70 percent in 1947—were what the Patil Report termed "newcomer independents"—those who had no prior connection with the film industry. Due to their lack of experience, the attrition rate of these independent producers, character-ized as "infant mortality" by the Patil Report, was quite high. It noted that, "Only 25 producers continued in the industry through all of the three years from 1946–48" (Patil 1951: 65). The Patil Report blamed new-comers for the problems besetting filmmaking: "The free entry of stray elements is generally held responsible for many of the ills of the industry, such as competitive bidding for stars, the sacrifice of quality in the hurry to complete a picture at any cost, payment of usurious rates of interest, mortgage of a film before it is completed, and also the many 'still-borns' among the production ventures that do not go beyond the stage of the first thousand feet or so of shooting" (Patil 1951: 65). From the Report's point of view, not only were there too many producers in India, there were also too many films being produced, judged by the high rates of commercial failure. It advocated reducing the number of films made an-nually: "It seems to us essential to find out ways and means to eliminate the production of useless pictures, which have not the slightest possi-bility of being certified for exhibition or of being screened successfully" (Patil 1951: 94).

The problem of the "free entry of stray elements" producing too many "useless pictures" did not resolve itself over time, and one finds similar criticisms in a later state-initiated inquiry about filmmaking—the *Report of the Working Group on National Film Policy*, published in 1980. The Working Group characterized film production in India as a highly specu-lative enterprise because of the large number of "ad hoc producers who are attracted to filmmaking, largely because of glamour, the possibility of making quick money, and the scope which filmmaking offers for sanitiz-ing black money" (Karanth 1980: 16). The consequence of a large number of new producers every year, according to the Working Group, is the ero-sion of professionalism, since these producers "do not have any expertise in the financial management of film production or an insight into the market for which their film is designed. They also have no definite in-volvement with the medium of cinema" (Karanth 1980: 18).

Both the Patil and Working Group reports suggested measures to rationalize and professionalize film production, which involved some form of regulation and erecting barriers to entry. For example, the Patil Report recommended the establishment of a Film Council of India, which would "superintend and regulate the film industry, to act as its guide, friend, and philosopher" (Patil 1951: 187). Additionally, the council would serve as an advisory body, offering guidance to the Central and state gov-ernments regarding film production, distribution, and exhibition. The

Patil Report also argued that a Production Code Administration needed to be set up in order to scrutinize scripts prior to production, "which would serve not merely to exclude objectionable material, but also to improve the quality of films" (1951: 102). Acknowledging the Patil Report's recommendations, the Working Group asserted that changes in filmmaking over the interim three decades necessitated a different approach to regulation, which did not involve control over the creative process of filmmaking, such as the vetting of scripts. Stating that regulation of film production was necessary "only to the extent that there is a need to discourage the entry of 'adventurers' in the area of film production" and to ensure that filmmaking met some "basic minimum professional business management standards" (1980: 20), the Working Group recommended that all film producers register with the National Film Development Corporation (NFDC). Since the NFDC was the government agency responsible for the import and distribution of raw stock at that time, the Working Group asserted that only producers who registered with the NFDC be allocated raw stock. The Report stated that when allotting raw stock, the NFDC needed to evaluate producers' past experience and how well planned and organized the current film project appeared to be. The Working Group's desire to severely curtail the entry of novice producers was apparent from its recommendation that even those producers who could have access to raw stock through a separate channel and licensing regime would be required to register with the NFDC; according to the Report, this regulation could be enforced by modifying the alternative importing license to include this requirement (Karanth 1980: 21).

Such recommendations never got implemented, however, and the high ratio of producers to the numbers of films produced by the Hindi film industry annually is an indication that stringent barriers to entry still do not exist. In my first year of fieldwork in 1996, 88 production companies, referred to as "banners" in the film industry, had produced the 96 Hindi films released that year, while the following year, 90 companies had produced the 92 Hindi films released. Even with the entry of the Indian corporate sector into filmmaking since 2000, film production has remained fragmented in Bombay. For example, in 2005, 177 production companies were involved in making the 187 films that were released, and in 2009, 128 companies produced the 135 films that were released, with the highest number of solo productions by a single company being 5.[4] The number of producers is potentially even larger, since a greater number of films are produced—as indicated by their certification for exhibition by the Censor Board—than are released theatrically every year. Even from the

TABLE 2   FRAGMENTATION OF THE PRODUCTION SECTOR

Year	Total Hindi Films Certified	Total Hindi Films Released	Number of Production Companies	Number of Successful Films	Number of Corresponding Production Companies
1995	157	99	97	16	16
1996	126	96	88	17	18
1997	117	92	90	27	27
1998	153	108	99	21	19
1999	137	112	106	16	16
2000	243	143	124	17	18
2001	230	156	143	13	14
2005	248	187	177	19	22
2006	223	153	147	23	21
2007	257	148	130	17	18
2008	248	127	124	14	18
2009	235	135	128	9	13

Source: Based on data compiled from *Film Information*, January 6, 1996–January 5, 2002; January 7, 2006–January 2, 2010.

perspective of commercially successful films, the ratio remains relatively stable. The number of Hindi films successful at the box-office from 1995 to 2009 and the number of companies involved in making them is shown in Table 2. The years where there are more companies than films are due to co-productions. The table demonstrates that while commercial success is concentrated with respect to the number of films produced, it is not concentrated in terms of the number of producers. The table also reveals that while it may be relatively easy to produce a film, it is difficult to have it released and even more difficult for it to be classified as a hit. Despite the reported high rates of commercial failure, Komal Nahta, the editor of the trade magazine *Film Information*, asserted that it was "hope and new money" sustaining the film industry. "It's the hope of every producer that he will get one *Hum Aapke Hain Koun!* or a *Sholay* and new money; [this is] the glamour which attracts people, who absolutely have no idea what filmmaking is or what they're getting into" (Nahta, interview, September 1996).

Although new infusions of capital sustain the industry financially, the high number of producers and high rates of turnover from year to year have been a source of anxiety—for the industry and the state—regarding the intentions and true identities of some producers. This is noted in the Working Group's reference to "black money" (Karanth 1980: 16). While black money refers to unreported, untaxed income that could be generated from legal enterprises, the intensely cash-based nature of the financial dealings of the film industry until the early 2000s made it possible for the world of organized crime to be involved with filmmaking. References to the underworld–film industry "nexus," as it was most commonly referred to by the Indian press, began in the late 1980s. The intersections between organized crime and filmmaking came into the national and international media spotlight in the late 1990s and early 2000s after the gangster-ordered murder of Gulshan Kumar, the founder and head of an audio company that expanded into film production, and the arrest of Bharat Shah, a diamond merchant who had become one of the most significant financiers within the industry, for his links to organized crime.[5]

While I did not come across explicit examples of, or references to, criminal involvement during my initial fieldwork, given Hindi filmmakers' desire for social acceptance by elites and their anxiety about respectability, I encountered more oblique statements in which filmmakers erected a distinction between themselves and those whom they did not consider legitimate filmmakers. For example, actor Sanjay Dutt predicted a better future for the film industry based on his sense that higher costs of production and an emphasis on quality would lead to a culling process: "I think people who love films will remain, you see. Filmmakers will remain. The riff raffs will go away. That's exactly what's happening today. There was a time, a couple of years back, when anybody was making a film. 'I've got so much of money, make a film,' but you're not making a film because you love to make films; you're making a film because you want to be known" (Dutt, interview, May 1996). Dutt's dichotomy of filmmakers with a genuine love and passion for cinema versus "riff raffs" with money, who make films for spurious reasons, can be understood as an indirect acknowledgment of the criminal presence within the industry, especially since so many of my other informants emphasized the participation of individuals from a variety of other businesses—jewelry, construction, textiles, hotels—that would not be regarded disreputable.

The involvement of individuals from legitimate businesses also posed potential problems, due to their lack of knowledge and experience in filmmaking. Producer Mukesh Bhatt described how the glamour of the film industry consistently attracted new investors from other sectors of the economy, who treated filmmaking as a form of speculation—an easy route to making quick money—rather than the difficult business that it was. "They come here for the glamour, more for fun than actually doing it in the proper way. They get caught with these con people, who tell them, 'Yes, we'll make a film for you.' They get duped and then they abuse the industry and go away" (Mukesh Bhatt, interview, October 1996). Not only did such individuals spread an undeservedly bad reputation of the industry, by paying stars much higher remunerations than established producers, they also upset its economics. "They muck it up," Bhatt complained, "because they're not producers, you see? So they do more harm than good. Apart from burning their own money, they also spoil the industry by giving the stars a ridiculous price they don't deserve. For a star, they're like a man-eater: once they taste blood, drawn blood, then he wants to, you know, once some fool comes and gives them, one *crore* rupees [10 million], they feel that's their price. Their price may not be actually worth more than 40 *lakhs* [4 million] of rupees, but they suddenly feel that, 'Mukesh Bhatt is exploiting me,' and this guy comes and pays me one *crore*" (Mukesh Bhatt, interview, October 1996). Bhatt likened such outside producers to NRIs (non-resident Indians) who came to Bombay and paid much more money for real estate than its market value and thereby drove up prices out of reach for local residents. "He spoils the market. He pays a ridiculous price, and you know, gets people's heads going [topsy-turvy]. Others suffer because of that" (Mukesh Bhatt, interview, October 1996). Bhatt's criticisms echo those found in the Patil and Working Group reports mentioned above, demonstrating the remarkable persistence over time of certain structural conditions and discourses regarding filmmaking in India. The representation of neophyte producers paying stars unwarranted salaries is a very longstanding criticism, one that is cited as the main reason for the demise of the studio system in India (Barnouw and Krishnaswamy 1980; Binford 1989). Bhatt's condemnation of stars as avaricious and undeserving is also part of a dominant discourse of criticism about them. His assertion that "they're not producers," and his reference to the "proper way" of making films forges distinctions between those who can be regarded as genuine producers and those who are not worthy of that occupational title. His criticisms operate as a sort of "boundary-work" (Gieryn 1983), which is part of a longstanding effort by members of the industry to cast filmmaking as a profession, with all of its attendant practices of exclusion.

In a scenario where anyone with money could conceivably produce a film, the most common discursive manifestation of boundary-work is the frequent use of the epithet, "proposal-maker," a term, deployed with great disdain by the vast majority of my informants, which describes a figure whom they regarded as the embodiment of the prevailing work ethic within the industry. In filmmakers' statements, a proposal-maker refers to a producer who is not interested in exerting the effort necessary for turning out a quality film, but simply runs after stars; this figure of the lazy, slapdash producer operates as a trope to showcase the conscientiousness and commitment of the filmmaker wielding the term. For example, R. Mohan, a businessman who made his fortunes with the nationally marketed Good Knight brand of mosquito repellant and then turned to Hindi film production in the early 1990s, after producing Malayalam films in his native state of Kerala, contrasted his style of producing a film in one shooting schedule with what he found to be the disjunctive mode dominant in Bombay. He attributed the fragmented production process to actor insecurity and producer complicity: "The Hindi stars are slightly nervous; they have this insecure feeling—'I don't know how many days I have.' So what happens is when one becomes successful, what they do is they generally sign fifteen to twenty films, so it gives them a broader base of income. They get fifteen advances and it suits the producer also, because most of the producers here, they don't want this one schedule business . . . because many of them are proposal-makers rather than really being filmmakers" (Mohan, interview, May 1996). Mohan then elaborated upon how a proposal-maker would go about financing and producing a film: first he would needle a star endlessly until he relented and agreed to allot a day or two in the future to shoot for the film; with this commitment, the proposal-maker approaches a music director (composer) who, because of the star's willingness, readily agrees to join the project; then the proposal-maker contacts an audio company and offers the audio rights to his film in return for an advance payment, which the company obliges based on the combination of star and music director in the film; the proposal-maker uses that payment to pay the star and cover the costs of shooting for a few days; the proposal-maker then edits that footage to show to distributors in order to obtain an advance from them, which he uses to fund shooting for another schedule, after which he repeats the process again with other distributors. "I wouldn't call this the right way of making films." Mohan asserted. "That means basically, you don't even have a script at the time or a subject." In the chapter four sketch, the producer—Vinod Lakhani—who approaches Vijay Khanna with an idea for a film, rather than a completed script, could potentially be regarded as a proposal-maker.

The epithet of proposal-maker, with its associations of being careless, uncommitted, and disorganized, primarily gains its meaning and value in relation to commercial outcome. Commercial success has been and continues to be the critical factor in establishing one's credentials and staying power as a legitimate filmmaker within the Hindi film industry. Commercially successful producers, though still criticized for a variety of reasons by members of the industry, are never referred to as "proposal-makers," no matter what the circumstances are of their production process and working style. The Working Group explicitly affirmed that in its report. After describing the broad categories of film producers in India— established producers, ad-hoc producers, director/producers, and producers of good-quality low- or medium-budget films, the Report states, "there is a certain amount of mobility [between the categories] and there are cases where a new person enters the field of film production as an 'adventurer' and if his film becomes a hit, he moves to the category of established producers" (Karanth 1980: 17).

Many of the filmmakers I met who were first-generation members of the industry exemplified this mobility. For example, the late B. R. Chopra, a producer/director who came to Bombay from Lahore during the Partition of India, characterized his entry into the world of filmmaking as completely unplanned. Chopra's early involvement with films was as a film journalist in Lahore. In 1947 some businessmen friends of Chopra's father approached him with the idea of making a film, and even though Chopra and his colleagues started working on the film prior to Partition, they had to abort the project due to the ensuing violence in Lahore. Once Chopra came to Bombay, he revived the project with the same partners, and hired a director as he had no experience in direction, but unfortunately the film, released in 1949, "bombed at the box-office in a very big way; it was thrown out by the public completely, and we were on the road" (B. R. Chopra, interview, 7 August 1996). Chopra relayed a fortuitous set of circumstances that lifted him out of his slump: he came up with an idea for a film that he was able to present to a wealthy friend from Lahore, who told him that he was willing to invest the money necessary to make the film. When Chopra responded that he would be unable to pay him back if the picture did not succeed commercially, his friend assured him that he would bear all of the losses, on the condition that Chopra direct the film. "I said, 'I don't know how to direct a movie! I've never been a director,'" Chopra recalled. "He says, 'I don't know, I have faith that you can do it.' So that's how I was made to direct the picture and I must say it's only a miracle and the divine grace that I was able to succeed in the very first picture . . . I was able to stay in the films and have continued to stay because of that one success. Once you are successful, then of course, things become easy: people start respecting you" (Chopra, interview, 7 August 1996).[6]

If commercial outcome is ultimately the criterion that distinguishes established filmmakers from all others, then why the persistent discourse about proposal-makers? The apparent rate of commercial failure does not dissuade new entrants into the industry from other businesses. Furthermore, since commercial success eludes most producers, including the established ones, box-office outcome is not an effective basis of distinction. The boundary-work of the sort discussed above differentiates filmmakers who possess the potential for commercial success from those who do not, which can translate into tangible benefits, such as attracting capital for future projects through distributors or new investors. Part of producer Mukesh Bhatt's complaint against people from other businesses trying their hand at filmmaking was that they did not choose the right people to collaborate with in the film industry. Describing new investors as susceptible to false promises of easy money and fame, Bhatt said, "They will not come to a genuine person, because a genuine person won't give them a picture which is only a bed of roses. They'll give them the clear picture, 'ki [that] listen, it's a tough job; it's hard work; and it's not a bed of roses, you have to really slog it out,' which doesn't suit their ears because they're coming here for fun more than business" (Mukesh Bhatt, interview, October 1996).

Bhatt's insistence that filmmaking is a "tough job" rather than "a bed of roses" points to another important function of boundary-work—to represent filmmaking as a challenging profession that requires specialized skill and knowledge. Training in filmmaking in India has primarily been through apprenticeship and heredity, which thereby garners much less symbolic capital—even among filmmakers—in comparison to professions that require formal higher education. If anyone can produce a film, then filmmaking does not possess prestige. This is akin to Shah Rukh Khan's point in chapter two about Hindi films' low cultural status resulting from their role as common entertainment. Just as Hindi films were not regarded as special because everyone saw them, filmmaking has been devalued because of the perception that anyone can do it. The effort to represent filmmaking as work and not "fun" also articulates with the concerns about respectability, discussed in chapter three, as it accords with filmmakers' valorization of middle-classness, exemplifying their concern with social status.

The lengthy exchange between Malhotra and Agrawal in the chapter four sketch represents the key role played by distributors in the filmmaking process. Historically, production and distribution have not been integrated in the Bombay film industry, and Hindi films have been distributed throughout India and the world by a decentralized network of independent distributors. These distributors have been one of the primary sources of finance for Hindi film production until the entry of media conglomerates and corporate producers around 2003. Producers have financed films primarily through the sale of their theatrical distribution rights, a process that begins from the moment a film is "launched," or its particulars announced at the *mahurat*—a ritual undertaken by a producer, marking the start of a new film project. From the time of the *mahurat*, producers start selling their film—or more accurately "the package," which at the bare minimum includes the director, the male star, and the music director—to distributors. Some producers, because of their past record and the marketability of the key personnel involved, are able to declare "all territories sold" on the day of the *mahurat*, while others have to work hard to acquire distributors for their films.[7] The somewhat hyperbolic manner in which Malhotra tries to convince Agrawal to buy the rights for his film was a practice that I encountered frequently throughout my fieldwork.

For the purposes of Hindi film distribution, India is divided into five major territories: Bombay; Delhi/U.P. [Uttar Pradesh]/East Punjab; C.P. [Central Province]/C.I. [Central India]/Rajasthan; Eastern; and South (Map 1). A sixth territory, known as the "Overseas Territory," was undifferentiated from the point of view of distributors in India, but by the late 1990s it became subdivided into North America, United Kingdom, Gulf States, South Africa, etc. The five territories in India are divided into fourteen subterritories (Map 2), which may be further subdivided.[8] Since a single distributor is unable to bear the cost of an entire territory, these subdivisions are the more salient distribution categories in terms of structuring film transactions, as depicted in the chapter four sketch by Agrawal, whose business encompasses the Delhi/U.P. subterritory of the larger Delhi/U.P./East Punjab territory. Until 2001, the Rajshri Group was the only national distribution company—referred to as an "all-India" distributor in trade parlance—while all other distribution concerns were specific to a territory or a subterritory. The significance of distribution territories for the creation of a taxonomy of the film indus-

MAP 1 Distribution Territories for Hindi Cinema.

try's audiences, raised in the lunchtime conversation between Chadda, Malhotra, and Menon, is addressed in greater detail in chapter eight.

Rather than encompassing India's 28 states in their current territorial integrity, the film territories that developed in the 1930s, after the arrival of the talkie, preserve a colonial geographical logic, both in terms of their boundaries and their names: Central Province; Central India; East Punjab; Nizam.[9] Thus, the territories do not correspond to the contemporary political division of India into linguistically organized states. For example, the political-linguistic state of Maharashtra, of which Bombay is the capital, is divided and portioned into the Bombay territory and the subterritories of C.P./Berar and Nizam. The Bombay territory, which is considered the territory with the highest revenue potential, includes the city of Bombay and its suburbs, the entire state of Gujarat, parts of

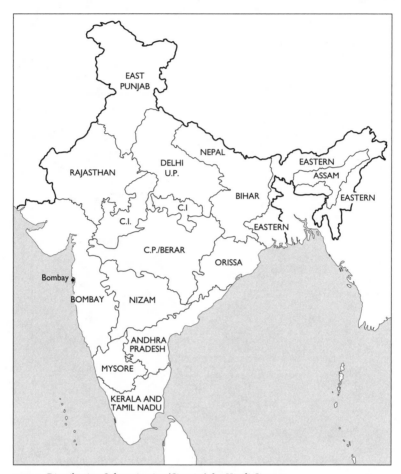

MAP 2 Distribution Subterritories (Circuits) for Hindi Cinema.

Karnataka, and only parts of Maharashtra. Another example of the distribution network overriding political boundaries is the inclusion of the independent nation-states of Nepal and Bhutan as parts of the domestic Eastern territory rather than the Overseas Territory.[10]

In addition to dividing India into territories and subterritories, the distribution network also subdivides each territory by revenue-earning potential into A-, B-, and C-class centers. A-class centers are generally more populated—cities and large towns—with more cinemas, thus generating the most revenues for the distributor. Another defining feature of an A-class center is the ability to fully collect revenues, for producers and distributors frequently lament that once their films are in B- or C-class centers, which include touring cinemas, they have no means of accurately tracking a film's earnings. In practice, such a division meant that films were first released in A-class centers to garner their full commercial potential, after which they slowly made their way to B- and C-class centers.[11] Over the years, due to numerous factors such as piracy and the increasing significance of satellite television, the temporal lag between A-, B-, and C-class centers has reduced drastically as producers and distributors try to recoup the greatest revenues as quickly as possible.[12]

Agrawal and Malhotra's negotiation over the price of the film referred to two of the three main types of distribution arrangements existing in the film industry: the minimum guarantee system, commonly referred to as an "MG"; and the commission system. The most prevalent arrangement in the Hindi film industry has been the MG system, where the distributor bids for and guarantees the producer a specific sum that is disbursed in installments from the onset of production. Distributors normally pay 30 to 40 percent of the contracted amount to the film's producer during the production phase and the remainder at the time of the delivery of prints. At the time of the film's release, distributors pay for the print and publicity costs as well as theater rental. After distributors cover their costs—rights, prints, publicity, theater rental—and extract their 25 percent commission, any remaining box-office revenue, referred to as the "overflow," is split equally with the producer. In such a system, distributors bear the majority of the risk of a film's commercial outcome, since the producer is guaranteed a certain price for the film's rights. As the box-office outcome of any film is highly uncertain, producers with clout and power in the industry have been known to price their films in order to make a profit even prior to the film's release—sometimes even before the onset of production—which is referred to as a "table profit." Although the minimum guarantee system ostensibly accrues profits to producers once there is an overflow, the chances of a film earning enough revenues at the box-office to generate an overflow are relatively small.[13] Another factor in producers' pricing decisions is their distrust of distributors with respect to sharing the overflow, since distributors frequently use the revenues from successful films to cover their losses from unsuccessful films. Such a scenario is a consequence of the absence of a transparent system of data collection, especially when distributors are based far from Bombay.

The other two common distribution arrangements—commission and outright sale—have varying levels of risk associated with them. When a film is distributed on a commission basis, distributors bear the least amount of risk because the most they may invest in a film are in its publicity and print costs. Distributors deduct a certain percentage (25 to 50 percent) of box-office receipts as a commission and remit the rest to the

TABLE 3 CLASSIFICATION OF COMMERCIAL OUTCOME

Classification	Super-Hit (AA)	Hit (A1)	Semi-Hit (A)	Overflow (BB)	Commission Earner (B1)	Average (B)
Distributors' Earnings	3x cost or more	2 to 3x cost	about 2x cost	1.25 to 2x cost	1.2 to 1.25x cost	1 to 1.2x cost

Source: Based on "Classification: 1995" (1996); Nahta (interview, September 1996); and Verma (1997).

producer. In an outright sale, distributors pay producers for the right to distribute their films for a given time period, during which all expenses incurred and all income earned are solely the distributor's. Not a very common practice within India, outright sale was the most common arrangement for overseas distribution until the late 1990s, when certain producers began to put in place systems necessary to recover profits from overseas markets.[14]

Distributors are not only critical to the production process, but also to the classification of commercial outcome. Whether a Hindi film is categorized as a "hit" or a "flop" by the trade is actually based upon whether or not distributors make a profit and how much of it they make (Table 3). For example, a film that earns twice its cost, by which is meant the distributor's cost, is categorized only as a "semi-hit." Furthermore, even though distribution is decentralized, and there are very few all-India distributors, the trade press tends to represent an all-India or "universal" hit as the benchmark, so that if a film does extremely well in one or two territories, earning more than thrice its cost for its distributors—which could be categorized as a "super-hit"—but does not fare as well in other parts of India, its ranking gets downgraded.

Thus, the determination of commercial success or failure is actually connected to the distributor and not the theatrical audience. It is the distributor's pricing decisions rather than the number of tickets sold that determines whether a film is classified as a box-office success or failure. Such a formulation is connected to the fragmented nature of production and distribution, where the sale of distribution rights has been the most common source of finance capital for filmmaking. In the MG system, the distributor's profit is a fact that could be independent of how many people actually saw a film, for a distributor could have paid a high price for the rights of a film, yet may not have earned as high a profit as anticipated; therefore, the amount of profit is not necessarily congruent with the size of the viewing audience. The auction system for allocating distributors to films produces what is known in economic theory as a "winner's curse," so the distributor who wins the rights has the highest chance of having overestimated what a film will gross and therefore has the highest chance for a flop.[15] As the buyers of films, distributors occupy the structural position of consumers—albeit a specialized one—within the filmmaking process, but they are rarely implicated in the wide-ranging discussions about the commercial outcome of a film carried out in the film industry, the media, and among viewers. Instead, box-office performance is discussed by filmmakers in terms of audience composition, tastes, and desires. Hits and flops are interpreted and represented as indices of audience subjectivities rather than of distributors' commercial predictions.

IMMEDIACY AND DISTANCE: THE PERSONALIZED NATURE OF THE INDUSTRY

Whether it was the distributor from Delhi visiting the set unannounced, the aspiring writer meeting the director, or the senior writer dropping by to give a pitch, the sketch in chapter four portrays the centrality of face-to-face interaction in the Hindi film production process. Films, deals, and commitments are made on the basis of personal communication and discussion between key players, rather than via intermediaries or written materials. What I was struck by early on in my research was the relative absence within the industry of professional mediators, such as casting agents, talent scouts, or talent agencies, as well as gatekeepers such as publicists, agents, or personal managers.[16] To my surprise—but consistent with everyday practice—I was able to set up meetings or interviews directly with informants, rather than having to go through any type of professional mediator. The figure of the professional mediator is the most immediate locus of difference encountered by Indian and American filmmakers during their attempts to cross the borders of their respective filmmaking worlds.

Sabbir Khan is a Hindi filmmaker whose directorial debut, *Kambakkht Ishq* (This Damn Love, 2009), was a big-budget spectacle set against the backdrop of Hollywood, and included cameos by Sylvester Stallone, Brandon Routh, and other American actors. He spoke in an interview with the online magazine *rediff.com* about the inordinate amount of time it took him to just meet people and clear permissions in the United States. "I met dozens of agents to get access to their actors. That's very difficult, as we have to go through many agents before you meet the star's real agent."

Referring to shooting in iconic locations like the Kodak Theater where the Oscars are held, Khan stated, "There are so many channels to go through. That one year was spent in organizing all this" (N 2009).

If Khan found all of the channels and agents frustrating, Sri Rao, the American filmmaker introduced in this chapter's opening anecdote, was frustrated by the lack of them. He spoke at length during the panel about how the extremely personalized nature of the Hindi film industry, especially in relation to discussions over remuneration, was a source of bewilderment and aggravation. He related that despite his entreaties to discuss all money matters with his agents, the Bombay producers would continue to contact him directly, so that the negotiations over money became a long and circuitous process. Addressing his agents Rao said, "As you guys know, it took a long time to get them to understand that they needed to talk to you guys and not talk to me directly about how much money I'm going to make and what's going to be the contract and all that sort of thing." Turning back to the audience, Rao continued, "It would always be the sort of thing where David and Suchir would call them and they would call me. And then I would have to call them [his agents] and tell them that they [Yashraj] called me and could you please call them" (MIAAC 2009a).

The root of Rao's and Yashraj's mutual unintelligibility is that except for actors, the other creative personnel in the Hindi film industry—directors, writers, or musicians—do not have any formal gatekeepers or mediators serving as proxies for attaining work. Even actors who have achieved star status in the Hindi film industry do not have agents; rather they have people known as "secretaries" who primarily manage their work schedule referred to as "dates." For actors at the beginning of their careers who do not have prior connections to the film world, secretaries can serve as agents, in terms of arranging introductions with filmmakers, just as Jignesh did with the London-trained actor in the chapter four sketch. While a few secretaries in the industry have reached some positions of power, using their connections with stars to become producers, most secretaries are marginal to the negotiations between a producer and a star. Producers with clout and standing in the industry would consider it an insult to negotiate or consult with a star's secretary. The other members of a star's personal staff—makeup men (for actors), hairdressers (for actresses), drivers, or man Fridays referred to as "boys" (for male stars)—mainly consist of people who look after his or her physical appearance and material comforts, rather than serving as mediators with other members of the industry. Sometimes these individuals do serve as gatekeepers on sets and public spaces with respect to industry outsiders, as with the journalist trying to interview Vijay Khanna in the chapter four sketch.[17] The other creative personnel in the industry are even less likely to have their staff, if they possess one, operate as gatekeepers.

The insignificance of professional intermediaries means that interactions and relations are much more immediate and direct; therefore, if producers want a particular star for their film, they speak directly with the stars. When journalists want to meet stars for a story, they contact them personally or simply show up at a film shoot, sometimes without any prior notice, to conduct an interview. During my research, I enjoyed a similar level of access to members of the film industry. I was able to approach some of the biggest stars personally for interviews; some even had no qualms giving me their cell phone numbers.

The relative absence of professional intermediaries and gatekeepers, however, does not mean that the industry is a completely open and accessible world. Instead, personal relations and Bombay-based social networks serve as the mediating and gatekeeping forces within the industry. In the chapter four sketch, the aspiring screenwriter who comes to meet Rakesh Chadda, with a screenplay in hand, is able to do so because his aunt is Chadda's neighbor. Journalists who write for the glossy English-language film magazines such as *Stardust*, *Filmfare*, or *Cineblitz*, among others, frequently have some sort of prior connection to a star, such as attending the same high school or growing up in the same neighborhood. Additionally, every film journalist I met had their own exclusive set of stars—their own "star beat"—they covered, which cultivated the personal relationships necessary for easy access to stars.

As I continued to meet members of the film industry, asking them how they became involved in filmmaking, their stories revealed the importance of social networks for recruiting and incorporating personnel into the industry. For example, Vashu Bhagnani was in the business of manufacturing audiocassettes, and during our interview he told me that he was inspired to turn to film production after watching the film *Aankhen* (Eyes, 1993) because he enjoyed the film immensely. By virtue of his friendship with the owner of a music company who produced both film soundtracks and films, Bhagnani easily met the director and star of *Aankhen*, convincing them that he was a serious and committed producer. They agreed to take part in his maiden production and, according to Bhagnani, he was able to finish the film in a relatively short period of time, despite his absolute lack of experience in film production.[18]

While in Bhagnani's case the requisite enthusiasm, resources, and contacts enabled him to become a filmmaker, in other instances, man's best friend can pave the way, as in the case of screenwriter Anjum Rajabali, whose induction into the Hindi film industry was by way of his dog. During our interview, Rajabali narrated the fortuitous manner by which he became a screenwriter:

> We have a dog actually; through the dog we met this family of the Azmis — actually Shabana Azmi's brother, Baba Azmi, the cinematographer, and his wife, Tanvi Azmi, who's also an actress.[19] We were looking for somebody who would help us look after the dog because both of us were working — my wife and I. We bumped into them, and it worked out: we sort of hit it off very well. Through them we began meeting people in the film industry, but socially — at parties and at dinners or at the gym. But this friend of mine, Baba Azmi, he had had ambitions of graduating to director also. He wanted to direct films. He and I used to discuss a lot. So he said, "Why don't you write something?" I said, "I don't even know what structure, I have no idea how to write." He said, "No, you're interested: you write about what you would like to see." That was the starting point. (Rajabali, interview, September 1996)

Even though he had no background or professional interest in screenwriting, Rajabali said he decided to write a sequence of scenes to humor Azmi, who was becoming vehement about it. When Azmi praised his skills as a writer, Rajabali decided to teach himself by reading books about screenwriting and watching more films. Another chance encounter through a common friend led Rajabali to meet director Govind Nihalani, who asked him for feedback on a script that he was writing. Rajabali ended up collaborating on Nihalani's screenplay and that led to further opportunities and more assignments. What Bhagnani's and Rajabali's examples attest to is that personal relationships can far outweigh relevant experience in gaining access to the industry.

Social and kin networks played a central factor in my ability to attain access to members of the film industry as well. The vast majority of people I met, whether they were stars, directors, producers, writers, distributors, or exhibitors, I met through their friends and families via personalized, face-to-face introductions, frequently on film sets. For example, my first encounter with Shah Rukh Khan, who continues to be one of the most powerful, sought-after, and successful stars in the industry, was on the set of the film *Duplicate* in March 1996. I was sitting on the steps of the set next to Tanuja Chandra, at that point an aspiring director whom I knew from Philadelphia, and observing the activity around me.[20] Chandra was hanging around the set because her mentor, Mahesh Bhatt, was directing the film. Having already introduced me to the film's choreographer and art director, Chandra turned to me and asked, "Have you met Shah Rukh?" When I shook my head, she simply called out to Khan, who was standing nearby. "Shah Rukh, meet my friend Tejaswini: she's come from New York and she's writing a book about the film industry." Khan nodded, smiled, and held out his hand to shake mine. "Hello, how are you?" While I had not anticipated meeting one of the biggest stars of the industry so early in my fieldwork, that casual and simple introduction allowed me to start interviewing Khan the next day on the set, and continue my interview with him over the span of a week in a variety of locales, from other film sets to rehearsal halls, his car, and his home.

Another outcome of meeting filmmakers by way of their friends and family was that two different directors offered me the chance to join the team of directorial assistants for two films. Akin to the narratives of chance encounters and unexpected opportunity relayed by Bhagnani and Rajabali, my first job offer came about at the end of an interview with director Aditya Chopra in April 1996. Although Chopra was known to be extremely shy and averse to granting interviews, he agreed to my request since it was arranged through his mother, whom I had also interviewed.[21] At the time, Chopra was busy with the scripting and pre-production of the film *Dil to Pagal Hai* (The Heart Is Crazy), which his father, Yash, was to direct beginning in June of that year. When I asked Chopra if I could observe the film under production, I was totally caught by surprise when he asked me if I would like to work as an assistant on the film. During our discussion about what being an assistant would entail, Chopra was vague about the specifics and kept assuring me that my most important qualification was that I seemed to have tastes similar to his, while the most important requirement was that I had to love films. I worked on *Dil to Pagal Hai* mainly keeping track of costume continuity.[22]

How do those individuals without prior friends or family in the industry, or the social networks that bring one into contact with film people, fare? The answer depends on the occupational role to which one aspires. In terms of acting, women without connections have more chances at a film career than men in a similar situation, through routes such as beauty pageants, modeling, or even being "discovered" by self-appointed star-makers. Ironically, the patriarchal nature of the film industry enables unconnected women to gain entry because the success or failure of a film is not perceived to be dependent upon the lead actress, just as in the chapter four sketch, where the actress is a beauty pageant winner whose inability to speak Hindi did not prevent her from getting the role.[23] Heroines are usually chosen after the male star, director, and music director have been finalized for a film project, and are frequently regarded as interchangeable. The narrative thrust of films and the financing structures of the industry are wholly oriented around the male star.[24]

Individuals who aspire to become directors encounter greater obstacles if they are outside the kin and social networks that dominate the work life of the industry. The example of Sridhar Kumar, who was an assistant director when I first met him in 1996, is illuminating in this regard. A graduate of a prestigious national institution, Kumar came to Bombay with the ambition of becoming a director. Intrigued by my research, Kumar made it one of his missions to help me as much as possible and was instrumental in introducing me to people who enabled me to get access to significant events or individuals within the industry. Ironically, by the end of my first year of fieldwork, Kumar was asking me to introduce him to important people. Although he assisted three different directors, none of them played a significant role in his own directorial debut in 2003, eight years after he first arrived in Bombay. Assistants who are either friends with or related to directors usually do not have to wait as long to direct their first features, and if an aspiring director's father is a producer or director himself, then working as an assistant may not even be necessary before one's directorial debut. Kumar's debut film, which fared poorly at the box-office, did not garner him much standing within the industry, and he continued to struggle to establish himself as a viable director. Commercial success is not the only determinant of further employment in the industry, however, as there are plenty of examples of filmmakers who, despite their many commercial failures yet because of their family connections or close friendships with stars, keep getting the opportunity to direct films.

In 2006, during my last trip to Bombay, Kumar expressed his frustration with what he saw as the increasingly impenetrable social world of the film industry, which closed off opportunities for outsiders like him: "You know, some people in this industry are never allowed to fail; they keep getting multiple chances, and then there are those of us who barely even get one chance." We were sitting in an auto-rickshaw, stuck in traffic while traveling between the western suburbs of Andheri and Santa Cruz. I asked him to elaborate and he pointed out that people whose families have been involved with filmmaking have the financial security and family support to keep trying their luck at various roles within the industry. "If a man fails as an actor, he then tries his hand at direction; if he doesn't succeed as a director, then he becomes a producer and produces films starring his brothers or friends. They keep it all in the family, so how does someone from outside have a chance?" He also explained that for a new director to have a shot at having his film produced, he needs to be able to convince a star to come on board the project, but for unconnected individuals like Kumar it is difficult to develop relationships with stars prior to becoming successful or noticed: "Producers want stars, but how do I get a star? They're busy working for their own or their friends' films. They won't say no to their friends. I mean will Abhishek say no to Rohan?"[25]

Since his chances of cultivating a relationship with a star appeared slim, Kumar's strategy was to try to convince a high-profile producer, who would have no problem attracting stars to a project, of his talent and ideas. He told me that he was so desperate to meet Aditya Chopra, who had become a very powerful and successful producer, that he had befriended Chopra's driver, cooks, and even washer-man, hoping for some inside information that could lead to a chance meeting with him. "Having that Y stamp [the logo of Yashraj Films is a stylized Y] on my film would get me noticed," Kumar said. I thought back to my interaction with Chopra and how easily he offered me a chance to assist his father. Although his college training, work experience, and passion would have appeared to prepare Kumar for a career in filmmaking, he did not possess the most important element: friends in the right places.

KINSHIP AS A RELATION OF PRODUCTION
AND REPRODUCTION

From Chadda following in his father's footsteps to Malhotra installing his sons as assistant directors and producing his nephew's debut film, the chapter four sketch presents filmmaking almost as a hereditary occupation in India. While the Hindi film industry is very diverse in terms of the linguistic, regional, religious, and the caste origins of its members, the unifying characteristic of the contemporary industry is its quasi-dynastic structure. Although there are other avenues for entering the industry, kin and social networks have become the most dominant, especially for lead actors—and increasingly for directors.[26] Nearly everyone I met during the course of my research had entered the film industry through a family or friendship connection, and my own navigation of the industry was facilitated through extended kin networks. Additionally, film people have been marrying other film people—across caste, religious, and regional lines—and their children also enter into filmmaking, so that, by the time I began my fieldwork in 1996, it seemed as if the Hindi film industry was physically reproducing itself in all spheres: production, distribution, and exhibition.

The dominance of families in the film industry fits in with the overall landscape of commerce in India where, according to financial journalist Sudipt Dutta, more than 99 percent of Indian companies are family firms, and about 75 percent of the 100 largest companies in India are family businesses (1997: 17). The apparent hereditary quality of filmmaking is also akin to much of the folk and classical performance traditions in India, which historically have been hereditary vocations. Filmmaking, however, is different in a few ways. First, for much of its history, filmmaking was not a hereditary occupation in India. The individuals hailed as the pioneers of Indian cinema in the early twentieth century did not establish filmmaking lineages or dynasties.[27] In 1996, most of the senior producers, directors, composers, writers, and stars of the Hindi film industry were first-generation filmmakers, having had no family connections when they started their careers in the late 1940s and early 1950s. Unlike other performance traditions and commercial enterprises in India, which have historically been the sole preserve of a few caste communities, from its inception filmmaking has attracted a great diversity of individuals from all across India and beyond.[28] Finally, narratives about the agentive power of innate talent feature prominently in filmmakers' characterizations of stardom, which work to downplay the significance of kinship and social networks in enabling access to the profession. Industry lore is full of stories of outsiders who became superstars, along with the inverse: children of stars who, despite their family connections, could not achieve stardom.

Hindi filmmaking began to take on the characteristics of a hereditary vocation beginning in the early 1980s with the phenomenon of "star sons"—a term used by film journalists to refer to the sons of former actors—making their debut as actors, mainly in films produced by their fathers. This hereditary trend intensified from the mid-1990s and, by 2008, a little over 60 percent of the actors who appeared in leading roles hailed from film families; of the top-ten male stars in the industry—those actors who generated the biggest box-office revenues and were the most sought after by producers—eight were either second- or third-generation members of the film industry.[29] Members of the film industry explain the consistent presence of second- and third-generation actors as a result of environment and habitus. In my conversations with writers, distributors, and trade experts, many brought up the example of the actor Dharmendra and his sons. A very successful star in the 1970s, Dharmendra began his acting career in the 1960s. He started a production company, Vijayta Films, in the early 1980s to promote his elder son Sunny Deol as an actor. In 1994, he produced the debut film of his second son, Bobby. Screenwriter Sachin Bhaumick explained how natural it was that both of Dharmendra's sons became actors: "From childhood, they are seeing Dharmendra acting and Dharmendra's pictures. Because the atmosphere in the house is movie-oriented, they started knowing things. You can say they're getting one type of education because they are star sons" (Bhaumick, interview, October 1996).

Aamir Khan, whose father and uncle were both producer/directors, affirmed this point when discussing the advantages he had by coming from a film family:[30] "You see, I never had to learn films. These things I have been hearing all my life, so I knew the technicalities of filmmaking. A person who is not involved with films would have to start from scratch, you know. So in that sense there are advantages, you get to know how things work; you get to know how to deal with people; there are certain norms, perhaps, in the industry which you get to be aware of. Also, people give you a little more regard because you are from a film family." When I asked him if understanding the technicalities of cinema helped him as an actor, he replied in the affirmative and elaborated:

> I've heard so many scripts being discussed in my presence by my father or by my uncle, and the emphasis on characterization and how those things come out in a scene. Then, my years as an assistant director have also taught me a lot of things. I've observed lot of actors closely while they're working . . . You get to learn not only by the good performances but also by their mistakes, because you're watching their shots on the screen and in the editing room, and you get to know, you get to learn from that: you should have done this actually; you looked a little late; you looked a little early . . . All these things have helped. (Aamir Khan, interview, March 1996)

Since the dominant mode of training within the industry is by apprenticeship, being the children of filmmakers is a process of training by immersion. Pamela Chopra, whose husband and two sons are involved in filmmaking, reiterated this point: "I've seen it with my children . . . From the time that they were born, they've not seen anything else! We literally live, breathe, eat, sleep films! How can they help but being influenced? They can't help it. So when you're brought up in an atmosphere like that, you have . . . an advantage over others. You have certain knowledge that you have information that you have imbibed, without even realizing it, without knowing it, which is a very, very big advantage" (Pamela Chopra, interview, 26 March 1996).

Sutanu Gupta, a screenwriter who entered the industry via the Film and Television Institute of India (FTII), stated that the children of stars have an advantage over absolute outsiders because their parents can guide them through the pitfalls of the industry:

> They can tell them, "Don't work with this guy." You see that is another problem for newcomers, they don't know whom to work with, and whom not to. Nobody is there to guide him. Whereas these people [the children of stars] have their parents, and they'll say, "No, no, that man will never be able to, he's lost his touch, don't do his film," or . . . "No, he is a good technician, though he has made six flops, tomorrow he can give you a hit; you must do his film, because through his film, you get to the other films." Being star sons, they get the help from the parents because the parents know the industry. (Gupta, interview, 18 November 1996)

The social networks and specialized knowledge of the workings of the film industry to which industry offspring have access through their families is the cultural capital that contributes to their success. Gupta pointed out that a further advantage star children have is an ease and self-confidence arising from their life-long encounter with fame: "They are not over-awed by stardom. They've not come through competitions, talent competitions. It's not that they're wanting—they're dying—to become stars and they want to, and it suddenly changes them—it's not that—because they have been stars from childhood. By being Dharamji's son, Sunny was a star from childhood, or Bobby has been a star even before he hit the screen . . . At the same time . . . they don't want to do just any film, because they're not insecure" (Gupta, interview, 18 November 1996).

Others in the industry, especially those who control the financial side of the trade like producers and distributors, interpret this form of training by immersion and instant name recognition as a type of guarantee in a very uncertain business. Thus, the offspring of stars possess symbolic capital with distributors and producers that outsiders do not. Komal Nahta, the editor of *Film Information*, characterized the attitude producers and distributors have toward star children, which allow these men and women to charge—and receive—much higher compensations than others in the same stage of their careers:

Maybe these producers think acting is in the genes, because other-wise—you're right—there is no justification till a person, a hero or heroine, has proved himself or herself—there is no reason, but Bobby Deol right from his first film, first film was his father's film, or other-wise right from his first outside film, he'd been commanding a big price—and people were ready to pay. I think it's all because they feel that since he's from a film family, his father or his brother has been an actor, [he will have] knowledge "He's been brought up on films, so [he will have] basic knowledge; we will have to work less hard on him" . . . since he's chosen this as a profession obviously he will also put in his best; it's not that he has an alternative. Film people have no alterna-tive. If you've decided to be a hero, you'll be stuck there. They treat that as some sort of a guarantee, and they don't mind betting on a film per-son's son or a film person's brother. (Nahta, interview, September 1996)

Nahta's statements reveal how kinship operates as a way of managing risk.

Shyam Shroff states how star offspring offer more assurance to dis-tributors because their lineages are a known quantity, akin to thorough-breds at a horse race:

As a distributor [I] know this guy is Dharmendra's son . . . When you bet on a horse, you take out the history: whose son; whose daughter; whose grandchild . . . First of all, basically they are in the glamour; they are in the news; you've heard of them; you read about them. You write about Bobby Deol—what he's been doing since the time he was a kid or something . . . you're aware of him; you know about him, which is not possible in an absolutely raw newcomer: you've not even heard of him; you've not even seen his pictures. That becomes risky from that point of view; here, you are aware: "Oh, this is Dharmendra's son, so he's bound to be dashing." Dimple Kapadia—Rajesh Khanna's daughter— "oh, she's got to be beautiful." Because you've heard about the parents . . . it becomes easier, plus distributors are willing to buy the pictures at any price, so why not? It would be foolish on Dharmendra's part to make a movie and not take Bobby Deol . . . You have the added advan-tage. (Shyam Shroff, interview, April 1996)

Through Shroff's remarks it is apparent that offspring of stars, because they are already celebrities before even starting their careers, are brands, which signifies their name recognition, reliability, and marketability to distributors.

It is not surprising that kinship networks have intensified in the Hindi film industry since the mid-1990s, following India's policies of economic liberalization. Rather than being inimical to capitalism, scholars of family firms argue that kinship logics are operative in capitalism and that the spread and transformation of capitalism has made the family more economically essential.[31] Many businesses become hereditary once there is something to inherit, and economic security results from consolidating one's investment within the kin group.[32] A consequence of the greater economic potential and increased cultural legitimacy of Hindi cinema since the mid-1990s has been the increasing attractiveness of filmmaking as a career option for filmmakers' own children.

Kinship relations and networks, therefore, play a variety of roles within the industry: providing a source of personnel and a ground for training; operating as various forms of capital—social, symbolic, and cultural; and serving as a mode of risk management. In a business as unpredictable as filmmaking, working with family members serves to reduce risk—both in terms of hedging against the capriciousness of the box-office and countering the fragmented structure of the industry. A dependence on kin networks also functions as a method of gate keeping, however, since the extremely personalized nature of the film industry creates barriers for those individuals who have no family or social connections within it.

THE SOCIAL AND MATERIAL MANIFESTATION OF HIERARCHY

A Hindi film set is a site rich with information, not only about the production practices and work culture of the Bombay film industry, but also about the various social relations within the industry. The most notable expressions of status and hierarchy on a film set are forms of address, since Hindi, like many other languages, possesses both formal and informal registers in the use of second-person pronouns.[33] In the chapter four sketch, some people are only addressed by their first names and spoken to using the informal familiar address, while others have the Hindi honorific suffixes of *ji* (sir/madam) or *saab* (sir) added to their first or last names—a practice that carries over into English—and spoken to in the formal address. Respect, deference, and intimacy are all encoded into the grammatical structure of Hindi.

Relative rank and power, therefore, are easily discernible by observing conversations. For example, while everyone addresses the producer as Malhotra-*saab* and speaks to him using the most formal register, he calls almost everyone else by his or her first name, speaking to them with informal address, reflecting his power and position as the boss. That the producer refers to the distributor as Agrawal-*saab* and uses the formal address in his conversation accords with the status of the distributor who, as a potential buyer and financier of the film, is treated with suitable respect and deference. The director is in a more intermediate position in the set's hierarchy. His assistants, the aspiring writer, the heroine's mother, and Jignesh (the secretary) all address him as Rakesh-*ji*, indicating their subordinate relationship to him. Others—the producer, dance director, and the veteran writer—address him by his nickname, Rikki, indicating the familiarity that comes with rank (in the case of the producer), seniority and social connections (in the case of the writer), or career-stage similarity (in the case of the dance director).

A set can also be a site for the display of gestures of respect and deference, revealing the reverence for seniority, age, and experience. For example, in 1996, when I was observing the shooting of a song for *Sar Aankhon Par* at Filmalaya Studios, which featured guest appearances of stars from the 1960s, Sanjay Dutt visited the set to convey his regards to yesteryear's star, Shammi Kapoor. Dutt walked over from the neighboring set, trailed by a huge crowd of onlookers, went up to Kapoor, and bent down to touch his feet—a very conventional South Asian expression of respect for elders. Kapoor quickly raised him up and embraced him. The two conversed for a few minutes, seemingly oblivious to the huge crowd that had gathered around them. Dutt then returned to his set, again followed by a large crowd. People around me remarked that, despite Dutt's highly troubled life,[34] his basic *sanskaar* (cultured upbringing) was solid—illustrated by his deferential manner toward the veteran star.

Outsiders who are unaware of the industry's codes of respect and unfamiliar with its key figures can commit serious blunders. This became very apparent one afternoon in November 2005, when I was visiting the shoot of *Kabhi Alvida Na Kehna* (Never Say Goodbye) at the Sleepy Hollow Country Club in Tarrytown, New York. In addition to the crew members from India, a number of Americans were hired for the production, since the film was being shot for over three months in New York, New Jersey, Connecticut, and Pennsylvania. The film, which was produced and directed by Karan Johar, was quite a high-profile project due to its star cast; thus, a number of men were hired to serve as bodyguards (gatekeepers). While the shoot at the country club did not attract any fans or curious onlookers due to its remote location, instances of gate keeping were still occurring on the set. The one that violated the norms of the film industry was when one of the American bodyguards commanded Javed Akhtar—one of the most prominent, successful, and respected screenwriters and lyricists of the industry, who had been involved in filmmaking since the early 1970s, and whom Johar referred to as "Javed Uncle," signifying both his respect and long-term kin-like relation with Akhtar—to move away as he was walking toward Johar, who was watching a shot on the video monitor. Though Akhtar good-naturedly took what in Bombay would have been considered highly disrespectful behavior in stride, the Indian members of the crew who witnessed the interaction did not. While one immediately pulled the bodyguard aside and started reprimanding him seriously, the other escorted Akhtar back to the monitor and brought a chair for him to sit next to Johar.[35]

Conversations and personal interactions are not the only way to discern rank and status, for even something as quotidian as a chair can reflect materially the hierarchy present on a film set. I noticed that there were never many chairs on a set, and only certain people—generally the producer, director, actors, and their guests—warranted them. I was always aware of, and intrigued by, the circulation of chairs on a set, as they appeared to follow the movement of the principal players: workers regularly shifted chairs to wherever the director, star, or producer was standing at the time. I experienced firsthand the difference that one's status makes in terms of having access to a chair on a set; as a scholar conducting research about filmmaking, I was treated as a guest on most film sets and accorded a great deal of hospitality—including a chair—but when I became a directorial assistant on a particular film, I found myself standing for hours on end as assistants rarely sat down while working, then never in a chair, and definitely not in front of their superiors. Only if the director appeared to be relaxed while seated did assistants occasionally perch or lean against areas of a set. In the case of a star's personal staff, they would never sit in the presence of their boss.

While a film's director is commonly characterized as the "captain of the ship" by members of the industry and accorded the most deference on a film set, each department and task contains its own hierarchy and chain of command. For example, camera attendants defer to the main camera assistant, who defers to the director of photography. Almost everyone is in a position of being a superior or a subordinate relative to someone else. Even among workers within the same department, a hierarchy is established based upon their age and years spent in the industry. By noticing who yelled at whom, I quickly discerned the various pecking orders. Ranking at the bottom of the hierarchy are the "spot boys" (Figure 9). This

FIGURE 9 Spot boys cleaning the set of *Kuch Na Kaho*, Mehboob Studios, Bandra (western suburb of Bombay), 2000. Photo by the author.

term refers to the men who do all forms of miscellaneous work, but who primarily take care of the most domestic of duties on a film set, such as bringing and moving chairs, serving drinks, setting out the food, cleaning up, and running errands. At the other end of the spectrum are the stars, who represent the apex of the film industry's hierarchy.

Spending time on a Hindi film set, it is hard to miss the stark contrast between stars and everyone else around them, especially the way stars are accorded a great deal more basic comforts than the rest of the cast and crew. My first encounter with a star was in February 1996, when I observed Juhi Chawla, a popular and successful actress at that time, on the set of the film *Daraar* (Chasm). I had finished interviewing Omar Qureishi, the editor of the film magazine *Stardust*, and he asked me if I would like to accompany him to Mehboob Studios, where he needed to meet Chawla for an upcoming issue of the magazine. I readily agreed, as this was to be my first visit to a film set. A song was being filmed with Chawla that day, and the set was what in Hindi movie parlance would be known as a "cabaret"—a combination restaurant/bar/nightclub, with space for a dance performance. The shooting floor was extremely hot and stuffy and constant attention was paid to keeping Chawla comfortable. When she was on the set, a fan was directed only toward her and not others. If she had to wait for a shot to be set up, she sat outdoors on the studio lawn while the other participants sat indoors in the heat.

While the chorus dancers were made to practice their dance steps continuously by the dance director, Chawla spent her time outside speaking to an assortment of film journalists. She rehearsed her steps just a few times before the sequence was filmed. Furthermore, by being seen with Chawla, Qureishi and I were accorded a fair amount of hospitality as well—without asking, chairs were brought for us and cold soft drinks were placed in our hands.

The physical space of a Hindi film set, along with its accompanying production venues like the old Bombay studios, reinforce the status differences between stars and others in a number of ways. Basic amenities, such as toilets, makeup rooms, air conditioning, seating areas, and shaded outdoor spaces, are all in short supply at the main shooting studios in Bombay, so while stars have access to such comforts, the rest of the cast has to make do with less or nothing. Chorus dancers and extras—referred to as "junior artists" in the film industry—often do not have access to makeup rooms or even bathrooms. If a shoot takes place somewhere other than a studio, air-conditioned trailer-vans equipped with bathrooms are hired for the stars, but not for others. When an outdoor shoot lacks areas with shade, individual stars are shielded from the sun by men holding umbrellas; everyone else is left to their own resources (Figure 10).

In August 2007, the Federation of Western India Cine Employees (FWICE), an organization consisting of 22 unions representing a variety of trades working in the film industry, issued an ultimatum to Filmistan Studios and Film City—popular shooting and production venues in suburban Bombay—to improve their basic amenities. Citing the lack of drinking water, changing rooms for junior and character artists, and sanitary or even functioning toilets, FWICE demanded that the two studios rectify the conditions by September 1 or it would issue noncooperative directives against the studios, which would mean that no producer would be permitted to shoot there. The manager of the state-owned and -operated Film City requested two months to carry out the necessary upgrades. Despite such assurances, no progress was made on the issue and almost a year later, on July 19, 2008, workers went on a four-hour "flash" strike to protest the lack of basic amenities such as clean toilets and changing rooms in Film City. The strike was called off when filmmaker Mahesh Bhatt intervened, assuring workers that he would bring the issue to the Maharashtra minister of culture's attention. On August 1, the management of Film City once again assured a delegation that the demands of workers would be fulfilled, adding that facilities would be provided for

FIGURE 10 Kajol, Juhi Chawla, Aamir Khan, and Ajay Devgan shielded from the sun on the set of *Ishq*, Film City, 1996. Photo by the author.

technicians, junior artists, and actors as well. As of January 2009, however, according to trade periodicals such as *Film Information*, these promises had yet to be realized.

The disparity in working conditions is taken for granted and often reinforced by producers. During my visit to a film shoot at Mehboob Studios in 2000, I noticed that there were trailers parked in the studio compound, an unusual sight since the studios had makeup rooms, bathrooms, and other standard amenities. Upon inquiring, I learned that since the makeup rooms at Mehboob were not air-conditioned, the producers procured air-conditioned trailers for the stars. When I mentioned to the director's sister, who was assisting him on his debut film, that such trailers seemed to be a new development compared to my previous trip to Bombay, she complained about the arrogance of the background dancers—because they were demanding makeup rooms with air conditioning as well. Indignant about their attitude, she kept asserting that she would like to do a "judo-chop" to them.

THE CENTRALITY OF STARS

The stark difference between stars and the rest on a film set are a material manifestation of the tremendous power that they wield within filmmaking, specifically in the conceptualization stage. It is important to note that all actors are not categorized as "stars" by the Hindi film industry, which has a particular taxonomy of actors related to narrative presence, commercial success, career trajectory, and tenure within the industry.[36] Furthermore, celebrity is not synonymous with stardom within the industry. Since 1996, at any given point of time, only about five to six actors are deemed top stars by the industry, based on their box-office draw and performance. Thus, stars are those select actors who not only essay the roles of male and female protagonists within a Hindi film narrative, but also are regarded as a scarce commodity by producers, distributors, and financiers, and thereby monopolize the finance capital of the industry.

Producers and directors are not the only ones with the power to greenlight a film in the Hindi film industry. Male stars frequently initiate projects—or are the first ones consulted about a project—as depicted in the chapter four sketch, where Lakhani approaches Khanna with an offer to star in a film, even though its script has yet to be written.[37] If aspiring writers, producers, or directors can persuade a male star about their story idea or script, the chances of it turning into a film are very high, since casting a male star is usually the first step in putting together a Hindi film. This characteristic is illustrated by the interaction between Chadda and the aspiring screenwriter Alok Sharma. Chadda asks who Sharma has in mind for the role of the "hero" of the film even before the writer finishes his description of the script. Sharma requests that Chadda speak to Khanna about the film, in the hope that Khanna's interest and approval of the script might translate into Malhotra's willingness to produce the film. A star's readiness to participate signals to producers, financiers, or directors the viability of a project, and once a star is on board, this fact is used in the pre-production stage—or in the early stages of production—to raise finance and sell the distribution rights of the film.

Producer/directors with standing and power in the industry do initiate their own film projects; these projects are usually conceived with a particular male star or set of stars in mind, however. All of the screenwriters I had met and interviewed impressed this fact upon me. Veteran screenwriter Sachin Bhaumick spoke to me at length about how he goes about writing a script, which is tailored to the particular star the producer has finalized for the film: "You need to know that nobody buys a story just by hearing a story here. The producer comes and says, 'I can get Akshay Kumar and Saif; have you got a two-hero subject?' Then I narrate a subject, because the picture's salability depends on the stars, not on the writer. Nobody hears the story and then selects the artist" (Bhaumick, interview, October 1996). Even if a script is written prior to selecting a star, a project can be shelved due to the star's lack of interest. Screen-writer Anjum Rajabali described a case that he felt was the correct way of planning a film—he wrote a script for which he was paid; a director had been finalized, but when the script was narrated to the star, he refused the part: "We had to abandon the project. I said, 'Go get somebody else; it's a damn good role,' but they [the producer and director] said, 'No, we want him, so abandon it.' So once a star says yes, it works" (Rajabali, interview, September 1996). Bhaumick reiterated the importance of a story appealing to a star: "See what happens, a producer will come to me and say, 'I can get Shah Rukh Khan, but with great difficulty, so I need a story that Shah Rukh will like.' I have to keep in mind Shah Rukh Khan and write a story and if he likes it, then they will make the picture" (Bhaumick, interview, October 1996).

In the chapter four sketch, the interaction between Chadda and Sharma also raises a series of issues about the gendered dimension of stardom and power in the industry. Although Sharma describes the film as a woman's struggle, Chadda searches for a hero in the film—asking Sharma about his preferences for a male star. When Sharma states he had Vijay Khanna in mind, Chadda immediately criticizes the choice, asserting that a star of Khanna's stature would not want to act in a film where the heroine's role is more significant than his. Films that have a woman as the protagonist or main narrative agent are referred to as "heroine-oriented," and a central truism within the industry is that such films have a hard time succeeding commercially at multiple levels. Producers are not interested in developing scripts with women at the center, since they would have a hard time bringing on board a top male star, thereby encountering difficulties in selling the distribution rights, which had been the main source of finance for a film until the advent of corporatization. Bhaumick lamented how the exclusive focus on the male star was a creative constraint: "Even if I have two or three ideas for a heroine-oriented subject, nobody wants to listen to them. I'll tell a producer, 'Look, I have a really good idea for a heroine-oriented film, Madhuri Dixit will be perfect in it,' but they're not interested. They always say, 'It won't sell, because the moment you take a heroine-oriented subject, I cannot go to Shah Rukh, Ajay Devgan, Sunny Deol [top male stars]; all of them will refuse. If you take a new guy, it will not sell'" (Bhaumick, interview, October 1996).

The reason that heroines "don't sell" is due to the second prevailing belief that female stars do not generate the huge first weekend box-office

collections, referred to as an "initial" or an "opening" in industry parlance, that has become a crucial barometer of a film's commercial success.
Female stars are simply not perceived as having the same box-office clout
as male stars. Screenwriter Sutanu Gupta explained, "The game today is
to get the initial, rake in as much as possible. Woman-oriented subjects
. . . don't have an initial. It is the word of mouth which spreads. A hero-
oriented subject gets an initial and that's why distributors find it safe"
(Gupta, interview, 18 November 1996).

Despite this dominant belief, a small number of films with women as
the central protagonist do get developed and produced, but each of these
films tends to be accompanied by a great deal of discourse about the difficulties that the film will face with distributors and audiences. Producers
also look for ways to mitigate the risks of these films by trying to re-
cruit a male star to act in the film, even as a special appearance. In 1996,
I was able to observe the pre-production process of the film *Dushman*
(Enemy, 1998), which was being produced by Pooja Bhatt, an actress who
had recently turned producer. *Dushman* was Bhatt's second film as a producer, and she had gotten one of the top female stars at the time, Kajol,
to play the lead in the film, which was about identical twin sisters, with
one avenging the rape-murder of the other. Although the film was very
mainstream in terms of its narrative, aesthetic, and use of music, Bhatt's
uncle, Mukesh, who was guiding her early efforts in production, kept displaying an ambivalence about the project. On the one hand, he would assert how unique it was that "one heroine has signed another heroine for
a film," encouraging Bhatt to trumpet this fact with distributors and the
trade, but on the other he would assert how heroines do not pull in the
crowds. Bhaumick, who was one of the writers of the film, told me about
Mukesh's worries about the film: "Even Mukesh Bhatt says, 'I will not be
able to sell without a big hero'" (Bhaumick, interview, October 1996). One
afternoon Pooja, her father, uncle, and Tanuja Chandra, who was directing the film, had a long discussion about possible male leads opposite
Kajol. They kept throwing out names of actors who were characterized
as newcomers. By the time the film went into production, the script had
been changed and leading male star, Sanjay Dutt, had been recruited to
play an important role, though his name was never mentioned during
the early phases of the film's planning. None of the actors from the initial
casting discussions were in the film, confirming Bhaumick's point that,
while films with established male stars and debutant actresses do not encounter difficulties in the trade, "new boys don't sell."

Sridhar Kumar, the struggling director, released his first film in 2003;

it starred seven actresses of varying stardom, but no male star. A testament to industry tenets, the film did not open well at the box-office. While Kumar acknowledged he was taking a risk with his directorial debut, he maintained that the risk would have been mitigated somewhat if the producer had requested that his friend, a top male star, play a key role in the film. What disturbed Kumar the most was the fact that the star frequently spent time on his set: "He was there every day, just sitting there and drinking tea and hanging out! How hard would it have been for him to do the role? I'm sure if my producer had asked him, he would have done it. I don't understand!" Kumar's lament points to two of the most important attributes governing success in the industry—male stars and personalized relationships.

The centrality of stars to the filmmaking process is further underscored by the tremendous amount of discourse—mostly negative and critical—about them within the film industry, and the frequency with which producers and directors tried to represent their creative autonomy by invoking the figure of the star as a foil. Producer/director Rakesh Roshan's exposition of his superior filmmaking practice, during our interview, focused a great deal on how he was able to handle infamously temperamental stars. He emphasized that a good director needed to exhibit clarity of vision and command over the filmmaking process in order to keep actors in line. He pointed out how an actor, with his fame, persona, and entourage, could overwhelm and intimidate directors: "Sometimes what happens is, if you are not clear, an actor can come and confuse you. See, because an actor is a very dominating personality—he comes in a big car; there are twenty people following him; he's got his spot boys—so the director's in awe of that actor, and if the actor suggests something, the director thinks, 'If I say no to him, he'll feel bad,' so he says, 'Haan yeh accha idea, aisa kar lete' [Yes, this is a good idea, let's do it like that], but he's not going with the screenplay; he's going with the actor. He's being dominated by his personality" (Roshan, interview, May 1996).

Roshan mentioned that he was very aware of the jockeying for power on a film set undertaken by actors, because he was once an actor and remembered criticizing his directors: "An actor on the very first day comes to know, like a [race] horse comes to know, whether he [has] a good rider or not: an actor comes to know [that] in the very first shot, 'Yeh kuch chalne waale nahin hai' [This guy isn't going to budge], so we have to do as he says; we have to be very punctual with this man, because he honors his commitment" (Roshan, interview, May 1996). Roshan further stated that a director's behavior and professional demeanor set the tone for actors' own behavior: "If am perfect, if I am honoring all my commitments, I don't see why an actor will not be punctual with me, [or] will misbehave with me" (Roshan, interview, May 1996). "Ninety-nine percent" of the time, according to Roshan however, actors were not handled properly by directors, which were why they became "dominant" and gave producers and directors trouble—defined mainly by perennial tardiness. He rounded out his discussion with a couple of anecdotes demonstrating his skill at managing stars who were noted for being difficult, thus revealing his exceptionalism as a filmmaker.[38]

If Roshan cited his firmness and authority over stars to express his greater creative autonomy in comparison with his colleagues, producer/director Subhash Ghai asserted his ability to make commercially successful films without established stars as evidence of his distinction and mastery within the industry. He represented himself as a revolutionary risk-taker, with casting decisions that bypassed prevailing stars. Referring to his film *Vidhaata* (1982), Ghai said, "I was fed up with stars, so I took the absolutely old man, Mr. Dilip Kumar, and absolutely new boy, Sanjay Dutt, and I deleted all of the middle generation of stars" (Ghai, interview, October 2000). He explained that he became frustrated with stars, specifically their sense of self-importance, and the hold they had over the industry. Describing the genesis of his film *Hero* (1983), Ghai stated that initially he was going to make a film with Kamal Hassan, a popular star from the Tamil film industry. After the commercial success of his debut Hindi film, however, Hassan had become so temperamental and inaccessible that Ghai decided to drop him from his project: "He made lots of *nakras* [frivolous complaints] and made me run for six months. One day I wrote him, 'Thank you very much; you're a good actor, but I'm making a different film.' Within six days I thought of an idea, which was *Hero*. I picked up a boy from some corner in Bombay, and next day I cast him as the hero of my film." *Hero* was a big commercial hit and the actor introduced by Ghai, Jackie Shroff, became a major star of the late 1980s and early 1990s. Ghai's discovery of Shroff—and Shroff's subsequent success—became a part of Ghai's self-representation and the film industry's lore, expressed in the trade and general press, about him as a powerful star-maker.

Ghai further elaborated upon his exceptionalism by mentioning a time when he began shooting a film with one of the top stars of the industry, then decided to abandon the project after ten days because he could not deign to laugh at the star's bad jokes. Ghai periodically asserted throughout our interview that he never wanted to laugh at a star's bad jokes, which emblematized the unequal status and hierarchical relationship between stars and producers or directors: "That will be my death, that is what I have always thought. Every ugly or boring joke of a star, I would not like to be a filmmaker of that stature." After he rejected working with the particular star, Ghai said that he received many accolades from his peers, for his action had "created a lot of confidence in the directors' community." Although Ghai cited this anecdote as an example of his autonomy and status as a producer/director, the fact that he asked me to not identify the star bespeaks the actual hierarchies existing with the industry. By the time I met Ghai in 1996, he was working with established male stars and has continued to work with them, while his "discovery" and introduction of new actresses has diminished over time.[39]

NOT-HOLLYWOOD: TO HOLD AS IT WERE THE MIRROR . . .

This chapter provided a broad overview of the structure of the Hindi film industry in order to disrupt universalist assumptions about mainstream feature film production that are primarily founded upon structures and practices specific to Hollywood. What insights about media production does the example of the Hindi film industry provide? First, that entrepreneurial capital and a decentralized network of production, distribution, and exhibition are capable of producing media forms that are as globally circulating, ubiquitous, and commercially successful as those produced by integrated media conglomerates funded by industrial and corporate capital. The next chapter illustrates that dominant media—big-budget large-scale feature films—can be produced under conditions that do not exhibit the characteristics of a Weberian bureaucratic rationality. Additionally, I hope the structure and organization of the Hindi film industry hold up a mirror to Hollywood's, which are beyond the scope of this book, and reveal how film production is always situated socially, culturally, and historically.

This chapter also demonstrated the prevalence of the sentiment of disdain in filmmakers' characterizations of the structure and organization of the film industry, which plays an important role in filmmakers' efforts at boundary-work. Additionally, the minimal barriers to entry and the significance of stars are features of the industry that continue to draw criticism from filmmakers and figure in their discussions about professionalism, quality, and commercial success. Perhaps an object of even more pronounced disdain and criticism is the work culture of the Hindi film industry, which is the focus of the next chapter.

CHAPTER 6

Sentiments of Disdain and Practices of Distinction

The Work Culture of the Hindi Film Industry

During the question and answer session with the cast and director of the film *The Loins of Punjab Presents*—a quirky comedy set among the Indian American community in New Jersey—which had been screened at the South Asian International Film Festival held in New York, in October 2007, one of the actors, Darshan Jariwalla, discussed how working in this particular film was such a pleasant departure from the standard "Bollywood" fare. He drew loud laughter from the full auditorium when he contrasted the director's working style with the norms of the Hindi film industry.[1] Stating that the whole process was very professional, because the film had a "bound script" (a completed script), which everyone read together, Jariwalla said, "There are none [scripts] in Hindi cinema. Whoever has the nicest handwriting writes the script; whoever comes on the set first directs the scene that day."

Jariwalla's sarcasm is not at all unusual, for the Hindi film industry has been a frequent object of mockery, ridicule, and parody—both by those unfamiliar with the industry as well as industry insiders—for its working style.[2] The dominant image of the film industry has been that of a chaotic, eccentric world populated with uneducated, uncouth, and at times, unsavory people. Even Hindi filmmakers are quite critical and disparaging of the industry's overall work ethic, representing the film industry as unprofessional and disorganized. For example, producer Firoz Nadiadwala declared at one point in our interview, "There's nothing that is organized in this place—right from the artist's dates, to the money that is paid, or to any of the technicians, nothing is organized. Everything is organized in a disorganized manner. We are organized to be disorganized" (Nadiadwala, interview, October 2000).

Throughout my fieldwork I heard similar statements from other filmmakers, who lamented the lack of discipline and professionalism among their peers and presented themselves in the forefront of trying to organize and professionalize the industry. I never met a single filmmaker who represented himself as the norm; nearly everyone in the industry represented himself or herself as harder working, more professional, and more quality-conscious than the "typical" Hindi filmmaker. Rather than being an empirical entity, the figure of the "typical" Hindi filmmaker, akin to that of the "proposal-maker," serves as a foil against which actual filmmakers define their own principles and practices of filmmaking; therefore, the sentiment of disdain expressed about the working style of the industry is another instance of boundary-work indulged in by Hindi filmmakers, as are their practices of distinction—by which I mean filmmakers' efforts to assert their difference from a generic norm, such as Jariwalla's mention of the "bound script."

In order to understand these sentiments of disdain and practices of distinction, however, it is necessary to know the working style of the industry. While the previous two chapters described the everyday life of Hindi film production and discussed some of the core features of the structure and organization of the industry, this chapter examines the work culture of the industry—an object of great criticism and disparagement by filmmakers, journalists, and sundry observers for decades. The inordinate amount of criticism and contempt about the working style of the industry expressed by filmmakers during my fieldwork was often articulated in conjunction with an equal amount of praise and admiration for Hollywood's perceived efficiency and organization. Although Hindi filmmakers are quite self-critical in their comparisons with Hollywood, they nonetheless manage to assert a form of cultural autonomy and exceptionalism: that despite the various constraints under which they operate, Hindi filmmakers are still able to produce films that have the potential to be wildly popular across the world. An acknowledgment of this popularity is the fact that Hollywood studios, since 2006, have become keen on partnering with Bombay producers to produce Hindi films in India.

Drawing and expanding upon the ethnographic material presented in chapter four, I first discuss the informality of the industry in terms of the blurred boundaries between work and home, as well as the absence of a clear-cut division of labor between the various occupational roles on a film set. Following that, I describe the tremendously oral nature of scripting, shooting, and negotiating. Then, I examine the reasons for Hindi filmmakers' highly flexible and improvisational style of working. After that, I detail filmmakers' relatively low-impact style of working and their prudent use of resources. Paradoxically, these very same attributes—informality, orality, flexibility, and minimal use of technology—are often the object of criticism and disdain by Hindi filmmakers in their representations and discourses about the film industry. Finally, I demonstrate how Hollywood—more specifically an imagined Hollywood—is invoked in filmmakers' discussions about professionalism, work discipline, and creativity.

INFORMALITY AND FLUID BOUNDARIES

Whether it is Malhotra negotiating a distribution deal, Debojit Das dropping by to pitch a story idea for a film, or the film journalist carrying out an interview with Vijay Khanna, in the chapter four sketch there is as much action off camera as there is in front of it. Even in a gated environment like a studio, a Hindi film set is a quasi-public space, where all sorts of activities occur in addition to the scene or scenes being shot: distribution rights are negotiated; other films are pitched, planned, or scripted; struggling hopefuls seek an audience with either a producer or a director; interviews are conducted by the media; and even fans turn up to obtain autographs or to be photographed with stars. In fact, while a film is under production, the set operates more as an office than filmmakers' actual offices. Since lighting a set takes a considerable amount of time, actors and directors have chunks of free time while on a shoot, during which they receive and interact with a steady stream of visitors. Additionally, a complex politics of status and respect exists between producers and stars, and the location of their meeting is an indication of relative status and power. Producers frequently meet stars on set when they are shooting a film, since sets—more than homes, offices, or makeup rooms—are regarded as neutral terrain. In the chapter four sketch, Lakhani chooses to wait for Khanna in the studio compound rather than meet him in his makeup room to discuss a potential film offer; this is an exemplary situation of these politics of space.

When I began research, I was unprepared for the informal working style of the film industry, with its lack of clear-cut spatial and temporal boundaries regarding different forms of work and leisure. When I approached members of the industry with a request for an interview, I was taken aback by their immediate willingness, especially if we were on a film set. I did not anticipate that actors or directors would speak with me while they were working, imagining rather that I would have to set up an appointment for a specific time and place—separate from the spaces of production—to conduct my formal interviews. I learned very quickly that I always needed to carry my tape recorder and lists of questions with me, because I never knew when a chance meeting could result in an interview.[3] I found myself conducting interviews—whether ad hoc or scheduled—in a variety of locations: film sets, makeup rooms, photographers' studios, recording studios, editing suites, homes, coffee shops, hotel bars, and even people's cars.[4]

This sort of immediacy of access and informality was not always viewed favorably by members of the industry, especially popular actors, who were the most likely to be visited during a film shoot. While discussing a star's relationship to his fans, during our interview that took place on the rooftop terrace of an apartment complex in suburban Bombay (where he was shooting for the film *Ishq* [Love]), Aamir Khan mentioned the challenges of working in an environment with minimal gate keeping: "There are times when you're trying to concentrate on your work . . . Unfortunately our office space is everybody else's public space, you know. Like we're shooting in this building now: this is my office. If twenty kids come and ask me for my autograph, what they are in fact doing is entering my office, opening my door, and while I am working coming in and saying, 'Sign those papers later, give that shot later; first, we want our autograph,' so that's a little unfair I guess sometimes, you know, it's disturbing sometimes" (Aamir Khan, interview, March 1996). Given Khan's popularity, there was a continuous stream of children and adults who lived in the complex visiting the roof to see him, ask for autographs, and pose for pictures (Figure 11).

A clear-cut distinction between work and home spaces, which exists in other modern urban professions in India, does not exist to the same extent in the film industry. The only formal offices I went to were those of exhibitors, some distributors, and a few producers. On the content-creation side of the film industry—in contrast to the business side—the people with offices, administrative staff, and other trappings of modern urban work-life are producers. Many of these offices are quite minimalist

FIGURE 11 Aamir Khan signing autographs during the shoot of *Ishq* in Tarapur Gardens Apartment Complex, Oshiwada (northwestern suburb of Bombay), 1996. Photo by the author.

in terms of staff and the amount of work taking place. Much of the preproduction of a film, such as scripting sessions, music composition, and discussions about production design, usually takes place in filmmakers' homes rather than their offices, a social fact alluded to by Malhotra telling his nephew and the screenwriter Debojit Das to meet at his home to discuss Das's idea for a film. Pamela Chopra, who is involved with her husband's and son's films, either formally as a writer or a co-producer, or informally in other capacities, described how the lack of defined work space enabled her to become involved in filmmaking as well.

> Our family is a completely *filmi* family, so we're all involved in various aspects of filmmaking. I am, you could say, involved with the writing, but I'm not actually writing. It's happened really because my husband likes to work at home. A lot of the work connected with making a film ... doesn't require office space or a certain set of people: nothing like that. You can—you could—very comfortably sit in your drawing room and discuss the subject, or the script, or the scene, or even the music of a film, which happens a lot in our house, so he used to work a lot at home, and after my children were born and they were slowly growing up, I found that I was getting involved in the process that was going on. (Pamela Chopra, interview, 28 February 1996)

The reminiscences of second- or third-generation members of the film industry, about witnessing scripting or music composition sessions as children, emphasized that filmmakers' homes were important spaces of production. This early exposure to processes of film production is one of the advantages of growing up within the industry.

When a film is under production, producers' offices tend to have a very quiet and deserted quality about them. In fact, it seems that the office is a place to go to when there is no other work to be done. A couple of my key informants, an actress, Radhika, and a director, Tarun—both in their twenties, and having grown up and worked together frequently—would go to the offices of Radhika's family's production company whenever they were not shooting or otherwise occupied with some aspect of film production.[5] They spent their time watching television, talking on their cell phones, or playing games on the computer. Sometimes Radhika's father, a very busy director, or her uncle, an equally busy producer, even used one of the office rooms to take a nap.

Along with the absence of discrete workspaces, the film industry lacks a strict division of labor among those responsible for the narrative component of films.[6] Given the close-knit nature of many production teams—referred to as "units" in Bombay—where people work repeatedly with friends or family members, strict boundaries between individuals and their assigned tasks are not maintained. For example, during the shooting of a song sequence for the film *Duplicate*, at Mehboob Studios in Bandra in 1996, I observed the producer's son, Karan Johar— as of 2010 one of the most successful and influential producer/directors in the industry—choreographing some of the movements for the background dancers; at the time Johar's only qualification was being a long-established producer's son.[7] Even after Johar established himself as a successful director, he would work on his friends' productions in other capacities—most notably as costume designer for superstar Shah Rukh Khan.

The lack of well-defined roles and duties among principal players can be disconcerting to those who are not accustomed to it. I recall my friend Sandeep's experiences as an executive producer.[8] While Sandeep's extended family had been involved in Hindi filmmaking for two generations, Sandeep grew up in Britain and went to college in the United States. He had moved to Bombay in 1996 with a desire to make films, quickly becoming a part of a new production company started by one of his grandfather's colleagues. Sandeep was utterly dismayed on the first day of a shoot when workers in the setting (set design) department asked him to place photographs in frames, since they were unable to do so. He kept protesting. "I can't believe I'm doing this! I'm the bloody executive producer!" The following day when one of the assistant directors told him that they needed a cushion for the living room, Sandeep exploded. "I'm the bloody executive producer! Why are you telling me? That's the setting department's job!" Clearly he did not recognize that specific titles, such as "executive producer," have not carried much import within the industry, and the operative occupational categories with creative decision-making power are that of star, director, producer, writer, dance director (choreographer), music director (composer), action director, lyricist, art director, editor, and cinematographer.[9] Indeed, since most people play multiple roles, the industry is filled with people who are both producers and directors, writers and directors, editors and directors, actors and producers, or even a combination of actor/director/producer.[10]

The fluidity of occupational roles translates even to the various workers on a film set, especially when a Hindi film is being shot on locations in the United States or Europe where crew sizes tend to be attenuated for the reasons of budget or international work regulations. For example, in the case of *Awara, Paagal, Deewana* (Wayward, Insane, Crazy) a film that I closely observed being shot in the United States in July 2001, the production's spot boys were denied visas to enter the United States; therefore, the lighting assistants carried out the work that spot boys normally did on a film set. Much like Sandeep, who was unsettled by workers not honoring his title of executive producer, Sri Rao described how he and his crew working on *New York* were thrown off by the Indian crew's indifference to maintaining a clear-cut division of labor among the various categories of film workers. "With us, it's very delineated. Every position has their specific roles, and the unions are very specific and you can't cross lines at all," he explained. "With them, it's sort of like a free-for-all. And if you're a grip, you're also a gaffer and if you happen to be standing around and happen to be near something, a stand or a mike or a prop or something, or someone needs help being changed or something, then you can be wardrobe all of a sudden. And that was really tough for us" (MIAAC 2009a). Positing the difference between the American and Indian crew, in terms of the values of professionalism and work quality versus efficiency and expediency, Rao asserted that the two crews were able to reach a "happy medium." He concluded his recollection by saying, "Ultimately we sort of drew lines, because we — the Americans — needed to draw the lines, but we drew the lines more broadly than we would have normally drawn them" (MIAAC 2009a).

The emphasis on face-to-face interaction, collaboration, and fluid work-spaces results in a highly oral and aural work culture, with a tremendous reliance on memory. Pitching ideas for a film—as Debojit Das did in the chapter four sketch—is one of the many examples of this working style. Whether it was a film being conceptualized, music being composed, a script being discussed, or production logistics being planned, I rarely saw anyone writing anything down. The pre-production process is mostly comprised of brainstorming sessions—referred to as "sittings"—attended by the director and key members of the production team, during which the script and music are finalized.[11] Sometimes these sessions, especially those involving the film's narrative in the early stages, were so casual and meandering—appearing to be a conversation between a few people—that it took me some time to realize that work was taking place. One afternoon, in November 1996, I was waiting in a producer's office while a writer and director were talking about how to represent most accurately the behavior of college students in their screenplay. The conversation began with a discussion of some young film stars and their sartorial preoccupations, then detoured through the writer and director's own college years, continued with the conservatism of contemporary Indian teenagers, followed by the problem with priests, and ended with the British suffragette movement, before returning to the topic of characterization and setting for their screenplay. During such story sittings, which are what scripting sessions are called, no one ever took notes. Even at the music sittings I attended, the music director composed melodies on his harmonium and recorded them directly onto a tape recorder, rather than writing down the music.

While screenplays are written, they are rarely read in solitude; instead, the key members of the production team gather to hear the writer or director relay the film's story or read the script aloud. These sessions, referred to as "narrations," are undertaken throughout the pre-production process as a way of bringing cast and crew on board a particular film; these can last anywhere from half an hour to several hours, depending on the completeness of the script. Narrating a film is in itself considered a performative skill, and certain directors and writers are renowned in the industry for their narrating prowess. The significance of narrations has to do with the fact that the script is often incomplete prior to casting. Even if a script is finished, writers usually read it aloud to small groups of cast and crew. It is very common to hear actors state in television interviews that they decided to do a particular film after "hearing the script," rather than reading it.

This sort of orality is devalued within the industry, however, which is demonstrated by the tremendous discursive emphasis on the "bound script." As the chapter's opening anecdote and the point in chapter four where Vijay Khanna appears reluctant to star in Lakhani's film demonstrated, the bound script—by which is meant a completed screenplay—is a highly fetishized object within the Hindi film industry. Although I interviewed many active and employed screenwriters, the dominant stereotype within the industry was that scripts were a rare commodity, as noted in Punkej Kharabanda's comment: "A script in a Hindi film is probably written at the time of its release, the only thing written ever" (Kharabanda, interview, 17 April 1996). The complaint about a lack of scripts had less to do with the actual absence of a screenplay than with the sequence of how a screenplay evolves. Since scripts are conceived with particular stars in mind, it does not benefit an actively employed screenwriter to write a complete screenplay prior to a go-ahead from either a producer or a star, as it could be rejected. However, the idea of a completed script is touted as a badge of distinction and professionalism by filmmakers, and stars especially, who profess to do roles only after consulting the script. Additionally, the phrase "bound script" is deployed as a marker of modernization and progress within filmmakers' and journalists' narratives about changes besetting the industry's work culture.

The paucity of documentation extends to a film's production as well, where typically the only written materials on a set are the continuity sheets, necessary for processing and editing the film, and the sheets of dialogues that actors have to memorize for a scene. Most Bombay directors do not storyboard their films, so decisions about lighting, blocking, and camera placement and movement are made in collaboration with the cinematographer once sets are constructed and shooting commences. During a post-screening question and answer session with producer/director Karan Johar, at NYU in February 2007, a member of the audience asked him about storyboards and decisions regarding camera placement. "We write the scene and I don't storyboard, contrary to popular belief," Johar responded. "Everybody thinks that we storyboard and it's all ready. It's far from it. It's confused and it's always chaotic. It's always through conversations with my Director of Photography that I work out my scene . . . There is really never any storyboarding. If we started to storyboard we would be doing that for a year." All of the directors I met asserted that they had their films "running in their heads," discussing them in very visual terms, commonly describing onscreen action in relation to camera angles and movements.

This oral style of working had a significant impact upon how I conducted fieldwork. Unless I was attending a large gathering or function where my presence went unnoticed, I was unable to take notes on-site because it was awkward to be the only person writing. In fact, in the early days of my fieldwork, whenever I wrote notes in public it was noticed and commented upon. One of the assistant directors of the film—for which Sandeep was the executive producer—was continuously curious about what I was writing in my notebook. At the end of the shoot everyday he would ask me in a teasing manner, "So how many pages did you fill today?" On another occasion, my note-taking was a cause for alarm: I had just witnessed my first music recording session and was sitting in the hallway of the recording studio, writing in my notebook, when the music director walked out of the recording booth—he sat down next to me and asked me what I was doing. When I said I was writing my notes, he asked anxiously, "What kind of notes?" Realizing that composers were ever fearful about their melodies being copied or stolen, I quickly explained my project, after which he relaxed considerably, readily answering my questions.

Another consequence of this highly oral work culture is that verbal commitments become the equivalent of contracts. If a producer discusses a film project with a star, the assumption is that unless the star states otherwise, he or she is in the film; therefore, producers approach stars one at a time, rather than several at once, in order to avoid any confusion or misunderstanding. Additionally, negotiations about money and salaries are also based on conversations rather than formal written contracts. Pamela Chopra characterized the negotiations between a producer and stars regarding payment: "When you're starting a film, you have, you know, formal conversations and decide, 'Okay, you're going to work in my film, and this is the film, and I'll pay you so much, and okay fine,' or, 'No, I'm sorry I want x amount more' or whatever, and that's fixed. And then the star keeps drawing money as and when he wants. And it's all sort of registered in some mental computer somewhere that this much has gone and this amount is still owed . . . and it works!" (Pamela Chopra, interview, 28 February 1996). During the late 1990s, written contracts did not play a significant role in the business dealings of the industry. Filmmakers emphasized the value of people's "word" or verbal commitments. Chopra described how all financial dealings were based on trust: "You're dependent upon that person staying true to his word. It's very strange that 90 percent of the time it works. You know that a lot of times contracts are never written" (Pamela Chopra, interview, 28 February 1996). Producer/director Rakesh Roshan described how a written contract could be easily altered and hence was not trustworthy, whereas a verbal assurance was immutable. He characterized the importance of one's word by asserting, "In this industry, only the tongue has a value" (Roshan, interview, May 1996).

The highly oral nature of contracts and financial dealings also has to be understood with respect to the centrality of the "black" economy in India as the main way of raising and disseminating capital for filmmaking, at least until industry status and the advent of corporatization. This point was amply demonstrated to me one afternoon in 1996, when I went to visit Sandeep in his production office. He was busy at the computer, working on an Excel spreadsheet to enter the salaries for all of the principal people involved in the film, both on the creative and the production side. Sandeep's entries of payments were part of his continuous effort to organize what he felt was a very lackadaisical way of operating: he would frequently make schedules, spreadsheets, and charts on his computer and post them around the office. I sat down next to him and read the computer screen: it was a schedule of payments that had been disbursed along with the amounts that were still outstanding. There were two columns under each payment date labeled "cheque" and "cash." In his zeal to be organized and efficient, Sandeep had assiduously recorded all of the "black" money or under-the-table cash payments in the spreadsheet. Ajay, the accountant for the company, walked into the room, and when Sandeep proudly pointed out his handiwork, he rolled his eyes in disbelief. Ajay said to him, in a tone of patient incredulity, "Sandeep, what are you trying to do to us, get us into trouble with the income tax-*wallahs*? We can't have all this on the computer." When Sandeep indicated that he was saving the figures on a floppy disk rather than on the hard drive, and that he would keep the disk at home, Ajay shook his head, telling him it was too risky and that he should erase all records of the cash payments.

FLEXIBILITY AND IMPROVISATION

In the chapter four sketch, not having the crane on the first day of the shoot, or an actress who could speak Hindi properly, did not pose any insurmountable obstacle to the production at hand. Being able to quickly come up with solutions, in the way that Chadda had in order to solve the problem of the heroine's inability to lip-synch, is a common feature of

Hindi filmmaking. Filmmakers are also quite adaptable to sudden changes in plan or setbacks. For example, in the case of the above-mentioned *Awara, Paagal, Deewana*, the cast and crew did not receive their visas for Spain in a timely fashion, so they decided to shoot the portions planned for Spain in the United States as well. A few different factors contribute to Hindi filmmakers' ability to be flexible: the visual style of popular cinema, the practice of dubbing, and the fragmented temporality of production.

Visual Style

Popular Indian cinema is very open and comfortable with the artifice that is at the heart of feature filmmaking. The visual style of popular Hindi films departs from the continuity editing, naturalistic lighting, and realist mise-en-scène conventions typical of Hollywood. Hindi filmmakers are not overly concerned with mimetic realism, even though a realist aesthetic is valued as a higher form of filmmaking by the state, media, and many filmmakers.[12] Unlike Hollywood films, which go to a great deal of effort to hide the fact that they are films—through their production design, editing, lighting, and camera practices—a Hindi film does not pretend that it is presenting an unmediated view of reality. The editing, lighting, art direction, and cinematography in popular Hindi films highlight the constructed, artificial nature of filmmaking, which is most apparent in the song sequences.

Locales, especially for song sequences, are chosen for their spectacle value rather than for their ability to blend in to the mise-en-scène of the dialogue portions of the film; therefore, for the producer and director of *Awara, Paagal, Deewana* (APD), who decided to shoot an additional song in the United States, since they could not go to Spain, it mattered less whether the song was shot in Spain or the United States than it did that it was shot against aesthetically pleasing backgrounds and landscapes. This point became very clear to me when, in the process of observing the shoot of APD in New York and New Jersey, I was recruited— by virtue of my friendship with the director, Vikram Bhatt—to help find suitable locations for the additional song they needed to film. As I was residing in Pennsylvania at the time, I took the film's director, producer, and cinematographer on a brief tour of southeastern Pennsylvania: Lancaster County, better known as Amish Country; Valley Forge National Park; downtown Philadelphia; and the campuses of Haverford and Bryn Mawr colleges, where I was teaching at the time. While lukewarm about Lancaster County and Valley Forge, Bhatt and his producer, Firoz Nadiadwala, were thrilled with the college campuses and downtown Philadel-

phia. They kept comparing Bryn Mawr's campus to Oxford's and Philadelphia to an Eastern European city like Prague or Budapest, deciding
to shoot on both college campuses and in parts of Philadelphia, such as
its city hall and art museum (Figures 12–13). What excited Bhatt and Nadiadwala the most was that, to their knowledge, no one from Bombay had
ever filmed there. They could not fathom how a city so close to New York
was not yet "discovered" by their colleagues in Bombay.

Dubbing

Not only can the visual style of Hindi cinema accommodate changes in
filmmakers' plans, the verbal and sound techniques are somewhat for-
giving of mistakes and oversights in the production process. The majority of Hindi films are not shot with sync-sound cameras, and all of the
sound in a film—from dialogues to music to sound effects—is added in
the post-production phase. While actors' speech is recorded separately on
the sets, for reference and editing purposes, due to camera noise, actors
must dub their own speech after a film has been shot and edited. Dubbing is carried out in special studios where actors watch their performance and repeat the dialogues to match their lip movements onscreen,
re-enacting the film without the interaction of co-stars, as dubbing is
done individually rather than in groups.[13] Orality is apparent during the
dubbing process as well. Instead of working from a script, actors use their
aural and memory skills: they listen to the lines that they had uttered
and repeat them verbatim.[14] Since an assistant director is responsible for
overseeing the process and making sure that pronunciation, grammar,
and syntax are correct, dubbing offers a chance to correct errors that occurred while shooting. Another advantage of dubbing is that filmmakers
can cast actors who do not speak Hindi, as in the case of Sulekha in the
chapter four sketch, having a professional dubbing artist or a well-known
Hindi-speaking actor dub for them; the reverse happens when Hindi film
actors appear in films made in other Indian languages.[15] There are also
instances where, even if the actors speak Hindi, filmmakers have used
someone else's voice in the film, because the actor's own voice was not
deemed suitable.[16] The practices of playback singing and dubbing mean
that in popular Indian films, the speaking voice, singing voice, and actor's
onscreen body can be a conglomeration of three different individuals into
a single apparent entity.

Although synchronous sound is not the norm, it is definitely valorized within the film industry as a more modern and higher quality filmmaking practice. When films have been shot in sync sound, that fact is

FIGURE 12 Preeti Jhangiani and Aftab Shivdasani at the Philadelphia Museum of Art during the shoot of *Awara, Paagal, Deewana*, 2001. Photo by the author.

FIGURE 13 *Awara, Paagal, Deewana* shoot at Bryn Mawr College, 2001. Photo by the author.

highlighted in trade and media discussions about the film. For example, Aamir Khan attracted a fair amount of media attention when he decided that *Lagaan*, the first film that he produced, should be shot with synchronous sound. In interviews with the press, Khan explained his preference for sync sound in terms of his commitment to cinematic quality, representing his decision as a practice of distinction: "Everybody I knew, including Karan Johar and Aditya Chopra, advised me against using live sound. It has never been used in a film from Mumbai. But it worked for us in *Lagaan*. I think sync sound makes a vast difference to the scenes, performances, everything" ("Aamir Khan denies re-shooting *Lagaan*" 2001). In the book *The Spirit of Lagaan*, which assiduously detailed the making of the film,[17] the author, Satyajit Bhatkal, characterized the system of dubbing as "much more than the technique of recording sound. It is part of a work culture" (2002: 51). As a result of dubbing, "actors have got used to being casual about their dialogue delivery on set, directors pumping up the emotional levels while dubbing, and the unit members to functioning in a noisy fashion during the shoot" (2002: 51). By this token, the decision to use synchronous sound in *Lagaan* is represented as a radical action, challenging the prevailing work culture of the film industry.

Fragmented Production Process

The third factor that has contributed to filmmakers' flexibility is the fragmented nature of the production process. A characteristic feature of the production phase of a Hindi film, until the early 2000s, has been that films were not completed on a continuous schedule, because often producers did not have all of the required finance at the outset. Thus, rather than being shot from start to finish over several weeks or a couple of months, most Hindi films were shot in a series of "schedules," ranging from two days to two weeks, over the span of months or even years as producers tried to raise finance throughout the production process. Even if the requisite finance was fully available, another impediment to a condensed production schedule was the unavailability of stars, who worked on multiple projects simultaneously and frequently did not have a large block of time to devote to one film.[18]

A consequence of such fragmentation was that a mishap or a delay in the production of one film could have a domino effect, affecting the production of other films. For example, in 1996, a number of films in which Shah Rukh Khan was acting had their production schedules thrown into disarray because his co-star's mother, who had accompanied the cast and crew of *Duplicate* to their on-location shoot in Prague, died in a road accident. Since the *Duplicate* shoot was waylaid by such unfortunate circumstances, the other films that Khan had to act in also got delayed. Filmmakers have to be capable of dealing with unforeseen circumstances during the production process.

The fragmented temporality of the production process was heavily criticized by Hindi filmmakers; it was often posited as the reason for the poor quality of films and thus the high rates of commercial failure. The practice of actors shooting for a number of films simultaneously, rather than sequentially, was especially criticized, including by actors themselves.[19] When I asked Sanjay Dutt how actors managed to work in a number of films simultaneously, he responded instantly: "I have stopped doing that." Although my interactions with Dutt took place at the sets of the two films that he was shooting for simultaneously, in his answers to my question he was critical of the practice, asserting that it led to a lack of effort. "I don't think you justify your work," he said. "There's no input from an actor nor a director. It's just that, 'Yes, I have to go there at that time, finish that scene by that time, because the other guy is waiting for me at that time, and you're running" (Dutt, interview, May 1996). He recalled a time when he was shooting at Filmistan Studios, and Shashi Kapoor—a popular actor from the late 1960s till the mid-1980s—was shooting for three different films on three different sets on the same day. Dutt humorously described the scenario: "He was doing a fight, a song, and a couple of scenes. So what he used to do was shake his ass out there, remove his shirt, by the time that lighting is going on he used to come and fight out here, remove that shirt, and come here and do a scene and go back! [laughs] Really crazy you know! But that had to stop, because there's no quality" (Dutt, interview, May 1996). He asserted that times were changing in the industry, and that actors who were concerned with the quality of their performance only worked one shift a day or devoted blocks of time to particular films, so that they could work serially, rather than simultaneously, in multiple films.

Pronouncing one's desire to work in one film at a time, reducing one's assignments, or appearing selective about one's projects are all ways for actors to assert their discerning taste and commitment to quality. Aamir Khan was (and continues to be) well known in the industry for his policy of working on one film at a time and being very choosy about the films he acts in—attributes that contribute to his widely media-disseminated public image as a highly conscientious and discerning actor. For producers, being able to shoot the entire film in one schedule, or finishing a film in a short amount of time, becomes a way to demonstrate one's exceptionalism as a filmmaker, revealing how temporality can be another mode to assert distinction.

Improvisation

In addition to flexibility, Hindi filmmaking has an improvisational quality, which I noted throughout my research. I experienced it firsthand in February 1996, my second month of fieldwork, while I was observing the production of the film *Sar Aankhon Par* (Your Wish Is My Command). One afternoon when I arrived at the bungalow, which was serving as a set for the film, some of the crew commented that I appeared more formally dressed than usual. They seemed suitably impressed that I had just attended the *mahurat*—a ceremony undertaken by a producer to mark the start of a new film project—of *Mrityudaata* (Angel of Death)—being touted at the time by the press as superstar Amitabh Bachchan's comeback film. While waiting for others in the cast and crew to arrive before we headed off to a preview theater to view the first rushes of the film, one of the production assistants looked at me and then turned to the director and said, "Why don't we cast her as Bubbly's friend?" I was a little taken aback by his question, and even more so when the director turned to me and asked if I would play a small role in the film, that of the heroine's friend.[20] This acting offer made me realize that casting for minor parts was not necessarily a matter of great concern in the pre-production stage and could occur while a film's production was already underway.[21] If an actor was required for only one or two scenes, casting could be done as late as a day or two prior to the shoot. In addition to on-the-spot casting, dialogues are sometimes composed on the set or written just prior to a shoot. Even if all of the dialogues have been written prior to the start of production, actors still learn their lines directly on the set, while waiting for the lighting and camera to be set up, rather than memorizing them prior to a shoot.[22]

During the U.S. shoot of APD, the director and other members of the crew would joke about how the film had no script, and that everything was ad lib or improvised because it was a comedy. While these were exaggerated claims, as I had observed the scripting process for the film a year before in Bombay, the two songs were choreographed basically on location.[23] The film's choreographer, Ahmad Khan, arrived in New York with his two assistants the day before the first song was to be shot. The day he arrived, a dialogue portion was being shot in Central Park (Figure 14), and during that shoot he and Bhatt (the film's director) listened to the song on the Nagra recorder, decided it was too long, and discussed where

FIGURE 14
Paresh Rawal,
Aftab Shivdasani,
and Akshay Kumar
in Central Park
during the shoot
of *Awara Paagal
Deewana*, 2001.
Photo by the
author.

FIGURE 15
Choreographer
Ahmad Khan
directing Aftab
Shivdasani and
Amrita Arora for
a dance sequence
in *Awara, Paagal,
Deewana*, Central
Park, 2001. Photo
by the author.

FIGURE 16
Aftab Shivdasani
dancing in front
of the aircraft
carrier USS
Intrepid during the
shoot of *Awara,
Paagal, Deewana*,
New York City,
2001. Photo by
the author.

to cut portions in order to trim it by one minute. The next day, having listened to the song on his Walkman—both on the previous day and on the morning of the shoot—Khan began to figure out the choreography based on the location, which was Bethesda Terrace in Central Park. He composed the movements for each verse and musical interlude on-site and directed the two actors in their steps (Figure 15). Since almost each verse of the song was shot at a different location, Khan was constantly thinking of other possible locations and backdrops for it, since every location had not been finalized. While shooting another verse for the song on the *Intrepid* (Figure 16), a decommissioned aircraft carrier permanently docked on the Hudson River in New York City, Khan decided that it would be nice to shoot a verse on the Circle Line Ferry, and the producer got on the phone to book a boat for the next day. I learned from one of Khan's assistants that nothing was ever written down, that the choreography was all mentally visualized, and that neither she nor Khan had any formal training in dance, but had learned from assisting another choreographer.

Even though Khan was composing the choreography for the two songs line by line and location by location, by no means did it mean that Khan or Bhatt were lax in their work. They both knew exactly what emotions and mood they wanted from the songs and were quite demanding of the actors, doing take after take until they were satisfied—in one instance, spending more than half an hour on a five-second phrase of a song that an actress was having trouble with—in terms of lip-synch, hand gestures, and facial expression—while shooting in front of Philadelphia's City Hall. Further evidence of filmmakers' ability to change course was that, after all of the time and effort to shoot and edit the Philadelphia area song, this particular song never made it into the final version of the film, since Bhatt felt that it slowed down the pace too much.

RESOURCES AND TECHNOLOGY

Over the years of observing Hindi filmmakers at work, two features have stood out for me: the relatively low-tech nature of the pro-filmic process; and the remarkably efficient use of resources. Although Hindi films exhibit high production values and are frequently elaborate visual spectacles, the production conditions are surprisingly simple and use minimal technology. With the exception of certain elaborate action or song sequences, Hindi films are shot with a single camera unit.[24] Equipment such as cranes and dollies are manually operated. Clapboards are not electronic, but handwritten with chalk. Ordinary sheets of black paper

FIGURE 17 Preeti Jhangiani and Aftab Shivdasani during the shoot of *Awara, Paagal, Deewana*, Philadelphia, 2001. Photo by the author.

and white Styrofoam boards serve as lighting equipment. When shooting abroad, filmmakers use natural rather than artificial light, relying on landmarks, cities, or natural landscapes rather than sets (Figure 17).[25]

Filmmakers did not start working with video-assist technology, where a video camera records the scene simultaneously so that it can be viewed on a monitor, until 1998. In the case of the APD shoot, even though the production team had brought along a video-assist monitor, Bhatt decided against using it since the rented portable generator made too much noise. On the third day of the shoot, when Bhatt remarked how surprised he was that they had only shot 6,800 feet of stock so far (out of their supply of 28,000 feet), his producer observed, "That's because you're not using the monitor; with a monitor there are always more re-takes." As raw film stock is imported and expensive, at one time comprising about 10 percent of a film's budget, Hindi filmmakers are extremely economical with their stock and do not waste it with unnecessary re-takes, re-shooting, or extra shooting.[26]

In fact, raw stock consumption can also be a site to express one's distinction, as I discovered during my interview with producer/director Rakesh Roshan who spoke in some detail about his use of stock to express his efficiency, planning, and organization. Roshan made an explicit connection between a properly worked-out screenplay and economic efficiency:

What happens most of the time, people . . . overshoot. They make their first length—it's 30,000 feet, 27,000 feet—then they have to cut 10,000 feet from the film. So when they are cutting, they are just chopping the film. Lots of money wasted. I shoot my raw stock—it varies from 100 to 132 tins—but people all around me, they use 400 to 500 tins.[27] I shoot for 100 days only, exactly 100 days—maybe 92 days, maybe 105 days, not more than that—but people shoot for 300 days, 400 days, because they are shooting on a trial-and-error basis. They shoot a scene and then say, "*Chalo yaar*, [Hey man] let's reshoot it." That's why there's so much reshooting in so many films, because nobody has time to [work] on the script. (Roshan, interview, May 1996)

Roshan further explained that his first assembly was always about 18,000 feet, which he then edited down to 16,500 feet, so his unused footage was minimal.

When shooting on location, Hindi filmmakers tend to work with the surroundings rather than trying to conform the surroundings to their shooting needs. The general working style of Hindi filmmakers counters the stereotypes held in the United States—of feature filmmaking always involving large, intrusive, disruptive, and troublesome film crews. This became very apparent to me while I was coordinating the logistics of shooting APD at the Bryn Mawr and Haverford college campuses, where I encountered officials whose perceptions of a film shoot were completely at odds with the reality of the APD shoot. While the administrators at both colleges gave their consent to the filming, they expressed a great deal of trepidation about the possible damage that the shoot could do to the grounds and landscaping. The officials were incredulous when I informed them that there were no generators, trailers, lights, or trucks and that the entire cast, crew, and equipment fit in one bus and one van. The American who had been hired by the producer as a local location manager kept commenting to me about how "low-impact" this production was, and that it reminded him of a documentary film shoot rather than a big-budget feature film. In fact, he surmised that even getting official permission might have been unnecessary, since the whole shoot was barely noticeable, even on the quiet and deserted campuses.

A minimal use of technology, however, is accompanied by a tremendous valorization and fetishization of technology. No matter how arcane, any introduction of technology is showcased. For example, during fieldwork in 2000, Sharmishta Roy and her assistant, who were production designers for *Mohabbatein* (Loves), a film directed by Aditya Chopra, proudly informed me that it was the first Hindi film to use CAD technology to generate the blueprints for the sets. The designation of being the "first" to use a particular technology was something I encountered often during my fieldwork and still come across while reading the trade press: the first film to utilize Dolby sound—*Ram Shastra* (1995); the first Hindi film with four-track, optical stereo sound—*Hum Aapke Hain Koun!*; the first Hindi film to digitally create the actor's double—*Duplicate* (1998); the first Hindi film to have a 90 percent CGI (computer-generated imagery) song—*Kartoos* (1999); the first Hindi film to shoot in synchronous sound—*Lagaan* (2001); the first Hindi film to feature an alien, created in a special effects studio in Australia—*Koi Mil Gaya* (2003).

Since the mid-2000s, the use of special effects, digital technologies, and complex post-production practices in Hindi filmmaking has increased immensely, reflected by the far greater number of animators, colorists, and other post-production personnel listed in a film's closing credits. By foregrounding their use of such technologies, Hindi filmmakers represent themselves as being aware of, and keeping current with, the latest technologies in filmmaking and asserting their exceptionalism within the industry. For example, in January 2010, I met director Tarun Kumar while he was vacationing in New York, and he related to me how he was using the online virtual world Second Life to do the entire set design, camera blocking, and storyboarding for his latest film. When I asked him if this had become the new norm in Bombay, he replied, "No, most Indian directors have no idea about Second Life. They are not so technically savvy."

HOORAY FOR HOLLYWOOD (AND BOLLYWOOD . . .)

In March 1996, while observing the shoot of Rakesh Roshan's *Koyla* (Coal) at Chandivali Studios, located in an outlying suburb of Bombay, I met Amrish Puri, a distinguished actor who had a prolific career playing a wide range of supporting roles in a very diverse filmography, including that of the villainous priest, Mola Ram, in Steven Spielberg's *Indiana Jones and the Temple of Doom*. After he finished his portion of the scene, Puri sat down next to me on the set and we struck up a conversation. I asked him about his experiences working with Spielberg, which became an opportunity for him to discuss the differences between the Hindi film industry and Hollywood. He characterized the two industries as diametrically opposed, both explicitly and implicitly. According to him, filmmakers from Hollywood were very focused, prepared, and disciplined in contrast to filmmakers in Bombay. He pointed out that in Hollywood "everything was prepared in advance," such as storyboards, shot breakdowns, and scripts, and the expectation was that everyone would be ready by the shoot. Puri attributed this readiness to a strong sense of duty and pride in one's work, which he contrasted with what he found to be the prevailing attitude in Bombay: "Here, even when you're paying people, you still have to plead with them to work. Everyone acts as if they're doing each other a favor. The hero and heroine act as if they're doing you a favor by giving the shot." He asserted that Hollywood filmmakers had no patience for star tantrums or unpreparedness, and because of its discipline and working style, Hollywood was able to produce films of a much higher quality than the Hindi film industry. Puri concluded his comments by shaking his head and saying, "There just isn't the same type of discipline here—just a few units have it—that sense of obligation and care for the finished product. Here most units don't even have respect for the director."

Puri's trenchant criticisms of the Hindi film industry and unqualified admiration for Hollywood—a phenomenon with a very long history, dating back to the 1930s (c.f. Majumdar 2009)—were a common occurrence throughout my fieldwork. I usually did not have to actively solicit comparisons from filmmakers, for in the course of talking about filmmaking, Hollywood usually came up in some sort of fashion—either as an object of admiration or a site of contrast. When I asked Pamela Chopra to comment on these frequent comparisons to Hollywood, she asserted that most filmmakers "looked up" to Hollywood. "Hollywood is more advanced technically; it is much more advanced content-wise, because they choose from such a vast range of subjects, and that's because their audiences are so mature. Plus it's a very alive industry. Things are happening, I mean, innovations take place every year. Every year in Hollywood something new happens. In the technical field, something new is happening. Either a new kind of film has been made, or a new kind of process has been made, or a new kind of camera has been made, or a whole new way of making films. I mean, imagine that film *Toy Story*, it's completely a computer film!" (Pamela Chopra, interview, 26 March 1996). Chopra's comments present Hollywood as a sort of techno-utopia and site of unlimited possibilities—a characterization that most people working in the actual sites denoted as Hollywood would not necessarily recognize.[28]

Hollywood did not always necessarily refer to the actual southern California–based film industry, but was used by Hindi filmmakers as a label for any English-language filmmaking that took place in a Euro-American setting,[29] which provided them the opportunity to comment both upon the conditions of their filmmaking and the intellectual and social development of their audiences. For example, during the lunch break of the shooting of *Ishq*, Aamir Khan was describing a fellow actor's experience working with a foreign film crew to a group of people, including the film's director, the cinematographer, the cinematographer's wife, a couple of Khan's friends, and me. "You know everything was planned out in advance and the daily schedule was posted every day, listing which car would pick up whom and at what time." He then aimed his remarks specifically at the director, Indra Kumar. "Indu, you know what he noticed was that the last reporting time was always for the director. The actors had to report earlier because they had to get ready, but the director could come to the location last because everything was planned in advance—all the shot lists, shot breakdowns were already done." In response, Kumar chuckled and said, "Here, the director comes first and waits for everyone else!"

The discourse about Hollywood within the Hindi film industry comprises two broad and interconnected themes that deal with the conduct and content of filmmaking. While Chopra's comments about innovation refer to the content of filmmaking, Khan's and Puri's statements about discipline and preparedness address the conduct of filmmaking, and the overwhelming representation of Hollywood—or its common synonyms "out there" or "out West"—by Hindi filmmakers is that it is more organized, more disciplined, more efficient, and more professional than the Hindi film industry. Hindi filmmakers articulate this contrast within the terms of their specific work practices and thus the features commonly singled out to signify Hollywood's discipline and organization were the singular (rather than fragmented) shooting schedule and the advance availability of the film's script. Shashi Kapoor, an actor/producer/director who had worked in a number of British and Merchant Ivory films, discussed how these features enabled better performances from an actor: "The advantage in working in Western films was that it was one schedule, and plus they had a complete script which they gave you, and they gave you advance notice. So four to five months, six months before the shooting would start—or a year—you were aware of what you were going to do, and you had enough time to prepare yourself for that particular character" (Shashi Kapoor, interview, 8 August 1996).

Other conduct-related characteristics of Hollywood admired by Hindi filmmakers were its greater division of labor and higher degree of occupational specialization. Director Mansoor Khan bemoaned the lack of casting directors—more specifically the notion that casting was a specialized task that required its own dedicated expert—and described how he often had his assistants help him, since casting was not his forte—mainly because neither did he come into contact with a large number of people nor did he watch much television.[30] "There should be a casting director, and that's what they have there, and they cast brilliantly," he said. "That's why it's so apt, you know? See, not that a director may not be able to cast once in a while, but it would take a lot of load off him if he [could] concentrate on something else" (Mansoor Khan, interview 1 April 1996). In addition to discussing his casting difficulties, Khan described how, as a director, he would be free to concentrate on the broad contours of the film if he were able to delegate the minutiae of certain tasks, like hunting for locations. Stating that such delegation of duties is only possible with a level of "technical expertise," which exists "abroad" but not necessarily in India, Khan spoke enviously of the level of specialization that existed in Hollywood films: "You look at the credits. The credits just reflect how much more structure there is, and even a simple film requires that amount of detail, you know?" (Mansoor Khan, interview, 1 April 1996).

Hindi filmmakers lauded Hollywood's attention to detail in numerous contexts, from casting to scripting to set design, but the one topic that epitomized the essential differences between the two film industries was the availability of technology. Firoz Nadiadwala contrasted the Hindi film industry as a technological backwater to Hollywood's techno-utopia: "How are we going to make films if we don't have the equipment? If we had good equipment, then we could train good people properly, and they would think about films in relation to that equipment. In America, according to the concept, they'll make the equipment. Panavision will make lenses according to your requirements. If you tell them what you need and you don't have the equipment, what will they do? They will make it for you; they will loan it to you at a certain agreed price, and then they will take the equipment back. Here it is not known. We're still using cameras that are fifteen years old" (Nadiadwala, interview, October 2000). Shah Rukh Khan also raised the issue of technology when discussing why Hollywood films were a continuous source of inspiration for Hindi filmmakers, especially when it came to action sequences. Citing the absence of technologies, such as back projection, morphing, and computer animation (that is, in 1996; currently, they are all available) Khan asserted, "I'm sure . . . if we had the cameras and the accessories they had, we would do better stunts and fights, because our stuntmen are much better, I think. But we don't have the technology, so we see a shot, and try to more or less

[to] copy it . . . so that it looks as grand and nice as in the foreign film. We do it at a much more dangerous level than those guys" (Shah Rukh Khan, interview, 21 March 1996).

Khan's statements, while acknowledging Hindi filmmakers' admiration and mimicry of Hollywood, also assert a form of distinction and implicit national pride that, despite the lack of resources, films continue to be made. This is made apparent in screenwriter Honey Irani's facetious assertion, "Every year America should give us an Oscar for making films with such bad equipment and bad printing—and bad this and bad that" (Irani, interview, May 1996). Thus, when discussing the material conditions of filmmaking, the contrast with Hollywood was deployed by members of the industry to point to the exceptionalism of their own industry. For example, Taran Adarsh asserted during our interview, "I know when you compare Hindi films with Hollywood films, people say *ki* [that]: 'What are we making?' But look at the conditions in which we're making, with no help from the government, yet we're coming out with films" (Adarsh, interview, September 1996). Adarsh went on to list a number of films that he thought were exemplary in terms of content, style, theme, and then mentioned a specific director whose big-budget multi-star war film was under production at the time: "Look at J. P. Dutta's kinds of films—brilliant! I mean I have seen portions of his latest film, *Border*, and I think it is [on] par with any Hollywood film. It's amazing to assemble a cast like that, and to spend so much on cinema is very difficult" (Adarsh, interview, September 1996).

The difficulty and challenges of filmmaking in India have been prominent and recurring themes articulated in a variety of ways in Hindi filmmakers' narratives and discourses about their work. When relating the difficulties posed by the Hindi film industry's work culture in contrast to the imagined ease with which films get produced in Hollywood, Hindi filmmakers sometimes convert the very same practices that are the source of disdain into marks of distinction. This rhetorical shift is noticeable in Subhash Ghai's reflections on the challenges he faced as a filmmaker in India, highlighting one of the main constraints as the shortage of qualified technicians and an absence of specialization of the sort mentioned by Mansoor Khan:

> The director in India needs to be a multi-faceted man. So I need to be a writer; I need to be a dialogue writer; I need to understand the gimmicks, punches, gags, story, characterizations; I need to understand the color scheme, the costumes; I need to understand the static sense

of art direction, settings, colors; I need to understand the choreography; I need to understand the music, the background music; I need to understand the mixing sounds; I need to understand the publicity, even the marketing, the strategy, and how it will take place. But in Hollywood it is not that, there the director needs to understand direction, that's it, and there are so many people who read his script, and they come with a brilliant idea to him, and he selects the best of them, but here he needs to give his best. (Ghai, interview, 10 December 1996)

From this point of view, the very ability to make films in India becomes a sign of an exceptional and qualified filmmaker. Hollywood—rather an imagined Hollywood—thus serves to showcase filmmakers' disdain for the work culture of the industry and demonstrates their distinction within a global landscape of filmmaking. The awareness Hindi filmmakers exhibit about Hollywood—or Western modes of filmmaking—and the contrast they draw with their own working style, can also be understood as an expression of their cosmopolitanism—their knowledge and consciousness of other ways of being, working, or carrying out the same tasks in the world.

WORK CULTURE AND ITS CRITICS

This chapter has examined the prominent features of the work culture of the Hindi film industry and discussed the sentiments of disdain articulated by filmmakers about that culture. In their self-criticisms and admiration for Hollywood, Hindi filmmakers imply that there is a correct way to make films; the very existence and nature of their filmmaking practices demonstrate exactly the opposite—that there is no one way or "right way" to produce feature films. The next chapter examines how the structure and work culture of the industry are implicated in filmmakers' understanding of risk and their practices of managing uncertainty.

CHAPTER 7

Risky Business

Managing Uncertainty in the Hindi Film Industry

And it is, in turn, the attempt of ideologies to render otherwise incomprehensible social situations meaningful, to so construe them as to make it possible to act purposefully within them, that accounts both for the ideologies' highly figurative nature and for the intensity with which once accepted, they are held.
—Clifford Geertz, *The Interpretation of Cultures*, 220

A producer prayed for 15 years, he did *tapasya* [intense meditation], and God appeared before him saying, "I'm very happy with you, tell me what do you want, what do you wish?" So the producer said, "My film is releasing next week, tell me if it's going to be a hit or a flop." God said, "Well I will have to go to the matinee show, see the film myself, and then predict whether it's going to be a hit or a flop."
—Taran Adarsh, editor of *Trade Guide*, September 1996

In a span of four weeks in May and June 2010, two highly publicized, promoted, and anticipated films—*Kites* and *Raavan*—performed well below expectations at the domestic and overseas box-office and were declared "flops" by industry analysts, events reported extensively in the trade and general press. Both were big-budget films featuring major stars of the Hindi film industry, directed by highly respected directors, produced by experienced banners—the term for production company in industry parlance—and distributed worldwide by Reliance Big Pictures, one of the few vertically integrated companies (production/distribution/exhibition) and one of the most significant players in the Hindi film industry since 2007. Both films had also generated a great deal of press and media attention while under production and were promoted by Reliance Big at the Cannes Film Festival in 2009 and 2010 — a fact that garnered further media coverage.

Each film had its particular "USPs" — industry parlance for unique selling points: *Kites* featured the Mexican soap opera star Barbara Mori and was shot extensively in the United States and Mexico; *Raavan* was touted as a modern twist on the ancient Hindu epic *Ramayana* and was produced simultaneously in Hindi and Tamil — its director, Mani Rathnam, was a leading filmmaker of the Tamil film industry. Each film also featured principal personnel or combinations whose previous ventures had been commercially successful. For example, the specific combination of actor, actress, director, composer in *Raavan* — Abhishek Bachchan, Aishwarya Rai, Rathnam, and A. R. Rahman — had achieved reasonable box-office success in 2007 with *Guru*. Meanwhile, *Kites* starred Hrithik Roshan and was produced by his father, Rakesh; every film produced and directed by the father and starring the son had been a top-grosser for that particular year. Although Rakesh Roshan did not direct *Kites*, its director, Anurag Basu, had become hot property in Bombay following three consecutive box-office successes; therefore, the weak box-office performance of both films attracted a fair amount of media attention and was represented as alarming in the trade press. For example, regarding the poor opening weekends of both films, *Film Information* commented, "The initial response of *Kites* this week has sent shock waves in the industry" ("Latest Position" May 2010); and "The unimpressive initial [gross] of this week's *Raavan* at many centres has come as a major disappointment for the trade" ("Latest Position" June 2010). Later issues of the trade magazine contained editorials lamenting the high rates of commercial failure, exhorting filmmakers to improve the poor quality of films — the most common reason posited for box-office flops.

The disappointing box-office performance of highly anticipated, big-budget, major star cast films is a phenomenon common to large-scale commercially oriented film industries across the world. Filmmaking has always been a very uncertain business, and in India the uncertainty encompasses both production — films may be aborted midway through production due to insufficient funds, or they may never be distributed once completed — and consumption, specifically the caprice of audience response as indexed by box-office outcome. This chapter examines how the Hindi film industry manages the uncertainty endemic to filmmaking, from specific production practices that attempt to reduce risk, to rituals that allay anxiety, to discourses that endeavor to explain the vagaries of box-office outcome. Hindi filmmakers aim to reduce the risks and uncertainty involved with filmmaking in a variety of ways, from the most apparently superstitious practices—such as always using the letter "K" to begin a film's title—to more perceptible forms of risk reduction, such as always working with the same team of people or remaking commercially successful films from the Tamil, Telugu, and Malayalam film industries. As the examples of *Kites* and *Raavan* illustrate, however, there are no guarantees that such efforts will be successful.

Even though "nobody knows anything" may be a rhetorical trope to characterize filmmaking that is aimed at wide audience appeal (Cassidy 1997: 36), in actuality filmmakers create and deploy knowledge to cope with the unpredictability of their enterprise; after all, films continue to be made despite the reportedly high rates of failure. I contend that these forms of knowledge constitute an ideology that allows filmmakers to make sense of, and enables them to act within, their highly uncertain environment (Geertz 1973: 220). A crucial feature of the ideology of film production concerns filmmakers' understandings and representations of their audiences, which I examine in great detail in the next two chapters. In this chapter, I focus on how Hindi filmmakers implicate specific production practices and features of the industry's work culture in their discourses about what is and is not necessary for commercial success. I term these mostly after-the-fact pronouncements "production fictions," which primarily serve the role of explaining commercial disappointments or failures. For example, a prevailing explanation for the failure of *Kites* was that there was very little Hindi spoken in the film, since the protagonists were an Indian American man, who primarily spoke in English, and a Mexican woman, who spoke only Spanish. Trade analysts pronounced that the film had a hard time at the box-office because Indian audiences do not like reading subtitles. Another more longstanding production fiction concerns the importance of stars, expressed in the dualism that stars cannot guarantee commercial success, yet commercial success is not possible without stars. Perhaps the most robust production fiction—the one that can be utilized to explain a large proportion of flops—is that of the absence of a "strong story" or script. Everyone in the industry asserts that the importance of good writing and good scripts is the foundation of a successful film; therefore, the root cause of commercial failure is frequently attributed to the script. As important components of the ideology of film production, production fictions are fluid and flexible discourses that can be consistently modified to account for new circumstances. For example, some films are said to have failed because there was not enough marketing and promotion, others because there was too much. Since their main function is to explain and rationalize inherently unpredictable and inexplicable events, production fictions constitute ever-shifting benchmarks that filmmakers must strive for in order to attain success.

My analysis of how Hindi filmmakers manage uncertainty begins with a discussion of specific ritual and discursive practices that appear to be centrally concerned with allaying the anxiety that accompanies the highly uncertain contexts of production and consumption. Then I turn to an examination of particular production practices and narrative elements deemed necessary to reduce risk. Songs, stars, and remakes of successful South Indian films are part of the Hindi film industry's standard repertoire of risk management, serving to reduce some of the financial uncertainty of the production and distribution process by ensuring distributors and exhibitors that commercial viability is an important consideration for producers. Stars and songs are important for attracting distributors due to the industry's presumption that such features are necessary to draw audiences; having already succeeded with one set of audiences, remakes of South Indian hits are perceived as reducing the risk of uncertain audience response. Since chapter five already addressed the centrality of stars within the industry, and I have discussed the phenomenon of remakes elsewhere (Ganti 2002), this chapter focuses on songs, particularly their commercial significance within Hindi filmmaking, and the ways they serve to reduce the uncertainties around finance, distribution, and consumption.

Among a wide range of production fictions, some refer to the content of films while others address the behavioral norms and working style of the industry. A prominent industry production fiction during my first phase of fieldwork was that its poor rate of commercial success had to do with its lack of professionalism, discipline, and organization; therefore, a prevailing sentiment existed: that in order for the industry's fortunes to improve, filmmakers needed to become more professional and disciplined in their working style, while the industry on the whole needed to become more organized. It is for this reason that I discuss the phenomenon of corporatization, which at one point was touted as the panacea to all of the problems besetting the Hindi film industry. I detail what this process has entailed exactly: both the changes it has brought about in the working style and structure of the industry and what has remained the same. As the rate of commercial success has not improved since the advent of corporatization, I examine the new production fictions that have been generated to make sense of the continued unpredictability of the film business.

CINE-MAGIC: RITUALS AND DISCOURSES
TO MANAGE UNCERTAINTY

> Magic is to be expected and generally to be found whenever man comes to an unbridgeable gap, a hiatus of knowledge or in his powers of practical control, and yet has to continue in his pursuit.
> —Bronislaw Malinowski, *Magic, Science, and Religion*, 68

> An Indian film producer is like a pariah dog trying to cross the road at Churchgate during rush hour. You have to dodge this way, dodge that way, and pray that you make it through.
> —Mukesh Bhatt, producer, October 1996

From conducting a ritual prayer to Ganesh, the elephant-headed Hindu god regarded as the remover of obstacles, to breaking a coconut to celebrate the first shot of the day, chapter four depicts how the everyday life of Hindi filmmaking is marked by a variety of Hindu ritual practices. I encountered other signs of religious practice, both generally South Asian as well as specifically Hindu, at the varied sites and spaces of production. For example, similar to standard practice at temples and mosques, many production and post-production spaces—like dubbing studios, editing suites, and preview theaters—require the removal of footwear prior to entering them. Chromolithographs of an assortment of Hindu deities, iconography, such as the symbol for *Om*, or images of Shirdi Sai Baba, a saintly figure revered by Hindus and Muslims, are a common visual presence across the sites of production and post-production. While these practices could be interpreted as expressions of the religious identity of members of the film industry, the appearance of religious imagery on the material items of production—*Om* stickers on a film camera; vermillion on the continuity notebooks—leads me to argue that these operate less as markers of religion than Malinowskian manifestations of magic.[1]

Malinowski, in his classic work, *Magic, Science and Religion*, argued that whenever humans engage in activities where there is a tremendous amount of uncertainty regarding possible outcomes, they resort to magic in order to be able to carry out their tasks with confidence. Drawing from his fieldwork in the Trobriand Islands, Malinowski juxtaposed the practice of lagoon fishing with open sea fishing to support his point; the former activity, due to its ease and reliability had no magic associated with it, while the latter, which was full of danger and uncertainty, had extensive magical ritual to secure safety and good results; therefore magic serves to "ritualize man's optimism," and "to enhance his faith in the victory of hope over fear" (1954 [1925]: 90). Certain ritual and discursive practices in the Hindi film industry serve to enact confidence and enshrine optimism within the vagaries of filmmaking. I focus here on two such practices: first, the *mahurat*—a ceremony that marks the commencement of a film's production—which has become far less prevalent since the advent of corporatization; second, a particular exclamatory mode of praise and encouragement mostly performed by producers, which I term "success-talk." While the first practice displays features that resonate with Malinowski's discussion of the mimetic and metonymic nature of magical rites, the second practice is analogous to his characterization of spells.

Mahurat, derived from Sanskrit *muhurtham*, in the most general sense refers to an astrologically calculated auspicious date and time on which to start any new venture. The word and concept are most commonly used in conjunction with Hindu wedding ceremonies. Taking place sometimes months in advance of any actual shooting, during my fieldwork I observed *mahurats* in the Hindi film industry ranging from simple ceremonies in studios or other production sites to ostentatious affairs in luxury hotels (Figure 18). One of the central features of a *mahurat* was the enactment of the filming process, during which the principal actors in the film performed a brief scene for the camera and the spectators present. The customary nature of the event was emphasized by the fact that the scene was written especially for the occasion, and the shot footage was never incorporated into the final film. The goal was to impart the essence of the film, since at this stage it was usually only a germ of an idea—a script had not even begun to be written. Other aspects of the event that highlighted its ritualized nature were the frequent incorporation of features from Hindu ritual worship such as the breaking of a coconut before the "Roll camera!" command, adorning a camera with flower garlands, or even the performance of an *arati*—the rotational display of an oil lamp or a camphor flame—to the film camera. Although the actual enactment of the scene is quite brief, the overall *mahurat*, attended by members from all three main

FIGURE 18 *Puja* (Hindu ritual prayer ceremony) being conducted with the producer, director, screenwriters, and music composer present as part of the *mahurat* for *Albela*, Film City, 1996. Photo by the author.

sectors—production, distribution, and exhibition—represents a space of sociality, celebration, and conviviality within the film industry.

The *mahurat*, although reported in newspapers, film magazines, and television shows, was not a significant form of publicity for the viewing audience. While it generated some expectations, the amount of time that elapsed between the *mahurat* of a film and its theatrical release was usually a couple of years, and in some cases many more. It was also a common feature of Hindi filmmaking that many films—and some very highly publicized ones—never progressed beyond the *mahurat* stage. The significance of the *mahurat* stemmed from its role in helping producers raise finance for their films, specifically in their efforts to sell distribution rights, which comprise an important chunk of the working capital for a film project. Often the most successful producers—either those who by virtue of their track record or star cast had no trouble raising finance, or those who were financially solvent enough not to have to rely on distribution rights as a source of working capital—did not have the ritualized *mahurats* to announce the start of a new film project.[2] The *mahurats* I attended during my fieldwork were for films that had some element of uncertainty associated with them: the lack of stars; the debut of a new actor; the return of a star after a several-year hiatus from acting; or the debut of a new director. In all of these instances, the lack of name recognition or the debut status of either actor or director comprised an unknown terrain, regarding both the availability of finance and box-office outcome.

The *mahurat*, in its enactment of the filming process, embodies both the mimetic and metonymic properties of magic. Malinowski categorized the various rites utilized in the practice of magic into two main types: those that simulate a certain emotional state; and those that perform a desired result, where the "rite imitates its end" (1954 [1925]: 72). By shooting a scene in one take, the *mahurat* ritual simulates a smooth, trouble-free film shoot; it also forecasts the successful onset and completion of production. Being performed in front of an appreciative and well-wishing audience, the *mahurat* reproduces a desired scenario of reception and audience response.

While the *mahurat* was a more spectacular ritual of managing uncertainty, a more common feature of the everyday life of filmmaking was "success-talk"—the hyperbolic articulation of praise and optimism by a film's producer at the various sites of production. Akin to Malinowski's discussion of spells, a distinguishing feature of success-talk is the use of words to "invoke, state, or command the desired aim" (1954 [1922]: 74).[3] We see examples in the chapter four sketch with Malhotra, the film's producer, during his verbal exchange with the Delhi-U.P. distributor and in his lunchtime conversation with his film's director. In both instances Malhotra's statements to the distributor, "It will appeal to everyone," and to the director, "Everyone will love it!" invoke a hypothesized audience response while forecasting box-office success.

Similar to the *mahurat*, I observed the most pronounced performances of such success-talk in situations of high uncertainty. One such example was the film *Sitaare* for which my friend Sandeep was ostensibly an executive producer.[4] The film had very little name recognition as it was being made by a first-time director and starred "newcomers" and "character artists"—industry parlance for novices and actors who play supporting roles—who had very little face value.[5] *Sitaare's* production schedule was very fragmented, since the producer constantly had to raise finance. A first-time director and the lack of stars posed a challenge in attracting distributors to the film. By the time I left Bombay at the end of my first period of fieldwork in 1996, the film was stalled due to a lack of finance. It finally released in 1999—three and a half years after it commenced production.[6]

Whether we were viewing rushes of the film or on the sets, *Sitaare's* producer, Kunal Madhvani, was indefatigable in his performance of success-talk.[7] After we had viewed the first set of rushes, Madhvani was exuberant. "It's singing! It either works or it doesn't!" he said to the cast and crew assembled in the preview theater. He then phoned his partner, an Indian businessman from London who had put up some of the initial finance for the film. "Congratulations, Sunny! The film looks great! We have a hit on our hands! And be ready for the Filmfare Awards, they're sure to come as well! The audiences will love it! The *taporis* downstairs will love it and the families upstairs will like it![8] It's so fresh!" Madhvani turned back to the group in the theater and discussed the plans he had for the film in terms of its theatrical release, making sure that the distributors would book the best cinemas for the film. At that time, I marveled at the over-confidence that Madhvani exhibited, since all we had seen were the silent rushes from six days of shooting, prior to color correction. When relating such expressions of buoyant praise against the larger insecurities and obstacles of this particular production, Madhvani appears less as a deluded optimist and more like Malinowski's fisherman battling the uncertainties of the open sea.

MUCH MORE THAN A SONG AND DANCE

> Music is such a part of our lives that, without music our lives are empty. If you don't have songs in a film, the film doesn't run. Music is a very necessary part of India.
> —Rumi Jaffery, screenwriter, November 1996

One evening in April 1996, alongside the cast and crew of *Sitaare*, I settled into my seat in the preview theater at Natraj Studios, located in Andheri—a northern suburb of Bombay dotted with a variety of film production sites—in order to view the rushes of the most recent shooting schedule of the film. We were watching a scene where the female lead, Tina (referred to as the "heroine" in Indian film parlance), goes to the library where the male lead, Anand—the "hero"—works, in an attempt to attract his attention. She asks Anand to retrieve books that are located on the topmost shelves, which requires him to climb a ladder. As the pile of books keeps mounting and unable to bear their weight, Anand finally falls off the ladder, and all of the books topple down. At that point, the dialogue writer of the film, Sandeep Desai, remarked to the director, "Forget the screenplay, Ganesh-*ji*, let's stick in a song right here. It'll be so appropriate. Let them just fall off that ladder and fall into Ooty.[9] We'll have this set with huge, huge books, and it will be this great song!"

Perhaps the most iconic and distinguishing feature of popular Indian cinema, when compared to other filmmaking traditions in the world, is the presence of songs sung by characters in nearly every film.[10] Regardless of genre—from gangster films to war films, from murder mysteries to period films, from vendetta films to love stories—popular Indian films contain sequences where characters burst into song (often accompanied by dance) for a variety of reasons having to do with narrative, characterization, spectacle, or viewing pleasure.[11] Desai's remarks above exemplify perhaps the most stereotypical image of such sequences—that they simply appear out of nowhere and are completely extraneous to the narrative. While there are plenty of examples of Hindi films where the songs seem very loosely connected to the narrative, such a lack of integration is considered sloppy, lazy, or simply bad filmmaking within the standards of the Hindi film industry. To those unfamiliar with popular Indian cinema, song sequences seem to be ruptures in continuity and verisimilitude. Rather than being an extraneous feature, however, music and song in popular cinema define and propel plot development (Prakash 1983: 115). Many films would lose their narrative coherence if the songs were removed. One scholar has described the popular film as operatic, where the dramatic moments "are often those where all action stops and the song takes over, expressing every shade of emotional reverberation and doing it far more effectively than the spoken word or the studied gesture" (Prakash 1983: 115).

While the near ubiquity of elaborately choreographed and lavishly produced song sequences have become the marker of Bollywood's distinctiveness in the global media landscape (Figure 19), rather than being a taken-for-granted feature of Hindi cinema, song sequences can be a site of tension, debate, and intense negotiation among members of the Hindi film industry. While I observed Hindi filmmakers spending a great deal of time and energy crafting the song sequences, I also detected a considerable ambivalence by screenwriters and directors regarding the presence of songs within a film's narrative. A few years after I had returned from my initial fieldwork in Bombay, I had a conversation with Tarun Kumar through the medium of ICQ, an early Internet chat platform, asking him generally what his feelings were about songs in films: did he like them? Did he feel constrained by them? Were they necessary? His immediate response was almost an academic explanation about the cultural antecedents of Indian cinema and cinema's similarity with other performance traditions. "Cinema in India has to be viewed differently because we belong to the *nautanki* art form and that has been the tradition of enter-

FIGURE 19 Song sequence with Aishwarya Rai, Abhishek Bachchan, and dancers during the shoot of *Kuch Na Kaho*, Mehboob Studios, 2000. Photo by the author.

tainment, so the natural occurrence of songs in our movies is but an extension of that art form. Whether you see a street play or you see the *Ram Lila* they are all incomplete without songs, so they are to be viewed in that respect" (pers. comm., May 1999). When I told him that I wanted to know his personal feelings about songs, remarking that I had observed him in Bombay during scripting sessions being periodically frustrated with them, he replied, "Of course one would love to make a movie without songs, but the only really hampering factor is the economic and marketing aspect of songs. I am all for movies without songs, unless you are making a musical,[12] because not only is it frustrating to conjure up situations, but I feel songs also, to an extent, change the characters in a movie and sometimes also retard the narrative" (pers. comm., May 1999).

Tarun's frustration was directed at the overwhelming role of music in the marketing and financing of popular Hindi films, rather than with its association with traditional performance genres. Since the beginning of the 1990s, film music has had an increasingly important economic function within the Hindi film industry. The sale of music rights became another source of finance for filmmaking, as audio companies vying for the top production companies in the industry were willing to pay sums that amounted to as much as 25 percent of a film's budget, since albums from successful Hindi films sold in the millions.[13] Many screenwriters and directors view having to create song situations as burdensome, however.

Most writers acknowledge that songs are not necessary to every film and can be awkward in certain genres, but point to the economic significance of music within the industry. Screenwriter Sutanu Gupta resigned himself to their presence, citing the pressure of music companies: "My kind of film, the kind of stories that I write—the song situations are difficult to find. I guess the songs have to be there and there have to be enough gaps between the songs, at least five or six songs are required, because the music companies want 40 minutes [of] recorded tape: that is the contract" (Gupta, interview, 18 November 1996).

The presence or absence of songs is the main way to categorize a film's appeal and its potential audience. The lack of songs, or a deliberate omission, is interpreted as a way of making a conscious statement against the dominant form and circumscribing one's audience. Songs are perhaps the single important element in denoting a film as "commercial," or aiming for box-office appeal; therefore songs, along with stars, are important tools for producers in their efforts to raise finance and promote a film among distributors. Songs are usually recorded before a film commences shooting, and a few song sequences are shot early on in the production phase in order to sell a film to distributors. Punkej Kharabanda, who has played a variety of roles within the industry from managing a star's career to producing, explained that filmmakers preferred to show a few well-produced songs rather than their entire under-production film to distributors. "Your songs are recorded, so they have an idea from the songs how good or bad they are. If they're good, that really helps. People don't like showing their films; they probably show a song or so, spend a lot on the song, show a good song, and that brings a lot of hype" (Kharabanda, interview, 17 April 1996). I noticed that during the four production schedules of *Sitaare*, comprising a total of 29 days, two schedules—13 days—were devoted to shooting three songs. Two of these songs were elaborate production numbers, which were then frequently screened for distributors in the producer's continuing search for finance and buyers for the film.

Song sequences are often a site for filmmakers to assert their distinction and exceptionalism within the film industry, which further serves to market their projects within the trade. One of the most common ways of adding production value and novelty to a film is to shoot song sequences in picturesque foreign locales. Switzerland—with its meadows, valleys, and mountains—has been a favorite of Hindi filmmakers since the 1960s.[14] Since the late 1990s, however, Hindi filmmakers have been traversing the globe, shooting song sequences in locations as diverse as Alaska, Egypt, Hungary, New Zealand, Norway, and Namibia. There is an element of the conquering explorer within producers who try to find locations. Filmmakers are constantly in search of locations that have never been shown on the Indian screen. Indeed, such an obsession with novelty led Philadelphia and the Bryn Mawr and Haverford college campuses to be the sites of the Hindi film shoot discussed in the previous chapter. Although some songs are set in foreign settings ostensibly because the characters are visiting or residing in that area, often foreign locations have a tenuous connection to the narrative and function more as spectacle and novelty. The producers of *Jeans* (1998) boasted how theirs was the first film to have a song that featured all "Seven Wonders of the World." This particular song, during which the two leads sing of their love for each other at the Great Wall in China, the pyramids in Egypt, the Taj Mahal in India, the Eiffel Tower in Paris, the Empire State Building in New York, the Leaning Tower of Pisa, and the Colosseum in Rome, became the main marketing point of the film.[15]

Hindi filmmakers' penchant for shooting songs in foreign locations has led to new and unexpected value for these sequences in the eyes of foreign governments, resulting in financial incentives that, in turn, reinforce the commercial significance of songs. Since Hindi films circulate all over the world, many governments view such sequences as a way to promote tourism; this is referred to as the "Bollywood effect," whereby dramatic increases in tourist arrivals from India are registered after several Hindi films have shot in a particular region. Thus governments have been courting Hindi filmmakers to shoot in their countries (Olsberg/SPI 2007: 82).[16] From Malaysia to Germany, South Africa to Scotland, and Florida to Finland, representatives of tourism promotion boards and film councils have been visiting India, trying to market their respective regions to Hindi filmmakers and offering incentives, such as all-expense-paid scouting trips, monetary subsidies, tax breaks, technical and logistical assistance, and co-production arrangements. In fact, as filmmakers increasingly scout out new locations—Switzerland is now perceived as passé and overexposed—the Swiss government has been aggressively trying to woo Hindi filmmakers back to their country by offering free scouting trips since 2006, which include round-trip airfare between India and Switzerland, hotel stay for a week, and chauffeured transportation for location-hunting (Miller 2006).[17]

In addition to their role in attracting finance and capital necessary for a film's production, songs play an important part in filmmakers' efforts to attract viewers. Nester D'Souza, manager of the erstwhile Metro Cinema, asserted that films needed "two good songs to bring in the public . . . those two good songs are your trailers that bring in [the audience], so your first four days are full" (D'Souza, interview, June 1996). Since the onset of cable and satellite television in 1992, with Indian television being packed with film-based programming, songs have become the most significant form of a film's publicity. Even before a film has completed production, sometimes months in advance, its song sequences start airing on the numerous film-based programs on television or appear as commercials in between other programs. At least two months prior to the opening of a film, its soundtrack is released into the market, which since the mid-1990s has been an event carefully orchestrated by the producer and the audio company. An event that seeks to maximize the marketing and publicity potential of a film's music is the elaborate and highly publicized "audio release" function in Bombay, to which the entire glitterati of the film industry is invited, along with distributors, exhibitors, music wholesalers, and journalists. The film's music is showcased by screening the clips of the song sequences, having the playback singers perform the songs for the audience, or putting on an elaborate stage show—with dancers performing to the film's songs. An invited chief guest for the evening, often a prominent member of the industry, officially "releases" the audio—unwraps a package of CDs and audiocassettes and hands them out—to the cast and key members of the crew, while photographers and television cameras capture every moment. The guests attending also receive a copy of the film's audio and occasionally other forms of promotional materials, such as press releases, posters, or film stills. Although this event is ostensibly for the industry and the trade, it also promotes the film to the general public, given the heavy media coverage, especially when famous film stars are present. Since 30–40 percent of the sales a film's soundtrack happen prior to a film's release (Chaya 1996: 42), filmmakers often interpret music sales as an early concrete indicator of audience interest in a film. Music sales also serve as the basis for the rankings of songs on television countdown shows, which function as another way to promote the film.

As music is absolutely essential to the marketing and financing of popular Hindi films, on certain occasions financiers or distributors have pressured filmmakers to include songs. One such example is a film that, for the sake of confidentiality, I have renamed *Darwaaza* (Door), which was originally planned as an entirely song-less film.[18] The film's screenwriter, Atul Rai, corresponded with me via email about how songs got added to the film. Rai explained that both the director, Jay Sinha, and he had agreed that there was no place for songs, because they wanted the film to be "gritty and dry, dramatic, and intense." Soon after, Rai described how "market anxiety" took over, as Sinha was assailed by the film's financier, distributors, and music companies about the folly of his ways: "'In India these things don't work, Sir!' 'Jay-ji, Music is a territory in itself; it will increase your recovery of money' blah, and more friggin' blah. So, Jay decides to include songs. We fight and fight; he agrees with everything I say, but the 'market' can become a bogeyman. So, we incorporate songs into the script." As Rai and Sinha continued to work on the script, they gained confidence with feedback from others about the strength of the screenplay and decided to revert to their original intentions. "Jay says, to hell with the songs; in any case we had conceived of the film without music and we have a point to prove anyway. So, out goes the music," wrote Rai.

By the time the film was completed, it had gone significantly over budget, and Rai described how songs ended up in the film as a form of insurance against box-office failure:

> Panic buttons again. How do we recover the money? Suppose no one comes to see the film, or if not enough people come? Distributors are getting shaky; smug smiles convey "we-told-you-sos." Now the financier steps in with a firm stride. Put the music back in. The director's position has been weakened by his lack of control over the budget, so he has to compromise. We need one song at least to promote the film through TV and cassettes. So, [the song] is conceived, written in, recorded, choreographed, a starlet contracted, and shot . . . it serves its purpose! It hits the top of the charts, makes for great TV promos, the film gets identified by the song and the music cassettes bring in some money, and everyone concerned is less depressed. (Email, 2000)

Darwaaza is not a singular case. Rumors and stories circulate periodically within the industry about distributors and financiers pressuring filmmakers to add songs to films to increase their prospects at the box-office. Not having songs signifies that a film is outside the mainstream of the Hindi film industry, possibly even an "art film," which to most people in the industry means death at the box-office. To anyone working within the dominant system of financing, distribution, and exhibition, songs are an indispensable element in films, which leads to a dominant production fiction: the necessity of songs for box-office success.

Nearly everyone I spoke to in the industry brought up the importance of songs for the commercial success of a film. In addition to drawing audiences into theaters, songs are also important for adding to a film's "repeat value." The most successful films of Hindi cinema have been marked by the phenomenon of repeat audiences—people seeing a particular film 10, 20, 50, even 100 times. Renowned contemporary painter M. F. Husain made news with reports that he had seen *Hum Aapke Hain Koun!*, which had 14 songs, 85 times. Songs are probably *the* critical element in a film's repeat value.[19] Screenwriter Sachin Bhaumick explained to me how with the presence of music even films based on suspense and mystery possessed repeat value and thus became hits: "Producers say that a suspense picture has no repeat value because you know who the murderer is after seeing it once, so why will people go back? The only suspense pictures which ran are those which have got good music; they came back for the music, like *Bees Saal Baad* [Twenty Years Later]: fantastic movie! *Woh Koun Thi?* [Who Was She?]: fantastic movie! Suspense picture with good music: these pictures ran. *Gumraah* [Without a Compass]: another picture with fantastic music. Music brought the repeat audience" (Bhaumick, interview, October 1996). The overwhelming commercial significance of music, however, can be frustrating, according to Tarun Kumar, who complained, "You see it should be a choice for the director to use songs or not, it is the compulsion that really wears us down" (pers. comm., May 1999).

Kumar's frustrations about conceptualizing song situations—the points in the screenplay where a song appears appropriate or necessary—have subsided somewhat with the advent of multiplexes and a sense of greater creative freedom filmmakers have, discussed in chapter two. Since 2006, Kumar's films have had far fewer instances of characters bursting into song or elaborately choreographed production numbers. Non-lip-synch songs continue to have a presence in his films, however, frequently expressing the psychological state of a character or the emotional tenor of a particular situation. As music's narrative significance has diminished with the decrease of lip-synch songs in many contemporary Hindi films, it has arguably taken on an even greater commercial significance within the industry, for it is primarily created for marketing, promotion, and ancillary revenue purposes.

While filmmakers assert that a commercially successful soundtrack is important for the success of a film, there have been plenty of examples where hit music did not translate into a hit at the box-office, or where the sales of a soundtrack increased after a film became a hit—that is, a soundtrack became a hit only after a film became a hit. The inability of music either to forecast or ensure box-office success leads to another prevalent production fiction within the industry: that a film's music alone cannot ensure its commercial success. The pair of truisms—songs are necessary for commercial success, but songs cannot guarantee commercial success—thus operates to explain a great deal of box-office outcome. If a film with successful music—indexed by strong sales, appearance on television and radio countdown charts, and dominant presence in the urban soundscape—ends up performing below expectations at the box-office, filmmakers can (and do) assert that music is merely one component of a film, and that a good story, narrative, and script are necessary for success. If a film's music does not register much impact in the market and subsequently the film fares poorly at the box-office, then the film's failure can be attributed to its music. A successful film lacking successful music, despite being relatively uncommon but possible, reiterates the truism that a film's story, narrative, and script are more important than its music.[20]

THE POWER OF CORPORATIZATION[21]

Going Corporate as a Mode of Distinction

"*Army* is the first corporate film of the film industry," Mukul Anand stated. "Our goal at Neha-MAD Films is to provide structure and security to everyone in the unit, from the technicians to the spot boys." In March 1996, I was attending the launch of United Music—a subsidiary of UTV, a television production company just beginning to make its forays into the film world—at the Grand Ballroom at the Leela Kempinski, a five-star hotel near Bombay's international airport. The event, attended by producers, writers, actors, journalists, and other members of the film industry, but devoid of stars, encompassed a series of presentations about UTV, United Music, and the Indian music industry, and the official release of the "teaser sampler" of *Army*'s music, which was listed prominently on the invitation as the evening's "added attraction."

A director highly acclaimed for his technical prowess, Anand was speaking on stage at the front of the room about *Army*, which he was producing but not directing, through the new company he had created in partnership with Nitin Manmohan, an established producer of reasonable commercial success at the time. Anand's individual production company MAD—an acronym for Mukul Anand Directs—joined with Manmohan's company, Neha Arts, in 1995 to form Neha-MAD Films Combine.

His claim that *Army* was the first corporately produced Hindi film had partially to do with the fact that 49 percent of MAD was owned by ITC, one of India's largest private corporations, and mainly to do with financial transparency, as Anand reiterated a number of times during his presentation: "It's the first film with checks and where we can produce all of the accounts." In June I interviewed Anand in his home, and he spoke at length about his plans and ambitions in filmmaking, as well as his overall vision for the film industry.[22] He was firm that the industry needed to be reshaped in terms of its structure and working style, and based on his experiences in the advertising world, he realized, "Bingo; this is what the film industry needs: it needs a corporate way of working" (Anand, interview, June 1996).

Although much media attention and reportage has been generated about the "corporatization" of the Hindi film industry from 2002 onward, as apparent from the above anecdote the term "corporate," to denote a particular organizational structure and work ethos, held a great deal of value and currency within the industry, even in 1996. During my initial fieldwork I encountered considerable discussion within the press and among filmmakers concerning the new trend of corporatization taking place within the industry, which was primarily identified with the establishment of two production companies, Amitabh Bachchan Corporation Limited (ABCL) and Plus Channel India Limited.[23] The significance of ABCL—and the reason it generated a tremendous amount of publicity and media attention—was that it represented a concerted attempt to convert the charisma and star power of its eponymous founder, Amitabh Bachchan, into a brand that could be leveraged across a variety of commercial enterprises involving entertainment: film production and distribution, television production, music production, and event management.[24] Plus Channel began, in 1995, as a producer of television programming and then turned to feature film production, releasing five films in 1996. It also had its own music division and branched out into event management as well.

The press hailed both companies as steps that promised to organize and discipline the chaotic world of Hindi filmmaking, and such representations were reaffirmed by their founders. A special feature story about Bachchan and ABCL that appeared in *India Today* asserted, "Bachchan says he is pursuing a dream: to bring order with ABCL into the chaotic, bad-money fuelled world of Bollywood" (Jain 1995: 111). In an interview with the journalist who wrote the feature, Bachchan explained his motivation for creating ABCL, "I felt the need for a professional attitude towards the entertainment industry. It was most disorganized, and I wanted to try to run it as a corporate entity" (Jain 1995: 119).

Amit Khanna, the founder and CEO of Plus Channel, stated in an article appearing about the company in the trade weekly *Screen*, that the goal of the film division of Plus was to "meet the crisis caused by the unprofessional approach to filmmaking" ("A Plus film" 1996). Speaking about the upcoming release of their first feature film, Khanna said, "If the experiment works, it will set a trend. It will free filmmaking from being the proposal-makers' gamble and make it professional" ("A Plus film" 1996). Once again the figure of the "proposal-maker" is deployed to assert boundaries between legitimate filmmakers and their others. The reason that Plus's first film was characterized as an experiment was because it was made without stars and on a very tight budget of approximately 8 million rupees, which was pretty low for the time; average budgets in 1996 ranged from 10 to 50 million rupees. Low budgets are only possible without stars, since the remuneration for the leading pair in a film, when played by stars, can often comprise up to 25 percent of a film's budget. "We will never sign stars who demand big money," Khanna declared, "though they are welcome to work with us if they are interested in making a good film" ("A Plus film" 1996).

The disorganization and unprofessionalism alluded to by Bachchan and Khanna referred to the star-centric nature of green-lighting film projects and the fragmented nature of production, but in 1996 the way that such terms were defined also had to do with the daily rhythms of work within the industry and the behavior of stars. For example, during our interview Taran Adarsh said, "Oh! I think our industry is the most disorganized industry, because we don't have any fixed rules. If you notice in other fields, they have a nine to six job, people entering an office at nine a.m., *nau baje kaam shuru pe lag jate hai* [people start working at nine], Right? *Yaha par nau baje kaam nahi hota* [here, work doesn't start at nine]*; yaha par* [here] production offices open at eleven o'clock, twelve o'clock, or one o'clock, or two. *Yaha par* [Here] evenings extend *hoti hai* [get extended]. It's not a normal job as such" (Adarsh, interview, September 1996). While Adarsh focused on the industry's overall sense of temporality in order to exemplify its disorganized nature, Komal Nahta homed in on stars and their mostly callous behavior as typifying the lack of discipline: "Stars, even today, you will be shocked to know . . . cancel shootings at the last moment. The stars are all-important, all-commanding, and of course, not that we don't have good stars, there are some good stars who are very disciplined, who come on time, before time and all that, but 80 percent of the stars have the producers at their mercy. It is rather sad. Now with corporatization, let us hope things change" (Nahta, interview, September 1996).

Nahta's point about "good stars," who "come on time," reveals how being "disciplined" within the film industry overwhelmingly had to do with punctuality. In fact, I discovered that "professional" was often synonymous with punctual; when members of the industry discussed stars who they felt were exceptional because of their professionalism, they consistently brought up the example of Amitabh Bachchan and the fact that he always reported to his shoots on time. Punctuality and the prominent discourse about it are deeply connected to issues of power and hierarchy within the film industry, as tardiness is a privilege only accorded to the powerful. The only people who could afford to be late, and not suffer any immediate repercussions regarding job security, were those with power and status in the industry—namely the stars. To keep people waiting requires a certain amount of confidence—most would say arrogance—in one's indispensability; therefore, punctual behavior by a star takes on tremendous meaning within the industry, for it signifies his or her commitment to the film, respect for the producer and director, and willingness to cede some autonomy over his or her time. For these reasons, punctuality has become synonymous with professionalism within the film industry, since it communicates a willingness to be a member of a group working toward a common goal—that of a commercially successful film.

Adarsh surmised how corporatization could possibly change working behavior within the industry: "The corporate people come in; they say, 'Fine, if you can't do that for us, we'll take you to court; if you don't stand by your commitment, we'll handle it in court; we'll meet you in the court of law'" (Adarsh, interview, September 1996). In 1996, corporatization was thus primarily perceived as a disciplinary mechanism that would transform the everyday interactions within the film industry, namely infusing an ethos of accountability. According to this perspective, such accountability would have an overall impact of reducing financial uncertainty within the industry, because if stars reformed their undisciplined ways, productions would not undergo undue delays, which would thereby hold down costs and increase the commercial viability of projects.

Some members of the industry were skeptical about the impact of corporatization because of what they regarded as the incommensurable working styles of the film industry and the corporate world. Shyam Shroff, whose distribution firm implemented the actual logistics of distributing some films in the Bombay territory that ABCL had bought the rights for, discussed how the film world and the corporate world were "not made for each other." He said, "The people in corporations are shocked to see the way film people behave here. The same way even film people are shocked to see the behavior, how corporations behave" (Shyam Shroff, interview, April 1996). When I asked him what were the differences between the two groups, his explanation primarily addressed the issue of personal interaction, gate keeping, and hierarchies of access:

> Corporations have their own set rules, and the film industry never works on set rules. If I have to meet you, if you have to meet me and you have to sign at three places, you have to write your name, designation, and then somebody goes in, comes, asks you to wait for ten or fifteen minutes—it doesn't work in the film industry. You just walk in here. That's the way the film industry works. If you tell some producer to wait outside for fifteen minutes—the CEO is busy or is talking to some subordinate or something, he'll get put off—what is this nonsense! That kind of system doesn't work in this industry. (Shyam Shroff, interview, April 1996)

Shroff's characterization of corporate culture primarily in terms of the modalities of personal interaction typifies the overall manner that filmmakers discussed concepts like professional, organized, and corporate, which had to do with individual behavior and personal conduct. Akin to the discussion, in chapter three, of the juxtaposition of "*filmi*" with "middle class," corporate is juxtaposed with an implied *filmi* in Shroff's remarks. The term "corporate" connotes rules, sharply delineated temporal and physical boundaries, and unnecessary procedures, which in Shroff's statements stand in stark contrast to the film industry's more personalized, flexible, and direct modes of operating.

While Shroff's skepticism was based on the issue of divergent working styles, Amit Khanna of Plus Channel was confident of his venture. During our interview, he represented Plus as "redefining the ground rules" of Hindi filmmaking, by focusing on low- to medium-budget films that would recover their costs in a variety of ways. Khanna characterized his company as distinctive from the rest of the industry, because of its focus, planning, and vision: "We're making self-sustaining films, not niche films, and we're making a film, not buying a lottery ticket, which is what 95 percent of the people do here. When I make a film I'm sure it should get me cost plus a reasonable amount of profit. And there are various avenues through which that profit or those returns can be generated. Music is one, television is another, exports are the third one, and there could be something as diverse as in-film advertising to in-flight screenings. Now people don't look at it in a holistic manner; we do, so it gives us that much more liberty" (Khanna, interview, June 1996). Khanna's remarks point to how reducing the risk of commercial failure—by introducing economies of scale and developing multiple revenue streams—was at the center of the early attempts to restructure and rationalize the industry, which is what the term "corporatization" represents. Khanna's point about earning a "reasonable amount of profit" suggests attempts to recalibrate ideas about commercial success as well, which Mukul Anand also discussed during our interview. Discussing the profitability of his company's first venture, Anand said, "We introduced films as a non-profit, non-loss medium. It's a profit medium with *Army*, but how profitable? We will see, but *Army* has shown us a profitable balance sheet, which is about 17 percent. It's not bad because it's the first time we are presenting a balance sheet, and within a year we have shown a 17 to 20 percent profit on a huge investment. Say on a 4 *crore* [40 million] investment we make 1 *crore* [10 million]: that's good enough" (Anand, interview, June 1996).

Despite Khanna's and Anand's modest expectations regarding commercial success, in contrast with the industry norms discussed in chapter five, both of their companies failed relatively quickly. The demise of Neha-MAD had to do with the untimely death of Anand, in September 1997, and it is hard to predict what Neha-MAD's trajectory would have been within the industry. Plus Channel produced a plethora of films in a very short time span—about 22 films in three years—none of which achieved any modicum of theatrical success; it became over-extended across its various spheres, going into a great deal of debt by 1999, and was dissolved by 2000.[25] ABCL's failure—its troubles began as early as 1997, and by 1999 it had declared bankruptcy—was exhaustively covered by the Indian press and attributed to several causes: the lower than expected demand for the company's stock during its first public issue; poor box-office performance of films starring Bachchan at the time; huge overhead expenses as a result of too many high-salaried employees; debts incurred by producing the Miss World Pageant in Bangalore in 1996; and overall poor management and business judgment.[26]

The initial response to the failure of companies like ABCL and Plus was the assertion, by some commentators, that attempts to corporatize the film industry were perhaps futile. Ashok Banker, a novelist, newspaper columnist, and television scriptwriter in Bombay, wrote an in-depth three-part story about the ordeal of ABCL, for the Internet newsmagazine *rediff.com* in June 1999. In it he stated, "ABCL's demise marks not just the end of one company, but of a campaign to corporatise the so-called Indian entertainment 'industry' itself. While AB's [Amitabh Bachchan] perennial high profile makes him an easy target for conjecture and controversy, the truth is, he's not alone. Other attempts at corporatising and bringing professional management standards to the hitherto disorganised, financially and professionally indisciplined industry have met with similar failure" (Banker 1999). Of course, subsequent media commentators look back, reinterpreting efforts like Plus and ABCL as ahead of their time (Jha 2005). The examples of Plus and ABCL reinforce the necessity of theatrical box-office success for a company's long-term existence within the film industry. These examples also reveal, especially in the case of Plus Channel and the sort of films it chose to produce, the significance of other structural factors—such as industry status, state policy, the advent of multiplexes, and the entry of entities with much greater capital reserves—to the larger project of rationalizing the film industry.

Post-Industry Status: The Arrival of the Corporate Era

As discussed in chapter one, the granting of industry status in 1998, and the subsequent recognition of filmmaking as an approved industrial activity by the IDBI in 2000, precipitated a number of structural changes within the contemporary Hindi film industry, which have come to be referred to as "corporatization." These changes ranged from the establishment of new production and distribution companies by high-profile Indian corporations and conglomerates, such as the Tata Group, Birla Group, and Reliance Industries, to the transformation of existing production, distribution, or exhibition companies into public limited companies—listed and traded in the Indian stock market—to the expansion of television production companies into film production, to the growing importance of private equity funds and venture capitalists as investors in the film industry.[27] An important result of these changes is that capital to finance film production has become more abundant and is available at a lower cost for filmmakers.

Unlike the mid-1990s, where some members of the film industry expressed their reservations about corporatization, "corporate" had become an adjective of complete distinction within the industry in the following decade. I found that the term "corporate" was being used to describe any sort of production company that appeared organized and successful, including veteran private production companies like Yashraj Films—established by producer/director Yash Chopra in 1970, and managed by his oldest son, Aditya—which were kin-based and not listed on the stock exchange. During fieldwork in Bombay, in 2006, I asked Shravan Shroff what "corporate" meant within the film world, relaying my confusion at the wide-ranging use of the term. "Over here it's being used interchangeably [with] transforming oneself from a sole proprietorship or partnership to a private limited company," he said. "That's what so-called 'going corporate' means—so that you can tap into organized funding" (Shravan Shroff, interview, May 2006). Shroff then discussed how his company, Shringar Films (founded by his uncle and father), was distinctive for its total transformation and reorganization: "When it comes to us, I think, we've gone the entire whole hog, from getting private equity money to going IPO, to having one of the best internal audit firms–KPMG does our audit—to having Temasek of Singapore as an investor. There are very few companies in the country that have done that" (Shravan Shroff, interview, May 2006). According to Shroff, one of the reasons so few film companies had fully refashioned themselves had to do with the overall inertia and sheer burden of the industry's past structure: "For many people, they're actually kind of grappling as to what it means, but I think we ought to be fair to them, because for 50 years the industry was disorganized; you can't expect people to organize themselves in 5 years" (Shravan Shroff, interview, May 2006). Shroff's statements once again point to how the term "corporate" is not simply about the structure or organization of a company, but also crucially represents a new way of being in the world, which became more apparent in his discussion of Yashraj Films: "I think Yashraj works as well as any other corporate in any other industry," he said. "You don't necessarily need to be a private limited company to be a corporately organized body.[28] When I say they're like a well-organized corporate, what I mean to say is that they put systems, people, processes, structures, the right way to do things, the right kind of audit processes, control systems, etc. That's what I mean by being a corporately run, well-run company" (Shravan Shroff, interview, May 2006). In Shroff's remarks, "corporate" operates as a normative category, signifying the right way of doing things; it is also a source of value when applied to entities that do not possess the requisite legal and administrative framework to be designated as a corporation.[29]

The new regimes of finance and organization within the film industry have transformed it from being a very undercapitalized enterprise to one where raising capital is not perceived as the main challenge or constraint. Shroff characterized the distinction between the present and the past: "Earlier, capital used to be the distinctive factor. If you had capital,

TABLE 4 CHALLENGES OF DISTRIBUTION

Year	Total Hindi Films Produced	Total Hindi Films Released	Percentage of Releases to Total Produced (Rounded)
1995	157	99	63
1996	126	96	76
1997	117	92	79
1998	153	108	71
1999	137	112	82
2005	248	187	75
2006	223	153	69
2007	257	148	58
2008	248	127	51
2009	235	135	57

Source: Based on data compiled from *Film Information*, January 6, 1996–January 5, 2002; January 7, 2006–January 2, 2010.

the other guy didn't have capital. Today, capital is there in abundance" (Shravan Shroff, interview, May 2006). The easier availability of funds (at much more reasonable interest rates) has mitigated the financial uncertainties, which often resulted in a very fragmented and extended production schedule that plagued the production process. As a result, films are being made much more quickly, with many projects having their theatrical release within a year to fifteen months of the onset of production rather than the eighteen months to three years — or even longer — that it used to take when I first began my fieldwork. The increased availability of capital is also enabling greater integration between the production, distribution, and exhibition sectors within the industry. For example, established production companies have expanded into distribution (Yashraj Films, Mukta Arts), distribution companies into exhibition (Shringar Cinemas), or exhibition companies into production (PVR Cinemas). One noticeable impact of the above changes has been the dramatic rise in the number of films being produced in the Hindi film industry. Table 4 shows the number of films produced and released theatrically between 1995 and 1999, as well as between 2005 and 2009, to depict the changes that have taken place over the span of a decade. While the total numbers of films being produced and released has increased, the percentage of films produced that are actually distributed has decreased, revealing that finding distribution, as in other film industries, continues to pose a challenge for new entrants into the field.

The entry of the "corporates," as these new production companies—such as UTV, Percept Picture Company, PNC, Sahara One, and K Sera Sera Productions—are commonly referred to by Hindi filmmakers, has led to certain changes in the overall and everyday work culture of the industry. Director Vikram Bhatt related that, with the advent of corporatization, filmmaking was "becoming more organized and industrial." He stated, "There used to be just one producer with production managers, and money was a big problem . . . you know every now and then there was some litigation or the other, but that is now more sorted out. It's getting more and more professional" (Vikram Bhatt, interview, January 2006). He mentioned that filmmaking was becoming more systematized, with written contracts, prompt payments, film insurance, completion bonds, and the use of both executive and line producers. Speaking about the new financial scenario, Bhatt said, "The corporates don't have problems with money . . . once they decide to allocate you a certain amount of money for a certain film, then that's like money in the bank; because they're playing with that amount of money, they have come into the business with that amount of money" (Vikram Bhatt, interview, January 2006).[30] When I remarked that such a scenario must be more desirable for directors, as they are assured of being able to complete their films in a timely manner, Bhatt assented, but then pointed out the disadvantages of working with corporate production companies. Unlike the traditional production companies—more commonly referred to as "banners"—that were identified with an individual producer or a producer/director who was responsible for overseeing all aspects of a film's making, corporate production companies had a greater number of people and multiple levels of procedure involved throughout the filmmaking process. Bhatt described his frustration:

> You're not dealing with one person, you're dealing with a complete corporate, so when you're narrating a script, and narrating it to fifteen people, then it goes through the procedure of them internally meeting and them deciding whether that's on their agenda. Then the casting becomes a problem, because then they have an internal assessment, so they have to assess whether the casting they're going for is going to be something that they're going to be able to distribute and cover, so then they have a different department that assesses that. You know, so they'll say, "Okay, this budget at this star cast: not possible." Like I'm doing a film for Percept/Sahara, so we've been talking for four months

now and they are very keen, but every time there's a change and there's a letter and then it goes to Sahara [headquarters] in Lucknow and then it comes back and the whole thing keeps going up and down. It's very bureaucratic. (Vikram Bhatt, interview, January 2006)

Intrigued by Bhatt's reference to an internal assessment that determines the commercial viability of a film's star cast, I asked him to elaborate:

> They have a distribution department, which assesses that if you're spending x amount of money with y amount of cast, are there going to be returns or are we going to lose money? So, for example, if you have, say, a Zayed Khan [a middle-tier male star], then you know what a territory [distribution] is going to go for, say 70 *lakhs*, 80 *lakhs* [7–8 million rupees], and then they say 80 *lakhs* into now three and a half and then the overseas and music and satellite and they say, "Okay, we're going to get in five *crores* [50 million rupees], that's what we estimate that we're going to get: five *crores* from this film, but the budget is seven and a half [*crores*: 75 million rupees] so it's not working." So they assess all these things before you go on. (Vikram Bhatt, interview, January 2006)

In the assessment that Bhatt outlines above, the "returns" are not box-office receipts, but revenues generated from a sale of distribution rights. The budget of the hypothetical film is not based on the potential revenues that the film could generate through the box-office, but on the revenues that could be earned from its theatrical distribution rights, based on the perceived marketability of a male star to distributors (signaled by the references to territories), and music, satellite, and overseas rights. In such a scenario, the male star takes on even more narrative and thematic significance than what was outlined in chapter five, for with the sort of budgetary constraints outlined above, certain stars can only result in certain genres of films. This form of assessment represents an attempt to systematize and concretize what essentially is subjective knowledge—for an actor's marketability is subject to a variety of factors that are highly variable—and translate it into an algorithm that converts a star into his potential revenues, irrespective of the project. Within this equation, the quality or track record of the director, the script, or the genre of the film is subordinate to the purported marketability of the actor.

Bhatt's description of the internal assessment is an example of how the new corporate production companies go about managing the commercial uncertainties associated with filmmaking. The other measures to offset the costs of production or recoup revenues prior to a film's theatrical release that have been instituted or have become more prominent since 2000 include product placement in films, merchandising tie-ups with Indian retailers, and co-branding with consumer products.[31] These practices are further highlighted for audiences, as a common feature of contemporary Hindi films since the mid-2000s are screens titled "Our Brand Partners," "Our Marketing Partners," and "Our Media Alliances" appearing prior to the opening credits or sequence of a film. The increase in marketing budgets for films, coupled with the explosion in satellite television channels and FM radio in India from the mid-2000s, has resulted in more elaborate and sustained marketing and promotion campaigns for films, which can be understood as practices that seek to reduce the risk of a poor opening weekend at the box-office.

Finally, since 2000, established and successful producers have been able to offset the risk of financial loss by pricing the distribution, satellite, and music rights for their films in such a manner as to earn a profit prior to the film's release. These "table profits," as they are referred to in the industry, have reached significant proportions because the corporates who have entered distribution are willing to pay enormous sums for a film's rights; these corporate distributors often recover—and profit from—their investment by selling the rights they have acquired from the producer to the independent territorial distributor, who is still necessary to implement the actual release of a film, especially in regions far from Bombay or other major urban centers. Despite all of these measures, a film's performance at the box-office continues to play a crucial role in determining future commercial transactions within the industry. A producer with a poor track record at the box-office will be unable to find distributors or unable to negotiate favorable terms for himself regarding the sale of his film's rights. One example that is being characterized as unprecedented by the trade press has to do with *Kites*. Its disappointing fate at the box-office prompted the satellite television channel that had bought the telecast rights of the film from its worldwide distributor to renegotiate the terms of its sale: the channel insisted on reducing the price by 33 percent or it threatened to back out of the sale completely ("Kites Satellite Deal Renegotiated" 2010).

Old Wine in Shiny New Bottles?

The advent of corporatization has either brought about or coincided with other changes in the working style of the Hindi film industry, such as the presence of more women in the spaces of production, more upscale and clearly delineated office spaces, and a greater attention to post-production and special effects. Efforts to represent filmmaking in India as akin to global norms is apparent in the shifts that have occurred in the job titles, noticeable in the opening and closing credit sequences: art director has become production designer; dance director has become choreographer; cinematographer has become director of photography; and spot boys have become production boys or "valets." Kinship and social networks, however, continue to remain strong in the corporatized scenario, extending beyond the creative sectors of filmmaking. Many publicly listed production, distribution, and exhibition companies have their founders' children or other family members working in key executive positions.[32] The family business quality of many of the companies involved in filmmaking is a phenomenon that continues to transcend the film industry and is part of the larger landscape of commercial activity in India.

Another feature of the industry that has not changed is the importance attributed to stars as a mode of risk management. When asked about the challenges that the film industry continued to face, Shravan Shroff responded, "The number of big actors that we have is very limited and those actors don't do too much work. So when you come down to the second rung of actors, unfortunately, those guys don't guarantee you a big box-office hit or opening. So you know you might pay a lot of money, but you are not guaranteed a sale of the movie or alternatively a big opening. So that's unfortunate, because there aren't too many big actors. So that's a constant challenge, about going after those — the big ones" (Shravan Shroff, interview, May 2006). Since the inception of my fieldwork, at any given point of time only about five or six actors are deemed top stars by the industry — "big actors," in Shroff's terms — based on their box-office draw and performance.[33] The "shortage" of top male stars was a lament that I heard, even in 1996, and appeared to contradict the assertion, repeated ad nauseum by industry members and journalists in the general and trade press as well as in conversations with me, that stars do not guarantee commercial success. *Film Information* editor Komal Nahta qualified the ubiquitous self-criticism within the industry about the undue prominence granted to male stars — signified by their power to green-light a project and the high remunerations they command — against the relative neglect of the script.

> The most important thing is the script, but to sell your film, to attract the audience inside in the cinema halls, for these two things, stars are very important. A distributor doesn't mind paying even a *crore* and 50 *lakhs* [15 million rupees] if it's a Shah Rukh Khan film, but if Hemant

Birje is there and the same story is made, he wouldn't even pay 5 *lakhs* [500,000 rupees] for that film. So [a] star is important for the producer to sell his film. [A] star is important for the distributor and exhibitor to sell their film to the public. When you see a Shah Rukh Khan poster, you say, yes, at least it might be good, you know? We may say stars are not important: what we mean actually is stars are important, but story is more important! (Nahta, interview, September 1996)

Unlike Plus Channel in the mid-1990s, which explicitly articulated its identity as a production company that would focus on narrative content rather than spending money on stars, the current crop of corporate producers are not interested in bypassing or undercutting the dominance of stars within the industry.

The greater financial resources of the corporate producers, and their ability to withstand some loss, are not being deployed to cultivate new acting talent, but to attract existing male stars with multiple film contracts promising unprecedented remunerations—anywhere from 100 to 350 million rupees per film, in contrast to rates in the early 2000s, which ranged between 10 and 30 million rupees per film for top male stars.[34] The "prices"—remunerations in industry parlance—paid to leading stars by corporate producers, are a constant object of criticism within the trade press. For example, an issue of *Film Information* had a special feature article detailing the experiences of two actors and how their fees skyrocketed after their interaction with corporate producers who were willing to pay any price the stars quoted. The article concluded with the following statements:

— Corporates are desperate to get the top-of-the-line actors to work in their films.
— Stars can demand any fancy price without being questioned. There's nothing [such] as his last price or [a] basis [for] his new price.
— Like there used to be music companies in the late-80s and early and mid-90s, there are corporates now [who] are offering highly skewed prices to actors. The difference is that audio companies never spoilt the market half as much as the corporates are doing today. ("A Tale of Akshay and Akshaye" 2008)

The criticism that corporates are "spoiling" the market harkens back to criticisms of "proposal-makers" and neophyte producers, who destabilized the social and economic structures of the film industry by wooing stars for their projects with large sums of money.

In fact, the representation of corporate production companies as agents that would radically revolutionize Hindi filmmaking, so rife in the international and Indian press between 2002 and 2004, was quickly revised by 2005, after the films produced by these new companies did not fare too well at the box-office. An article in *Variety* titled "Suits stumble at B.O." asserted, "Corporate is still a Bollywood buzzword, but the transformation hasn't produced bigger grosses or better movies . . . despite the big bucks, streamlined operations, and nattily dressed execs, corporate entities have still not managed to bowl over the box-office. The blockbuster remains the property of Bollywood's old guard" (Chopra 2005). Table 5 lists the top box-office hits from 2003 to 2010, along with their producers and banners; among these 33 films, only 3—listed in bold— have been solo productions by the new corporate production companies that entered the industry in the early 2000s. The rest of the films have been made by individual producers or producer/directors with many years of experience within the film industry many of whom are second- or third-generation filmmakers (the names marked by an asterisk in the table).

Rather than a lack of organization, professionalism, or discipline, the corporates' commercial failures were attributed to bad judgment and inexperience. In this manner, there was a remarkable similarity with the criticisms, leveled in an earlier era, about the ease with which individuals became producers. In 1996, the first attempts at corporatization were hailed as transforming filmmaking into a properly exclusive activity that would rightfully be the domain of the truly competent and knowledgeable. For example, Sunil Manchanda, a joint managing director of MAD Entertainment, asserted in *Outlook*'s feature about the corporatization of the film industry, "No longer is it viable for a rich farmer from Punjab to produce a film at random and partake in the glamour world of films" (in Annuncio 1996). Nearly a decade later, Indu Mirani, a trade magazine journalist, asserted in an international wire-service story about the poor rate of success of corporate producers: "These companies were worse than some of those truck transporters who put their surplus money into films" ("Bollywood's attempt to escape murky past" 2005). Such criticisms are completely connected to commercial outcome, for if the films made by these new companies had succeeded at the box-office, then these companies would have been lauded for transforming filmmaking, along with their organizational structure and working style, as the reason for their success. A text box appeared in the issue of *Film Information* from June 19, 2010, which offers a snide and critical commentary about the

TABLE 5 TOP BOX-OFFICE SUCCESSES 2003–2010

Year	Film	Producer	Banner
2003	*Koi Mil Gaya*	Rakesh Roshan*	Filmkraft Productions
	Kal Ho Na Ho	Yash & Karan Johar*	Dharma Productions
	Baghbaan	Ravi Chopra*	B.R. Films
	Munnabhai M.B.B.S.	Vidhu Vinod Chopra	Vinod Chopra Films
2004	*Main Hoon Na*	Shah Rukh Khan	Red Chillies Entertainment
	Veer Zaara	Yash & Aditya Chopra*	Yashraj Films
	Dhoom	Aditya Chopra*	Yashraj Films
	Murder	Mukesh Bhatt*	Vishesh Films
2005	*No Entry*	Boney Kapoor*	S.K. Films
	Bunty aur Babli	Aditya Chopra*	Yashraj Films
	Kya Kool Hai Hum	Ektaa Kapoor*	Balaji Telefilms
2006	*Dhoom 2*	Aditya Chopra*	Yashraj Films
	Krrish	Rakesh Roshan*	Filmkraft Productions
	Lage Raho Munnabhai	Vidhu Vinod Chopra	Vinod Chopra Films
	Vivah	Kamal Kumar, Rajkumar, Ajit Kumar Barjatya*	Rajshri Productions
	Fanaah	Aditya Chopra*	Yashraj Films
	Malamaal Weekly	**Percept Picture Company**	Percept Picture Company
2007	*Chak De! India*	Aditya Chopra*	Yashraj Films
	Om Shanti Om	Shah Rukh Khan	Red Chillies Entertainment

corporate production/distribution houses, asserting that those working in these new companies do not have the requisite knowledge or experience of filmmaking (statements ii and iii) and are culturally alienated (statement xii). Asserting that it "comes from a keen observer of the corporate culture in the film industry," the text box stated:

> Looking for a Job in a Film Corporate?
> Qualifications You Need to Possess
> Q: Who is fit to join in a top post in a film corporate house? What should his qualifications be?
> A: Only he can apply for a job which offers an annual pay packet of Rs. 50 lakh and above who:
> (i) is an MBA; (ii) does not understand [the] film business at all; (iii) doesn't know which centre comes in which circuit; (iv) is confident

TABLE 5 CONTINUED

Year	Film	Producer	Banner
	Welcome	Firoz Nadiadwala*	Base Industries Group
	Partner	Sohail Khan*	Sohail Khan Productions
	Taare Zameen Par	Aamir Khan*	Aamir Khan Productions
	Bheja Fry	Sunil Doshi	Handmade Films
2008	*Ghajini*	Allu Arvind, Madhu Mantena	Geetha Arts
	Rab Ne Bana Di Jodi	Aditya Chopra*	Yashraj Films
	Jaane Tu . . . Ya Jaane Na	Aamir Khan & Mansoor Khan*	Aamir Khan Productions
	Singh Is Kinng	Vipul Amrutlal Shah	Blockbuster Movies Entertainers
	Golmaal Returns	**Shree Ashtavinayak Cine Vision Ltd.**	Shree Ashtavinayak Cine Vision Ltd.
	Jannat	Mukesh Bhatt*	Vishesh Films
2009	*3 Idiots*	Vidhu Vinod Chopra	Vinod Chopra Films
2010	*Dabangg*	Arbaaz Khan* **Dhilin Mehta**	Arbaaz Khan Production **Shree Ashtavinayak Cine Vision Ltd.**
	Golmaal 3	**Dhilin Mehta**	**Shree Ashtavinayak Cine Vision Ltd.**
	Peepli Live	Aamir Khan & Kiran Rao*	Aamir Khan Productions **UTV Motion Pictures**

Note: * represents individuals from film families; **boldface** represents corporate producers.
Source: Based on data compiled from *Film Information*, January 7, 2006–January 7, 2011.

that he will not pick up the business very fast; (v) can wear different ties every day, neatly knotted; (vi) can prepare reports on Excel sheets; (vii) can send out e-mails at the drop of a hat; (viii) believes in communicating with his colleagues only through e-mails, even if his female or male colleagues are all seated next to him; (ix) has the ability to not answer his cell phone when any caller calls for the first time or, better still, has the ability to never take calls and also never call back; (x) is always in meetings; (xi) can all the time plan, but is incapable of executing the plans; (xi) can talk about Hindi films, but only in English. ("Looking for a Job in a Film Corporate" 2010)

As the overall hit-flop ratio has not improved since the advent of corporatization, illustrated by Table 6, and in fact, with more films produced the percentage of hits has actually decreased, certain production fictions

TABLE 6   RATIO OF HITS TO FLOPS, 1995–2000, 2005–2010

Year	Total Hindi Films Released	"A" Hits (Doubling or More of Distributors' Investment)	Percentage of Hits (Rounded)	"B" Earners (Coverage of Distributors' Investment)	Percentage of Earning Films (A & B)
1995	99	6	6	8	14
1996	96	6	6	10	17
1997	92	8	9	19	29
1998	108	6	6	15	19
1999	112	4	4	13	15
2000	142	2	1	15	12
2005	187	3	2	16	10
2006	153	9	6	14	15
2007	148	7	5	9	11
2008	127	9	7	7	13
2009	135	3	2	6	7
2010	156	4	3	9	8

Source: Based on data compiled from *Film Information*, January 6, 1996–January 5, 2002; January 7, 2006–January 7, 2011.

have remained resilient within the industry: stars alone cannot guarantee hits; the script is "king"; proper marketing is necessary for a film; or too much promotion can ruin a film's chances at the box-office. Since corporate producers have not been more successful in their ventures than independent producers, some new production fictions have been articulated to make sense of this scenario. While industry members asserted, in the late 1990s, that poor planning and the haphazard way of making films were the reasons for the poor rates of commercial success in the industry,[35] since the mid-2000s, the lack of knowledge and absence of "passion" have been offered as the reasons for the continued commercial disappointments, despite the introduction of organization, discipline, and professionalism into the industry.

A feature titled "Are Corporates Helping the Film Industry or Harming It?" written by Komal Nahta for the Diwali special issue of *Film Information* in 2007, articulates these new production fictions. While pointing out the benefits that have accrued to the film industry because of corporatization, namely the large infusions of capital—or "money power" in Nahta's words—which have enabled production to be more streamlined, post-production technology to be improved, and exhibition infrastructure to be upgraded, Nahta also asserts that money corrupts and leads to substandard filmmaking. "Corporatisation has also resulted in the content of films taking a backseat," Nahta claims. "Excess money has made several creative people lax, and secondly money is being thrown around for anybody and everybody to make films, as a result of which even mediocre and below-average directors and writers are churning out films which are sub-standard" (2007: 31). Thus, too much money can be as much of a reason for box-office failure as too little money, which was the scenario in the past. The second criticism of the corporates has to do with their lack of knowledge and experience with filmmaking, apparent from statements like, "Most of the corporate houses don't have the ability to separate the wheat from the chaff"; or "The problem with corporates is that they've appointed outsiders in top creative posts" (2007: 31). In pointing out that the "film business is not so easy that rank newcomers can learn it," Nahta indulges in the longstanding practice of boundary-work discussed in chapter five.

Perhaps the most intriguing criticism has to do with the corporates' lack of passion and their excessive commercialism: "The greatest harm the corporate culture has done to the film industry is to have made film production and distribution a trading business. Of course film production and distribution are commercial businesses, but there's art involved, at least in production. Where there's art, there must be passion. But passion has gone out of the window after corporates have made an entry into Bollywood. With an eye on profits and only on turnovers and top lines, corporates are trying to make more money by trading in films rather than by making and releasing films" (Nahta 2007: 32). The "trading" that Nahta is referring to is the practice of buying and selling distribution rights as a profit-generating enterprise on its own: that is, a company buys the distribution rights for a film and then sells it to another company for a profit, rather than undertaking the logistics of distributing the film itself. This sort of buying and selling of rights is a well-established practice within the film industry, but in the past these transactions were undertaken to generate working capital rather than profit.[36]

According to Nahta, the corporate trading in films is a major reason for the departure of passion from filmmaking. He does not, however, single out corporate producers, but holds others accountable as well: "For the corporate producer, the lack of passion is still somewhat understandable, but what is unpardonable is the missing passion of the creator or the director, and also the actor. Directors these days are trying to amass as much wealth as possible, actors are busy running to the bank with fat pay cheques, and producers whose films are acquired by corporates are only interested in wrapping up their projects so that they can plunder another corporate for their next film" (Nahta 2007: 32). As an analyst of what is most commonly referred to as "commercial cinema," Nahta's criticisms are curious, for they in essence argue that the reason for commercial failure is excessive commercialism, that is, films are not making money at the box-office because filmmakers are only interested in making money. If more films were deemed as hits, then these very attributes would be celebrated as legitimate modi operandi, for they would be interpreted as signs of filmmakers' commitment or "passion."

THE IDEOLOGY OF FILM PRODUCTION

Such assertions about passion, knowledge, experience, and quality are all ways that members of the film industry attempt to make sense of the uncertainty of the film business—to impose some meaning and order on the highly unpredictable and disorderly commercial universe in which they operate. These production fictions enable filmmakers to continue with their enterprise, for they provide a way to explain the randomness that marks commercial filmmaking. While the insecurities around finance capital and distribution outlets have been resolved in the Hindi film industry, due to the phenomena of corporatization and growth of multiplexes, the ultimate site of unpredictability, which continues to vex filmmakers, is that of the audience. From a discussion of the Hindi film industry's production fictions and its practices of managing uncertainty, I now turn to an examination of the industry's audience fictions and practices of audience-making in the following two chapters.

Part 3

DISCOURSES AND PRACTICES OF AUDIENCE-MAKING

CHAPTER 8

Pleasing Both Aunties and Servants

The Hindi Film Industry and Its Audience Imaginaries

In October 2000, during one of my visits to Bombay, I dropped by an editing studio to watch Tarun Kumar put together television trailers, referred to as "TV promos," for his upcoming film. The film was a sexually charged thriller/murder mystery, which Tarun kept referring to as his "*Last Tango in Paris*." Discussing the commercial prospects of his film, he declared, "You know this *Last Tango in Paris*; I know Bihar will get sold immediately."[1] The 30-second spot Tarun was editing was a provocative one, where it was clear that the lead characters were engaged in sexual activity, though nothing explicit was being depicted.

Tarun then seemed to have second thoughts about how he had cut the spot: "You know, I think the family audience is not going to go for this. What will happen to my family audience with this kind of trailer?"

He turned to one of his assistants and asked, "What would your mom think about this film if she saw this promo?"

The assistant said, "I don't know, but she'll definitely raise one of her eyebrows."

Tarun responded, "I know my servant will definitely want to go see this. You know, if I try to please the aunties, I'll end up disappointing the servants."

In this chapter and the next, I examine how Hindi filmmakers imagine, classify, and discuss their audiences as an essential manifestation of all three features of the film industry's production culture: sentiments of disdain, practices of distinction, and efforts to manage uncertainty. Peppered with references to distinct audiences with distinct taste cultures (Bihar, family audience, aunties, and servants), Tarun Kumar's conversation in the editing studio illustrates the relevance of social categories, such as region, generation, gender, and class, as well as the dominance of binary oppositions—Bihar vs. family audience, aunties vs. servants—in the Hindi film industry's creation of a taxonomy of the film-viewing public. Rather than originating from the well-established tradition of market research utilized by the print media, television, advertising, and consumer product industries in India, the film industry's audience classifications, which are broadly encompassing and highly imprecise, emerge from a combination of intuition, regional sterotypes, and developmentalist perceptions of how education, occupation, and residence shape subjectivities and thus taste cultures.[2] All of the various fragmentations of the audience reproduce a larger and more enduring binary of the "masses" and the "classes" as the two main audiences of Hindi cinema. Filmmakers regard these constituencies as fundamentally in opposition, with completely incommensurable tastes and worldviews, which is the basis of Kumar's frustration in the editing studio. Despite this great divide between its audiences, for most of its history the Hindi film industry has aimed to bridge or transcend these gaps, rather than exclusively target any particular audience category.

Underlying the film industry's audience classifications is a theory of film spectatorship, which is intimately associated with commercial outcome. Commercial outcome is regarded as an accurate barometer of social attitudes, norms, and sensibilities, and therefore serves as a source of knowledge to filmmakers about audiences. Box-office success or failure either reinforces or revises filmmakers' assumptions about audiences—from their composition and tastes, to intellectual abilities and codes of morality; therefore, I argue that for Hindi filmmakers the box-office serves as a metonym for the practice of film consumption and operates as a technology of "social envisioning"—a phrase coined by John Durham Peters to refer to modern mass media's promise of representing unseeable social totalities, which "make society imaginable to itself" (1997). Box-office figures represent the unseeable totality that is the cinemagoing audience, and thus mediate Hindi filmmakers' relationship to abstract collectivities such as "Indian society."[3] This view is manifest in the industry both in the way that commercial outcome produces a sociology of the viewing audience, and in the manner in which that outcome is consistently interpreted through culturalist, rather than economic, logics.

An important site for the operation of culturalist logics is the category of commercial success known as the "universal hit," which refers to a film understood to have had broad audience appeal based on its uniform box-office performance throughout India. Rather than a transparent economic classification, however, the category serves as a social index for Hindi filmmakers—signifying a collective experience rooted in a shared, essential identity that transcends differences of class, region, gender, and generation; yet the ideal of a universal hit is very difficult to achieve in practice, and I detail filmmakers' discourses about the challenges and obstacles involved in attaining such a hit. The challenges articulated by filmmakers reveal their understandings about the relationship between film consumption and subjectivity, demonstrating their role as cultural theorists producing "neighboring epistemologies" to anthropologists;[4] even though their pronouncements about audiences appear paternalistic and reductive, the underlying premise (rather than the conclusions)— interpreting film consumption as an expression of subjectivity or identity—is not dissimilar from the scholarship on audiences and media consumption.[5]

This chapter begins with an elaboration of the film industry's theories of spectatorship. My use of the term "spectatorship," which has been closely associated with the discipline of film studies and a particular mode of formal textual analysis, is intentional—just as the construction of the spectator in classical film theory bears little resemblance to the actual viewers of films (Hansen 1991; Mayne 1993; Willemen 1994), Hindi filmmakers' ideas about audiences are equally distant.[6] Whereas the former analyzes the formal and narrative properties of a film text to delineate an ideal type or imagined spectator, the latter analyzes box-office outcome to construct particular spectators. After discussing how filmmakers theorize spectatorship and interpret commercial outcome through culturalist logics, I detail the various modes of classifying and categorizing the audience for Hindi cinema. Finally, I describe the desire expressed by filmmakers in the late 1990s, both to make a film that resonated with diverse audiences and the constraints they faced in trying to achieve a universal hit. In addition to describing the dominant assumptions and beliefs Hindi filmmakers hold about their audiences, this chapter also lays the foundation to comprehend the full impact of the discussion in the following chapter on the shift in audience imaginaries that occurs after 2000, including the changing significance of the universal hit.

Members of the industry discuss viewers' relationship to, and engagement with, cinema through the related concepts of identification and acceptance. While identification encompasses a range of meanings, from literal similarities between audiences and the characters onscreen to a familiarity with the circumstances, scenarios, and conflicts depicted in the film, it is represented as the basis of audience pleasure; therefore it is integral to commercial success. Javed Akhtar, a highly successful screenwriter, lyricist, and poet, explained the concept as a delicate balance of the familiar and the fantastic: "Whatever is happening on the screen should make him laugh, should make him cry; he should be able to identify with it. He should be able to fantasize and at the same time: if it is too real, then he won't like it. If it has nothing to do with reality, then too he won't like it!" (Akhtar, interview, November 1996). From a Hindi filmmaker's point of view, identification is not dependent upon an aesthetic of social realism—or even a realistic mise-en-scène—which could impede pleasure according to Akhtar; it is more dependent on whether the portrayal of the joys, sorrows, and dilemmas faced by the characters are able to resonate with—rather than replicate—audiences' own experiences.

The concept of acceptance, despite being located more in the realm of moral codes and kinship norms, is related in that it is often the precondition for identification. As apparent from Tarun Kumar's comments about the family audience and "aunties," filmmakers operate with a distinct and internalized sense of boundaries and limits to what is and is not permissible.[7] Acceptance, by which filmmakers mean audiences' lack of objection to a film's plot, theme, or characterizations, is most palpable and salient when it appears to be absent, signified by a film's poor showing at the box-office. Pamela Chopra discussed the disappointing commercial performance of Silsila (Affair) and Lamhe, directed by her husband, Yash, in these terms. Characterizing both as "good films," Chopra surmised that they were not successful because they were a "tad bit extra different." She asserted that one had to be very careful with, and sensitive to, dominant codes of morality. Referring to Silsila, which was about an extramarital affair, Chopra said, "You cannot afford to ride roughshod over very, very basic emotions. The marriage is a very, very sacred institution in India, and when the director created sympathy for the two lovers who were willing to go outside their marriage and continue their love affair, he didn't carry the audience with him" (Pamela Chopra, interview, 26 March 1996). She speculated that those audiences who did feel sympathy for the pro-

tagonists would still not accept the film, because their potential identification made them feel guilty and uncomfortable. She offered a similar
reasoning for *Lamhe* where the plot of a much older man falling in love
with a much younger woman was posed as another morally uncomfortable situation for audiences.

Both forms of engagement with a film are therefore understood and
measured by members of the industry in terms of the commercial performance of films; commercial success ("hit") or failure ("flop") is read as
evidence of viewers' propensity to accept, or identify with, a particular
film. Director Vikram Bhatt elaborated on how commercial outcome provides filmmakers with the necessary feedback about audience likes and
dislikes: "They constantly reject what they don't want, till they accept
that one film, and the filmmakers understand—'Oh so this is what they
want.' And that's why every Hindi film that becomes a hit . . . is a pointer
in the right direction that tells you—'Oh this is what they want; this is
what they're feeling right now,' which doesn't mean that the repetition
of the same thing will work, but at least it's a step in the right direction"
(Vikram Bhatt, interview, January 2006). Bhatt's remarks reveal how hits
and flops are the main way that Hindi filmmakers know, understand, and
relate to their audiences.

Commercial outcome carries such heavy social significance because
the ratio of hits to flops is very low, and members of the industry until
the early 2000s acknowledged that the majority of viewers could not afford to see each and every film in the theater. Komal Nahta, the editor of
the trade weekly *Film Information*, stated bluntly, "India is basically a poor
country. Everybody has limited purchasing power—especially the worker
category: they cannot be expected to see every film" (Nahta, interview,
September 1996). While film viewing is represented as entertainment,
the decision to see a particular film is not viewed as frivolous. Since going
to see a film in a theater involves an investment of time and money, the
act of choosing a film is accorded tremendous agentive power and symbolic significance by filmmakers. Producer/director Aditya Chopra characterized how movie-going in India, in contrast to the United States, was
not a trivial matter, due to the limited discretionary income most Indians
possessed:

> For Indians, everything is money-oriented. Why? Because they're
> not, they don't have so much of it, so they can't afford to be casual
> about it. Like you go abroad and you see a flick and think, "Eh, it was
> okay, I didn't like it." You don't think of those four or five dollars that

you spent on it. Here, you think about those 50 rupees, and you feel, "Oh God!" It feels that way because there are people here who work throughout the day, earn daily wages, and probably skip a meal to see a film! So he has the right to take his films very seriously, and he does take his films very seriously, so that's why you need to take it very seriously. (Aditya Chopra, interview, April 1996)

The most noticeable manifestation of this serious attention to commercial outcome is that filmmakers interpret film consumption through culturalist rather than economic logics. The act of purchasing a ticket is understood as an endorsement or appreciation of that particular film and its stars. For example, in an interview published in *Film Information*, Shah Rukh Khan related that a director had once told him, "As soon as someone has bought a ticket to see your film, he has already treated you as a god, he has put you on a very, very high pedestal" (Nahta 2000b: 32); therefore, a film designated as a hit signifies that it enjoys wide-ranging popularity and adulation, while a flop signifies broad displeasure and censure on the part of viewers. Producer/director/star Aamir Khan discussed how commercial outcome operated as a form of imperfect communication between audiences and filmmakers:

Nobody really knows what the audience wants to see. You're trying to figure out for yourself what the audience wants to see. So one of the basic rules that a lot of people follow in the industry—a lot of financers or film producers follow—is that they go by the last previous hits, and what is the present trend going on . . . So if a stupid and junkie film becomes a major hit, then the audience is sending a certain signal to the producers and the people who are financing films, and they may not be intentionally sending that signal that, "Ah, we are making this film a hit because this is the kind of films we want to see." No, but that is the signal that the producers pick up whether it is sent or not, and they say, "Fine, if this is what the audience wants to see today, this is what we want to give them." (Aamir Khan, interview, March 1996)

However, as I discussed in chapter five, the classification of commercial outcome and the determination of box-office success is entangled with the distributor and his pricing decisions rather than gross box-office receipts or number of tickets sold. The categories of hit and flop are generated when distributors' expectations are disrupted. High expectations can yield a flop, while low expectations can yield a hit. The issue of mismatched expectations is very common in the case of stars, as Taran Adarsh, the editor of *Trade Guide*, made explicit, "If a big star cast film fetches 75 percent [occupancies in a cinema] in the first week, it's termed disaster. You have to have 95 percent . . . to have the hit category. On the other hand, a small picture, if it fetches 80 percent, it is considered good, but for a big film to fetch 75 percent or 85 percent is very bad!" (Adarsh, interview, September 1996).

By highlighting the distributor's role in order to question the avowed transparency and the culturally indexical interpretation of commercial outcome, my intention is not to imply that a different mechanism to measure commercial outcome would somehow yield truer insights or more accurate knowledge about film audiences. Media scholars have long pointed out that audiences for large-scale culture industries such as television are literally unknowable (Ang 1991; Hartley 1987), and the same conclusions can be applied to film audiences. Even if aggregate tickets sold or gross box-office receipts are the criteria for categorizing commercial outcome, all that they quantify is the act of purchasing a ticket, which at the most measures awareness and interest in a film, but not the more complex processes of reception. Box-office data does not yield information about viewers' intentions, perceptions, experiences, likes, or dislikes; in fact, displeasure with a film, once it has been viewed in a theater, can never really be quantified, since the action of purchasing a ticket gets registered and interpreted as audience approval.[8] While box-office outcome at best can be understood as an index of a commercial transaction, Hindi filmmakers interpret it as an indexical expression of social identity and subjectivity.

The case of *Hum Aapke Hain Koun!* (HAHK) and its success offers a good example of this sort of socially indexical interpretation. As discussed in chapter two, the film's stupendous success took the industry by surprise. I asked members of the industry about why they thought the film did so well, especially since it had initially been dismissed as a "wedding video," by many filmmakers and commentators. Rather than focusing on the carefully planned release strategy of the producers, who were also the film's distributors, everyone I spoke with explained the film's success in culturalist logics. For example, screenwriter Sachin Bhaumick asserted, "We've progressed so much; we're sending rockets in the sky, but still a family picture like *Hum Aapke Hain Koun!* is doing very well, because audiences still value these things" (Bhaumick, interview, October 1996). The fact that the producer/distributors released a limited number of film prints, introduced a new form of television publicity, were allowed to raise ticket prices significantly, went against the prevailing norms of the time by withholding the videocassettes, and instituted safeguards to curb video piracy, were not as relevant to filmmakers' explanations for the film's success as the discourse of "Indian values and emotions."[9] For members of the film industry, the overwhelming success of HAHK demonstrated an affirmation of traditional Indian values—that despite all of the changes occurring in post-liberalization India, certain core values about the importance of the extended family—as well as traditional gender and filial roles—remained the same.

Although the unique release strategy of HAHK was remarked upon, it was never put forth as the central explanation in the film's overall success, and neither was the fact that the film's producers, Rajshri Productions, also happened to be its India-wide distributors. According to Komal Nahta of *Film Information*, HAHK was a "slow starter" and written off by the industry as a flop in the first week, but gradually its business picked up and screenings were running at full capacity. Nahta explained how, despite a disappointing opening, the film remained in theaters because, "Rajshris are the distributors themselves; they don't sell their film to anybody, so they had the holding capacity. They were so confident: they couldn't care less what people were saying" (Nahta, interview, September 1996). While the example of HAHK demonstrates the commercial advantage achieved by integrating production with distribution when feasible (not all production companies have the necessary access to, or reserves of, finance capital to self-distribute their films), it did not set a precedent in restructuring the relationship between production and distribution, nor did it initiate a wide-scale discussion about the importance of release and marketing strategies within the industry. Although certain practices associated with the film's distribution and publicity, such as delaying the release of videocassettes and new types of television trailers, became the norm within the industry, the main impact of HAHK was at the thematic, narrative, and aesthetic level.

The discussion precipitated by HAHK's success was mainly carried out in a cultural and social register, revising ideas about audience tastes, preferences, and demands. Several filmmakers related to me that the success of HAHK communicated that audiences were fed up with the standard fare of sex, violence, vendetta, and action. Although Komal Nahta mentioned the importance of the Rajshri's persistence in keeping the film in theaters, despite its weak opening, he explained the film's success by stating, "*Hum Aapke Hain Koun!*: it was just our roots, Indian weddings, and plain emotions that made it a big hit" (Nahta, interview, September

1996). I argue that this reliance on culturalist explanations is linked to the tremendous uncertainty of the business of cinema, where it is nearly impossible for the film industry (and others) to predict box-office outcome. This very uncertainty can also entice individuals into the film industry, like R. Mohan, the entrepreneur introduced in chapter five, who decided to dabble in film production after making his fortunes in paper goods and mosquito repellent. Mohan explained that unlike other businesses, filmmaking had the potential for incomparably high returns: "One *Dilwale Dulhaniya* can get 200 *crores* [2 billion rupees] or something . . . that's the figure they're talking about, which happens in no other business. There, input is fixed; return is also fixed. We know that from one kilo of paper how much we make, so in order to break even, we know this many kilos have to be sold. You won't get returns like a *Dilwale*—you'll not get a jackpot out of that. Only Hindi films are jackpots" (Mohan, interview, May 1996).

The "jackpot" quality of box-office outcome lends itself more readily to culturalist explanations than commercial accounts, which lack the necessary explanatory power to make sense of a highly uncertain business environment. For example, the incredible success of HAHK took industry members by surprise, not only because they were skeptical of its success, but also because of the competing sources of entertainment options— from satellite and cable television to home video—available to audiences. Its success was inconceivable from the standpoint of the market conditions at the time. In commercial explanations for box-office outcome the onus falls on filmmakers, since their actions and practices are held accountable, while in culturalist explanations the onus shifts to audiences and their subjectivities.[10]

Finally, commercial explanations for box-office outcome do not possess the same affective power as social and cultural explanations. Throughout the world, films viewed by large numbers of people tend to get labeled as cultural phenomena and seem to generate social and cultural explanations (as well as anxieties) in a variety of spheres—media, scholarly, and everyday life. The Hindi film industry's theories of spectatorship and its own representation as a mainstream industry are predicated on an affective relationship between cinema and its audiences. The very label "commercial cinema," which has a system of market relations and consumption embedded in it, is based on the notion that film is an important source of entertainment and pleasure to vast numbers of people. As mentioned above, entertainment and pleasure are understood in terms of the concepts of identification and acceptance, both of which rely on an affective engagement with films. The only mechanism for filmmakers to discern such engagement is commercial outcome, however, which is why box-office results are interpreted in a sociological fashion. This is apparent in how members of the industry describe, discuss, and classify their audiences.

MAPPING THE AUDIENCE

Tarun Kumar's confidence that his sexy trailer would ensure that his film was bought by distributors for the Bihar territory demonstrates how the geography of the distribution network for Hindi films produces a social imaginary of difference (Dàvila 2001; Himpele 1996), whereby taste is ascribed onto place, implicitly mapping film-viewing preferences in a vast and culturally diverse country like India onto ethnic and linguistic markers of identity.[11] While Kumar's comment about Bihar is based more on assumptions about the class composition of audiences in the state, much of the regional classification of audience preference is predicated upon an idea of literal identification: that certain stars or films may fare better in some territories than others because of the ethnic and linguistic affinities between stars and audiences. Punkej Kharabanda, who in 1996 was the secretary for a few leading actors and actresses, offered Dharmendra—an actor whose career has spanned over three decades—and his two sons, Sunny and Bobby Deol, as examples: "Any film of theirs in Punjab can never do badly. Punjabis think of them as their own—'It's our family; *Sade puttar hai*' [they're our sons]" (Kharabanda, interview, 17 April 1996). Although a large number of the actors in the Hindi film industry are of Punjabi origin, this particular family of actors has always been overtly identified as Punjabi in film magazines and other modes of disseminating news and gossip about the film industry.[12]

In addition to imagining affinity between film stars and their audiences based on shared ethnicity, regional identity, or linguistic community, members of the industry assume that films depicting a specific regional milieu in terms of theme, dress, music, dialect of Hindi, and other markers of ethnicity will be more successful in the regions that they depict. Reviews in the trade press, which always assess a film's commercial potential, often negatively value a film that appears too rooted in a particular regional milieu, for that would preclude identification from a broad spectrum of viewers. For example, the trade magazine *Film Information*, in its review of the 2001 film *Chandni Bar*, asserted, "The film is too Bombay-centric in the sense that the story is entirely about Bombay's dance-bar culture and the underworld." While praising the director's efforts in familiarizing himself with the specific milieu, the review declares, "too much emphasis on presenting the truest picture of Bombay's underbelly rules out universal appeal for the film." The review went on to predict that the film "has appeal only for Bombay and parts of Maharashtra," and thereby would do much better business in Bombay than anywhere else.[13] The fact that the film was a modest commercial success primarily in Bombay reinforces the reviewer's projections about the links between regional identity and film consumption.

In my conversations with distributors and trade journalists, entire territories were assigned a singular character based on the commercial performance of films. For example, according to my informants, "modern" films, or those that feature a contemporary urban setting and are less melodramatic, did better in the Bombay territory and the South,[14] while "social" films—films that focus heavily on family relationships that could be either in an urban or rural setting—did better in the North and the East. Thus within the film industry's social imaginary, the fact that modern films do better in Bombay and the South signifies those territories as modern, while the sort of films that succeed in the North and the East signifies them as traditional. Although the Overseas Territory is generally described as beholden to romantic films, replete with song and dance sequences, sometimes the territory is divided according to preferences that correspond with specific territories in India. For example, distributors have observed that films that do well in the cities of Bombay and Delhi also do very well in the United Kingdom, United States, and Canada, while films that do well in Punjab also do well in the Gulf. One major difference between the territories in India and the Overseas Territories is that not all Hindi films will be distributed overseas. Films made with lesser-known actors or lesser-known directors are less likely to be released in the Overseas Territory, so that it is basically dominated by big-budget, highly publicized films with popular stars.

In addition to producing ethno-linguistic audience categories, the distribution network generates the scalar residential binary of "city" and "interior" audiences, which corresponds to the division of distribution territories into A, B, and C class centers. Within this binary, the city refers to A-class centers, while the interior is comprised of B- and C-class centers. While each territory and subterritory has its interiors, entire subterritories in central and northern India, such as C.P., C.I., U.P., or Bihar, are regarded as the "interiors" from the perspective of Hindi filmmakers in a cosmopolitan city like Bombay. The interior audience is understood as poorly educated, culturally conservative, economically marginalized, and socially backward. For example, during the shooting of a scene for the film *Sar Aankhon Par* (Your Wish Is My Command) when the protagonist tells his father that he has an interview at the *Times of India* (a nationally circulated English-language newspaper), the scriptwriter, Sanjay Chhel, suggested to the director, "Gyan-*ji*, I think he should say *akhbaar* [the Urdu word for newspaper] after *Times of India*, because people in the interiors won't know what it is." When explaining the poor box-office fate of the film, *1942 A Love Story*, which is set against the backdrop of the Indian independence movement, the head of a leading distribution firm in Bombay articulated the main differences between audiences in cities and the interiors in terms of education, intellectual curiosity, and the rhythms of daily life:

> Those are intelligent movies . . . in the sense that [the] city-based audience would like to see it again and again. They'll pay you a higher rate of admission to go in, but the same movie, if it has to go to a smaller station, people don't understand it. [This is] because . . . [in the city] you're well educated—you understand what is happening in the world; you are in a big town. Smaller town people say, "Oh we just need . . . two [or] three hours of entertainment, [a] normal action movie, and go to sleep." It makes a lot of difference that way. The standard of living—see Bombay is different; now you go 100 miles away, it's different: there, priorities are different. (interview, 1996)

The condescension expressed toward small-town audiences in the above statements is similar to stereotypes of the "heartland" or "middle America" expressed by U.S. media professionals (Zafirau 2009a). I frequently heard the Bombay equivalent of "Will it play in Peoria?" which was "Will this run in Jhumri-Talayya?" In addition to the opposition between city and small-town audiences, the other dichotomy established is that between intelligent movies and action movies, implying that these categories are mutually exclusive.

When I had the chance to meet Lala Damani, a distributor for the Bengal and Bihar subterritories, I asked him about the perceptions I had heard from others that audiences in those regions only wanted to watch action films. Rather than questioning the normative judgments made about the genre, he asserted that viewers in his territories had no alternative, because the other genres of films being produced by the Bombay industry were not of the sort with which they could identify. Quoting a Hindi proverb, which roughly translates to "It's better to have a one-eyed uncle than no uncle at all," Damani pointed out that the block-buster films of the previous years like HAHK and *Dilwale Dulhaniya Le Jayenge* also had done very well in his territories. To reinforce his point about audiences in his region wanting something more than action, Damani told me to watch the film *Nadiya Ke Par* (Across the River) an older film upon which HAHK was based. He pointed out how that even after HAHK's release, the older film was still doing well in repeat runs, signaling to him that audiences in his territories had more diverse tastes than what was generally attributed to them by Bombay filmmakers. "*Nadiya Ke Par* has got no action," Damani said, "but it is still running for five weeks in the repeat run. It means that the people's taste is not the action picture. Action pictures run for one week only." The main problem from his point of view was, "The people in Bombay take it for granted that only action pictures run. They don't have time to sit down and create universally appealing stories" (Damani, interview, October 2000). I will discuss Damani's tribulations further in the next chapter, as well as the over-determined status of Bihar in filmmakers' discourses. It is not happenstance that Tarun Kumar alluded to Bihar in the editing studio when surmising that images that could be potentially offensive and scandalous to women and families would be appealing to viewers in this region. Similar to those addressed in chapter two's discussion of "front-benchers," Kumar's comments arise from assumptions linking gender, social class, and filmic preferences.

CLASS-IFYING THE AUDIENCE

Tarun Kumar's hesitation about mothers and "aunties" illustrates how gender is an important mode of classifying audiences. "Ladies audience" is an operative category within the film industry, and until the advent of multiplexes, it was perhaps the only niche audience from the point of view of the industry. Working with a literalist idea of identification, most members of the industry (who are predominantly male) presume that women prefer "heroine-oriented" films — those that have a woman as the central protagonist or main narrative agent. The prevailing belief in the industry is that actresses do not guarantee a good opening at the box-office, however. Most filmmakers asserted that heroine-oriented films depended on word-of-mouth to succeed, implying that the audiences who frequented movie theaters in the opening weekend of a film were primarily male. Nonetheless, female audiences are perceived as much harder to please. Scriptwriter Sutanu Gupta expressed his views about what he thinks women want to see in a film: "You see *yaha pe kya hota hai* [what happens here], if you're writing an action picture, then the hero kicks one fantastic blow on the villain's face, people clap. Women don't: they are not interested. You have to give them a solid story. They're impressed by story; they're impressed by characterization; they're impressed by touching moments, which is more difficult to write" (Gupta, interview, 18 November 1996). Aside from heroine-oriented films, other films thought to appeal to women are those that contain narratives centered around kinship relations and devoid of violence, action, and "vulgarity." The following excerpt from *Film Information*'s review of *Raja Hindustani*, the highest-grossing film of 1996, provides a glimpse of how women's film-viewing preferences have been imagined: "These two scenes—the hero's refusal to sign the divorce papers and the heroine's refusal to divorce her husband—reaffirm one's faith in the institution of marriage and are so reassuring that they will be fantastic scoring points to make the ladies audience love—nay adore—the film. The refusals, of the husband first and the wife later, come at moments when one actually expects that they would sign the divorce papers. The shock value coupled with the heart-warming feeling one experiences after these two scenes are enough to bowl the ladies audience over and make them patronise this film in a very big way" (Nahta 1996).

Trying to draw women into theaters was viewed as a desirable challenge by filmmakers, since women were seen as more likely to view films with their families. Komal Nahta stated that films that have been "long runners" were those with "good emotions"[15] and music, "Because good emotions means ladies will come in, and ladies [coming] in means [that] they will [bring] their children along and their husbands along. Then, you know, it becomes like a whole cycle" (Nahta, interview, September 1996). What is apparent from the review—and from the way that the viewing practices of women are characterized—is that the "ladies audience" essentially refers to married women. From the point of view of filmmakers, unmarried women do not exist as a separate demographic group, and—even if thought about—would get subsumed into other large categories, such as "student," "youth," or "family."

"Family audience" is a significant audience category, which is seen as having similar tastes to the ladies audience, predicated primarily on viewing practices, but not requiring heroine-oriented films. The key characteristic for a film to appeal to family audiences is cross-generational propriety: everyone should be able to watch the film together, which means there should be nothing in the content or treatment that makes it uncomfortable or embarrassing for parents, children, siblings, or other kin to view as a group. It is in this respect that Kumar was concerned about driving away potential viewers with his trailer. Films suitable for family viewing are also described as "wholesome" or "vegetarian," which denotes their sanitized language and lack of highly suggestive song sequences, bawdy humor, or graphic violence. Nester D'Souza, the manager of the erstwhile Metro Cinema—which turned into a multiplex in 2006—one of the oldest theaters in Bombay, explained the importance of the family audience for his business and how he tried to cater to that segment:

> I have to show a film that would assure me 524 seats in the balcony at the rate of around about Rs. 70, dead on, in advance,[16] and 400 in the stalls. If I get this—I get the family audience—everything else runs. I can't go for sex; I can't go for horror. Families don't come. I can't afford spot booking; I can't afford straggler bookings—straggler bookings means singles and doubles. I need people to buy tickets in fours, tens, fifteens, and twenties. I need people to buy them in advance . . . If I don't get those, I'm in trouble, so I blend my choice of pictures that give you a lot of entertainment, [a] little bit of violence, but also at the same time caters to the families. (D'Souza, interview, June 1996)

In D'Souza's statements, it is clear that the family audience refers to a mode of viewing rather than a specific genre of films. His remarks about the balcony and stalls are a reference to the differential pricing of tickets and the spatialization of class hierarchy in the single-screen movie theater.

The ladies, family, Overseas Territory, and (sometimes) city categories make up the larger audience category known as the "classes," whose other is the "masses." The masses-classes binary has been the dominant interpretive framework—by filmmakers, the state, the press, scholars, and social elites—for discussing and understanding audiences in India. The elaboration of this framework is rife with assumptions about class and taste, where taste is most notably expressed as distaste for certain aesthetic conventions, narrative styles, and thematic concerns (Bourdieu 1984). Until the early 2000s, the masses were regarded as the primary audience for Hindi cinema. Members of the industry define the masses vaguely in terms of occupation—domestic workers, manual laborers, rickshaw drivers, taxi drivers, factory workers—implicitly gendering them as exclusively male and characterizing them as either illiterate or having had very little formal education. Other terms for the masses are "laboring classes" or "the common man" in English, or "*janta*" (people) in Hindi. Writer/director Rumi Jaffery, who had written many films for David Dhawan—a director frequently characterized by the film press as "having his finger on the pulse of the masses"—described the theatrical audience for Hindi cinema as comprised primarily of the masses; he asserted the centrality of their viewership for the commercial health of the industry: "The upper class, they watch films at home on video. Our films run because of the masses—the rickshaw-*wallahs*, *tanga-wallahs* [horse-carriage drivers], labor classes. They are our providers. We have to be aware of their tastes, what they want; poor guys, they work so hard all day: they earn 500 rupees and spend 50 of it to see a film, so he should get his money's worth" (Jaffery, interview, November 1996).

When I asked Jaffery how he comes to learn their tastes, he said that it was difficult and that he tried to talk to people he encountered during the course of his daily routine, such as rickshaw drivers or domestic workers. I noticed that filmmakers frequently used their own personal domestic workers and staff as proxies for the mass audience during the collaborative scripting sessions referred to as "story sittings."[17] For example, one evening I had accompanied Tarun Kumar to a producer's home for a story sitting where Kumar, three writers, and the producer were hashing out the details of a screenplay. The film was a sort of madcap adventure comedy, with multiple protagonists, subplots, and plot twists, and at one point in the discussion Kumar said, "We might understand it, but will Asif understand it?" referring to the domestic worker who had just entered the room to serve everyone tea. "After all, he is the one who goes to the cinema to see the film. We'll watch it on cable at home." Before the others could answer, Kumar chortled, "I wonder what Aseem-bhai, my driver, would think? Poor guy, he got pretty confused by my last film!"

Jaffery's claim about the need for working-class audiences to get the most value for their money was a very common refrain in filmmakers' discussions of the masses and their filmic choices. Such value was defined through the idea of entertainment, which filmmakers characterized mainly in terms of an escape from the harsh realities of everyday life. Citing film viewing as the cheapest and only source of entertainment for the masses, producer/director Aditya Chopra attributed poverty as the reason for the masses' purported penchant for escapism: "Here, the common man—his ultimate dream is an escapism, is to watch films. He goes for three hours; he sees a world which he probably will never get, or he'll see women whom he'll never meet, or he'll see stuff where he's never going to go to, and for him that's it. That's his ultimate, because you're dealing to a country of have-nots" (Aditya Chopra, interview, April

1996). One of the most cited elements of escapism are the song and dance sequences, which frequently take place in sylvan locales both in India and abroad. Producer Mukesh Bhatt explained the penchant for foreign locations that became the norm for song sequences from the mid-1990s: "Basically, we are selling dreams. We are making them feel that they are doing something, which they, in normal life, would not be able to do. That's why we go to these beautiful places, like Switzerland, and all that. It's the common man's dream. He can never go to Switzerland, Paris, or Australia. So when he sees the songs in which we show it, with that 20 rupees he's taken his wife and children to Australia. He's shown them the Alps" (Mukesh Bhatt, interview, October 1996). Other elements of escapist entertainment, according to filmmakers, include high doses of action, slapstick humor, bombastic dialogues, titillation, and a fast narrative pace. This notion of film-viewing as "escape" is a very common characterization and criticism of popular cinema in India, expressed across a variety of domains — state, journalistic, intellectual, and in everyday parlance among people who comprise the "classes" side of the masses-classes binary.

The classes are defined as the exact opposite of the masses: educated men and women; usually English-speaking; sophisticated; preferring realism; able to handle a slower-paced film; open to innovation in subject matter; and more likely to view films in the comfort of their homes. Screenwriter Anjum Rajabali felt that this segment of the audience was the most underserved by the Hindi film industry. "I feel, in fact, the neglected segment, ironically, of this country is the most privileged segment . . . in terms of entertainment. There's nothing being made in this country which fulfills their wishes — the educated, so-called, English-speaking, urban-based audience" (Rajabali, interview, September 1996). Rajabali surmised that elite audiences therefore patronized Hollywood films and American television out of a lack of Indian options. He conceded that certain films drew such viewers sporadically, "I mean Hindi films? They try to go — *Rangeela-wangeela, thoda sa jazz-wazz dedo* [show some style and slickness], they go and sort of see that, but they have been a neglected lot, not the man from Matunga" (Rajabali, interview, September 1996). The "man from Matunga"[18] was Rajabali's shorthand reference to how producers and distributors always criticized him for not thinking more explicitly about audiences in terms of the industry's matrix of region and class — taking into account tastes of the interiors and the masses — when writing his scripts.

While the mechanism for ascertaining overall audience choice was commercial outcome, the means by which filmmakers gauged specific tastes was centered upon the class-based spatial hierarchies present inside the single-screen movie theater. Producer/director Subhash Ghai's response to my question about how he kept in touch with audience preferences relied on this spatialization of class hierarchy. "We come to know the box-office collections. You've got balcony, stall, upper stall. *Kahi baar* [Sometimes] the balcony is always full and [the] stall is always empty. It means the masses have not understood; the movie is running on the strength of the classes . . . Sometimes the stall is full and balcony is empty, so you come to know the trend—who is appreciating, which class? Ladies? Students? Masses or classes? [The] masses . . . feel very offended by the class production, so somewhere we have to bring optimum balance between the class movie and the mass movie" (Ghai, interview, 9 December 1996). As evident in Ghai's statements, Tarun Kumar's comments in the opening anecdote, and the discussions in chapter two about *Lamhe*, the tastes of these sweeping categories are usually represented in opposition—the masses versus the classes. Since the masses were thought to constitute the bulk of the theater-going audience, trade reviews of films were always assessing whether a film was "too classy"—lacking elements that would make a film popular among these broad categories of viewers and hence impede commercial success, which is what Ghai was referring to in his own comments. For example, *Film Information*'s review of Ghai's 1999 film *Taal* (Rhythm) pronounced, "On the whole, *Taal* is high—very high—on gloss, glamour, grandeur, style, music, but is low on racy screenplay, pacy drama, and mass-appealing ingredients . . . It will appeal to the gentry audience more than the masses and will, therefore, do well in A-class centres. Considering its high price on the one hand and city appeal on the other, it can hope to fetch returns only in Bombay, Maharashtra, Delhi (not U.P.), South, and Overseas. Business in Bengal, Bihar, and Rajasthan in particular and in small centres in general will be dull" (Nahta 1999).

Further conversations with filmmakers revealed how masses-classes was not a neutral binary, but one imbued with value judgments. Such judgment was apparent in Ghai's discussion of the distinction between comedy and humor, whereby he associated the former with the masses and the latter with the classes. "Humor [differs from] comedy. The gentry like humor, not cheap comedy. [A] man falling, [or a] girl falling on banana and her skirts fall out, those kinds of things, masses may like it but these people do not like it." In his remarks, Ghai wielded comedy as a pejorative term, using words like "vulgar," "loud," and "caricature" as descriptors, while humor was described in terms of witty repartee between the protagonists in a film. Ghai was particularly critical of the inclusion of a comic figure or a separate comedy track running parallel to the main narrative, which was a common feature in many mainstream Hindi films from the 1950s to the 1990s. Positioning himself as a filmmaker with taste and distinction, Ghai ended his remarks with, "We don't need those buffoons, but there are many directors who believe the buffoon has to be there for those buffoon audiences" (Ghai, interview, 9 December 1996).

As noticeable from Ghai's statements, a discussion of the masses-classes binary often devolved into a general criticism of the masses for their filmic preferences. This sort of criticism was readily apparent in the trade press as well. For example, *Film Information*'s review of the film *Mela* (Carnival) illustrates how the masses and particular territories are associated with bad taste and poor aesthetic judgment:

> The story offers absolutely nothing new . . . The second half is lengthy, repetitive and boring. The main negative aspects are the almost dull music, the lack of repeat value and novelty, a weak romantic track and a dacoit[19] who is supposed to spell terror in the village, but is actually hardly menacing or intimidating in his performance . . . Not only is the script routine, the making is also quite crude. Nevertheless, the crudeness will appeal to the mass audience, especially in the Hindi-speaking belt . . . On the whole, high-priced *Mela* has mass-appealing masala for circuits like Bihar, Rajasthan and C.I., but not enough for many of the other circuits. (Nahta 2000a)

Trade journalists who write these reviews present themselves as omniscient viewers, able to predict and speak for the variety of audience reactions. Since the elaboration of audience taste is drawn mainly from observing the commercial outcome of films, it frequently results in circular assertions, such as the masses are crude and vulgar because they like crude and vulgar films or that intelligent films do well in cities because city audiences are intelligent.

The separation posited between the reviewer's judgment of the film and the hypothetical response (reviews are written on the day of a film's release) of the mass audience in parts of northern India demonstrates how members of the film industry locate themselves firmly within the "classes" side of the masses-classes binary, positing their own tastes and aesthetic standards as distinct from the majority of audiences. Producer/director Rakesh Roshan, in describing his filmmaking practice, asserted an inherent difference between himself and his audience: "I don't try to make difficult screenplays. I don't like to confuse people, because I know when a common man comes to see a film, he doesn't want to put pressure on his brain, though we like to see such films sometimes. I see some films and there are some complications and then you know you have to think over it, but a common man in India? I don't think we should put that pressure on him" (Roshan, interview, May 1996). While Roshan represents himself as the more cerebral and engaged viewer in contrast to the "common man," the following excerpt from my interview in 1996 with Rahul Agrawal, the director of marketing for a production company, reveals how the masses-classes binary serves as an opportunity to define the classes-self in opposition to the masses-other.[20] I had asked Agrawal to describe the different audiences for Hindi films, and he asked me which film I had seen most recently. When I told him *Saajan Chale Sasural* (Lover Goes to His In-laws)—a film that was a slapstick comedy about bigamy—he asked me whether I had enjoyed it, and when I said "not particularly," he immediately responded, "It's not for you. It is for the mass audience, absolute mass audience, maybe your servant at home, or your driver, or rickshaw-*wallah* will enjoy that film because that's for him. *Saajan Chale Sasural*, though this is on [pointing to my tape recorder], it insulted my sensibilities. It is so stupid. I just couldn't digest it, because it is not for me." After establishing our common social and aesthetic distance from the presumed mass audience based on our dislike of the film, Agrawal went on to posit our shared class-linked cinematic preferences: "I'm thinking of a film for the elite audience and not for the mass audience. Have you seen *Lamhe*? [I nodded] Yes, *Lamhe* is a classic example. It's a beautiful film. I loved it, I'm sure you loved it, because it is for us. It is not for the mass audience."

Lamhe (Moments) was an eagerly anticipated film that turned out to be a major box-office disappointment; members of the industry at the time attributed its commercial failure to the class composition of the theatrical audience—an explanation offered by Agrawal too that afternoon. "Unfortunately, films [that] have appeal for the mass audience run in the cinemas today, because they are the actual, they are the 90 percent audience, we are just 10 percent, and we don't go twice and thrice to see a film; they go ten times" (interview, 1996). Even though it was my first ever meeting with Agrawal, and he really had no knowledge of me other than that I was an NRI (non-resident Indian) from New York University, who was conducting research for my PhD, my level of education, English-speaking ability, and diasporic location positioned me as a member of the "classes" audience. Prior to his remarks about audiences, Agrawal had informed me that he had spent two months at Harvard University, enrolled in a summer international business program, and that he desired to pursue an MBA abroad rather than in India. Thus his continual assertion of our presumed shared aesthetic disposition was predicated upon his own educational aspirations for a post-graduate degree and his use of the pronouns "we" and "us" in his answers signaled his own location within the classes audience as well.

In Agrawal's castigation of the masses for their tastes and excessive film-viewing, along with his distress over their sizable proportion of the viewing audience, we see the curious instance of a member of an industry—one that is overwhelmingly described as only concerned with the bottom line—lamenting the very existence of a sort of consumer and type of consumption that has sustained it financially over time. This is an example of the sentiment of disdain that underlies the production culture of the Hindi film industry and belies any simple portrayal of its commercial nature. The problem that 90 percent of the audience poses for Agrawal is an example of the tremendous ambivalence with which members of the industry regard the bulk of the viewing audience. While the masses brought in the revenues for the film industry, the classes earned the industry symbolic capital and cultural legitimation. Although these two audience categories were described dichotomously, it was still possible—according to filmmakers in 1996—to make a film that transcended their differences and appealed to both. "The film [that] is a super hit like *Dilwale Dulhaniya*," Agrawal added, "or *Hum Aapke Hain Koun!*, or *Maine Pyar Kiya* [I Have Loved], these sort of films appeal to both the elite and the masses. That's why they are super hits" (interview, 1996).

FROM "6 TO 60": AIMING FOR UNIVERSALITY

The Significance of Universality

Tarun Kumar's dilemma in the editing room—of working out how to please both the classes and the masses, represented by the figures of aunties and servants—was an example of how Hindi filmmakers aimed to make films that appealed to the broadest audiences possible. "From 6 to 60," which referred to the age span of filmgoers, was a phrase I heard uttered frequently during my early fieldwork that encapsulated this goal. Traditionally, a Hindi film was deemed an unqualified success only if it was a nationwide or an "all-India" hit, communicating to the industry that linguistically, regionally, and religiously diverse audiences were able to identify with the film. Taran Adarsh, the editor of *Trade Guide*, impressed upon me the necessity of a Hindi film doing well all over India and especially in the smaller centers, the ones referred to as the interiors, or the B- and C-class centers. "Those are the centers which decide if your film is going to be a success or not; that's where you recover your investment from . . . the biggest of films may not be doing so well in the cities, in the metros, but they do phenomenal business in the interiors, in the B- and C-class centers" (Adarsh, interview, September 1996). When I asked him if films could be economically viable just on the strength of the large urban areas, referred to as A-class centers in distribution parlance, Adarsh responded, "We make films for not just Bombay, Delhi, or Calcutta. We make films for centers in Raipur, Bhilai, Gujarat, in Bihar, or Punjab . . . It is more important that a film does well there, than it does well in cities. A hit film in Bombay does not mean that it is accepted on an all-India basis. You have to have universal acceptance. You have to appeal to not just people in the balcony class; you have to appeal to the people— the hoi polloi also; you have to appeal to B- and C-class centers also. That's where you realize that *aap ki* picture *mein kitna dum hai* [how strong your picture is]" (Adarsh, interview, September 1996).

I encountered the concern about universal acceptance during the pre-production process of *Ghulam* (Vassal), a film on which I worked as an assistant in 1996. The film, which was an adaptation of the Hollywood film *On the Waterfront*,[21] had as its backdrop the problem of extortion that is rampant in Bombay. In *Ghulam*, the particular neighborhood in which the protagonist resides is completely under the mercy of the local crime boss and his gang, who collect protection money weekly from all of the shopkeepers in the area. Vikram Bhatt, the film's director, and some of his crew members initially were worried as to whether the problem of extortion depicted in *Ghulam* was as "universal" as the problem of labor in *On the Waterfront*. While *Ghulam* did extremely well in the Bombay territory, earning more than three times its cost for its distributor, and was categorized as a "super-hit" within that territory, since it did not fare as well in other parts of India, it did not earn the coveted title of a "universal hit."[22]

Since a film had to appeal to everyone, the audience categories I described in the previous section operated more as boundaries than niches; that is, rather than thinking about audience taste as templates for making specific films, Hindi filmmakers regarded audience taste as constraints that needed to be navigated and negotiated. Subhash Ghai described his task as a balancing act of taking elements that he believed would appeal to the masses and presenting them in a manner that would appeal to the classes. He articulated this "optimum balance" as that between the "earthy" and the "aesthetic," where the former appealed to the masses and the latter to the classes. Referring to his earlier films, which were all big box-office successes, Ghai asserted, "*Karma, Vidhaata,* and *Saudagar* were liked by masses and classes both, [because] the gentry appreciated the cinematic expansion and dimension, whereas the earthy people liked the aggressiveness of Dilip Kumar and Raj Kumar" (Ghai, interview, 9 December 1996).

While Ghai presented his box-office success as a result of his judicious balance of cinematic elements, Aditya Chopra, whose first film, *Dilwale Dulhaniya Le Jayenge,* was one of the biggest commercial successes of Indian cinema, described his method for achieving universal appeal as one of transcending social difference: "You just realize that you're making a film for people who are going to be different, and you have to try and thread them in some way, link all of them together. That is actually what *Dilwale* was—this belief that, even if they come from different classes, this guy might ride an auto-rickshaw and we might go in a Mercedes-Benz—but he's also going to cry if his mother dies, he's also going to react when his sister gets married. Okay, so what you need to do is get to the essence of being Indian and strike that chord that will somehow or the other have a place in everybody's heart" (Aditya Chopra, interview, April 1996). In Chopra's words, the "essence" of being Indian appears to be a focus on the affective power of kinship relations. The idea that kinship relations overrode differences of class was expressed by other filmmakers as well and contrasted sharply with the discourse about the masses-classes binary, where clear-cut distinctions are drawn between filmmakers and their audiences. Mukesh Bhatt, who mentioned how filmmakers were selling dreams (of European travel) to the common man, posited himself as a member of the audience who shared an emotional bond with the implied mass audience due to the essential nature of kinship: "I believe, that 'I' as an audience, and a man of the street, we are no different. Just because I'm sitting in an air conditioned room, or sitting in a Mercedes-Benz, [that] does not make my heart and my emotion different from the man who is pulling the cart on the streets of Bombay. His emotion for his mother will be the same as mine for my mother. His emotion for his child will be the same as mine for my child. It's only the bank balances that are different." Thus according to Bhatt, films focusing on kinship relations, referred to as "emotions" (Ganti 2002) within the film industry, were the ones with universal appeal. Standing in again for the audience he asserted,

When you're catching subjects which deal with human relationships and emotions, it's universal, so if . . . you have an emotional scene where it involves your mother, and it brings tears to your eyes, it'll definitely bring tears to his eyes. Something which brings joy to your face, and a scene where your child is doing very well, or your sister is getting married, and you're very happy . . . and you smile as an audience, even that man on the street, when he sees the film, he will also identify with the character, feel that his sister is in the same situation, and he will also react the same way, so you should make films which are basically universal, and that is emotion. Emotions are universal, irrespective of whether you have money in the Swiss Bank, or you don't have money at all. (Mukesh Bhatt, interview, October 1996)

Bhatt's professed psychic solidarity with the audience undergoes a drastic change a few years later, which I will discuss in the next chapter.

The Challenges to Achieving Universality

Although Hindi filmmakers strived for universal hits, by no means did they view it as an easy task. During my early phase of fieldwork (1996–2000), the dominant sentiments that I encountered were, "We can't!" or "In India it is not possible"; producers, directors, and writers were constantly articulating what they could not make in terms of plots, themes, characterizations, and genres. There was an elaborate narrative of constraints mediated mainly through the figure of the audience, which hinged on the concepts of identification and acceptance. Subhash Ghai described the audience's need for identification—a need, if may I remind, that filmmakers themselves ascribed to the audience—as restrictive: "In India, all of the stories, the ways that films get made, it has to be stories that audiences can relate to, they have to feel, '*Ki* yes, this is our story.' People should be able to imagine that this is a story that they could have lived, a familiar story. However, in the West, you don't have that problem, because people are educated. Educated people can imagine beyond their own lives so they can enjoy watching other people's stories" (Ghai, interview, October 2000). The distinction that Ghai draws between Indian viewers and Western ones, premised on the level of formal education, demonstrates how the problem of identification for filmmakers is really one posed by the class composition of their audience. The fact that the majority of the Hindi film audience was comprised of the masses—90 percent, according to Agrawal—appeared to be the root cause for the variety of challenges articulated by filmmakers as constraints on their filmmaking practice. For the remainder of this section I examine the three main obstacles expressed by filmmakers with respect to their audiences: cultural diversity, moral and kinship codes, and social conditions.

Filmmakers perceived the vast linguistic and cultural diversity within India as a significant hurdle for achieving broad-based appeal. The trade press is critical of Hindi films that appear too specific in terms of their cultural milieu, for that is thought to impede audience identification. Komal Nahta asserted that Hindi films were "more national in character" and that it was risky to depict anything too regionally specific: "You have to make them understandable to everybody"[23] (Nahta, interview, September 1996). Screenwriter Sachin Bhaumick characterized Hindi cinema as full of artistic compromises because of its need to cater to such a diverse audience: "Now we want to cater from Assam to Madras, to so many languages, so our picture becomes full of compromises" (Bhaumick, interview, October 1996). Bhaumick defined "compromise" in terms of the variety of elements that producers and directors insisted be included in a Hindi film in order to please audiences all over India. He related the attitudes of filmmakers that he encountered while writing a script (the italicized portions in quotation marks indicate where Bhaumick is imitating producers' and directors' instructions to him):

> You must think that if you don't put [in] a bhangra,[24] [a] Punjabi audience will run away. "*So somewhere put a bhangra dance there, and now what about some Manipuri kind of, put some Manipuri dance.*" I cannot put Manipuri dance. "*Achcha [Okay] do something about it: Eastern people must like; Bengali people also like; and Orissa people also like, and put some little action and some horse-riding sequences, as they go very well in Punjab because they like slightly crude things, and it will also go very well with the South, because they cannot follow the language, so they'll follow the action.*" Now we are asked to write like this: it becomes a formula now. You have to cater [to] all-India. We show in Bombay only, then our picture is a flop. It should run in Calcutta also; it should run in Bombay also; it should run in Hyderabad also; it should run in Bangalore also. So you're working within so many limitations. (Bhaumick, interview, October 1996)

Unlike Nahta's comments, which describe Hindi films as abstracted from any specific regional milieu, Bhaumick characterizes Hindi films as a potpourri of regional customs and features. Whether it is one thing for everyone or something for everyone, either approach is premised on the centrality of identification for the film-viewing process. Bhaumick's representation of striving for universal appeal as limiting and compromising is an example of the disdain that filmmakers express toward their own practice.

In addition to the difficulties of audience identification, filmmakers represented audiences as possessing clear-cut moral boundaries, usually pertaining to ideal kinship behavior, which could not be transgressed. *Lamhe* kept surfacing in my discussions with filmmakers as an example of a film with all of the ingredients of a successful film—a strong story, stars with drawing power, hit music, high production values, proper marketing—which still failed at the box-office. Vikram Bhatt, a director who was in his late twenties when I first met him, interpreted *Lamhe*'s failure as a sign of the moral conservatism of audiences in India:[25] "Indian audiences are quite stuck up with age old moralities and ideas, so one has to be definitely sensitive to those . . . A film like *Lamhe*, however good the film was, the people could not accept that a man in love with the mother could settle for the daughter. So lets say that what the audience is sensitive about sometimes can restrict us" (email communication 1999). Like Bhatt (and Rahul Agrawal), everyone I spoke to in the industry mentioned what a "good" film it was, and how they personally enjoyed it, but that audiences had "rejected" the film because its theme was unacceptable to them. This particular analysis of *Lamhe*'s failure is different from the reasons suggested by filmmakers and journalists in chapter two, which centered on the class-differentiated response to the film. Since the film-going audience is fundamentally unknowable, filmmakers' theories about audience taste, preference, and desire constitute an elastic and flexible discourse, which nevertheless governs the basis of future decisions and transactions.

According to many members of the industry I spoke with, *Lamhe* failed at the box-office because the relationship between the male and female protagonists was perceived by the audience as incestuous. The film's narrative centers around Viren, a wealthy NRI who falls in love with Pallavi, a woman slightly older than he, on one of his trips to India from England. Pallavi, oblivious to Viren's feelings for her, is in love with someone else and gets married. Pallavi and her husband are injured in a car accident when she is pregnant, and although both die, Pallavi first gives birth and exacts a promise from Viren to take care of her daughter. Viren leaves the child, Pooja, in the care of the nanny who had brought him up, and goes back to England, but returns to India every year for a day to commemorate Pallavi's death anniversary. Pooja grows up into the spitting image of her mother—the roles of the mother and daughter are played by the same actress—and falls in love with Viren who, after a great deal of personal turmoil, finally reciprocates her love.

Sachin Bhaumick, articulated what he felt was the Indian audience's disapproval (the italicized portions in inverted commas are to indicate Bhaumick speaking as an audience member): "*Lamhe* did very well abroad, but not here because they say, '*I see one woman giving birth before my own eyes, by my money, and now the mother is gone, and the child has been kept in my house brought up by Waheeda Rehman* [the actress's name] *who also brought me up. Then I can marry her? In India it is not possible. She's like my daughter, because I have seen her from birth to her growing up. She was brought up in my house, so how can I think of getting married with her?*' People didn't like it at all" (Bhaumick, interview, October 1996). By mentioning that *Lamhe* did well abroad but not in India, Bhaumick constructs the difference between overseas audiences and those in India as being based upon an adherence to, and awareness of, proper kinship behavior. Bhaumick reinforced his point about how seriously Indian audiences view appropriate kin behavior, even when the ties are fictive, by discussing the failure of an older film, *Bambai ka Babu* (The Gentleman of Bombay, 1960). In this particular film, the protagonist (played by actor Dev Anand) enters a house to rob it and is mistaken by the elderly couple and their daughter (actress Suchitra Sen) for their long-lost son; he then starts living with them as their son. Anand falls in love with Sen, who thinks of him as her brother. During *Raakhi*—the festival where sisters tie colorful bands (*raakhi*) around their brothers' wrists as a symbol of the bond of love and protection between them; when Sen tries to tie a *raakhi* around Anand's wrist, he refuses her, for then he would have been bound to her as a brother and would not have been able to consummate his romance. According to Bhaumick,

> [The] picture flopped first day itself. They said, "*This bloody bastard can call the father a father, mother a mother, he may be an imposter, but why will he not call the sister a sister? When he came in this house, he's posing as the brother, he's impersonating a man, so his relationship should be the same relationship! Why should he fall in love with Suchitra Sen? He cannot! He can fall in love with a village girl, another girl.*" [The] picture did not do well. *Moo boli bahen bhi* importance *hota idhar* [Even a sister by word (rather than blood) has a lot of importance here]. *To kya hai,* [So what it is] these are the values. That's why you cannot change that. (Bhaumick, interview, October 1996)

Coming back to the issue of *Lamhe*, Bhaumick related that after he saw the film he had warned the director, Yash Chopra, that it was "dangerous." He felt that if the script had been written in such a way that the two characters had no contact with each other while the girl was growing up and met later on in life, fell in love, and then discovered their prior connection, audiences might have accepted the fact that a man once in love with a woman could fall in love with her daughter. He reiterated his point about the importance of being sensitive to the dominant kinship idioms through which such a plot would be interpreted in India: "*Ab ghar mein bada hua*, [Now she grew up in his house] he knows her development, then she's like a daughter in the house. *To woh* India *mein jamega nahin, nahi jama, nahi chala* [So that doesn't gel in India; it didn't gel; it didn't run]. Like *Bambai ka Babu* flopped that way. People will not accept [it]" (Bhaumick, interview, October 1996).

By referring to the older film's failure, Bhaumick asserted the immutability of kinship codes and principles. Bhaumick's explanation of *Lamhe*'s box-office failure is an example of a culturally indexical interpretation of commercial outcome, which is the primary way that filmmakers impose meaning upon box-office results and make sense of the uncertainty of audience response. For if *Lamhe* had succeeded commercially, it might have elicited from filmmakers (and the press) narratives about social change—about how audiences were less beholden to the ties of fictive kinship and what was previously taboo (as registered by the commercial failure of *Bambai ka Babu*) was no longer so. It is also entirely plausible that *Lamhe*'s success would have been simply attributed to its stars, music, director, and other details specific to the film.

While Bhaumick brought up *Lamhe* and *Bambai ka Babu* as examples of filmmakers' lapse of judgment regarding deep-seated beliefs, he discussed his own insensitivity to, and lack of reflexivity about, social conditions at the beginning of his screen-writing career. He had written a film titled *Lajwanti* (1958) where a woman leaves her husband, a hard-working lawyer, because she feels neglected by him. Bhaumick narrated how Nargis, one of the leading actresses of that time and who was to play the part of the woman, told him that the picture would not run because the conflict presented in the film would not be meaningful to viewers.[26] According to Bhaumick, Nargis said to him, "Who understands that here? That a husband should spend time with a wife, nobody understands that. The husband comes from Bihar, he comes here for three years, earns, doesn't see his wife's face at all, only sends her money. She buys a cow with the money. He goes back home two or three times, stays for seven days, fathers a child, comes back, and doesn't meet her for another three years. All the wife thinks is, 'my husband is great.' It is not a Western country. Economically, there are so many problems, who the hell is thinking of their time with the husband?" (Bhaumick, interview, October 1996). The use of "understand" in the above comments could easily be replaced with "identify," as Nargis's statements present audiences in India, for reasons of economic hardship, as incapable of identifying with a woman's need for companionship in a marriage.

Nargis suggested to Bhaumick that if he portrayed the husband as cheating on his wife, then audiences would be sympathetic to the wife's plight. Regarding audiences' reactions to the film, she said (in Bhaumick's words), "The audience will accept her sorrow if she's a good girl, but her husband is going to another one. Then only the audience will accept . . . companionship: this is not an Indian concept. Companionship is only a rich people's concept. Poor people always stay separately . . . It won't run, I'm telling you it won't run" (Bhaumick, interview, October 1996). In addition to Nargis's admonitions, Bhaumick described how Mehboob Khan, one of the top producer/directors of the time, responded when he heard about the script. Like Nargis, Khan also told Bhaumick to make the husband unfaithful to his wife in order to elicit audience sympathy and provide an appropriate rationale for her departure. Bhaumick narrated Khan's criticism of the script, which paralleled Nargis's in terms of articulating a hierarchy of needs:

> Such a beautiful wife—a wife like Nargis—and he is cheating on her? I can leave. I cannot leave because he's working and earning. It is India. What bloody companionship! [She leaves him] because he did not go to a party with her? Ninety-nine percent of the people here do not know what a party is. Have you ever seen the poor have a party? Do they know about birthdays? We see birthday parties in the movies, but they don't know anything about birthdays. They're like "I don't know, I must be 20 or 22 years old. Remember the year of the hurricane, my mother told me that I was born two years after that." This is the country you're living in. What are you thinking? You're not with the roots of the people. (Bhaumick, interview, October 1996)

When Bhaumick related these sentiments to the film's producer and expressed his doubts about whether the film would be successful or not, the producer disagreed and reassured him that the film would be successful. According to Bhaumick, the producer, Mohan Sehgal, said to him, "No, Sachin, it's very nice. The wife is sitting there all dressed up ready to go to a party and the husband doesn't come. It will run." The film flopped, confirming to Bhaumick that Nargis and Khan were right in their assessments of the irrelevance of such a theme to the majority of audiences. He said, "It didn't run because he's not doing anything wrong. He's working all night to pay off debts. He's doing hard work, earning money for the family. He gave her such a big house; he's giving her jewelry. In India, this is happiness. In India, companionship is not understandable because the economy is so poor" (Bhaumick, interview, October 1996). According to Bhaumick, the onscreen depiction of material comfort and the fulfillment of kinship obligations (being faithful) worked against the narrative logic and rendered the conflict in the film meaningless, as the majority of audiences were poor. In his view, poverty was a constraint, not in the obvious manner of preventing or limiting consumption, but in terms of being able to identify with certain themes and narratives. Poverty appeared to preclude the desire for companionship in a marriage, but not the desire to see films, since Hindi films were posited as a form of escape or fantasy for poor and working-class audiences.

The other major constraint, also connected to poverty, posed by the mass audience was their low level of formal education, indexed by low rates of literacy. The issue of illiteracy was frequently brought up in my discussions with filmmakers as a major reason for the self-professed formulaic nature of popular Hindi cinema. As apparent in Subhash Ghai's contrast between Indian and Western audiences in the beginning of this section, for filmmakers illiteracy signified the inability of audiences to comprehend, appreciate, or identify with a greater variety of themes, subjects, or genres. Thus, filmmakers stated that they felt limited in the kind of films they could make. "The level of the audiences' understanding binds us," Vikram Bhatt asserted in an email. "A filmmaker like me, who would be dying to make a sci-fi film, could never make it. Audiences here are so illiterate that they don't know all about our very own country. Making a film about the fifth moon of Mars is unthinkable. Though that looks like no great loss, it really is when you look at the fact that a whole genre of film has become useless for us" (1999). Bhatt's statements present a very circumscribed definition of knowledge and awareness, predicated upon solitary acts of literacy, and completely ignores and discounts the variety of oral and social means by which knowledge is disseminated in India. In his statements, we also see the effect of the imagined audience on his own sense of self: "filmmaker like me."

Unlike the other constraints posed by filmmakers, however, illiteracy is a condition that can be rectified tangibly. Aditya Chopra was optimistic during our interview that, as literacy increased, Hindi filmmakers would be able to make films that were more diverse in their subject matter. Feeling hopeful about the near future, Chopra asserted that literacy levels were rising slowly but surely in India: "You are coming to know of people also in villages who now know English; it will take time, but it will definitely happen. It's just that it will take a few years" (Aditya Chopra, interview, April 1996). Chopra then launched into an explanation of how an increased awareness of the world associated with rising literacy levels was a necessary precondition for diversifying filmmaking: "You see Hindi film is commercial art, so everything will have to be done when you know there is a promise of making money. You understand? Nobody is going to make a quality film about an AIDS victim when nobody's going to come to see it, so you need to first educate them about AIDS. First, tell them that AIDS is there, okay, then when everybody knows about it, and you make a film about AIDS, then it makes sense, but here people don't even know about AIDS" (Aditya Chopra, interview, April 1996). As often happened, filmmakers' discussions about the inadequacies of the Indian audience culminated in a celebration of Hollywood and its purported freedom to make any sort of film it desired. Chopra ended his remarks by asserting admiringly, "That's why where Hollywood scores is that they just don't have any limit, any *bandish* [restriction] on their expression. They can make a film on anything! They make a film on—I mean I've seen films on just one line . . . and they're good films . . . it will definitely happen, but it will take some time" (Aditya Chopra, interview, April 1996). In addition to literacy being defined as literacy in English, what is striking about Chopra's statements is how discourses about audiences, film-viewing, and filmmaking are intertwined with the teleological discourses of development and modernization. Chopra presents a narrative in which once audiences become literate, Hindi filmmakers, like their counterparts in Hollywood, will have more creative and artistic freedom. Unlike the state's frequent exhortations to the industry—oft echoed by the earlier generations of filmmakers—to make films that can serve as tools to spread knowledge about social issues and problems, Bhatt and Chopra—both in their mid- to late twenties when these interviews were conducted—explicitly rejected any developmentalist or pedagogical role for commercial cinema and assigned that responsibility to other institutions and structures.

While it is easy to hold up Chopra's discussion about the incongruity of making a film about an AIDS victim as an example of how market-driven forms of cultural production are inherently conservative and risk-averse,

Chopra's assessment of audience interest is not markedly different from that espoused by Khan, Nargis, or Bhaumick regarding *Lajwanti*. In both cases, material conditions — that is, poverty and its concomitant, illiteracy — are presented as the dominant force in shaping the interpretive frameworks through which audiences can (or cannot) understand, identify, or relate to a film. In Bhaumick's example about *Lajwanti*, audiences' struggles to eke out their existence renders certain conflicts as incomprehensible, while in Chopra's example, audiences' ignorance about certain issues reduces their interest in films made upon those topics. Unlike moral codes and kinship norms, which are represented as arising from cultural essences and thus appear immutable, however, poverty is a condition that could be ameliorated, allowing filmmakers to imagine a future when they may be less constrained in their filmmaking.

These discussions, about box-office failures and what films should not be made, illustrate a variety of issues about the Hindi film industry. They reveal how talking about the commercial prospects of a film, or analyzing the commercial performance of a film, is the primary method for transmitting knowledge about audiences and socializing novices into dominant ideologies about audience subjectivities, behavior, tastes, and desires circulating within the industry. Screenwriter Anjum Rajabali, who had just started his career a few years prior to my initial fieldwork, related his frustration with how the discussion about commercial outcome became received knowledge within the industry. He brought up *Lamhe*, as an example to illustrate what he felt was the superficial manner in which industry members interpreted commercial outcome:

> You don't want to strain your intellect. You don't want to look at the complex issues in why a film has been accepted or rejected. A film like *Lamhe*? Every other idiot will meet you and tell you, "*Boss, don't want to do anything different.*" At least a year after *Lamhe*, "*See what happened to Lamhe?*" My dear friend, *Lamhe* failed for various different reasons, let us look at them. "*Tsk, tsk, all this you know alag had ke* [off the beaten track] *young woman falling in love with an old man: it won't work, don't do that man! See they tried it: good director, everything was great about it, but the audience didn't like it!*" I don't agree with that and I certainly, with my limited knowledge — I don't believe it, that is why *Lamhe* was rejected. (Rajabali, interview, September 1996)

Rajabali was unusual among his peers for his desire to probe deeper into the issue of audience response.[27] The axiom that is still left unquestioned, however, is that box-office outcome signifies an audience mandate or verdict over a film, illustrating how this understanding of commercial outcome operates as "doxa" (Bourdieu 1977) — that which is completely naturalized and taken for granted — within the film industry. The categories of hit and flop are an outcome of disrupted expectations: high expectations often result in flops, while low expectations often result in hits. In the case of *Lamhe*, distributors would have bought it at a very high price since producer/director Yash Chopra's previous film, *Chandni*, was declared a blockbuster two years earlier. Given that *Lamhe* had the same actress and music team as the previous film, as well as one of the bankable actors of the time, expectations were high.

As Rajabali recounted his colleagues' warnings about *Lamhe*, such discussions also demonstrate how commercial outcome operates on filmmakers as a disciplinary mechanism — as a way of curbing any flights of fancy and bringing them back to the "reality," or in Mehboob Khan's term, the "roots" of their audiences. The fact that the producer of *Lajwanti* was confident about its commercial prospects reveals the unpredictability and uncertainty that is at the heart of film production. Not only do the anecdotes about the various films make explicit how commercial outcome is interpreted as a direct, unmediated reflection of social reality, it also demonstrates how for filmmakers commercial outcome *produces* the very social reality of their audiences.

I contend that a significant feature of the film industry's discourse about audiences and box-office outcome is an "erasure of the economic" when interpreting commercial outcome. By economic, I am not referring to Sachin Bhaumick's use of poverty as an explanation for the lack of identification with certain themes. What I mean is the absence of attention to exhibition conditions (decrepit cinemas, not enough cinemas), regional economic variation, state taxation, diverse rates of admission, and the role of distributors' pricing decisions. Economic discourses do not possess the same affective or explanatory power as culturalist discourses, which are flexible enough to continuously generate explanations and offer ways of making sense of the unpredictability intrinsic to the film industry's production culture.

BRIDGING DIVIDES

This chapter elaborated Hindi filmmakers' representations of their audiences, including the variety of ways that filmmakers imagined their audiences constraining their filmmaking practice. What is clear is that when I began my research in 1996, filmmakers were highly aware that groups designated as "the masses" comprised their primary viewing audience. The challenges posed by cultural diversity, morality, and social conditions were not applicable to segments of the audience identified as "the classes." Despite the essentialism, criticism, and paternalism expressed toward the masses, Hindi filmmakers sought to make films largely with these audiences in mind. In filmmakers' discussions about the significance of universal appeal, we see a concern for trying either to bridge or transcend the divisions that separate the various audience categories. Statements about the necessity of finding the "essence of being Indian" (Aditya Chopra) reveal how the discourse about super or universal hits is imbricated with the discourse of the nation as an Andersonian imagined community (Anderson 1983). Although the audience is divided into binary oppositions of classes/masses and city/interior, producers, in their quest for a "super-hit" picture, try to encode into their films what they see as some shared cultural norms, common to everyone in India. That quest for the super-hit is thus a quest for some shared identity, which expresses itself periodically through the phenomenon of the "universal hit."

In the next chapter, I describe how by the turn of the millennium, the variegated business of films in different distribution territories was interpreted by trade analysts as a sign of the increasing assertion of discrete taste cultures and attendant difficulty of making a universal hit. Ideas about the importance of bridging divides, universal hits, and the masses as the primary audience for cinema were all radically transformed after 2000. Events that had been lauded as necessary and important for the health of the film industry, such as industry status, corporatization, and the advent of the multiplex, have all played an important role in changing the Hindi film industry's relationship to its audiences.

CHAPTER 9

The Fear of Large Numbers

The Gentrification of Audience Imaginaries

In January 2006, I met Tarun Kumar while he was vacationing in New York City. During dinner, I asked him about the changes that had taken place in filmmaking over the last five years. His immediate response was that audiences had changed drastically. The incommensurability of audience taste that had seemed so inherent and vexing to him seemed to have been resolved: "It's now the gentry—the people with cars—who come to see movies." Kumar elaborated that, whereas in the past such people were only a small proportion of the film-going audience, with the entry of multiplexes over the last couple of years, the "gentry" had become the main audience for Hindi cinema: "Films are now either being made for masses and classes, or only for the classes. Films were earlier made for either the masses and the classes, or if your subject did not go that way then you would say, let's stick with the masses, but now it's gone the other way around."

Kumar's statements exemplify one of the main changes characterizing the post-millennium Hindi film industry. His trajectory as a filmmaker who did not want to disappoint the servants, to now only caring about the gentry audience, represents a momentous departure from how Hindi filmmakers had articulated their relationship to audiences when I first began my fieldwork. It is in the realm of audience imaginaries that the gentrification of the Hindi film industry is most pronounced. The nature of this shift is most perceptible in the changing significance accorded, within the industry, to the category of commercial success known as the "universal hit," which refers to a film that is understood to have had broad audience appeal, based on its uniform box-office performance throughout India.

Although in 1996 filmmakers had complained about the difficulties of attaining a universal hit, they nevertheless strived to create films of broad appeal. A decade later, the discourse within the industry about universal hits had changed from being regarded as indispensable to the economic well-being of the industry to a fortuitous happenstance that cannot be planned. Although the proportion of films being designated a universal hit has not altered over the course of my research—every year since 1995 there have been one or two films that have been wildly success-ful from the perspective of distributors—filmmakers' representations of this category have changed. In this chapter, I detail the transformations in attitudes about the necessity and significance of universal hits, situat-ing these changes in the shifting structures of production, distribution, and exhibition characterizing Hindi filmmaking since 2000. The chang-ing significance of this category indexes particular moments in the his-tory of capital formation and political economy within the film industry. The structural changes taking place in the film industry introduced in chapter seven and the growing significance of multiplex theaters, which I discuss in this chapter, have produced new definitions of success that enable filmmakers to restrict their imagined audience, yet still earn capi-tal—both financial and symbolic—within the industry. I use the phrase "imagined audience" to mark the distinction between filmmakers' discur-sive constructions of the vast film-going public, and socially and histori-cally located viewers who are infinitely more complex than filmmakers' characterizations.

Although filmmakers offer a market-based argument for targeting a particular fraction of the (imagined) audience, changing audience imagi-naries are as much about symbolic capital and cultural legitimacy as they are about simple profit. As the discussions surrounding coolness in chap-ter two demonstrated, the reputation and status of Hindi cinema and the film industry are integrally connected to the social status and class loca-tion of its audiences. Restricting one's imagined audience to the middle and upper classes, referred to as the "gentry" or the "classes" by film-makers, resolves the dilemmas of disdain and uncertainty arising from Hindi cinema's longstanding identification with poor and working-class audiences. In fact, the shift from targeting mass to targeting niche audi-ences is celebrated by filmmakers, journalists, and economic analysts as a sign of the maturation and modernization of filmmaking within India.

The first part of this chapter describes the drastic transformation in audience imaginaries that I encountered between 1996 and 2000. This transformation is evident in who comprised the main audience for Hindi cinema. Central to these changes was the territorially divergent box-office outcome of films in conjunction with the growing significance of South Asian diasporic audiences, along with new sources of revenue for producers. The issue of widely heterogeneous audiences, with incommensurable tastes that has always been at the heart of Hindi filmmakers' audience imaginaries—which filmmakers tried to transcend in the past—becomes a more entrenched division with the arrival of the multiplex movie theater. The second part of the chapter examines the impact that multiplexes have had on filmmakers' relationships to their audiences and their ideas of commercial success. This chapter locates these reconfigured relationships within the structural reorganization of the film industry, revealing how the idea of the audience is not only implicated in the micro-practices of production, but also within the material properties of exhibition and the larger political economy of filmmaking.

CHANGING AUDIENCE IMAGINARIES

From Masses to Classes: Local to Global Indians

The January 1, 2000, issue of *Film Information* opened with an editorial asking, "Is the Film Industry Y2K OK?" a reflection on the Hindi film industry's performance in 1999, which pondered whether the film industry was ready for the new millennium. Two phenomena of the previous year—both of which centrally involved the question of audiences—were cited as portending trouble for the industry's future: the absence of a universal hit, and the growing attention paid to the Overseas Territory. While the film *Hum Saath Saath Hain* (We Are All in This Together) was categorized by the trade journal as "the blockbuster of the year," it was not deemed a universal hit, because its net earnings were not uniform throughout India. "Time was when, in 1977, there were not one or two, but three mega hits in a single year. Time is in 1999 when there's no film qualifying for the title of 'universal blockbuster'" ("Is the Film Industry" 2000). The other related trend, which the editorial characterized as "dangerous," was making films primarily with the Overseas Territory in mind. This apprehension arose over the incidences of certain Hindi films becoming hits in the United States and the United Kingdom while earning much less, or even flopping, in India. Positing the difference between audiences abroad and those within India as that between style and substance, the editorial asserted, "The films of such Overseas-conscious film-makers are tops in style. While style is fine, it cannot be so at the cost of substance." The editorial ended by exhorting filmmakers to work harder to make films that would be widely appealing to audiences across India and the world.

During fieldwork in Bombay in 2000, I perceived both of the above-mentioned trends in my discussions with filmmakers, who character-ized the main changes in filmmaking in terms of audience composition. Whereas earlier someone like Rahul Agrawal lamented that he and others like him only comprised a small percentage of the film-going audience, it appeared now that socially elite viewers comprised the majority audi-ence for Hindi cinema. I was struck by the stark contrast in attitudes ex-hibited by the very same people whom I had observed and interviewed four years earlier. For example, screenwriter Anjum Rajabali, who had as-serted in 1996 that educated, English-speaking, urban viewers were the most neglected segment of the Hindi film audience, told me in 2000 that no one was thinking about "front-benchers" or working-class audiences anymore in their filmmaking.

When I asked producer/director Subhash Ghai his sense of the main changes that had occurred in filmmaking between 1996 and 2000, he as-serted that Hindi cinema had transformed from being a form that ex-hibited and appealed to "rural" sensibilities to one that was "urban and global." This evocation of "the rural" was a new feature of filmmakers' dis-courses about audiences, one that I had not observed in 1996. Throughout this chapter, however, readers will encounter the trope of "rural India" or "rural audiences" in filmmakers' statements, despite the fact that cinema-going is overwhelmingly an urban phenomenon in India. Akin to Dipesh Chakrabarty's discussion of the "peasant" as an overdetermined signifier of all that was not modern or bourgeois in the nationalist histo-riography of India (2000: 11), "the rural" in filmmakers' discourses refers less to some sociological reality than as a trope to signify social worlds and markets that are regarded by filmmakers as backward, traditional, outmoded, and unprofitable. Ghai defined rural sensibilities—a charac-terization that he used to describe the urban wealthy as well—as an in-difference to production values and quality, with an overriding interest in melodrama, good music, and three-hour-long running times. He felt that contemporary Hindi films were being made about topics and char-acters befitting what he referred to as the "global Indian," rather than the "local Indian." One reason for these changes was satellite television, which functioned as a type of pedagogical device, training viewers to appreciate technical quality and inculcating media literacy. The other reason centered on the changes in the class composition of the theatrical audience:

> Before, Indian cinema belonged to masses: 75 percent were masses and 25 percent were classes at that time. You could hardly find audiences who were educated, who had graduated [from college] to come to the cinema hall. Now the story is different. Now you see 70 percent classes and 30 percent masses. Why? Because masses have enough entertainment on television and they don't have the purchasing power to buy a ticket and go to the cinema hall, so they will go for a very selective film—one or two films in a year, you see, as a special outing. But people who are middle-class or upper-class, they like to go out to restaurants and movies and all that. They want to go to the movies and see a good film, with good content, of better quality, so that is why the cinema also has changed. (Ghai, interview, October 2000)

Like filmmakers' statements discussed in chapter two, in Ghai's statements, we see how the class composition of the audience is explicitly linked to the improvement in cinema. Ghai's reference to the prohibitive costs of film viewing demonstrates cinema's significance in the new realms of elite leisure and consumption brought about by the postliberalized Indian economy. Additionally, Ghai's categorizations and representations about audiences would have been based primarily on the commercial outcome of his past couple of films, *Pardes* (Foreign Land, 1997) and *Taal*, which did not enjoy the same pan-Indian success as his earlier films.

The other main change regarding audiences was the increased attention paid by filmmakers to the Overseas Territory. The distinct preferences of this territory—understood in terms of South Asian diasporic audiences in North America and the United Kingdom, rather than audiences in other parts of the world—became a source of discussion and debate after the sharply divergent commercial performance of Subhash Ghai's *Taal*, which witnessed unprecedented success in markets outside of India, but did not fare even half as well in India. The film, released in August 1999, was hugely successful in the United States and United Kingdom, becoming the first Hindi film to debut at number 20 in *Variety's* weekly listing of the 60 highest grossing films in the United States.[1] When I met him in Bombay about a year after *Taal's* release, I asked Ghai whether he had anticipated its success in the Overseas Territory. He replied, "I could never imagine that *Taal* will be such a big hit abroad." Based on what he felt was the overriding sensibility and tone of the film, Ghai made sense of its divergent commercial performance in terms of the classes/masses audience binary, whereby audiences overseas were wholly classes, while audiences in India were, by implication, wholly masses. Ghai explained that the film worked overseas, albeit unexpectedly, because it was a "very mature and sensible love story," where the protagonists were open and frank in terms of their feelings and desires, rather than a clichéd narrative full of melodrama, violence, and stock villains, which, he implied, worked better in India. He stated that overseas audiences "appreciated the content and the technical finesse."

With the ongoing devaluation of the Indian rupee in the late 1990s, the fact that audiences abroad bought tickets in dollars or pounds—revealing the very circumscribed notion of overseas markets on the part of Hindi filmmakers—meant that markets like the United States or United Kindgom were seen as disproportionately lucrative in comparison to India. Comparing ticket prices in India to those in the United States, Ghai pointed out, "The quantum of the audience may be less, but the quantum of the money is much more. Ten years back, only 10 percent of the revenue was from the overseas market, but now it is 60 percent" (Ghai, interview, October 2000). He went on to assert that a film's maximum revenue potential in India—the money that a filmmaker could get for selling distribution rights—was only half of that of the Overseas Territory. When I asked Ghai whether the increased significance of overseas markets meant that audiences in India were being ignored, he denied it, stating that a filmmakers' duty was to care about all audiences: "to make everyone happy from the class to the mass." He immediately stated that it was difficult to live up to this obligation, however: "We make one section happy, the other gets annoyed, so there are two things which you look into . . . First, your own growth, because you can't make everybody happy. Somewhere some section is left out, but at least you're making some section happy and yourself happy . . . You should make a film [that] you believe in, and you want to enjoy, and you really feel that is your growth" (Ghai, interview, October 2000). Ghai's statements reveal an ambivalence about trying to appeal to a broad spectrum of audiences—an evident tension latent in filmmakers' discussions about the difficulty of creating universally appealing films. With the changing economics of filmmaking in the early 2000s, however, filmmakers were better able to justify how they resolved this ambivalence.

Although Ghai's claims about the size and strength of the Overseas Territory were somewhat premature in 2000, his assertions about the significance and value of the territory were hotly debated in the trade press. As many distributors in India were not even able to recover their investment in *Taal*, a week after its release *Film Information* ran an editorial titled "Overseas Market: Is Its Bigness Eclipsing Home Market?" It asserted, "The Overseas bug seems to have bitten some of the bigger film makers. Not just in terms of shooting their films abroad. But in making films which cater to the tastes of audiences in foreign lands more than to Indian audiences" ("Overseas Market" 1999). The dominant characterization of overseas audiences was that they were excessively star-struck, hesitant regarding unknown actors or directors, only interested in love stories, and terribly nostalgic for a sanitized and romanticized portrayal of Indian extended families and Hindu weddings, rituals, and festivals.[2] This profile of the diasporic audience, like all of the other profiles discussed thus far, was based on the commercial outcome of Hindi films in the United States and United Kingdom. Detailing the growing business of the Overseas Territory, the *Film Information* editorial went on to quote an unnamed filmmaker, "Our under-production monies mostly come from the Overseas distributor and the music company holding the audio rights. If we make a musical for the Overseas market, are we wrong?" and then criticized this claim by stating, "But it is also a fact that while these makers make films for the Overseas market, they don't charge their Indian territorial distributors any less. Having thus taken heavy MGs from the all-India circuits, isn't it necessary to also keep the interest of the all-India distributors in mind? Bihar is not what Overseas is, but if the Bihar distributor is paying through his nose, he expects the film to have something for his circuit too" ("Overseas Market" 1999). In addition to illustrating how distributors were in one sense the main audiences for film producers, the editorial's main criticism leveled at the Overseas Territory was that it was skewing the prices at which producers sold their films' rights to distributors. Within the minimum guarantee (MG) system, producers basically tried to raise the finance capital, and perhaps even make a pre-release profit for their filmmaking, by selling the distribution rights to their films. The prices for the various subterritories are set as a proportion referred to as ratios—based on the expectation of a film's potential business—of the price of a major territory, usually Bombay. For example, the ratio of a subterritory like Bihar is set at 50 percent, so that if the rights for Bombay were sold for 10 million rupees, then Bihar would be sold for 5 million rupees. The editorial objected to the fact that the high prices some producers received from the Overseas Territory were being used to determine the prices of the other territories. According to subterritory distributors, however, these prices were not commensurate with the limited business that such overseas-oriented films generated in their territories.

Lala Damani, the distributor for the Bengal and Bihar subterritories, complained to me about how the existing ratios generally overestimated the potential business of most films in his territories. "What I found is that for the super-hit films, the Bihar territory's ratio, which was supposed to be 50 percent, is hardly 20 percent" (Damani, interview, October 2000). Referring to the film *Fiza*, which he had just released, Damani estimated that the revenues earned in the Overseas Territory would be five to six times more than what he would earn in his own territory. Periodically throughout the interview he lamented how it had become very difficult for him to distribute films, since all of the big-budget high-profile films had flopped in his territories. Calling his territories "peculiar," Damani recounted how films that were successful in Bombay and other major territories over the past three years usually turned out to be losing propositions for him. When I asked him why he thought such films failed in his territories, he responded with his own taxonomy of audience taste: "What I analyzed is that there [are now] two tastes in Hindi pictures: one is the producers making the pictures for the Overseas, Bombay City and its suburbs, Delhi city, and South—meaning Bangalore and Hyderabad. These territories have got one taste; the rest of India—it has got some other taste" (Damani, interview, 20 October 2000). Damani's assertion of a bifurcation of taste, which lumped the major urban centers of India with overseas audiences, was a common refrain among members of the film industry in 2000, and continues to be a recurring trope in the industry's discourse about its audiences.

Although Damani conjectured that the majority of India had cinematic tastes in opposition to the Metro and Overseas minority, most of the producers I spoke to isolated the state of Bihar (one of Damani's subterritories) as the ultimate figure of backwardness, representing its tastes as aberrant. During my interview with producer Vashu Bhagnani, I asked him about Damani's assertion that producers were only making films for urban and overseas audiences. He responded by affirming the opposition Damani posited between overseas audiences and those in the interiors, and then went on to describe what he felt was the problem with audiences in territories like Bihar. Referring to the fact that films of A-list producer/directors such as Yash Chopra and Subhash Ghai have successful runs all over the world, except in Bihar, Bhagnani claimed, "The audiences in those centers are not used to seeing such sophisticated films. They want a run-of-the-mill, clichéd film with violence, blood, and gore, which appeals to baser instincts.[3] This sort of film doesn't work anywhere in the world, but we have places in Bihar where even today that stuff runs. Films that don't run in the rest of world, run in Bihar" (Bhagnani, interview, October 2000). Having rendered Bihar as completely abnormal in terms of its tastes in cinema, Bhagnani explained how the territory did not generate any profits either. He surmised that the cinema-going population comprised a small proportion of the highly populated state, and contrasted it with New York, where an even smaller proportion of Hindi film viewers generated much greater revenues for filmmakers: "We're getting so much money from them, so why should we think about Bihar?" Confirming Damani's claims, Bhagnani stated that producers did not think about territories like Bihar when making their films, for they saw no potential for growth in the interior, in contrast to the overseas and Bombay markets, which were both perceived as high-growth territories. Bhagnani summed up his disdain by stating as a matter of fact, "Good filmmaking is when you earn both money and respect. You earn neither from Bihar" (Bhagnani, interview, October 2000). This concern with respect is a key motivating factor for Hindi filmmaking practice.

While Bhagnani was categorically contemptuous and dismissive of Bihar, Damani outlined a number of reasons for the diminished business potential of the territory. First, he pointed out that audiences in his sub-territories were very poor, noting that the lowest per capita incomes in India were in the states of Bengal, Bihar, and Orissa. He also reasoned that the business in these territories had depreciated, in his view, "500 to 1000 percent," due to the closure of industries and the desperate economic circumstances. Articulating a hierarchy of needs, Damani asserted, "Movies can't be the first preference. First preference is always food; second preference is clothes; third preference is residence; fourth preference can be movies, entertainment." Another factor limiting growth was that the state government in Bihar had not allowed ticket rates to increase for over a decade. Damani quickly pointed out, however, that even if ticket rates were allowed to increase, audiences could not afford to come to the theater: "Ultimately our businesses depend on the audiences—when the maximum numbers come to the theater—and it should be well in their reach, so that they can afford to buy the tickets" (Damani, interview, October 2000).

From Audiences to Consumers

However, the inability to consume was almost posited as a character flaw on the part of some filmmakers, which was a sharp departure from my earlier fieldwork, where filmmakers articulated a somewhat ethical imperative to entertain poor and working-class audiences. Producer Mukesh Bhatt, whose statements I presented in the previous chapter, appeared to have undergone a complete volte-face. While in 1996 he described the main audience for Hindi cinema as the "common man," in 2000 he was explicit that the main audiences for Hindi cinema were urban elites. I had asked him his opinion about the allegations—made by the trade press and distributors—that producers were only making films for urban and overseas audiences and he responded in the affirmative. The reason he gave was a simple matter of economics: "They are the consumers who got money to buy, you see. I have no point in making a film for rural India, which is of course a very huge population, but then my cinema halls are not taking me there. Because they have no cinema halls there, they don't have the buying capacity; the ticket rates are so high, so why should I make films, which are not affordable, to that man there sitting in Bihar or Orissa? Why should I stoop down my sensibilities to his level of thinking, when he doesn't have the money to buy my tickets?" Whereas earlier Bhatt argued that the only difference between him and the man on the street was that their bank balances were different, for him poverty is not just the inability to consume, but emblematic of a social and psychological divide so broad that it cannot be bridged. While the psychic unity that Bhatt had formerly expressed for the "common man" appeared somewhat disingenuous, what I want to foreground is the dramatic shift in his discourse about audiences, especially non-elite filmgoers. Delineating a dichotomy of taste based on class, Bhatt firmly located himself within the classes, city, and overseas side: "I am catering to the city audience, to the audience which has got the money to buy my tickets, to the NRI, whose sensibility . . . [matches my own], to the satellite channels, and all who are big corporate houses who are totally influenced by the Western culture and also happen to be a part of that; so we relate to each other's sensibilities and they are the people who have got the money, and obviously you have to make films that cater to the tastebuds of people who have money, because it takes a lot of money to make a film" (Mukesh Bhatt, interview, October 2000). Four years later, it was obvious that bank balances mattered a lot in Bhatt's imagination of the Hindi film audience. While filmmakers earlier had located themselves along the class-axis of the masses/

classes binary, they were clear that the bulk of their audience was on the mass side of the binary. Bhatt's statements not only indicate a change in target audiences, but also reveal how changes in the Indian media land-scape—his references to satellite television and corporate production companies—have had an impact on filmmakers' understandings of their audiences.

What is also noticeable about Bhatt's statements is that the social distance between filmmakers and their target audiences appeared to have reduced drastically. This collapsing of distance was most apparent when Bhatt discussed how it is that he came to know the tastes of the urban "youth"—defined as viewers between 18 and 25—who he argued were the demographic that most frequented the cinema. He responded to my question about how he gauged the tastes of this group by invoking his own teenage children and their preferences, "I see them watching television. I see what sort of films they [enjoy], what sort of serials . . . what sort of books they are reading, so from that, I know . . . you don't have to go into some agency house. Your own son, sitting right under your nose, he is teaching you: just watch him; what is he watching? That's an indication, that's a pointer" (Mukesh Bhatt, interview, October 2000).[4] From the common man on the street to the teenagers in his home, from universally appealing stories based on kinship relations to "high-adrenaline" films targeting the elite urban youth market, Bhatt's transformed perception of his audiences is an example of what I have been characterizing as the gentrification of the Hindi film industry. Bhatt explained his changed attitude by evoking the binary of two Indias, which became an increasingly prevalent trope, proffered by the media over the course of the decade, to describe social and economic conditions in the country: "There are two different worlds; there are two different Indias. The rural India and the urban India are two countries living in one country, and the gap is getting wider and wider and wider" (Mukesh Bhatt, interview, October 2000).[5]

Bhatt's assertions, that India was increasingly riven by deep social and economic divisions, meant that the probability of attaining a universal hit had also diminished. I asked him about filmmakers' desires to appeal from "6 to 60" that I had observed four years earlier, and he qualified it by asserting how only a select genre of films possessed the capacity for broad appeal: "'Six to 60' is only with family socials, you know, *Hum Aapke Hain Koun!*—films about a middle-class Indian family with tradition, family values, and all that. They, of course, become block-busters, but they can't be made every year . . . They come once in four to five years. Otherwise there is not that much scope in that" (Mukesh Bhatt, interview, October 2000). While Bhatt was skeptical, he allowed for the infrequent possibility of films becoming universal hits. Subhash Ghai was much more definitive in his claims that filmmakers could not appeal to such a broad spectrum of audiences. We were discussing the absence of a universal hit in 1999, and I asked Ghai if it was possible for a film to appeal all over India. He answered: "It cannot . . . because there is a contrast in the segments now. I told you initially when there were mass people, *rikshawalla-tangawalla* [rickshaw drivers, horse-carriage drivers] but even the class people had a rural heart, a rural mind. When this new generation has been educated, their sensibility is different, so now there are definitely two sensibilities. So it is not a filmmaker's fault; a filmmaker has to speak one language. You cannot bring an optimum point between sense and nonsense" (Ghai, interview, October 2000). Ghai's statements above are in direct contrast to his earlier ones, where he spoke of the necessity of finding the optimum balance between masses and classes. From Ghai's remarks, it is apparent that the binary mode of thinking about audiences had not changed, but the practice of managing this binary had changed. Rather than balance, Ghai now described his filmmaking in terms of fulfilling his own artistic sensibilities, which happen to be congruent, according to him, with the tastes and preferences of the class audience.

Profits Without Audiences

What accounts for this transformation in attitude? What are the factors that enabled filmmakers to narrow their target audience? As apparent from filmmakers' statements, the growing significance of diasporic markets played a crucial role. What had changed between 1996 and 2000 was that producers, and not simply distributors, were able to profit from these territories, either by establishing the infrastructure to recoup revenues directly—for example, producer/director Yash Chopra set up his own distribution offices in London and New York and began to distribute his own films, along with some others, directly in North America and the United Kingdom—or more commonly by being in a position to enter an MG distribution arrangement, rather than an outright sale of distribution rights. Another key factor was the expanding revenue potential of a film's music rights. Since the beginning of the 1990s, when new entrants into audio production challenged HMV's monopoly, film music played an increasingly important economic function within the Bombay film industry. By the late 1990s, the sale of music rights had become another source of finance for filmmaking, as audio companies vying with the top production companies in the industry were willing to pay sums that amounted up to as much as 25 percent of a film's budget. Audio companies were ready to part with sums because the soundtracks from successful Hindi films sold in the millions. Finally, the rapidly expanding presence of satellite television in India benefited film producers as well. The profusion of channels made Indian television networks look to the Hindi film industry to fill their ever-increasing demand for content, and networks began competing aggressively to buy the telecast rights for Hindi films. The networks' willingness to pay substantial sums made satellite broadcast rights a significant source of revenue for producers, offering them a chance of recovering monies even if a film did poor theatrical business.

During my fieldwork in 2000, a variety of members of the industry relayed how overseas, satellite, and audio rights were regarded as "territories" unto themselves, indicating the extent of revenue they were capable of generating for producers. For established high-profile producers, the sales of these three categories of distribution rights brought in enough working capital to cover the cost of production, so that the revenue earned by the sale of distribution rights within India worked out to be pure profit. One feature of these new circumstances was the ability of powerful producers—those with a successful track record—to earn large sums prior to the advent of a film's production, which was referred to as a "table profit." When I had arrived in Bombay in October 2000, the industry was abuzz with the news that producer/director Karan Johar had already made a table profit estimated between 150 and 200 million rupees from the sale of the distribution rights for his film *Kabhi Khushi Kabhie Gham* (Sometimes There's Joy and Sometimes There's Sorrow), which just began shooting that same month.[6]

From the perspective of Indian distributors, these new sources of revenue made it feasible for producers to be less concerned about pleasing the vast majority of audiences in India. Lala Damani, the Bengal-Bihar distributor, complained that the potential profit margins for producers had become excessive, leading them to be unconcerned about the box-office fate of a film. Differentiating between a film and a "proposal," where the former signaled effort and commitment to quality while the latter indexed a calculated avarice, Damani stated, "The earnings [are] too much. Producers of the big proposals are earning 20, 30 *crores* [200–300 million rupees] on table. On table, before [a film's] release, whether the picture is a flop or the picture is a hit." He characterized producers as unfeeling mercenaries, likening distributors' losses to murder: "It doesn't bother them that the money they are earning is a result of many murders. Even if all the distributors are totally wiped out, the producer still makes money!" (Damani, interview, October 2000). He gave me the example of the 1998 film *Dil Se* (From the Heart) where, according to him, only the producers, audio company, and overseas distributors made a profit, while the distributors in India had suffered "heavy losses," in the tens of millions of rupees.

The fact that distributors were willing to outbid one another to pay producers their asking prices reveals that distributors perceived the potential for immense profit from the very films that they criticized. Distributors' readiness to buy certain films, from which they do not recover their investment, demonstrates the highly uncertain knowledge environment in which they operate and their inability to predict audience response. The expansion of producers' sources of revenue reconfigured the relationship between producers and territorial distributors, whereby the balance of power shifted toward the former from the latter, which is another way of understanding Damani's criticisms.

As indicated by the editorials in *Film Information* at the beginning of this section, and even by Tarun Kumar's dilemma in the editing studio that opened the previous chapter, the notions of universality and striving for broad appeal still had value in the industry in 2000. During fieldwork at that time, I encountered discussions—during scripting sessions—about audience identification, acceptance, and comprehension, which invoked the figure of the mass audience, as well as criticisms of certain films that appeared to be too niche in their appeal. While 1999 may not have had a universal hit, both 2000 and 2001 witnessed tremendous box-office successes, which were hailed as universal. The overwhelming domestic success of *Gadar: Ek Prem Katha* (Revolution: A Love Story), and the commercial, critical, and global success of *Lagaan*, deferred further discussions of niche and fragmented audiences. What really cemented the acceptance of social inequality and truly allowed the film industry to "escape the masses," rather than offer an escape to them, was the entry of corporate producers and the advent of multiplex theaters.

THE MULTIPLEX: REDEFINING AUDIENCES AND COMMERCIAL SUCCESS

The opening anecdotes of this chapter and of chapter two reference the impact of multiplex theaters on Hindi cinema, film-viewing, and the film industry, revealing how changes in the material properties of the spaces of exhibition can engender new patterns of production and consumption. Tracing the debates and struggles over the development of movie theaters in colonial Nigeria, Brian Larkin has argued that the space of the cinema is never neutral, but one marked by specific histories and particular social practices (2002). Similarly, the emergence of the multiplex indexes a particular sociopolitical and economic configuration in India and signifies a transformation of media practice. Not only has the multiplex created new modes of sociability and reordered public space (Larkin 2002), but it has also reshaped filmmakers' audience imaginaries. The move away from the masses and toward niche audiences, which began discursively in the previous section, is realized materially with the arrival of the multiplex. My discussion of multiplexes first addresses the material nature of the changes affecting film exhibition, and then examines how this very materiality produces new imaginings of film audiences and revises definitions of commercial success.

Twenty-First-Century Movie Palaces

The most noticeable feature of multiplexes is their sheer dazzling splendor, with immaculately maintained lobbies, cornucopia-like concession areas, and plush-carpeted auditoriums, with wide velvet or leather seats, which stand in great contrast to the older single-screen theaters (Figures 20–22). While single-screen theaters are stand-alone establishments occupying a prominent physical and landmark-like presence in the urban landscape, the vast majority of multiplexes are located in the interior of shopping malls that have been proliferating all over urban India since the early 2000s (Figure 23). In fact, multiplexes are an integral element of shopping malls, serving as the anchor business. Rashesh Kanakia, the chairman of Kanakia Constructions—a commercial and residential real estate developer that created the Cinemax chain of multiplexes— explained that malls and multiplexes were completely interdependent: "If the mall culture didn't come into the country, multiplexes wouldn't have come either, because if I make only a multiplex, it's not a viable proposal. If I make an entire mall, in order to attract good footfalls, I require a multiplex; then it becomes a viable proposal. If I make my multiplex on the third floor, my first and second floor [will] rent for a very high premium rate, because people see that at least 2000 or 3000 people are surely going to come into the mall" (Kanakia, interview, May 2006).

The symbiotic relationship between multiplexes and malls that Kanakia alludes to demonstrates how cinema has been employed to play an integral role in promoting and inculcating a newly consumerist dispen-

FIGURE 20 Entrance to Fame Cinemas Multiplex in Inorbit Mall, Malad (northwestern suburb of Bombay), 2005. Photo courtesy of Shyam Shroff.

FIGURE 21 Corridor of Fame Cinemas Multiplex, Vashi (Navi Bombay), 2008. Photo courtesy of Shyam Shroff.

FIGURE 22 Metro Cinema when it was still a single-screen theater, Marine Lines, Bombay, 2000. Photo by Pankaj Rishi Kumar.

FIGURE 23 Interior of Inorbit Mall, Malad, 2006. Photo by the author.

sation in India. The links between cinema and consumerism are most apparent in the lobbies and concession areas of multiplexes, which feature advertising for cell phones, cell phone services, credit cards, banks, financial services, jewelry brands, clothing brands, air conditioners, and even airlines. Some multiplexes have kiosks selling CDs and DVDs, or even small stores selling clothing and jewelry (Figure 24). All of the publicly visible spaces in a multiplex are potential sources of advertising revenue for the theater (Figure 25). BIG Cinemas' brochure, "The Power of BIG Cinemas: connecting brands to 65 million consumers in 116 cities, 500 screens across the world," details the potential advertising options for companies, revealing how every inch of their multiplexes, both interior and exterior—from doors to walls, staircases, elevators, parking lots, theater seats, and even the restrooms—is for sale to a brand (BIG Cinemas 2010).

With their location in malls, multiplexes have fundamentally altered the nature of cinema-going in India, from being a highly visible feature of the urban streetscape to a much more gated experience, marked by class privilege (Figures 26–27). The design and location of shopping malls are characterized by what I call "an aesthetic of intimidation": uniformed security guards; English-speaking staff; wide, expansive entrances set at a considerable distance from the street; driveways only open to elite forms of transport, such as private cars or taxis; and inaccessibility of public transportation. The aesthetic of intimidation ensures that the clientele patronizing the malls, and thereby the multiplexes, are only those drawn from that small fraction of Indian society that exhibits the class privilege and confidence to enter and inhabit these spaces.[7] When discussing the demographics of who frequents their theaters, multiplex managers in suburban Bombay listed call-center workers, IT professionals, families, college students, and members of the film industry. In promotional literature targeting potential advertisers, BIG Cinemas described their customers as "aspirational," "discerning," and "young, upwardly mobile people with high disposable income."[8]

Based on their target demographic of viewers comprising the "middle and upper income strata,"[9] a prominent characteristic of multiplexes is their explicitly articulated concern for customer service, which manifests itself rhetorically in their marketing and materially in terms of the diverse options to reserve and procure tickets. The language used in promotional literature by the main multiplex chains, such as PVR Cinemas, Fame Cinemas, BIG Cinemas, and Cinemax, focuses heavily on the material and physical comfort of viewing films in their establishments, as

FIGURE 24 Clothing and jewelry store inside the lobby of Fame Cinemas multiplex in Inorbit Mall, 2005. Photo by the author.

FIGURE 25 Citibank kiosk inside the lobby of Fame Adlabs multiplex in Citimall, Andheri, 2005. Photo by the author.

FIGURE 26 Entrance to Inorbit Mall, Malad, 2005. Photo by the author.

FIGURE 27 Security guard in the lobby of Cinemax Versova, 2006. Photo by the author.

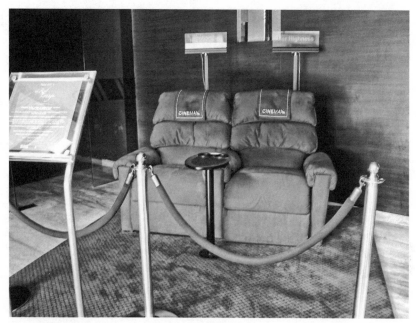

FIGURE 28 Advertising the seating in the Red Lounge, the Cinemax chain's exclusive and ultra-premium auditorium, 2006. Photo by the author.

well as on the sensory experience of cinema, detailing everything from their seat design to their sound and projection systems (Figure 28). In addition to comfort, the other main articulated attribute of multiplexes is the ease of obtaining tickets, which is enabled by modern communication technologies: viewers can buy tickets online, reserve tickets via text-message (referred to as SMS in India), or reserve tickets by phone. Multiplex chains like Fame Cinemas and Cinemax even offer free home delivery of tickets in Bombay. Communicating through a vocabulary of quality, service, and luxury, as well as catch-phrases like, "Enjoy, relax @ Cinemax" or BIG Cinema's "*Ab Bada Mazza Ayega* [Now we'll have a lot of fun]," multiplex marketing strategies rely on an implicit opposition to single-screen theaters in terms of their physical infrastructure, material conditions, and experiences of film-viewing. The poor state of movie theaters, even in a cine-centric city like Bombay, was a constant object of criticism by filmmakers when I began my research in 1996, and was posed as yet another challenge for filmmaking in India.

All of the amenities and luxury of the multiplex come with a hefty price tag; the ticket rates at multiplexes are significantly higher than those at single-screen cinemas. Between 2007 and 2010, the average ticket prices at the main national chains ranged from 110 to 130 rupees, compared with 20 to 60 rupees at single-screen cinemas.[10] In a high-cost city like Bombay, average ticket prices in 2009 at both types of theaters were even higher—ranging from 175 to 300 rupees at multiplexes and 50 to 110 rupees for single-screens.[11] The practice of assigned seating, which marks the Indian film-going experience, is maintained in multiplexes, and the differential pricing of tickets is taken to a new level, with completely elastic or demand-sensitive pricing. Ticket prices can vary by film, time of day, day of week, seat location, choice of screen, and week of a film's run.

While the architectural distinctions between balcony, dress circle, and stalls (orchestra level) that segment the physical space of the monumentally large single-screen theaters—thus providing the basis for the differential ticket rates—do not exist in the much smaller individual auditoria of multiplexes, distance from the screen still serves as a form of distinction for ticket prices. Most multiplexes have two or three rates of admission, based on seat location even in theaters with seating capacities as low as 150. Unlike the standardized single-screen categorization of "stalls, upper stalls, dress circle, and balcony," however, the language used by multiplexes to describe their different classes of seating varies across chains and conveys a sense of luxury and top-quality treatment. For example, Fame Cinemas classifies its seating using terms like "premier," "silver," "royal," "gold," "executive," and "jubilee," where the ticket rates—rather than the designations—reveal the internal spatial hierarchies of the theaters. Many multiplexes escalate their level of luxury and exclusivity by offering premium seating, such as single or double—referred to as "couples"—leather recliners at the very back of the auditorium, along with pillows and blankets to ward off the chill of the air conditioning. In the case of the large urban centers of Bombay, Delhi, or Calcutta, the scale of exclusivity is boosted further with the creation of entirely separate, ultra-upscale auditoriums with even smaller seating capacities and attendant premium amenities such as leather loveseats, seat-side food and beverage service, and separate waiting or lounge areas. The description on Fame Cinema's website of one of their multiplexes in Calcutta (Kolkata) communicates the extent to which cinema-going, specifically the multiplex version of it, is envisioned, packaged, and marketed as a highly elite and privileged experience: "The palace is built; the butlers are ready. Your Throne is waiting. Welcome to Fame South City: the first 6-screen ultra-luxurious multiplex in Kolkata. Far removed from the ordinary, with elegance and opulence tastefully made for Kolkata's supreme appetite. The Gold Class Screen is one of the six screens luxuriously spaced out . . . with [only] 74 lavish fitted recliners that stretch to 150 degrees at the press of a button. Butlers serve you at your seat in the screen and at the attached Gold Lounge, exclusively for Gold Class patrons."[12] The references to gold, thrones, palaces, and butlers reveal how the marketing aphorism "the customer is king" is realized literally in the space of this particular multiplex. The cost for such a cinematic experience was 400 rupees per ticket ($29.80 — PPP) for an evening or night show time in 2010. Since cinema-going is a deeply social experience in India, however, usually involving large groups of people who are frequently kin, the price of one ticket does not adequately convey the expenses incurred in seeing a film; therefore, when estimating the average expense involved in seeing a movie at a multiplex, it would be necessary to multiply the ticket cost at least four to five times, resulting in a considerable outlay of money.

Citing the high cost of admission, during my research visits to Bombay in 2005 and 2006 I asked the owners of multiplexes whether cinema-going was being transformed into an exclusively elite pastime. Many pointed to the existence of single-screen theaters as evidence that cinema-going was still affordable, not acknowledging the pressures facing single-screens: either to close down or convert into multiplexes. Shravan Shroff, the managing director of Fame Cinemas, argued that cinema-going was generally an expensive proposition anywhere in the world. Reminding me that, as a New York City resident, I definitely should understand that cinema-going is not a cheap enterprise, he focused on the necessity of recovering the investment in constructing multiplexes:

> Unfortunately in India it's always been looked upon as a cheap way to get entertained, but it's not necessarily cheap to make these things. They are very very expensive, and you see them — they are on par with any of the multiplexes that are there anywhere in the world, maybe better. So, you know, we have to break that mold of that it's always been cheap. They have been cheap because no new investments have been made thus far, but with the new investment . . . we need to recover the costs, so it is going to be expensive. I think it is important that people understand that it's not going to be cheap to go to movies in multiplexes, because of all the costs that are associated with it. (Shravan Shroff, interview, May 2006)

In terms of the expenses in building a multiplex, the land itself is usually leased rather than bought, and the costs of the structure are calculated either in terms of a per-seat cost or a per-screen cost. In 2009, the average cost was 70,000 rupees per seat or 20 million rupees per screen. Shroff stated that a "really nice, fancy facility" cost about a 100,000 rupees per seat. With regard to their cost and location, multiplexes are obviously identified with and cater to the "classes" segment of the film industry's audience binary.

While Shravan Shroff cited the costs of building and maintaining multiplexes as a reason for their high rates, his father, Shyam Shroff, focused on the quality of the entire viewing experience at multiplexes. He criticized the longstanding view in India that films were the cheapest form of entertainment: "See, unfortunately we've been taking our movies, treating them as dirt. We thought it's our birthright to see movies at whatever price we want to pay—that was wrong, after all it's a business." Shroff argued that multiplexes were able to charge higher rates because of a superior quality of service, as a result of the class and education levels of its employees and the willingness of customers to pay:

> If you feel you have an audience who's willing to pay you more, you are charging them. Now there are certain cinemas [that] don't provide you with basic facilities; nobody is going to go there. People go where you provide a service and they are willing to pay for the comforts and the service now. In our multiplexes—we have staff who call you "Sir" and "Ma'am." When we used to go to a cinema, staff used to say, "*Eh, bait-jao; chalo utho!*" [Hey you, sit down; get up!] They were so rude and filthy. In multiplexes, we have management students who are taking jobs and we train them; they get a certificate, so things have changed and you have to pay for that. (Shyam Shroff, interview, January 2005)

Shroff likened the distinction between watching a film in a multiplex versus a single-screen as similar to the different classes of train travel—first class, second class, and third class—that exist in India, wherein the multiplex was like the first-class compartment of a train and the single-screen was akin to the second- and third-class areas of a train. Just as passengers pay more to travel first-class with the expectation of a more comfortable and pleasurable journey, audiences pay for a more pleasant viewing experience in a multiplex. Part of that pleasant viewing (or traveling) experience is based on the absence of working-class audiences, whose mode of inhabiting the space are represented as abhorrent to more elite patrons. "If I'm watching a good movie, like a well-educated guy, well-established, I don't want the taxi-driver or the *rikshaw-wallah* [rickshaw driver] to come and sit next to me, chewing *paan* [betel leaf] and spitting. I want a better atmosphere, so what will I do? I'll spend more and go to a better outlet" (Shyam Shroff, interview, January 2005). Shroff's statements are similar to *Film Information* editor Komal Nahta's observations about prohibitively expensive ticket rates in the balcony sections of single-screen theaters producing a better viewing experience for social elites.[13] In the case of single-screens, however, while wealthier viewers were assured that members of a lower socio-economic stratum would not be sitting next to them, their presence was still perceptible within the larger space of the theater. Multiplexes ensure that a "better atmosphere" for socially elite viewers involves the complete erasure of poorer and working-class viewers from the space of the movie theater.[14]

While the multiplexes have been praised for their amenities, customer service, and material comforts, some members of the film industry have not been as sanguine about the larger social impact of the multiplex. Although a minority perspective, it is worth noting because it speaks to the larger social experience of cinema. Screenwriter Anjum Rajabali was ambivalent about the emergence and growth of multiplexes in India. Acknowledging that multiplexes had expanded the possibilities of more unconventional filmmaking, Rajabali nevertheless was critical of their overall impact: "What is it doing in the long run according to me? It has somehow taken the charm of democratic viewing away—I mean rubbing shoulders, within an Indian community: it was a microcosm. You attack any theater and you would find such a nice cross-section of people enjoying the same fare, maybe with different kind of rigor and different kind of externalization, but it was there and you related to that. *Arre, is baar seeti bajayenge, aah, maza aayega* [Hey, this time we'll whistle; and yeah, it'll be fun]. It's gone, you know? And that is my personal grouse" (Rajabali, interview, May 2006). Aditya Khanna, the manager of the Chanakya Cinema—a stalwart single-screen cinema located in an affluent part of New Delhi—made a similar point in an op-ed piece he wrote for the English-language daily *Indian Express* as a part of its feature commemorating the tenth anniversary of Delhi's first multiplex: "From a business standpoint, it's not rocket science: running a multiplex in India is a far better economic proposition than a single-screen cinema, but from the cinematic standpoint . . . a movie watched at a multiplex cannot be compared to one watched in a single-screen theatre. That is because cinema itself is a community experience. It's about watching a film with many other people in a given ambience" (Khanna 2007). Distinct from the discourses of comfort, service, and class segregation outlined by Shroff, Khanna defined viewing pleasure in terms of the presence of large numbers of people who hail from diverse class backgrounds:

Hearing 1000 people laugh together is a different experience from hearing 300. When the director wants . . . silence, the silence can be felt more if you are sitting in a larger hall. The small multiplex cannot give you the elevated feeling that you can get from sitting in the balcony of a single-screen theatre. There you feel like you are overseeing the proceedings. Also, because of the price, there is a like-minded crowd in a 300-seater, but in a big hall, there are so many people. Sometimes, a remark from the front stall can get the whole hall laughing . . . these are moments that add to the community experience of watching a movie! (Khanna 2007)

The large seating capacities of single-screens, which allow for varied audiences and the community experience that Khanna celebrates, is the very feature that has been heavily criticized by most quarters of the film industry and the Indian press. By contrast, the smaller seating capacities of multiplexes that Khanna criticizes are hailed as the impetus for a cinematic revolution.

The Emergence of a New Audience Binary

In my conversations with members of the film industry, the impact of multiplexes was not only articulated in terms of narrative-aesthetic practice, but also in terms of audience imaginaries. Multiplexes were attributed with expanding the base of theatrical audiences, drawing people in who never used to patronize movie theaters. Shyam Shroff explained that after his company's first forays into exhibition, which involved renovating an existing cinema and a joint venture in building one of the first multiplexes in Bombay, "Suddenly we saw a kind of audience that never used to visit cinemas because of the condition of cinemas. You realize that there is a totally new audience—the doctors, the engineers who never went to cinemas because they thought it's all bad and they always hired a DVD, VCD, or VHS cassette" (Shyam Shroff, interview, January 2005). Producer/director Vikram Bhatt reiterated similar sentiments about the effect of multiplexes on the class composition of the industry's audiences:

I think what the multiplex has done is it has brought into the theater the audience that, till now, was basically watching films at home, or they were not going to the theaters because they didn't like the ambience . . . Now going to the theater has become like an evening of enjoyment, and they've made theater the place to be, so a lot of gentry comes in, and also you must understand that the entrance is very expensive, it's 125 or 150 rupees, and sometimes for a very good film they hike it up even to 200, so if you have a family of four, you're talking about a 1000 rupee outing, so not everyone is going to be able to afford it. (Vikram Bhatt, interview, January 2006)

I reminded Bhatt that a similar narrative about socially elite audiences returning to theaters was produced in the mid-1990s, after the successes of *Hum Aapke Hain Koun!* and *Dilwale Dulhaniya Le Jayenge*, and asked him what was different about this contemporary moment. He responded by asserting that audiences in the mid- to late 1990s were only coming to theaters to see big-budget films with popular stars by well-known directors, whereas with the advent of the multiplex, films without well-known stars made on a smaller budget were able to draw audiences. He said, "Now the audiences are coming back, and if your film is even halfway decent, you can do a decent amount of business in the multiplex." Bhatt's remark about a "decent amount of business," or Shyam Benegal's relief at having smaller theaters, points to how the measurement and understanding of commercial success have been transformed with the advent of multiplexes.

Bhatt described this new audience as a more cosmopolitan and cinematically literate one, which posed new challenges for filmmakers in terms of genres: "With the coming of the multiplex, an audience which is very exposed to foreign films has come into the theaters. So, let's say the films that we used to make for the overseas market, that has come to India, so what that means is that action films don't do well, because if you've got an action film then you have to compete with a *King Kong* or a *Terminator 3* showing in the same multiplex, so you have to be better than that, and Indian films don't have the budget to be better than that" (Vikram Bhatt, interview, January 2006). Bhatt's reference to "the films that we used to make for the overseas markets" has to do with the perception in the film industry that only certain genres of films are successful among diasporic audiences in the Overseas Territory. By stating that a similar sensibility has developed within India, Bhatt attributes a convergence of tastes between certain audiences in India and those abroad as a result of the multiplex. He believed that love stories were going to continue to be popular and he predicted that "emotional films, thought-provoking films, sci-fi, and futuristic films" were all going to become regular industry genres.

Additionally, according to Bhatt, the audience frequenting multiplexes was also perceived as less socially conservative and more open to themes that in earlier eras would have been regarded as taboo. In that sense, the distance between the sophisticated sensibilities of filmmakers and their more conservative audiences had disappeared for Bhatt: "The target audience is more the filmmaker now; by that I mean, first we used to say things like 'I don't think this will be accepted in India,' but that has changed, because the audience is now very mature, very educated" (Vikram Bhatt, interview, January 2006). For filmmakers, the advantage of such an audience was that they were much less constrained in the types of stories and themes they could make films about than in the pre-multiplex past. Bhatt cited the production and exhibition of two recent films that had homosexual characters as a sign of the audience's maturity and ability to accept unconventional subject matter. He even surmised about *Lamhe*, "I feel that Yash Chopra made *Lamhe* a little early. If he had made it today, it would have been a big hit. At that time it was still a single-screen age, and he was thinking multiplex. If he had made *Lamhe* today and released *Lamhe* today, it would have been a big hit, because the audience [doesn't] find anything wrong with someone who is in love with the mother, the mother died, and now the daughter is there, so big deal. I mean, you have *Rumor Has It*, which has just released here [United States] in which you have the same man sleeping with the grandmother, mother, and the daughter. It's okay; it's fine" (Vikram Bhatt, interview, January 2006). Leaving aside the fact that when *Lamhe* was being conceived and produced in 1990, the concept of multiplexes was nowhere on the horizon in India, Bhatt's statements are in line with others discussed in earlier chapters, where media infrastructure like video, satellite, and now multiplexes, produce a discursive environment and provide a vocabulary to discuss social change.[15] *Lamhe*'s commercial failure, which was cited by many in the industry, including Bhatt, as a sign of Indian audiences' moral conservatism, is recast as a problem of temporality rather than of the immutability of kinship codes. The basis for Bhatt's judgment about *Lamhe* is founded upon the culturally indexical interpretation of the box-office outcome of the Hindi and Hollywood film, which allows him to reflect on the changing social mores of one segment of the Indian audience.

As a result of these new audiences and their new tastes and sensibilities, Bhatt asserted that multiplexes had transformed the way filmmakers conceived of and marketed their films to distributors. He pointed out that English titles for Hindi films were *de rigueur* for a multiplex audience and a cursory review of titles of Hindi films since 2006 — *Gangster, 36 Chinatown, Tom Dick and Harry, Life in a Metro, Welcome, Singh Is King, Partner, A Wednesday, New York, Luck, Do Knot Disturb, Wake Up Sid, Blue,*

3 Idiots, My Name Is Khan, Karthik Calling Karthik, Kites—indicates the rising popularity of English for film titles. Bhatt explained that from a film's conception, filmmakers discuss whether a film is a multiplex film or a single-screen film and that categorization extended itself even to titles. He narrated the experience of one of his films, where its content and style was more apropos of multiplexes, while its title connoted single-screen theaters, producing a dissonance that he felt led to its poor box-office performance:

> A case in point is my film *Jurm* [Crime], which didn't do well. There were two brothers, the producers—Ashish Singh and Anurag Singh. Anurag was of the opinion that *Jurm* is not a multiplex title and Ashish was that it is, and Anurag proved to be right, because with Bobby Deol in *Jurm*, they [multiplex viewers] thought it was an action film, so the single-screen viewers would like to see it. If the same film had a different title—like right now I'm doing a very dark thriller—a very passionate kind of thriller [that] is called "Red," and that is very exciting suddenly to the distributors! If I had said "Red" four or five years back, they would have said, "He's out of his mind!" So that's how things have changed. (Vikram Bhatt, interview, January 2006)

Bhatt's explanation for his film's poor commercial performance is an example of how filmmakers make sense of the uncertainty of box-office outcome. In this instance, the advent of the multiplex enables new sorts of production fictions, such as the significance of a film's title for its success, within the film industry.

Bhatt's discussion reveals the operation of a new audience binary within filmmakers' discourses about audiences—multiplex versus single-screen—that has basically supplanted the dominant classes/masses binary. An issue of *Film Information* laid out the distinction between the multiplex audience and single-screen audience: "A marked segmentation of the audience for Hindi films is being noticed these days. There is one section of the audience which likes what is known as 'different cinema,' but there's another which is still fond of the cinema of the '80s and '90s; The former section may be loosely referred to as the multiplex audience, whereas the latter can be termed the single-screen audience" ("Why No Universally Appealing Film" 2009). Although the above remarks posit a distinction in taste and cinematic preferences between audiences, locating those distinctions within the spaces of the different types of movie theater, in reality, both sites contain nearly the same programming. Whereas their multiple screens enable multiplexes to screen a larger selection of films, the films that are exhibited in single-screen theaters are also exhibited in multiplexes. The main distinction between the single-screen theater and the multiplex theater is not necessarily the films that are screened, but in the class composition of their respective audiences.

When I went to Bombay in the summer of 2006 and visited a number of multiplexes, I was most struck by how they were all screening exactly the same big-budget mainstream Hindi films and mostly the same mainstream Hollywood films.[16] I had come across comments in the Indian press about how initially the multiplex offered a space for filmmakers who did not conform to the conventions of mainstream cinema, but that was a short-lived period and in the words of one journalist, "Size matters. When a Yash Chopra production or a Hrithik Roshan vehicle comes along, it floods the multiplex screens and blanks out the smaller releases" (Chatterjee 2006). Rashesh Kanakia of Cinemax explained that their programming was in sync with the release schedules of the large producers, acknowledging that lesser-known filmmakers would have difficulty in obtaining screen time, unless they had well-known stars in their film. He said, "If the movie is not very big then they have trouble in exhibiting the film because they don't get a good slot then. We'd probably give them a matinee show" (Kanakia, interview, May 2006). Therefore, despite being touted as an agent of narrative and aesthetic change in filmmaking, the multiplex's significance also emerges from its role in transforming filmgoing practices and the industry's audience imaginaries.

Film Information's review of the film *Wanted*, the Hindi remake of a blockbuster Tamil film, released in September 2009, utilized the new audience binary, which still carried the traces of the older one:

> The film, despite all the gloss, looks like a typical South Indian film of the '80s and '90s, something which will not go down too well with the multiplex audience. On the plus side for the masses is the abundant action in the drama. While the violence, bloodshed, and gore in the film would be lapped up by the audience frequenting single-screen cinemas, the overdose of it would put off ladies, families, and a section of the multiplex audience . . . The tastes of the multiplex audience, especially, have undergone such a sea-change that they would not quite approve of such loud . . . excessive action and stunts. However, the action scenes will be simply adored by the masses and frontbenchers. On the whole, *Wanted* will be loved by the masses and the single-screen audience, but it will not find favor with a large section

of the multiplex-frequenting public due to excessive violence, dated making, and lack of a convincing story. (Nahta 2009b)

Certain features of this review are familiar, such as its use of audience categories like "masses," "front-benchers," "ladies," and "family," which are a standard part of the film industry's audience taxonomy, as well as its assertion that the masses "adore" action and violence, which other segments of the viewing audience find distasteful. It also expresses a certain level of disdain for films produced by the southern Indian film industries. What is different, of course, is how the single-screen cinema seems to have been emptied of its "classes" audience, at least at a discursive level, despite the continued existence of differential ticket rates at the single-screen theaters. What is distinctive about this review, however, is that the benchmark of assessing a film's commercial viability has shifted from the masses to the classes. While the previous chapter discussed how trade analysts were always assessing whether a film was too "classy," and therefore limited in its commercial potential, in the above review, the apparent mass appeal of the film is posited as the limiting factor. Here, pleasing the multiplex audience appears paramount for a film's commercial success. This concern for whether a film would appeal to audiences who frequent multiplexes more than a mass audience who attend single-screen cinemas has to do with the changing economics of film exhibition. The next section discusses how the advent of multiplexes has restructured the relationships between exhibitors, distributors, and producers, which has had an impact on how filmmakers define commercial success and how they relate to their audiences.

Multiplex Economics

According to a variety of reports carried out by a number of global consulting firms,[17] in 2009 multiplexes comprised about 8 to 10 percent of the total exhibition sector in India, but accounted for anywhere from 35 to 70 percent of box-office revenues.[18] Vikram Bhatt explained how these new economics transformed the way filmmakers conceived of their films and audiences, referring to films made in the mid- to late 1980s: "You know films like Coolie and Mard [Man] and all those other films a few years back—they were hugely mass-y films, but there are no returns to that anymore. So, you know like a 30 percent full theater in a multiplex gives you what a 60 or 70 percent single-screen theater does, so it's better off going the classy way" (Vikram Bhatt, interview, January 2006). This disproportionate share of revenues was due to significantly higher ticket prices, rather than increased rates of occupancy—noted in Bhatt's comments about the commercial equivalence between a minimally populated multiplex and a two-thirds full single-screen—since average occupancies at multiplexes ranged from 27 to 43 percent between 2007 and 2010 (Shah and Boob 2009). Bhatt proceeded to give me a more specific example of the inordinately large revenues that could be earned from multiplexes: "I was sitting with Ratan Jain, the producer of *Main Hoon Na* [You Can Count on Me] when his film released. *Main Hoon Na*'s first three-day collections, in two multiplexes of Bombay, was seven and a half *lakhs* [750,000 rupees] in one, and six and a half *lakhs* [650,000 rupees] in the other multiplex. I'm talking about two screens [and] close to thirteen *lakhs* [1.3 million rupees], and in Punjab the first three days was twelve *lakhs* [1.2 million rupees]; all of Punjab with the single-screen theaters! So he's better off making . . . *Main Hoon Na*, let's remember was a mass-y and classy film, so we're talking about full houses even in the masses" (Vikram Bhatt, interview, January 2006). Bhatt's comments about uneven box-office earnings reflecting the disproportionate power and value of smaller numbers of multiplex audiences mirror sentiments articulated earlier in the chapter about the commercial importance of overseas audiences, which buy tickets in dollars and pounds, versus Indian audiences buying in rupees. From Subhash Ghai's description of the overseas market—"the quantum of audience is less, but the quantum of money is more"—to Bhatt's equation of multiplex audiences being worth twice as much as those in single-screens, the driving commercial logic of the film industry since 2000 is characterized by an inverse relationship between the numbers of viewers and the amount of revenue; in other words, filmmakers have been striving to make more money from fewer people.

In addition to higher ticket rates allowing filmmakers to reap profits from smaller numbers, multiplexes have also introduced a level of transparency in the measurement and tabulation of commercial outcome that had not existed earlier. When I began my fieldwork, I encountered a great deal of criticism and resignation about the lack of reliable empirical knowledge regarding a film's fate at the box-office. Rajjat Barjatya of Rajshri Films asserted, "Basically, nobody knows how much business a film has done. Under-reporting? There is no reporting. What is reported is just the box-office collections of the film, that too at the main stations of India, maybe that would be 10 percent or 20 percent of the total. Nobody knows how much the film has done, and because a normal film is sold to different distributors in different parts of the country, you can never come to know" (Barjatya, interview, April 1996). The problem of verifiable data was connected to the undercapitalized nature of the film industry prior to the early 2000s, the fragmented relationship between the production, distribution, and exhibition sectors, and the high rates of entertainment tax borne by exhibitors. Such a production-distribution scenario presented numerous incentives for various agents located at different points in the circulation of a film to under-report or misrepresent the amount of revenue a film had earned. For example, the exhibitor had an incentive to under-report box-office receipts to evade paying entertainment tax. The distributor had an incentive to under-report a film's earnings and not share it with the producer, as per the arrangement of the MG system. A producer had an incentive to downplay his profits in order to pay lower salaries. Producers and distributors were very matter-of-fact about the deception and characterized it as the nature of the film business. Shyam Shroff asserted humorously in 1996, "You see there is cheating from stage one to stage last. You cheat producers; you cheat the government; you don't pay taxes. There are no figures anywhere, and Indians are masters at cheating others" (Shyam Shroff, interview, April 1996). He pointed out that the only way to ascertain information about a film's business was by constant personal interaction and monitoring, "I don't sit down here with my computers and start getting figures. Nobody sends figures over here. I don't know what is happening unless I go there. If I'm not on the spot, people take you for a big ride here" (Shyam Shroff, interview, April 1996).

Multiplexes represent the entry of organized industrial and finance capital, with its associated regimes of financial transparency and accountability, into the film industry. Either as divisions of larger conglomerates (BIG Cinemas), or as autonomous companies whose shares are listed and traded on the Bombay Stock Exchange (PVR Cinemas), multiplexes are located within a political economic framework where the visibility of revenue is privileged and rewarded. In fact, if the earlier structure of distribution and exhibition encouraged under-reporting of revenue, the current conjuncture offers incentives to show profit and growth, which are prized attributes of companies listed on stock markets. With computerized systems of ticketing and data collection, multiplexes enable a monitoring of a film's business that is not solely dependent upon face-to-face interaction and social relations. This financial transparency works to the advantage of producers who are able to recover revenues due them from distributors, or in many cases by the exhibitors, because several commercially powerful producers have forgone the distributor and dealt directly with the multiplex chains since 2005.

The figures generated by these systems represent a form of concrete and verifiable knowledge contrasted with the ambiguity associated with single-screen theaters in regions outside large urban centers.[19] Shroff characterized the issue of data collection in large cities as one of utmost ease as a result of multiplexes: "Everything is computerized, you punch in a button and you get all the information out" (Shyam Shroff, interview, January 2005). While he asserted the complete veracity of data from multiplexes, stating that "you can take the figures blindfolded," he also acknowledged that accurate information was still difficult to obtain from certain parts of India: "Certain cities, certain states, like Bihar . . . don't disclose correct figures. It's a vast country. You can't just keep on tracking each and every cinema and each and every exhibitor" (Shyam Shroff, interview, May 2006). This inability to ascertain a comprehensive picture was a point of frustration for Shroff's son, Shravan, who complained about the dearth of data regarding the entire exhibition sector: "Unfortunately what's not happening in India up till now is that you don't have an agency which is actually collecting all the information from the theaters. They are actually collecting all the information from the multiplexes, but they aren't collecting the information from the rest of the theaters" (Shravan Shroff, interview, May 2006). This lack of data was framed as a problem of technology, anachronistic attitudes, and disorganization, where the fault lay squarely with the single-screen theaters. He continued, "Now the problem is that the rest of the theaters are manual, so an agency can't sign off till the time they organize themselves. It's a classic problem of being in the twenty-first century, but with many of the old screens being back in the eighteenth or nineteenth century. That's going to continue being a problem till the older guys organize themselves or the number of newer guys is much more than the older guys. That's the reason that all the multiplex data is publicly available and that's what the Yes Bank reports and the FICCI reports actually base themselves on, but unfortunately for the older screens we don't have that data" (Shravan Shroff, interview, May 2006).

Set against the backdrop of the difficulty of data collection and the dearth of accurate empirical knowledge about aggregate box-office outcome in India, multiplexes operate as sites of financial discipline and empirical visibility. I contend that the economic and symbolic value of multiplexes and their audiences arise from their position within new regimes of accounting and data production, which impart the semblance of objectivity, rationality, and modernity. Multiplex audiences are important to the film industry not simply because they represent higher revenues, but because they can be *counted accurately*; the ability to be enumerated is converted into knowledge that operates as a form of capital within the world of organized corporate finance and its discursive production of company annual reports, red herring prospectuses, and investment analyses. This knowledge capital is then used to attract investment capital into the film industry through the media of formal research reports prepared by investment banks and consulting firms, which since 2000 have been projecting the immense economic potential of filmmaking in India.[20]

Not only have multiplexes made it easier for producers and distributors to monitor box-office earnings, they have also restructured the relationship between distributors and exhibitors for the former's benefit. Until the advent of multiplexes, the dominant exhibition arrangement was the practice of fixed theater rental. Due to a shortage of screens, exhibitors had the upper hand, and regardless of occupancy rates they charged distributors a fixed rent. This practice was cited by filmmakers in my early fieldwork as one of the reasons that films had to be successful outside of large urban centers like Bombay, where onerous theater rentals limited the revenues accruing to distributors and producers. Producer/director Rakesh Roshan declared, "A movie that just does well in Bombay is not a hit. If a movie does well even 100 percent, 70 to 80 percent goes in the theater hall. What you get is nothing—moneywise. You only get a reputation in Bombay. It's in those places where the theater rate is 10,000 rupees, and the collection is 1 *lakh* [100,000 rupees]. Here it's reverse. The theater rate is 90,000 rupees; collection is 10,000 rupees" (Roshan, interview, May 1996). With the emergence of multiplexes, the expansion of screens in urban centers recast the supply and demand equation in favor of distributors and producers, leading to a system of percentage-based revenue sharing with exhibitors. This has had a major impact on distributors' and producers' earnings, because it enables them to recoup revenues even in situations of low theater occupancies, which they were unable to do earlier. Shyam Shroff asserted, "Even if your movie is flopping, you're getting something out of it." The idea that a "flopping" film—which in this context refers to lower than expected audience turnout—could still garner revenues for the distributor, demonstrates how multiplexes have crucially recalibrated notions of commercial viability within the film industry. These altered understandings have an impact on how filmmakers regard the necessity and attainability of universal hits, which I address in the next section.

Escaping the Masses

A small editorial titled "Why No Universally Appealing Film?" appearing in an issue of *Film Information* from October 10, 2009, discussed the divergent fate of several films of that year, noting that the films that succeeded with multiplex audiences did not succeed with single-screen audiences and vice versa. It ended by posing the following questions: "With the tastes of the two kinds of audience being very different, and the difference seeming to be only growing with each passing week, is it becoming difficult for filmmakers to make a universal hit—a film which appeals to every class and section of the audience? Or is it that nobody is trying hard enough?" ("Why No Universally Appealing Film?" 2009). The contrast with the January 2000 editorial, discussed at the beginning of the chapter, is telling: while the earlier editorial predicted dire consequences for the health of the film industry if filmmakers did not work harder to try to make more universally appealing films, the comments from 2009 pose the issue as a set of rhetorical questions rather than as an imperative. The reasons for the remarkable change in tone has to do with the restructured relationships between production, distribution, and exhibition within the Hindi film industry, which in turn have redefined notions of success within the industry.

Just as the growing importance of overseas markets and increased revenue potential of satellite and music rights had reduced the value of certain distribution territories within India, the multiplex has diminished the significance of the mass audience in filmmakers' imaginations. With the multiplex's skewed economics, filmmakers do not even have to attempt to appeal to the "masses." Screenwriter Anjum Rajabali affirmed my hunch that filmmakers appeared unconcerned with the majority of audiences in India. As I was starting to ask a question about this, Rajabali jumped in:

> I will interrupt your question, right away. They actually, verbally, avowedly . . . don't care. As a strategy, as a market, they don't care at all. They really don't. They in fact feel so *liberated* . . . so relieved that, "I don't need to look at what the Bihar distributor is saying; they don't need to hold me to ransom and all that, these illiterate bastards," but the fact is that the Bihar distributor, the film was not meant for him!

He was trying to be the sort of conduit that controls what goes in. *You* had the capacity to independently relate to the Bihar audience; you never did, you became a slave of this and now you feel that, "Oh I can be liberated from that!" (Rajabali, interview, May 2006)

In addition to reproaching producers and directors for narrowing their target audience, Rajabali is also critical of how filmmakers regard territorial distributors as metonyms for specific audiences. He continued to discuss how most filmmakers had become concerned with what he termed "a very narrow band of the audience," and did not attempt to think about what it entailed to appeal broadly across India. With the advent of multiplexes, he felt what was previously regarded as a limitation—the inability to make films that appealed to diverse audiences across India—had been turned into a virtue: "Okay, what is the Indian script? What is a pan-Indian script? Can we at least think of that? Instead of doing that, they said, 'Let's work out a way where we don't need to think about it,' you see, and the multiplex culture lent itself very, very admirably and very eagerly to that and they grasped it . . . Your observation is absolutely spot-on that they don't feel the need to do that and they feel very relaxed about it" (Rajabali, interview, May 2006).

The marginal nature of mass audiences in filmmakers' imaginations corresponded with the reduced aspiration for universal hits as the penultimate criterion of success. When I asked Vikram Bhatt whether a universal hit was desirable or possible, he replied in the affirmative, but then qualified the idea of a universal hit by differentiating between an "all-India hit" and an "A-B-C center hit." The A-B-C classification of regions within distribution territories refers to the revenue earning and revenue-collection potential of particular areas, as well as an audience category within the film industry's taxonomy. He explained that while an all-India hit was still possible, the A-B-C center hit was nearly impossible, because of the vastly different taste cultures between audiences who frequent multiplexes in the A-class centers versus those audiences in the other two centers, who are mired in the past—as evident from their taste in films. Bhatt stated, "It is more difficult to make it an A-B-C center hit. An all-India hit would also include Patna, which is now a multiplex center. But to make an A-B-C center hit is very difficult. I mean look at the films that Suneel Darshan makes—*Dosti* [Friendship] and all these kinds of films, they do well in the Hindi belt, North belt, but then they completely miss out on the multiplex, because the multiplex audience thinks these are some films from the '70s or '80s, which has an old connotation" (Vikram Bhatt, interview, January 2006). In Bhatt's statements, the advent of multiplexes in Patna, the capital city of the state of Bihar, upgrades and recasts at least one site in this most reviled and belittled region into a valued entity.

In discussing his reasons for why he did not think it possible for a film to be successful among the various class segments and the urban-rural divide implied by the A-B-C classification, Bhatt deployed the trope of the two Indias:[21]

> We must understand that India is going bipolar as a country: the buying power; the per-capita income; the progress; everything is so different. The divide between the cities and the villages of India is ever increasing so it's becoming more and more difficult to kind of please both audiences. When you just close your eyes and imagine Bihar and the interiors of U.P. and then when you're talking Bombay, Hyderabad, Bangalore—it's completely different; it's like two different countries you know? So when the people are so diverse, it's very difficult to bring everybody under one umbrella, so obviously the filmmaker is going to go for what seems to be a more profitable option. (Vikram Bhatt, interview, January 2006)

In Bhatt's statements, we encounter continuities with ideas expressed in the previous chapter and earlier in this chapter: the location of audience taste within socio-economic conditions; and the necessity of appealing to regions and audiences that accrue greater revenues for filmmakers.[22] Unlike the filmmakers presented in chapter eight, who discussed how successful filmmaking either lay in locating the essence that was common to audiences or judiciously balancing elements in order to appeal broadly, Bhatt, like Subhash Ghai, argues that such differences of taste, class, and social location cannot be transcended.

This idea of a vast insurmountable taste divide between audiences was echoed by producer/director Karan Johar, during the post-screening discussion of his film *Kabhi Alvida Na Kehna* (Never Say Good-Bye) at New York University, in February 2007. Replying in the affirmative to my question about the possibility of achieving a universal hit, Johar quickly asserted that it was not something that could be planned beforehand. Johar then went on to explain how the changing demographics of filmmakers and audiences mitigated any certainty of this category of success, since the audience was getting "more and more sectioned in a certain sense." Johar, like Bhatt, deployed the A-B-C center taxonomy to elaborate on these social and taste divides:

We have three centers: the A-class centers, the B-class centers, and the C-class centers. B and C are the smaller towns and villages. Now, films that work and appeal to them, will not appeal at all to the A-class centers. A very few connect like a *Dhoom*, because B and C will react to maybe the sex-appeal of it and the action of it, and the A will react to it and call it cool, and the Overseas will like the star power of it. But those are really only one or two films in the entire year. If you look at 2006, *Dhoom* and *Munnabhai*, and maybe *Krrish* are the three films that worked all over, but that is three films in the entire year. (Johar 2007)

The way Johar positions the three films above that had achieved wide-ranging commercial success is a stark contrast from the last chapter, where such types of success were sought after and valorized within industry discourses. His comments reflect that such successes are fortuitous—almost accidental—in nature. Johar's dismissive tone—"three films in the entire year"—reflecting a somewhat underwhelmed reaction, presents an interesting contrast to the *Film Information* editorial of January 2000: this had contrasted the poor showing of 1999 with that of 1977, which witnessed "three mega hits in a single year!" The films that Johar mentions were all tremendous box-office successes in 2006—either garnering AA or AAA classifications by the trade press, which meant that distributors had at least tripled their investments. Regardless of filmmakers' pronouncements, universal hits have always been difficult to achieve, and there are never more than a few every year. Rather than asserting that it has become more difficult for filmmakers to make universal hits, I am arguing that the relationship of filmmakers toward this category has changed.

Despite the fact that some films still enjoyed wide pan-Indian commercial success, the fact that both Bhatt and Johar did not think it was a consistently attainable goal reveals how much attitudes are changing regarding universal hits. I argue that the change is less about the widening social chasm between different categories of audiences than about the changing conditions of production, distribution, and exhibition in the film industry. A universal hit simply does not hold the same economic and symbolic significance it once it did in the Hindi film industry. This is due to the structural transformations of filmmaking with the entry of corporate production companies and multiplexes, which have altered ideas of commercial success in the industry. As already mentioned above, multiplexes, with their high ticket rates, revenue-sharing arrangements, and financial transparency, have managed to transform even low to moderate audience attendance or ticket sales into a sign of success. Additionally, major urban and overseas markets are more prized by filmmakers than the smaller, provincial ones, so if a film appears to be doing reasonably well in multiplexes simply in Bombay or Delhi, it gets represented as a hit by filmmakers and the media.

The large infusions of capital and the rationalization of film financing initiated by the entry of the corporate sector into film production have reduced or removed the reliance on the traditional territorial distributor as a source of finance capital for filmmaking, at least for the influential producers of the industry. Historically, raising capital was one of the main difficulties for the Hindi film industry, and distributors were an important source of funds through the MG system. When distributors throughout India provided the main source of finance capital for filmmaking, they bore a significant share of financial risk; therefore, it was imperative for the overall functioning of the industry that films were positioned to succeed commercially all over India in order to project their ability to earn healthy profits for their territorial distributors. The idea of the universal hit was critical for the general financial health of the film industry.

The entry of the Indian organized industrial sector into film production, and the ability of established producers to raise money from the Indian stock market by transforming their production companies into public limited companies, have diminished the role of the traditional territorial distributor from a source of finance and power to being a middleman between producer and exhibitor. Anjum Rajabali's description of filmmakers' relief at not being "held ransom" by the Bihar distributor represents the dominant perception of distributors as a tremendous constraint on the creative process. Screenwriter Sutanu Gupta characterized distributors as extremely risk-averse, especially when it came to backing films with newcomers: "Distributors are people who are a scared lot; they are shit scared; they're afraid . . . if they had their way, besides Ashok Kumar,[23] nobody would have come in, because they go by whoever is running, whoever is on the screen. They are afraid of new faces because they don't know how the audience will react" (Gupta, interview, 18 November 1996).

There is a sense that the new corporate producers are less risk-averse than traditional distributors, although as the discussion in chapter seven indicated, the star-centric nature of the film industry has not diminished with these new production houses. Many corporate producers have also ventured into both all-India and overseas distribution, and possess a much higher threshold for financial risk. These corporate distributors can either rely on profits from some territories to offset losses from others or profit from their investment by re-selling distribution rights to the individual territorial distributors. A universal hit is simply not as necessary within this new financing and distribution scenario; therefore, the diminished significance of the universal hit is correlated with the decreased importance of the independent territorial distributor within the contemporary Hindi film industry.

The reduced value of the universal hit within the industry has expanded the criteria of success to the benefit of filmmakers. While the previous structure of the industry only rewarded—in terms of both economic and symbolic capital—filmmakers who strived for universal hits, the contemporary structure, after the advent of corporate producer/distributors and multiplexes, enables those filmmakers who are unable to achieve, or are unconcerned with broad appeal, to raise finance and earn prestige and status within the industry.[24]

This chapter has delved into great detail about how these new regimes of production, distribution, and exhibition are enabling filmmakers to consciously restrict their market, at least in the short term. Aiming to please all audiences does not actually garner filmmakers any symbolic capital within the industry, and may in fact reduce it. Although Bhatt and Johar raise the issue of profit and commercial outcome to explain the turn toward certain themes and audiences within the current generation of Hindi filmmaking, a portion of Johar's remarks regarding my question revealed a great concern with issues of symbolic capital as well. Discussing the neglect of certain categories of audiences, Johar asserted, "What is happening is that the hardcore rural-based audiences are being ignored. These audiences are just not helping the elevation of cinema at all, because films that appeal to them don't make you feel proud of them in the wider context. So again, there is a divide. You want to make a mark and you want to take Indian cinema many steps ahead. You want to put it [onto] the global map, [onto] the world map. You want to do that because you feel proud of your country and proud of the work you do" (Johar 2007). Thus, the desire to appeal to urban elites and overseas audiences is not simply about profit, but also about garnering distinction (Bourdieu 1984).[25] The causal link between the type of cinema and the social class of its audiences is asserted here once again, mixed in with a certain politics of national pride and prestige based on the vilification of the majority of the Indian population—"rural-based audiences"—whose tastes are represented as an obstacle to the development of Indian cinema as a globally prestigious form. Johar's remarks are not singular, but emerge from the framework of disdain that characterizes the Hindi film industry's production culture. Multiplexes and corporate production companies have resolved the dilemma of disdain that arose from having to produce films for mass audiences by making profitable—what would appear to be a counterintuitive economic logic—the conscious narrowing and restricting of audiences.

This logic of restriction, usually described as making films for niche audiences, is frequently hailed by the Indian press and financial analysts as a sign of progress and quality, indicating the modernization of the Hindi film industry. These discussions are rife with developmentalist tropes of "mature markets" and "mature audiences." For example, an article in the *Financial Times* newspaper about the marketing and distribution strategy of the 2003 Hindi film *Jhankaar Beats*, which had only 40 prints release across ten cities, hailed multiplexes and developed audiences for enabling a film of this nature to be a commercial success: "A more mature audience is now willing to sample new fare, even if it is devoid of big stars" (Chandran 2003). An article from the *Financial Express*, a few years later, was more measured in its praise for multiplexes, pointing out that mainstream Hindi films still commanded the lion's share of screen time. It depicted the Indian cinematic landscape as childlike and not fully developed: "A mature distribution-exhibition system should be able to embrace all sorts of cinema, which, alas, still isn't the case in India" (Chatterjee 2006). The 2009 FICCI-KPMG Media & Entertainment Industry Report's portions about filmmaking herald the emergence of multiplexes as giving "a new lease of life to the niche category of cinema in India." Describing how smaller seating capacities allow exhibitors to screen non-mainstream movies, the Report paints an image of the "mature" distribution-exhibition system that the previous article desired. Multiplexes are represented as the key technology for improving cinema in India insofar as they reduce the reliance on large numbers of audiences: "The theater can manage reasonable capacity utilizations even with [a] lesser number of people. This helps them maximize the potential of any film, irrespective of its budget and star cast. Ticket prices in multiplexes are also much higher as compared to single-screens, with no under-declaration of revenues. This provides a platform for thematic exclusivity and creativity to the producers, since they can now make movies keeping only a particular class of audience in mind" (KPMG 2009: 56). The logic of narrowcasting and the idea of segmenting markets are not inherently imbued with ideologies of gentrification, but the fact that "niche cinema" is completely associated with multiplexes and their higher ticket prices demonstrates how such cinematic practice is deeply embedded in structures of social inequality. Speaking of the growing divergence of taste between urban and rural audiences, because of the changing demographics of filmmakers themselves, Karan Johar predicted, "Eventually, in ten years, I think, every cinema will be a multiplex, and catering just to these will be the prime concern" (Johar 2007).

WHICH AUDIENCES MATTER?

Whereas for much of its history, the Hindi film industry regarded all of India as the primary market for Hindi films, what this chapter has demonstrated is that, since 2000, only certain audiences and certain regions in India have mattered to Hindi filmmakers. Just as it regarded all of India as its primary market, the film industry at one point considered everyone residing within the geopolitical boundaries of the Indian nation-state as a member of the cinema-going audience. While the previous chapter illustrated how the Indian audience was once a metonym for the nation and its diversity, this chapter has shown how the audience has become a metonym for a globalized India and its modernity. With the advent of industry status, corporatization, and multiplexes, the parameters of the imagined audience have constricted, counting only those who can actively take part in the consumerist dispensation that is valorized in a post-liberalization India. It is in these respects that audience imaginaries have been gentrified within the Hindi film industry.

I want to remind readers, however, that this and the previous chapter have discussed filmmakers' audience imaginaries—the discursive production of audiences by the film industry—and not the actual people who go to see films. While the Hindi film industry's valorization and celebration of the multiplex is troubling, as it is a palpable material expression of the disdain they feel for the majority of viewers, the gentrification of audience imaginaries has a more complex trajectory. As made apparent in this chapter as well as in chapters two and eight, the majority of Hindi filmmakers have an extremely condescending attitude toward the "masses" and the "interiors." When filmmakers were consciously targeting the masses, or aiming for a universal hit, they deployed a theory of spectatorship that was based on a combination of literalist identification, developmentalist paternalism, and moral and culturalist allochronism. Filmmakers' representations of poor and working-class audiences, or the inhabitants of non-metropolitan regions of India, did not accord these viewers any sort of complex subjectivity; instead, such viewers were primarily represented as enormous constraints on the creative process. Another way to regard the gentrification of the audience imaginary is that filmmakers have liberated themselves conceptually from their own self-imposed audience fictions. The phenomena of reception are much more complex than filmmakers' discourses and theories allow for. To lament too much that Hindi filmmakers are ignoring the masses or the diverse film-going public, based on the content of films, would be to replicate the essentialist and literalist theories of the Hindi film industry.

The shift in Hindi filmmakers' audience imaginaries parallels shifts in other spheres of cultural production in India, brought about by the neoliberal restructuring of the state, media, and society, in which citizens have been reconfigured as consumers.[26] The ideology of the universal hit represents a particular Nehruvian nationalist vision located within an economic imperative: broad audiences were necessary for the continued existence of the Hindi film industry. However, the pursuit of mass audiences and broad public appeal were the very logics that brought opprobrium upon Hindi cinema by intellectuals, journalists, and other social and cultural elites. For years mainstream Hindi cinema was criticized as rootless, culturally inauthentic, and brazenly commercial because it aimed to please diverse audiences. In contrast to the filmmaker statements presented in this chapter, the quest for a shared cultural expression, represented by the universal hit, now appears curiously utopic. The shift from targeting mass to niche audiences is celebrated by filmmakers, journalists, and economic analysts as a sign of the maturation and modernization of filmmaking within India. It is this logic of gentrification that is at the heart of the Hindi film industry's transformation into Bollywood.

My Name Is Bollywood

It was a familiar fanfare—the staccato drum-beats, followed by a drum roll, overtaken by the clear, penetrating sound of trumpets, joined by the string section swelling to a crescendo—that preceded the screening of many a film in the United States. This time, however, the recognizable strains of the 20th Century Fox fanfare filling up the auditorium at Village 7 Cinema in Manhattan, on February 12, 2010, was followed by a series of opening credits—"Fox Star Studios and Fox Searchlight Pictures Present . . . A Dharma Productions and Red Chillies Entertainment Production"—that ended with the title of the Hindi film, *My Name Is Khan*, starring Shah Rukh Khan, directed by Karan Johar, and co-produced by Khan and Johar.

My Name Is Khan (MNIK) attracted a great deal of media attention in India in 2009 for the unparalleled sum that Fox Star Studios, the Indian subsidiary of 20th Century Fox, paid to acquire the global distribution rights of the film—purportedly between 800 and 850 million rupees.[1] In press conferences and interviews, Khan and Johar represented their decision to sell the film to Fox as a step toward bringing a new global visibility to Hindi cinema, by partnering with an institution that would take their film to new, untapped, and untraditional—that is, non-diasporic—markets. Johar stated in an interview with *rediff.com*, "Because of its vast network, Fox was able to show this film in the best of theaters worldwide, from Canada to Poland to Indonesia. Even in countries where Indian films are very popular but not well distributed, Fox did a remarkable job. From Egypt to Jordan to Malaysia, the film has performed strongly to a large extent because of the Fox distribution strategy and its ability to engage leading film writers in various countries to run stories on *My Name Is Khan*" (Pais 2010).[2] The film's box-office performance in India was more checkered, and in the year-end accounting of commercial outcome, MNIK was not classified as a hit, but as a "coverage to commission-earner" by *Film Information* (see Table 3, p. 190) which meant that the territorial distributors to whom Fox resold the rights covered their costs, and some may have earned their 25 percent commission, but none had profited greatly on their investment.[3]

Starring Shah Rukh Khan and Kajol—Johar's favorite onscreen star pair—the film centered on the ethnic profiling and discrimination faced by American Muslims in the aftermath of 9/11, as experienced by a Muslim man (played by Khan) with Asperger's syndrome. In terms of its content, treatment, and narrative style, which eschewed lip-synch song sequences, MNIK represented a radical departure from Johar's previous films. He characterized it as emblematic of his evolution as a filmmaker: "This is not the usual *masala* film. This is not even a typical Karan Johar film. It is a more thought-provoking and deeply psychological film than anything I have done before. Making this film made me grow more as a person than ever before" (Pais 2010). In Johar's remarks we encounter the traces of disdain, the assertions of distinction, and the entanglement of film production with the production of filmmaker subjectivity, which have been a central focus of this book.

While Johar's remarks focused on how MNIK differs from the norms of Hindi cinema—or even his own filmmaking practice—Khan's comments at another venue focused on the distinction that accrues to Hindi films from their circulation amidst sites and audiences considered "Western." "We have hit upon a kind of cinema that's brave," said Khan, "and the kind of pop cinema that India stands for today. Internationally, we need to work on the kind of cinema that would respect the tastes of the Western audience also" (Shetty-Saha 2009). From his comments during our interview, over a decade ago, to the statements above, Khan has appeared centrally concerned with the global reputation of Hindi cinema over the course of his career. MNIK thus exemplifies Khan's desire of making films that are "less tacky" in order to "reach the international market." Following the dominant logic of interpreting commercial outcome as indices of audience identification and acceptance, Johar touted the film's global box-office grosses—about $39 million, including a little over $4 million in the United States—as concrete evidence of the film's international appeal.[4]

MNIK also represents a new phase that began in the Hindi film industry in the late 2000s: one of greater interaction and formal partnerships being forged between Hindi filmmakers and Hollywood studios. For example, studios such as Sony and Warner Bros. have co-produced and distributed mainstream Hindi films,[5] while Disney has invested in UTV and partnered with Yashraj Films to co-produce animated films for the Indian market.[6] The flow of capital is not simply unidirectional from the United States to India, however. Reliance Big Entertainment, a subsidiary of the Indian conglomerate Reliance ADA Group, made news in May 2008 when it signed deals to produce and develop movies with prominent Hollywood actors, such as Tom Hanks, Brad Pitt, George Clooney, Jim Carrey, and Nicolas Cage (Lakshman and Grover 2008; Timmons 2008).[7] Reliance further solidified its position as a significant player in Hollywood when it announced an $825 million production and distribution deal in August 2009 with Steven Spielberg's DreamWorks Studios, of which $325 million was an equity investment on the part of Reliance (Jamkhandikar 2009).[8]

While Hollywood's interest in "Bollywood" is definitely interpreted and registered by Hindi filmmakers as a validation of the Hindi film industry, and as a sign that it has indeed "arrived" on the global stage, the collaborations to date have not yielded the sort of commercial success that Hollywood studios may have been hoping for. I believe this is partly due to the very different motivations each industry has for collaborating with the other. Hindi filmmakers regard Hollywood's interest and resources as a way to expand into new and untapped markets, while Hollywood studios are interested in profiting from what they perceive are the Hindi film industry's vibrant domestic markets. This leads to an irony: Hindi filmmakers see Hollywood studios as agents in their continuing gentrification—their partners in going "global" at the same time that Hollywood appears to be interested in going "local" in India.

Although MNIK did not garner the sort of box-office success in India that earlier films featuring the director-star duo had, Johar nevertheless characterized it in his acceptance speeches at various awards ceremonies as the "most important film I have ever directed."[9] That MNIK had garnered a great deal of symbolic capital for Johar within the Hindi film industry and the national media establishment was evident at the seventeenth Annual Star-Screen Awards, held in Bombay in January 2011, when the film was bypassed for the best film and best director award, but won the Ramnath Goenka Memorial Award, characterized as the "most special award" of the night, which went to "the biggest movie of 2010."[10] Shekhar Gupta, the editor-in-chief of the *Indian Express*, announced the winner, describing the award as one that recognizes "boldness and courage of imagination" in filmmaking. Prior to Johar going onstage to receive the award, a montage of clips from the film was accompanied by a voice-over that proclaimed in Hindi, "There are only a few films that spread their magic beyond boundaries and time. We have such a film this year, which not only broke records on a global platform, but also raised the stature of Hindi films throughout the world. This memorable film presented a current problem through such a touching story. This is the first film to be appreciated in so many countries around the world—*My Name Is Khan*." In his acceptance speech, Johar stated, "*My Name Is Khan* has truly been the most special experience of my life. It has been the most important film I think I have ever directed. I really thank the cast and crew of *My Name Is Khan* who have stood by me through thick and thin—everyone—but more importantly I think to the content of the film, which has travelled globally, and I thank *Screen* and the Indian Express Group for honoring the film for its endeavor."[11] The way MNIK was positioned within film industry discourses was that the social, cultural, and reputational value accruing to the film, from its distribution deal with Fox and its global circulation in non-traditional markets, more than made up for its lackluster commercial performance within India.[12]

While I encountered many Hindi filmmakers who harbored global ambitions, specifically the desire to win over non-diasporic audiences in Euro-American contexts, the incredible commercial and critical success of British filmmaker Danny Boyle's *Slumdog Millionaire*, in 2008 and 2009, had a significant impact on the Hindi film industry's perceptions concerning their horizons of possibility with respect to success among non-traditional audiences. That a film set and shot completely in India, with an all-Indian cast, a mainly Indian crew, inspired by the narratives and idioms of mainstream Hindi cinema, and with nearly one-third of its dialogue in Hindi, could win eight Academy Awards, including Best Picture, and earn over $377 million globally would have been inconceivable to most members of the Hindi film industry.[13] The film's critical acclaim in sites such as the Academy Awards, Golden Globe Awards, and BAFTA Awards, the individual awards and continuing global recognition garnered by the film's composer, A. R. Rahman—a highly acclaimed, respected, and successful composer working in the Hindi and Tamil film industries—and the subsequent participation of Anil Kapoor, a well-established star of the Hindi industry, in mainstream American films (*Mission Impossible 4*) and television (season eight of *24*) are interpreted by members of the film industry as signs that Indian filmmakers are no longer restricted to domestic or diasporic audiences in their appeal and reach.

When I began my fieldwork in 1996, neither my informants nor I could have predicted any of the above occurrences. The dynamism of contemporary mass media—the quality of it being a moving target—makes it both an exciting and challenging topic of research. Over the course of finishing this book, certain other trends within the Hindi film industry have emerged that warrant attention as sites for future inquiry. Since 2006, a trend of making sequels has been gaining momentum—something that had been unheard of within the Hindi film industry prior to this period. Sequels, along with the more established practice of remaking earlier Hindi films, which became heightened from 2002 onward, represent new methods within the industry to manage the commercial uncertainty of filmmaking, especially the caprice of audience response. An associated trend is the tremendous nostalgia among contemporary filmmakers for earlier eras of Hindi cinema—particularly the 1970s—and since 2007 there has been a spate of period films set in that decade.[14]

An even more intriguing instance of nostalgia is manifest in *Dabangg* (Fearless), which was the biggest hit of 2010. Starring Salman Khan, the film is about a corrupt Robin Hood–esque police officer in provincial Uttar Pradesh; it tells the story of his battles against an even more corrupt politician and his goons, and of his own dysfunctional family, which includes an asthmatic mother, a stern step-father, and a sickly weak-willed half-brother. *Dabangg* is striking for the confidence with which the film displays the very features of Hindi cinema, albeit in an ironic and much slicker style—with spectacular violence, earthy humor, bombastic dialogue, mannered acting, and erotic song sequences—that during my fieldwork were derided as déclassé. With a narrative centered on betrayal, revenge, and redemption—which also includes elements of romance, comedy, action, and filial piety—the film unabashedly embraces the narrative form and aesthetic style of the *masala* film, reminiscent of the 1970s and 1980s. *Dabangg* received quite favorable reviews from the English-language press, and its smashing commercial success was celebrated by the film industry, evident from its garnering of four best film awards from four different awards ceremonies.[15]

For a film to unapologetically embrace—and be celebrated for—a style of filmmaking that earlier was characterized as only suitable for the "masses," and thus be cited as a source of Hindi cinema's low social and cultural status, demonstrates the vast transformations that have occurred within the field of Hindi film production. The processes of gentrification that I outlined in this book, which reduced the symbolic and economic importance of poor and working-class audiences and accorded Hindi films respectability, cultural legitimacy, and "coolness," made it possible for a film like *Dabangg* to be produced by second-generation members of the film industry, and for it to receive the Indian government's National Award for Best Popular Film, which cites "wholesome entertainment" as its main criteria for judgment. The very decade, the 1980s, that was decried by my informants when I began my fieldwork—and which was a basis of disdain and anxiety—has become a source of novelty and nostalgia.

Another noticeable trend is that low-budget films made without stars have begun to appear as not just commercially sustainable, but as genuinely profitable. Two of the biggest hits of 2010, *Peepli Live* and *Love Sex aur Dhokha* (Love, Sex, and Betrayal)—classified as "A1" and "A," respectively, by *Film Information*—deviated from the prevailing norms of the Hindi film industry in terms of narrative and aesthetic style, content, theme, and casting; both films featured mostly nonprofessional or debutant actors without any name recognition, and *Peepli Live* was directed by a female first-time director, which continues to be an exceptional occurrence within the industry. Neither film was expected to garner the success that each did; this was due to their lack of stars coupled with their cynical and dark perspective about the nature of contemporary urban India.

Peepli Live presents a satirical perspective on the Indian news media, government bureaucracy, and electoral politics; it comments upon the growing social and economic inequality between urban and rural India. The narrative centers around two brothers who are poor farmers, and the media and political circus triggered by the younger brother's decision to commit suicide, so that his family can collect government-mandated compensation to pay back the mortgage on their ancestral land and save it from being seized by the bank. *Love Sex aur Dhokha* (LSD) is a digital film that contains three loosely related vignettes within it, each pertaining to one of the topics in the title, and each representing a different mode of seeing associated with specific technologies: the highly mobile video camera, the stationary surveillance camera, and the restricted view of the hidden camera. Inspired by a variety of salacious and brutal news stories—the casting couch scandal in Bollywood; clips of secretly recorded sex circulating on cell phones and the Internet; the murders of young couples who attempted to marry across the social divisions of caste, class, or religion—LSD paints a very dark portrait of kinship and gender relations in urban North India. Like *Peepli Live*, it presents a jaundiced view of the broadcast media, specifically television, in India.

While industry members attributed LSD's success to the titillating appeal of its title and topic, its low budget and low price to distributors played an important factor in enabling distributors to double their investment. *Peepli Live*'s success, on the other hand, was attributed overwhelmingly to the marketing savvy of its producer, superstar Aamir Khan. Khan seemed to spare no effort to promote the film, which resulted in a high amount of visibility and media attention paid to the film. During a roundtable discussion titled "New Directions in South Asian Cinema," held in conjunction with the Engendered I-View Film Festival in New York City in September 2010, the overall consensus among the Indian filmmakers present was that *Peepli Live*'s success in the overseas market, which in their view was more conservative and star-struck in its film-viewing preferences, was solely due to Aamir Khan's association with the film. According to producer/director/composer Vishal Bharadwaj, "For the NRI, overseas market, if you didn't have Aamir Khan promoting it, it wouldn't have done that kind of business."

Although *Peepli Live* disrupted some of the film industry's dominant production and audience fictions—namely that films set in, or about, rural India were not viable at the box-office, because urban elite audiences, the "classes," were not interested in rural issues and poorer audiences, the "masses," would not see films that resembled too closely their harsh lives—its success did not necessarily revise these fictions. Instead, the film's commercial performance was explained through the prominent production and audience fictions that a male star and a strong story are necessary for box-office success. Through my many years of research, the star-centric nature of the Hindi film industry has not changed; in fact, even the leading male stars have not changed. When I began my research in 1996, the top box-office draws were Shah Rukh Khan, Aamir Khan, and Salman Khan, and in 2011, these three actors continue to be the most popular, successful, and powerful stars in the industry.

Boundary-work is another feature of the industry's production culture that has remained persistent, especially in relation to discussions of work culture. Abhishek Chaubey, an upcoming director whose first film *Ishqiya* (Romantic, 2010) was critically acclaimed but not commercially successful, drew a distinction between the "old Bollywood" and the "new Bollywood" when discussing his observations of the industry's working style and his own filmmaking practice during our interview in New York, where he had arrived to screen *Ishqiya* as part of the I-View Film Festival. "Old" and "new" were not temporal boundaries in Chaubey's remarks, but evaluative ones, where the new signified greater organization, professionalism, and rationality in the production process. Stating that he spoke for "the 50 percent of Bollywood that functioned in the new manner," Chaubey argued that the changing social and class backgrounds of filmmakers also played a role in constituting the new Bollywood. He pointed to his own middle-class background, college degree, and parents' professional and occupational backgrounds—a bank manager and a schoolteacher—as providing him with the cultural capital to navigate the industry. Describing his first forays into the film industry around 2000, Chaubey said, "Around the time I came, before that, a boy like me from a service background, *pade-likhe log* [educated folk] hardly came into the industry; when I come in—I'm a English lit student—I could have been an MBA. Compared to the guys who came in say, '88, who were from . . . different economic strata, we had it slightly easier because we were more worldly aware, had more education . . . It is because of people like us that the industry is also seeing a change—we, from our disparate backgrounds, with education, and a lot of self-respect: because you can't take us for a ride" (Chaubey, interview, September 2010). Although Chaubey presented himself and his peers as atypical, his statements fit into a broader discourse—discussed in this book and dating back to the 1930s—that links cinematic quality with the class position of its producers.

Finally, the desire for global recognition and distinction continues with each subsequent generation of Hindi filmmakers. However, the ground against which this desire is framed appears to have shifted from wanting to showcase Indian exceptionalism (Aditya Chopra in 1996) to demonstrating one's ability to transcend the nation-bound categories of global distribution and exhibition.[16] This is apparent in Abhishek Chaubey's closing thoughts during our interview, "I think in this generation of filmmakers, there is an aspiration to reach out, to be as well known as— not the Indian Scorsese—but *the* Scorsese. I think the new generation of filmmakers—we consider ourselves as not only people from India, but also people of the world. We'd want our films to be seen and appreciated everywhere" (Chaubey, interview, September 2010). This desire for global circulation and recognition will continue to shape and transform Hindi filmmaking in the years to come.

Introduction

1. For the millions of fans of Hindi cinema around the world, Khan requires no introduction. The first time I met him in 1996, his position as a bankable star had been established by four solid box-office successes between 1993 and 1995: *Baazigar*, *Darr*, *Karan Arjun*, and *Dilwale Dulhaniya Le Jayenge*.

2. Although Bombay was officially renamed its Marathi equivalent "Mumbai" in 1995, and the print and broadcast media use the new name, the city is still referred to by its former name in daily parlance by the vast majority of Indians, especially filmmakers. The name change was effected by the Shiv Sena—a Hindu and Marathi chauvinist political party—soon after they came to power in Maharashtra in 1995, as an attempt to alter the diverse and cosmopolitan character of the city. My choice to use "Bombay" rather than "Mumbai" throughout the book reflects common usage, but is also driven by a distaste for the nativist politics represented by the name change and the continuing efforts to enforce the change, which experienced a resurgence in 2009, when an even more extreme offshoot, the Maharashtra Navnirman Sena (MNS) went on the rampage against public figures using Bombay rather than Mumbai. The MNS disrupted the screenings of the Hindi film *Wake Up Sid* in October 2009 because the characters referred to the city as Bombay rather than Mumbai. Some theaters even canceled screenings of the film for fear of damage to their property. The film's producer, Karan Johar, had to issue an apology and promise to change those portions of the audio. For more about the cultural politics of the naming of Bombay/Mumbai see Ganti (1998) and Hansen (2001).

3. In his biography, *King of Bollywood: Shah Rukh Khan and the Seductive World of Indian Cinema* (Chopra 2007), commissioned and published by Warner Books, the author hails him as the new face and persona of a new type of Hindi cinema. The book was positively reviewed in the *New York Times Book Review*, in which the reviewer pointed out that the larger significance of the book was that "a major American publishing house is bringing out a biography of a major foreign star, largely unknown in the United States" (Taylor 2007).

4. The Bharatiya Janata Party (BJP)-led coalition government, from 1999 to 2004, had an important role to play in promoting an image of India as an emerging economic power with its "India Shining" advertising campaign prior to the 2004 general elections. At the center of this representational transformation was the BRIC Report, prepared by Goldman Sachs in 2003, which predicted that by 2050, India, along with Brazil, Russia, and China, will challenge the G7 and U.S. econo-

mies, because of the sheer market size and dynamism of its economy. For more, see Vicziany (2005).

5. Infra dig is a colloquial abbreviation of the Latin phrase *infra dignitatem*, which means "beneath one's dignity." The online edition of the *Oxford English Dictionary* states that the source of the expression is obscure, but dates its usage in English to the mid-nineteenth century. Although not commonly used in American English, the phrase is quite prevalent in the Indian English-language press when discussing popular cinema.

6. As the term "producer" is a specific occupational category within the film industry, to avoid confusion, I use the term "filmmaker" broadly to refer to members of the industry—producers, directors, actors, writers, distributors—who possess the power to make creative or financial decisions.

7. While a moment of prior liberalization occurred under Rajiv Gandhi in the mid-1980s, in the popular press, 1991 has been represented as a much more watershed moment, probably because it was more perceptible, mainly because of the appearance of satellite television.

8. See Ganti (1994) for a discussion of the dominant themes in the discourse about Hindi cinema. Indian novelist Khushwant Singh best encapsulates the derision in an article appearing in the *New York Times Magazine* in 1976, "India's movie industry makes the worst films in the world—and the Indians love them" (Singh 1976: 42). This sentiment was not unique to Hindi cinema, but also a feature of the discourse surrounding Tamil cinema discussed by Dickey (1993).

9. Hindi filmmakers are increasingly circulating in the Euro-American academy, either as invited speakers—Aamir Khan at Cambridge in 2005; Karan Johar at NYU and Harvard in 2007; Rohan Sippy at Princeton in 2005—or as recipients of honorary degrees: Yash Chopra from the School of Oriental and African Studies, England, in 2010; Shah Rukh Khan from the University of Berfordshire, England, in 2009; Akshay Kumar from the University of Windsor, Canada, in 2008; Amitabh Bachchan from De Montfort University, England, in 2006. Premier cultural institutions such as Paris's Pompidou Center ("Did You Say 'Bollywood'? A Retrospective of Popular Indian Cinema" in 2004), London's Victoria and Albert Museum (Cinema India: The Art of Bollywood in 2002) and New York's Lincoln Center (Amitabh Bachchan: The Biggest Film Star in the World in 2005) have all had programming featuring popular Hindi cinema. Since the premiere of *Devdas* at Cannes in 2002, many high-profile mainstream Hindi films have premiered at international festivals: *Kabhi Alvida Na Kehna* at the Toronto International Film Festival in 2006; *Om Shanti Om* at the Venice Film Festival in 2007; *My Name Is Khan* at the Berlin Film Festival in 2009.

10. See Binford 1983, 1987, 1989; Das Gupta 1991; Jain 1991; Khanna and Dutt 1992; Nandy 1981, 1987; Prasad 1998; Saari 1985; Thomas 1985, 1995; Valicha 1988.

11. While earlier films went to some effort to depict how the protagonist fell into a life of crime, usually arising out of dire circumstances and sheer desperation—for example, *Awara* [Vagabond] (1951), *Gunga Jumna* (1961), *Deewar* [Wall] (1975)—contemporary films are more matter-of-fact and do not offer elaborate moral justifications or rationalizations—for example, *Satya* [Truth] (1998), *Company* (2002), *Kaminey* [Scoundrels] (2009). Whereas in older films, characters turned to a life of crime for basic survival when all other avenues of employment were exhausted, films from the late 1990s onward represent organized crime as a pragmatic employment choice for poor and working-class men.

12. Kapur and Pendakur (2007) makes a similar point about how the city of Bombay has disappeared from Hindi films.

13. Wartime shortages in basic goods and commodities led to a thriving black market, and by 1944 war profiteers increasingly laundered their illegal earnings by investing in film production. As a result, budgets skyrocketed, as did stars' salaries, which studios were unable to match, and gradually the studios went out of business by the mid- to late 1950s.

14. Sometimes what remained was the spatial and physical infrastructure, which continued to be utilized by independent producers. Examples include Filmistan Studios, located in Goregaon, and Filmalaya, located in Andheri.

15. Producer/director Mehboob Khan established Mehboob Studios in Bandra; actor/director/producer Raj Kapoor established R. K. Studios in Chembur; actor/director/producer V. Shantaram established Rajkamal Kala Mandir in Parel; and producer/director Kamal Amrohi established Kamalistan in Andheri.

16. Kajri Jain, in her work on the calendar art industry (2007), encountered similar sentiments regarding the "masses."

17. Even though the Indian media dates the multiplex era to 1997, when the first one was built in Delhi—many years passed before others were built, and the first one in Bombay was not built until 2001. Multiplexes have differentiated rates of admission but this is not based on any implicit sociological reasoning like the single-screens, where the cheapest seats enabled film viewing to become a mass phenomenon. The multiplex's differentiated ticket prices are instead based on an economistic logic of audience demand, where prices can vary based on film, time of day, day of week, and proximity to the initial release date. I discuss multiplexes in greater detail in chapters one, two, and eight.

18. The ban's impact was quite far-reaching. For example, the Eagle Theater, which showed Hindi films in Jackson Heights, a neighborhood with a large number of South Asian businesses located in the borough of Queens in New York City, had to shut down during that period.

19. See Allor 1996; Anderson 1996; Ang 1991; Bennett 1996; Blumler 1996; Ohmann 1996; Traube 1996.

20. There appear to be multiple origin stories of how this term got coined. Madhav Prasad (2003) states that the neologism "Tollywood," to refer to Calcutta's film production center—located in its suburb of Tollygunge—was first coined by an American sound engineer working in Calcutta in 1932. He points out that the Bengali film industry was nicknamed "Tollywood" by a specific English-language magazine in Calcutta and speculates that could be the etymology of "Bollywood." The *Oxford English Dictionary* cites the first attestation of the term in British mystery writer H. R. F. Keating's 1976 novel, *Filmi Filmi, Inspector Ghote*. Keating wrote a series of novels set in Bombay featuring an Indian detective, Inspector Ghote. In the above-mentioned novel, Ghote has to investigate the murder of a famous Hindi film actor. The way "Bollywood" appears in the novel references my more common understanding of the origin of the term: that it was coined by the English-language film magazines and fanzines like *Stardust* to refer to the Hindi film world in a tongue-in-cheek manner. For example, in the early part of the novel, Ghote interviews one of Bombay's prominent gossip columnists, and she uses the term "Bollywood." When Ghote professes ignorance of this term, she replies, "'Do you not read at all Inspector?' She demanded. 'The Bombay film set-up is called Bollywood in simply every film magazine'" (Keating 1976: 45).

21. For example, see the Press Trust of India article, "Calling Us Bollywood Is Derogatory."

22. This informal experiment was done on July 11, 2009. The exact figures for Amazon .com: Bollywood, 4,030 results; Indian cinema, 1,616; Hindi cinema, 486; Bombay film industry, 265; Hindi film industry, 186. The exact figures for Google: Bollywood, (more than) 62,000,000 results; Indian cinema, 15,300,000; Hindi cinema, 3,380,000; Bombay film industry, 15,200,000; Hindi film industry, 17,300,000.

23. Other examples of the increasing legibility of the category within the United States include the growing popularity of "Bollywood workout" DVDs and dance classes at gyms across the country, cited by the American Council on Exercise as a major growth area for gyms and dance studios. The Associated Press carried a story on February 19, 2009, "Bollywood-style dance classes drawing big crowds," which was syndicated in a number of U.S. newspapers, detailing this newest trend in exercise (Wyatt 2009). More unusual are the Bollywood contests sponsored by insurance companies like State Farm and Esurance in 2009. The March 2010 issue of *Time-Out Kids* NYC (Tidwell 2010) listed the top Bollywood dance classes in New York City.

24. Examples of this tendency include the Independent Film Channel's website's "Bollywood Starter Kit" labeling the first feature film made in India in 1913 as a "Bollywood" film. Vasudevan (2008) calls to task certain U.K.-based scholars for their uncritical and anachronistic deployment of the term.

25. Although filmmaking in India is a private enterprise, in order to have a theatrical release, films have to be cleared and rated by the state's Central Board of Film Certification, more commonly referred to as the Censor Board, which was a practice initiated by the British in 1918 to protect the image of the colonizer, where perceived threats to the reputation of white women and any allusion to self-governance, the Indian nationalist movement, or Indian independence were heavily censored by the colonial authorities.

26. See Ganti (2002) for a discussion of how Hindi filmmakers adapt Hollywood films—a process referred to as "Indianization."

27. Members of the Indian diaspora settled in Africa, the Caribbean, Southeast Asia, and the Pacific—locations that index colonial migrations of peoples from the subcontinent—are usually referred to as PIOs—person of Indian origin. NRI is a legal status defined by the Indian state under the Foreign Exchange Management Act, 1999 and also applies to Indian citizens living outside of India.

28. Bachchan comes from a social background marked by a high degree of cultural and symbolic capital. His father, Harivanshrai Bachchan, was a highly respected and noted Hindi poet. After graduating from college with a bachelor of science degree, Bachchan took up a job as a manager in a shipping firm in Calcutta. Bachchan was close friends with the late former prime minister, Rajiv Gandhi.

29. See Deshpande 2003; Fernandes 2006; Mazzarella 2003; Oza 2006; Wyatt 2005.

30. See Assayag and Fuller 2006; Derne 2008; Fernandes 2006; Ganguly-Scrase and Scrase 2009; Lukose 2009; Sharma 2008.

31. See Chakravarty 1993; Pendakur 1989; Rajadhyaksha 1992; Vasudevan 1990.

32. See Hjort and Petrie (2007) and Miller et al. (2001) for a representation, discussion, and critique of such narratives.

33. The more apt comparison would have been to a start-up company financed with venture capital.

34. For example, in a special edition of the American news program *Nightline*, on

January 14, 2005, titled "Bollywood 101," *Time* magazine's film critic Richard Corliss asserts, "It's best to think of Bollywood films now and forever as Hollywood films of the '30s and '40s" (ABC NEWS 2005).

35. See Binford 1983, 1987; Das Gupta 1981; Rangoonwalla 1983; Sarkar 1975; Vasudev 1986; Vasudev and Lenglet 1983.

36. See Gopalan 2002; Mishra 2002; Nandy 1998; Prasad 1998; Rajadhyaksha 1993; Thomas 1995; Vasudevan 1995, 2000; Virdi 2003.

37. See Athique and Hill 2010; Bhaskar and Allen 2009; Booth 2008; Dwyer and Patel 2002; Gopal and Moorti 2008; Govil 2005; Hughes 2006; Jacob 2009; Kaur and Sinha 2005; Kavoori and Punathambekar 2008; Majumdar 2009; Mazumdar 2007; Rai 2009; Rajadhyaksha 2009; Rajagopalan 2008; Srinivas 2009; Vasudevan 2010; Vitali 2008; Wilkinson-Weber 2005, 2006.

38. See Abu-Lughod 2005; Booth 2008; Condry 2006; Dàvila 2001; Deger 2006; Dickey 1993; Dornfeld 1998; Ginsburg 1993, 1997; Ginsburg, Abu-Lughod, and Larkin 2002; Hannerz 2004; Himpele 2008; Larkin 2008; Mankekar 1999; Martin 2009; Matzner 2010; Mazzarella 2003; Miller and Horst 2006; Miller and Slater 2001; Pinney 1997; Strassler 2010; Wilkinson-Weber 2005, 2006.

39. Abu-Lughod 2005; Caldarola 1994; Dickey 1993; Gillespie 1995; Lull 1990; Mankekar 1999; Rofel 1994; Salamandra 1998; Yang 2002.

40. See Caldwell 2008; Cantor 1988; Ettema and Whitney 1994; Mayer et al. 2009; Ohmann 1996; Zafirau 2009a.

41. This was a recommendation by a scholar on a panel about the anthropology of media at the AAA meetings in the late 1990s.

42. See Ang 1991; Cantor 1988; Crawford and Hafsteinsson 1993; Dàvila 2001; Dornfeld 1998; Espinosa 1982; Gans 1957; Kapsis 1986; Mazzarella 2003; Ohmann 1996; Zafirau 2009a, 2009b.

43. See Barnouw and Krishnaswamy 1980; Binford 1983, 1987, 1989; Das Gupta 1981, 1986; Nandy 1987, 1995; Rangoonwalla 1983.

44. John Hartley argues that the U.S. television industry is a "paedocratic regime" where "the audience is imagined as having childlike qualities and attributes." He contends that the larger the target audience, the more it will be paedocratized (1992: 108). See also Cantor 1988; Hartley 1992; McQuail 1997; Miller et al. 2001; Ohmann 1996; Zafirau 2009b.

45. See Larkin 2002, 2008; Miller and Horst 2006; Miller and Slater 2001; Pinney 1997, 2002; Pinney and Peterson 2003; Spitulnik 2002.

46. Another example to demonstrate the disproportionate relationship between a small group within the industry and commercial success took place in the year 2007. While the percentage of successful films was about 11 percent, the overall accounting of that year determined by the trade press was that the industry as an aggregate made more money than it had lost, which was only the second time in ten years that it had done so. This feat was attributed to five films, which according to the trade magazine *Film Information*, had generated a combined profit of 1.25 billion rupees, without which the industry would have been in the red yet again ("Bollywood Out of the Red" 2008: 6). Each of these films—*Chak De! India, Om Shanti Om, Welcome, Partner*, and *Taare Zameen Par*—featured the biggest male stars and were produced by leading production houses.

47. Although I did spend time with and interview one prominent art director.

48. A *mangalsutra* is a special necklace, with features that vary by region, worn only by married women. The gold chain with black beads and two circular pendants that

I wore during my entire fieldwork period was a recognizable symbol of marital status — equivalent to the wedding ring in Euro-American contexts.

49. The preface went on to assert that the report was prepared based on information obtained from consulting a variety of sources such as "key industry players, trade associations, government agencies, trade publications, and industry sources" (Pricewaterhouse Coopers 2006a).

Chapter One

1. India is politically organized as a federal structure; the national level of government is referred to as the Central government, or Center, and the individual states are referred to as state governments.

2. Although television has also played an important role in these discourses as the state invested in television specifically for pedagogical and modernization purposes, cinema has existed and flourished in India as a mass medium for a much longer period. Television did not become significant in India until the mid-1980s. The first telecast began in September 1959, as a pilot UNESCO-sponsored educational project, and the initial range of transmission was only 40 km and educational programs were broadcast for 20 minutes, twice a week beginning in 1961. Throughout the 1960s, there were various pilot projects oriented around education, but no systematic program of television broadcasting. It was not until 1976 with the formation of Doordarshan, the state-owned single-channel network, that television programming was broadcast to a wider (but still relatively small) audience. Color broadcasting as well as national transmission via low-power transmitters and satellite began in 1982, because of India's hosting of the Asiad games. Commercial sponsorship of programs began in 1983, as did the first major expansion of Doordarshan's network. See Mankekar (1999) and Rajagopal (2001) for more on the history and development of television in India.

3. While the introduction of commercial satellite and cable television in 1991 has changed the television landscape considerably, the only network television — which is free, unlike cable and satellite — is still the state-controlled Doordarshan, which in the 1990s consisted of only two channels, but since the mid-2000s has expanded to seventeen channels.

4. Examples include the 1951 Film Enquiry Committee, the Sangeet Natak Akademi Film Seminar of 1955, the Khosla Committee on Film Censorship in 1968, the Symposium on Cinema in Developing Countries in 1979, the Working Group on National Film Policy in 1980, and the National Conference on Challenges Before Indian Cinema in 1998.

5. The Emergency was a two-year period from 1975 to 1977, when Prime Minister Indira Gandhi declared a state of emergency, suspended the constitution and civil liberties, imprisoned many political opponents, and nationalized banks and other key sectors of the economy.

6. On the early relationship of the Indian National Congress and cinema, also see Bandyopadhyay (1993). For more on Phalke and his nationalism, see Barnouw and Krishnaswamy (1980), Kaul (1998), and Shoesmith (1988).

  Swadeshi was a principle articulated by Indian nationalists with respect to imported goods, especially mill-made cloth. The call by Gandhi and others to reject foreign goods and use only indigenously produced goods culminated in a movement where a form of protest against colonial rule was to burn British cloth.

7. What Gandhi meant by "losing his caste" is that he would lose his respectable social status.

8. The letter is reprinted in its entirety in both Bandyopadhyay (1993) and Kaul (1998). As far as I can determine, Gandhi never responded, which is not surprising, since it would be very unlikely that he would be reading a film magazine. The letter should be taken as Abbas's attempt to address the common perceptions and criticisms of cinema prevalent during that time.

9. In addition to *Mahatma* (the great soul), *"bapu"* was the other most commonly used appellation for Gandhi.

10. Not everyone was as deferential as Abbas about Gandhi's criticism of cinema. Baburao Patel, the editor of *Filmindia*, retorted in the issue dated January 1940: "Let this Champion of the *Daridra Narayan* [Godly Poor] come down and meet us and we shall try to convince him, or be convinced. Surely as workers in the film field, we are not worse than the poor untouchables, for whom the old Mahatma's heart so often bleeds. And if he thinks we are, the more reason why he should come to our rescue" (in Kaul 1998: 51).

11. Reportedly Gandhi saw his first film in 1944—*Ram Rajya* (The Rule of Ram)—which was based on the Hindu epic *Ramayana*. For more details about the screening see Kaul (1998). He wrote to a cousin about the experience: "It was a depressing experience and I felt like running away from the place, but I could not do so. It was sheer waste of time" (in Jeffrey 2006: 211).

12. The complete list: *Life of Louis Pasteur*; *Life of Emile Zola*; *Boys' Town*; *Lost Horizon*; *Juarez*; *Sant Tukaram*; *Sant Tulsidas*; *Seeta*; *Vidyapati*; *Janma Bhoomi* (Birth Land); *Dharti Mata* (Mother Earth); and *Admi* (Man). Abbas also provided brief (one- to two-sentence) descriptions of each film.

13. In fact according to Kaul (1998), Nehru was an avid viewer of films, as a result of his education in England.

14. For more about film censorship see Ganti (2009).

15. Prior to 1960, Bombay was also the name of the state (derived from the colonial-era Bombay Presidency) in which the city of Bombay was located. This region became divided into the states of Gujarat and Maharashtra following much agitation and the continuing process of states' reorganization that began in 1957.

16. Uttar Pradesh, located in northern India, is the most populous state of the country.

17. This phrase is not my coinage but taken from media theory to characterize the model of media influence developed in early mass communications research that drew upon the Frankfurt School's overtly pessimistic view of mass media.

18. Miller et al. (2001: 179) terms this view of film as a technology that can enter viewers' minds either to edify or pervert as the "domestic effects model" (DEM).

19. This statement, which is prominently displayed on the Indian Censor Board's website, is taken from the Supreme Court's judgment dated March 30, 1989, in a civil appeal relating to censorship of the Tamil film *Ore Oru Gramathile*.

20. This attitude is prevalent even within Western media reports and articles about filmmaking in India, exemplified by writers' incredulity at the sheer volume of film production and lavish production values of mainstream Indian films—a type of surprise that a country like India—poor, overpopulated, developing—could actually have thriving film industries when so many Western countries do not.

21. There are two widely noted influences for this group of directors: the Italian neo-

realist movement; and the earlier "art" film directors such as Satyajit Ray, Mrinal Sen, and Ritwik Ghatak, who were all working in Bengali-language cinema.

22. New Cinema generated its own stars, specifically Shabana Azmi, Smita Patil, Naseerudin Shah, and Om Puri, who appeared in film after film.

    While filmmakers working outside the dominant paradigm received loans from NFDC to make films, many of these were never released theatrically because of a lack of an alternative distribution and exhibition network. NFDC-funded films have been the ones that tended to receive the National Awards granted by the Indian government.

23. This total includes touring cinemas, which comprise almost one-fourth of the theaters. The most current figures based on the Government of India's Ministry of Statistics—6,607 permanent cinemas and 1,914 touring cinemas—which is a total of 8,521 cinemas for all of India. Movie theaters are unevenly distributed throughout the country, with many more in the southern states of Andhra Pradesh and Tamil Nadu than in the northern and most populous states of Uttar Pradesh and Bihar. The United States, which has a much smaller theater-going population (1.363 billion tickets sold in 2008, including Canada), had 39,233 movie screens in 2009 (NATO 2009).

24. A Department of Culture, set up in the Ministry of Education, oversees the National Gallery of Modern Art that opened in 1954 in New Delhi. Three national academies were established in the 1950s to deal with the visual, performance, and literary arts: the Lalit Kala Akademi for painting and sculpture, the Sahitya Akademi for literature, and the Sangeet Natak Akademi for music, dance, and theater. All three are entirely state-funded, but autonomous, organizations with an India-wide representation of artists, critics, and scholars. The Indian Council of Cultural Relations was formed in 1950 to promote international cultural activity. The National School of Drama was founded in 1959 to serve as an all-India institution for higher learning in theater.

25. *Chalachitra* is the Hindi word for films. The word is a coinage that literally means moving (*chal*) picture (*chitra*), but is never used in daily discourse or conversation. The English words—picture, film, or cinema—are much more commonly used in ordinary speech, no matter what the language.

26. The Nehru Centre is located in Worli, north of downtown Bombay, and is home to the NFDC and is a frequent venue for film festivals, exhibitions, and other cultural events.

27. See Ganti (1998) for a full discussion of the cultural politics of this particular event.

28. Watsons Hotel is currently referred to as either the Esplanade Mansion or the Army-Navy Building.

29. The ceremonies began with a moment of silence for the remembrance of Hindi film actor Raaj Kumar, who had died two days earlier, and for all those before him. The minister for cultural affairs, Pramod Navalkar, then presented renowned playback singer Lata Mangeshkar with a big bouquet of flowers and led her to a tall brass oil lamp. Navalkar and Mangeshkar lit the lamp together, officially initiating the program. State minister for cultural affairs Anil Deshmukh "released" the official program of the film festival by unwrapping a package tied in red ribbon, taking out a brochure titled in English, "Celebrating the 100th Year of the Arrival of Cinema in Mumbai," displaying it to the audience and then distributing it

to all of the guests present on stage. See Ganti (1998) for a detailed description of this event.

30. The first Indian sound film—*Alam Ara*—was released in 1931. The publications associated with these industry-initiated commemorations are *Indian Talkie 1931–56: Silver Jubilee Souvenir* published by the Film Federation of India, and *50 Years of Indian Talkies (1931–1981)* published by the Indian Academy of Motion Picture Arts and Sciences.

31. Just a sampling of this trope: a book titled *Satellite Invasion of India*, D. C. Bhatt, 1996; and a news article from the Malaysian *New Strait Times* with the headline, "India Battles Invasion by Satellite TV" (1993). See Mankekar (1999) for a further discussion of the anxieties and debates provoked by the entry of satellite television in India.

32. The FICCI was established in 1927 and represents itself as the "largest and oldest apex business organisation in India." On its website it also characterizes its history as "closely interwoven with India's struggle for independence." See http://www.ficci.com.

  My description of the conference is based on documents produced by FFI and FICCI, which include the conference schedule and the text of speeches and presentations. I thank Shyam Shroff of Shringar Films for providing me with these materials.

33. It comprised an inaugural session filled with introductions, welcomes, keynotes and special addresses by representatives of FICCI and FFI, four substantive sessions dealing with issues of taxation, intellectual property rights, institutional finance, and industry status, and a closing session with speeches by FICCI representatives, actors, and the union minister for information and broadcasting. Union minister refers to a cabinet member at the national level, whereas state minister refers to the cabinet member at the individual state level.

34. For years filmmakers had been putting forward a list of demands to the finance minister before the yearly budget asking for certain concessions. These demands included the reduction or removal of import duty on raw stock since raw stock was not produced within the country, and therefore there was no domestic industry to protect. Another longstanding demand had been the exemption of filmmakers' export earnings from income tax; the exemption only applied to corporations that exported goods and since production companies were mostly limited partnerships or proprietary concerns, they were not eligible for such exemptions.

35. Khanna is currently the chairman of Reliance Entertainment—a unit of Reliance ADA—one of India's largest conglomerates.

36. For example, see "Industry Status Granted to Films" (1998); and Mathur (2002).

37. It is important to understand the distinction between black money and the extent of organized crime's involvement in filmmaking. Black money is basically unreported and therefore untaxed income; black money is about tax evasion and not money-laundering. Organized crime launders money through filmmaking, but businessmen from a variety of enterprises—real estate, construction, diamond trading, etc—invest untaxed income into filmmaking.

38. For more on this topic see Chopra (2007).

39. In fact, one of my informants in 1996 was R. Mohan—a businessman who made his fortune in a variety of sectors who decided to venture into film production first in his native state of Kerala and then in Bombay. In his interview with me he

represented his foray into film production both as a business decision—the one sector where one could earn fantastic profits—as well as a personal, creative decision: he was "bitten by the film bug."

40. Some of the earliest states—prior to 2003—to offer incentives for multiplex development were Gujarat, Maharashtra, West Bengal, Rajasthan, and Uttar Pradesh.

41. This was the Adlabs Multiplex, which was part of the IMAX Adlabs Theatre Complex in Wadala, a northern suburb of Bombay. The particular set of exemptions was for the city of Bombay; for the rest of Maharashtra the category of multiplex was defined as three screens with a cumulative seating of 1,000 seats.

42. The only exception is Big Cinemas which is a national chain of both multiplex and single-screen theaters. Big has been following a mixed construction and renovation policy—in some cases building new structures and in others buying older properties and renovating them either into multiplexes in the case of Bombay's Metro Cinema or retaining the single-screen structure in smaller towns—for example, Muzaffarnagar, U.P.'s Alankar theater. See http://www.bigcinemas.com/in.

43. It has been notoriously difficult to find any exact or even consistent statistics about the number of permanent movie theaters in India. Much of the data is collected at the aggregate all-India level, which does not correspond to Hindi film exhibition sites, as that would only comprise one segment of the sector—due to the diverse filmmaking traditions that exist. Sixty percent of the theaters are in southern India, which is disproportionately high for the population; therefore northern India, which comprises Hindi cinema's main markets, is even more severely under-screened than an all-India statistic would communicate.

44. "Films and Cinemas," Indiastat.com, http://www.indiastat.com/media/21/films andcinemas/61/stats.aspx.

45. Precipitated by the government's multiplex policy, the first strike started on May 16, 2003, but was called off immediately after assurances that their grievances would be addressed. The main demand on the part of single-screen theaters was a 50 percent reduction in the entertainment tax rate (from 60 percent to 30 percent). The second strike occurred on October 17, lasting three days and included demands for an exit policy—whereby theaters would be allowed to convert to other uses if the cinema business was not lucrative—in addition to the demands for a reduction of entertainment tax. The third strike began on March 19, 2004, and lasted for three weeks; it was sparked by the government's failure to implement its promised new tax policy that reduced the entertainment tax rate by 10 percent.

46. Bajaj told me "South Bombay King" was his appellation, which was confirmed by one of my distributor informants. Bajaj controlled Eros, New Empire, and Excelsior in South Bombay.

47. One of the prominent multiplex theater chains in Bombay, Adlabs, had bought Metro. Adlabs—one of the few companies that was vertically integrated in terms of production, distribution, and exhibition—had the majority of its stock bought by Reliance Capital in 2005. In 2009, Adlabs was renamed Reliance MediaWorks, and its chain of cinemas got rebranded as Big Cinemas.

48. From Ravi Shankar Prasad's, the minister of information and broadcasting, inaugural address at FRAMES 2003, http://www.bisnetworld.net/ficci/BUSINESS/entertainment.htm.

49. For example, during the FRAMES 2002: Global Convention on the Business of

Entertainment, the president of FICCI asserted in his opening remarks, "The entertainment industry in India has historically grown in a somewhat unstructured manner, and if I may say so without much government support or incentive" (http://www.bisnetworld.net/ficci/march-frames-lodha.htm).

Chapter Two

1. Tarun Kumar and Asha Mehta are pseudonyms.
2. From the mid-1990s, Hollywood films began to be dubbed into Hindi and some other Indian languages and released in a wider scale theatrically, but even then foreign films occupy a small percentage of domestic box-office. "Proportion of Gross Box Office collections of foreign films lies between 5 and 10 percent of total GBOC of all Indian films. Outside of the United States, India is probably the strongest local film market in the world" (Kheterpal 2005: 10). Shroff is probably referring to video and laser disc as media to watch Hollywood films in the 1980s — as the reference to *Top Gun* would suggest — the media technologies and the fact that these films would not have been dubbed or subtitled in Indian languages points to the circumscribed nature of such consumption.
3. Shroff's family has been involved with the film industry for two generations: Shroff's grandfather started a film financing business and then his father, Shyam, and uncle, Balkrishna, transformed that company into a film distribution business. Shroff then added exhibition to the company's portfolio in 2001.
4. The ubiquity of the term "cool" globally makes it notoriously difficult to define. The use of the term as a form of slang to denote a certain style and attitude has its roots in African American jazz culture of the 1920s. For the history and evolution of the term see Moore (2004), Pountain and Robins (2000), and Nancarrow et al. (2002).
5. See Ganti (2002) for an earlier instantiation of this point.
6. Johar had been shooting his film, *Kabhi Alvida Na Kehna* (Never Say Good-bye) (2006) for three months in the New York, New Jersey, and Connecticut area. Ranjani Mazumdar, who was teaching a class on Indian cinema — at the time through the NYU Cinema Studies department — had organized the trip for her students. I thank her for including me in this excursion.
7. *Kabhi Alvida Na Kehna* shoot at the Sleepy Hollow Country Club, November 18, 2005.
8. *Himmatwala* (The One with Courage) (1983), directed by K. Raghavendra Rao, starring Jeetendra and Sri Devi, was a big box-office success and can be seen as starting this particular trend.
9. For example, the directors Mani Rathnam and Shankar, and actor/director Kamal Hasan, have often been hailed as cinematic pioneers and are held in highest regard by members of the Bombay industry and film press.
10. This perception appears to be a longstanding one. I came across an interview with Telugu director K. Vishwanath in the July 3, 1982, issue of the trade magazine *Film Information* where the writer introduces the director as an anomaly: "K. Viswanath baffles you. He is a maker from South — where loudness and crudeness are the order. Even the 'bests' like Dasari and Rama Rao are hardly aesthetic, but K. Viswanath is a highly sensitive director" (Kathuria 2007 [1982]: 11).
11. See Mankekar (1999) for a discussion of the motivation behind this policy move and its impact.
12. Actually this issue has not been studied in great depth as to why filmmakers with-

held the sale of domestic video rights. Pendakur (1989) explains it as the Indian film industry's shortsighted position. He asserts that the "film industry must be blamed for having created an adversarial relationship with the emerging video business. Instead of treating home video as a source of new revenues, Hindi film producers took an "untenable" stand" (Pendakur 1989: 73). The issue is more complicated than that, however, given the fragmented nature of the industry, which I will examine in greater detail in subsequent chapters. During the period Pendakur refers to, and until the mid-2000s, distributors served as the main source of capital and finance for filmmaking. It would appear that distributors would be the ones against the sale of video rights, rather than producers. From reading the trade press of the early years of the advent of video (1982–84), it is apparent that dissension existed—there are strong statements by distributors threatening boycotts of producers who sell domestic video rights and denials by producers about having sold said rights. Producers started selling domestic video rights in 1984, and "officially" from 1987 onward. Videocassettes of films were released simultaneously with their theatrical release. The disagreement between producers and distributors over the sale of rights has continued till this day with the issue of satellite rights and telecasts. Distributors have always wanted to be able to have a longer period to exploit films theatrically, whereas producers have an incentive to sell the satellite telecast rights much earlier.

13. Mark Liechty (2003) discusses a very similar narrative emerging from the same set of circumstances taking place in Nepal.

14. The article quoted a housewife from an affluent neighborhood in New Delhi asserting, "After a really long time, we have a movie that is different. I am really fed up of the crass violence in today's movies. *Lamhe* is a film that you can see with your family without being embarrassed" (Khanna and Dutt 1992: 68).

15. *Masala* is a Hindi word that means a blend of spices, but has frequently been used to describe popular Hindi films, denoting their unabashed goal of entertainment as well as the inclusion of a variety of narrative and aesthetic elements: songs; dances, comedy, action, romance, and drama. *Nautanki* is a form of traditional musical theater originating and performed in northern India—in the present-day states of Uttar Pradesh and Bihar. For a detailed history and study of this form, see Hansen (1992).

16. His surprise and statements evoke in a peculiar way Ravi Vasudevan's argument about Hindi films doing well and being popular in "transitional societies" (1995).

17. The standard length of Indian films ranges from 150 to 165 minutes. In 1996, producers and directors told me how exhibitors prefer such running times for the sake of standardized exhibition practice, which divides the screening day into four shows: at 12:00, 3:00, 6:00, and 9:00 p.m. (or at the half-hour). HAHK's length necessitated a readjustment of the standard exhibition times, either from four shows to three, in which case the distributor compensated the exhibitor for the revenue lost from the reduced number of shows, or if keeping four shows, then starting the first show of the day as early as 10:00 a.m. The film was later re-released with two more songs, which increased the running time to 205 minutes. The advent of multiplexes did away with the standardized exhibition times that for decades had marked the experience of seeing a film.

18. HAHK is a story of two families: one with two sons, Rajesh and Prem; and the other with two daughters, Pooja and Nisha. Rajesh and Prem's uncle, who has been their guardian and parental figure ever since their parents died many years

before, arranges Rajesh's marriage to Pooja, the daughter of his old college buddy, thus transforming a friendship into kinship. The main narrative focus of the film, however, is the unfolding of a clandestine (to the families) love story between Rajesh's younger brother, Prem, and Pooja's younger sister, Nisha. Pooja discovers their love and is ecstatic that her sister will marry into the same family, and hence join the same household, as Rajesh, Prem, and their uncle (who never married) live together as a traditional Indian joint family. Unfortunately, before she can spread the good news, Pooja suffers from an untimely accident and dies suddenly. Rajesh's uncle and Pooja's parents decide that Nisha should marry Rajesh, so that his infant son will have the benefit of a mother's care. Fortunately, Rajesh discovers his brother's and Nisha's love for each other in time, and Prem and Nisha are married and presumably live happily ever after.

19. The word *crore* is derived from Sanskrit and is used in Indian English. One *crore* represents 10 million.

20. Until HAHK, filmmakers, in order to minimize their losses from piracy, released the videos of their films at the same time as their theatrical release. The producer/distributors of HAHK withheld the videos and went to great lengths to stave unauthorized circulation of their film. I will address HAHK's unique release and distribution strategy in chapter eight.

21. See Derne 2008; Deshpande 2005; Ganti 2004; Inden 1999; Kapur and Pendakur 2007; Kazmi 1999; Mazumdar 2007; Uberoi 2001.

22. I want to remind readers that I am discussing the dominant trends in filmmaking, but such trends do not preclude other types of films from being made, especially given the prolific nature of the Hindi film industry. For example, the fascination with the world of organized crime and gangsters, which has had a long history in Hindi cinema, also gained prominence in the late 1990s. The representations of mafia bosses and their gangs changed from the glamorous, Westernized, and sanitized representations of earlier Hindi films, however, to grittier and more ethnically and regionally specific portrayals, a trend that began with Mukul Anand's *Agneepath* (Path of Fire, 1990), which became a standardized feature of the genre after the critically acclaimed and modestly successful *Satya* (Truth, 1998) by Ram Gopal Varma. While Varma's films and aesthetic style could definitely be regarded as "cool" by viewers and scholars, his self-proclaimed iconoclastic position within the industry (furthered by both critical and media representations of him) associate him with a more conventional understanding of coolness—of rebellion, opposition, or defiance to authority. My discussion of coolness, however, points to how the category of cool within Hindi filmmakers' own discourses is about becoming culturally mainstream and socially desirable within a more elite social world.

23. One can argue that this trend goes as far back as *Devdas*—the film based on Sarat Chandra's novel of the same name—and the enduring popularity of this narrative. Even *Awara* (1951) is an example.

24. See the Rajshri Productions website, http://www.rajshriproductions.com.

25. For a detailed discussion of the emergence, development, and growth of multiplexes in India, see Govil (2005) and Athique and Hill (2010).

26. The panel was titled "Urbane themes, gloss, and technical savvy topped with high-end pricing: is Hindi cinema increasingly the preserve of NRIs and multiplex audience?" It was organized by the film weekly *Screen* as part of its 58th anniversary celebrations. The panel was comprised of directors Kabir Khan, Sujoy Ghosh, and Sooni Taraporewala, as well as distributor Shyam Shroff (Pillai 2009).

27. *Awaaz* is a pseudonym.
28. Kumar's reference to "cross-over films" was another generic designation that gained purchase in the industry after the global success of South Asian–themed films made by diasporic filmmakers like Mira Nair's *Monsoon Wedding* and Gurinder Chadha's *Bend It Like Beckham*. Although both of these films were made by diasporic South Asians living and working outside of the Bombay film industry, their success opened up new imaginative horizons for some Hindi filmmakers in terms of thinking more specifically of a global audience, hence the label, "cross-over."

Chapter Three

1. Although the international press kept referring to Kapoor as a "Bollywood star," he would not be regarded as a "star" by audiences or industry members. Kapoor was mainly known for his roles as villains and comic sidekicks and never as a leading man.
2. See Chaudhury (2005), Sanghvi (2005), Venkatesan (2005).
3. According to some news reports, the actresses Kapoor named were Rani Mukherji, Aishwarya Rai, and Preity Zinta; the producer/directors were Yash Chopra, Subhash Ghai, and Yash Johar. Not all of the media outlets chose to divulge these names.
4. Susan Seizer (2005) also discusses the issue of managing stigma in her ethnography of special drama artists in Tamil Nadu.
5. On the emergence of middle-class identity see Chatterjee (1993), Joshi (2001), Mosse (1985), and Strathern (1992); on contemporary formations of middle-class identity see Liechty (2003), Mankekar (1999), and Skeggs (1997).
6. I thank Bambi Schieffelin for suggesting this particular analytical framework and reintroducing me to Goffman.
7. During my first stint of fieldwork in Bombay, films were never shot from start to finish in one continuous shooting schedule, but rather in increments — sometimes a schedule would be as short as two days or as long as three weeks. Due to the constraints of my own funding schedule, I was unable to participate as an assistant for the entire length of the production process.
8. For a discussion of the stigma attached to the performance of Hindustani (North Indian classical) music see Bakhle (2005); for Carnatic (South Indian classical) music see Weidman (2006); and for theater see Banerjee (1998), Hansen (1992), and Seizer (2005).
9. This was not such an unusual occurrence, since in many folk performance traditions in India men played the parts of women.
10. Viewing them as cultured and refined women, nobility would frequently send their sons to the best-known courtesans for training in etiquette, manners, the art of conversation, and the appreciation of literature, poetry, and other arts. Compared to prostitutes, a courtesan had more control over her body and sexual activity, often entering into a monogamous relationship with her patron. The patron would provide for any children he had with his courtesan, and the children would carry on the profession into the next generation — boys being trained as accompanying musicians and the girls in all of the arts of their mother (Oldenburg 1991).
11. As women holding property and wealth, courtesans were seen as an integral part of the ruling elite the British were trying to displace. Many of the native rulers

in India were portrayed by the British as decadent and unable to govern properly. The British waged campaigns against courtesans to reduce their influence by taking over their property, discrediting their patrons as immoral and debauched, and using many of the women as prostitutes for British soldiers, which stripped the women of their cultural function and exposed them to sexually transmitted diseases (Oldenburg 1991).

12. For a rich and engaging exposition of the anxiety around actresses' social and class background in the 1930s see Majumdar (2009).

13. The adjective of the western state of Maharashtra; actually in her autobiography, Khote, whose maiden name was Laud, mentions that her family "originally" belonged to Goa and the elders spoke Konkani at home. Khote grew up in Bombay, however, and mentioned that Marathi and English were spoken at home.

14. The film was *Farebi Jaal* (Web of Deceit), and Khote appeared in it for about ten minutes (Khote 2006).

15. Khote had agreed to act in the film out of economic necessity, because her husband's family had lost all of their wealth by speculating in the stock market and she was trying to supplement their meager income; however, acting in a film caused her to lose her main source of income as a private English tutor. She subsequently joined Prabhat Studios and acted as the lead in a number of Marathi and Hindi films. Due to her elite social background, Khote's presence in the film profession has always been remarked upon in film histories as anomalous for her time.

16. An obvious exception was the actress Shobana Samarth, popular in the 1940s, and her two daughters, Nutan and Tanuja, who both became actresses in the 1950s and 1960s.

17. For example, Rishi Kapoor's son became an actor in 2007, while his daughter was married in 2005; Dharmendra's two sons, Sunny and Bobby, became actors, while his daughters from his first wife have nothing to do with filmmaking. Sunil Dutt's son, Sanjay, is an actor while his two daughters are not. Amitabh Bachchan's son, Abhishek, is an actor, while his daughter, Shweta, is married into a prominent business family, the Nandas who are related by marriage to Raj Kapoor as well. Raj Kapoor's daughter, Ritu, married Rajan Nanda and their son, Nikhil, is married to Shweta Bachchan.

18. Mussoorie is a town in the foothills of the Himalayas in the state of Uttarakhand. Her first film was *Kurbaan* (Sacrifice) (1991), in which she played opposite Salman Khan.

19. Beauty pageants have been an important source of actresses for the contemporary film industry since the 1970s: Zeenat Aman, Juhi Chawla, Aishwarya Rai, Sushmita Sen, Lara Dutta, Priyanka Chopra, Neha Dhupia, and Tanushree Dutta are all Hindi film actresses who were former beauty queens.

20. Chatterjee 1989, 1993; Joshi 2001; Mayo 1927; Sangari and Vaid 1989; Sarkar and Sarkar 2008; Singer 1972; Sinha 2006.

21. Imran is a pseudonym.

22. I discuss the dominance of face-to-face interaction and personal relationships, along with kin and social networks in shaping the structure and work culture of the film industry in chapters five and six.

23. For an interesting parallel, but in a very different context see Seizer (2005) and her discussion of the attempts at respectability by Tamil special drama artists in southern India.

24. Mukherji is not Muslim; while I can't comment on how widespread the practice is

of industry women donning *burqas* to avoid being noticed in public spaces, it is a common feature of actors' anecdotes about being able to see films with the general public.

25. Rai has been seen in British and American productions such as Gurinder Chadha's *Bride and Prejudice* (2004), Paul Berges's *The Mistress of Spices* (2005), Doug Lefler's *The Last Legion* (2007), and Harald Zwart's *The Pink Panther 2* (2009).

26. I had been spending time at photographer Rakesh Shreshta's studio observing photo shoots of film stars for a variety of English-language film magazines; Rai's shoot was a pretty elaborate affair with multiple outfits and, unlike others, it was not commissioned by a magazine. Shreshta decided on his own to take photos of Rai and then sell them to film magazines.

27. Dixit comes from a Maharashtrian Brahmin family whose immediate and extended members consist of highly educated professionals settled in the United States. Dixit married a U.S.-based Indian doctor—also of the same caste and regional background—through an arranged marriage and she resettled in California and then Colorado.

28. Aditya's father, Yash Chopra, has been one of the most consistently successful producer/directors of the Hindi film industry for over four decades. Aditya's late uncle, B. R. Chopra, was also a well-respected producer and director in the industry.

29. The "training" that Dutt is referring to involved taking lessons in horse-riding, Hindi and Urdu diction, dancing, and fighting.

30. Whistling Woods divided its curriculum into eight disciplines: acting; animation; business of film and television; cinematography; direction; editing; screenwriting; as well as sound recording, design, and music production.

31. The catalog I obtained during my visit in 2006 listed the tuition fees both in rupees (for Indian residents) and dollars (for NRIs and expatriates). The annual tuition for NRIs and foreigners ranged from $7,500 to $13,750, depending on the course of study and year of study; for example, the first year of the screenwriting program cost $7,500 while the second year cost $10,000. In terms of the fee structure for Indian residents, the most current information on WWI's website lists total costs for their two-year programs in cinematography, direction, editing, producing, screenwriting, and acting, ranging from 750,000 rupees (screenwriting) to 1.3 million rupees (direction), plus a 1 million rupee security deposit. Additionally, a 10.3 percent service tax is levied upon the tuition amount (http://www.whistlingwoods.net).

32. Sridhar Kumar is a pseudonym.

Chapter Four

1. Back in 1996 even some scholars, both foreign and Indian, could not fathom what I could learn about Indian cinema from observing the production of films rather than analyzing the finished product. I remember being asked, "Do you learn anything interesting from visiting the sets?" Of course such attitudes have changed in the scholarly community, both with the increase in media ethnography and with shifts away from a text-centric approach in film studies.

2. The material is drawn from my observations of film sets and shoots in Bombay in 1996, 2000, 2005, and 2006, as well as in the United States in 2001 and 2005. The conversations are a combination of actual speech and my rendering of the

discussions that took place on a daily basis during my fieldwork. The characters are based on actual individuals but do not correspond directly to any one person in particular. The events all took place but not necessarily in the same day or on the same set. With the exception of the names of the production spaces, all of the names in the sketch — of the film, the production company, and the people — are completely fictitious. My intention with this strategy is to protect the identities and privacy of my informants, most of whom are celebrities — or quite well known — within and outside India. Given the high profile of the Hindi film industry and the tremendous media attention it garners, a simple use of pseudonyms could still tip off the identity of people and films to those who are familiar with this world.

3. I tried to represent some of this diversity in the vignette; for example, Malhotra, Chadda, and Khanna are Punjabi; Das and Sen are Bengali; Sulekha is from Andhra Pradesh; Menon is from Kerala; Lakhani is Sindhi; Sharma is from U.P.; Arif, Iqbal, and Khan are Muslim; and Jignesh is Gujarati.

4. For example, terms such as gaffers, grips, best boy are not commonly used in Bombay.

5. Diwali or Deepavali is often described as the "festival of lights." It is a very important pan-Indian Hindu festival that takes place in the lunar month of *Karthik*, falling between late October and early November.

6. Filmistan is not a pseudonym, but the name of a production facility which used to be a studio in the traditional sense in the 1940s and '50s.

7. Dance director is the term used for choreographers in Indian filmmaking.

8. The system of Hindi film distribution will be explained in chapter five.

9. Malhotra and Agrawal's entire conversation would be in Hindi. Any English words — other than "film," which has become so incorporated into Hindi that its endings [*filmein, filmon*] suit Hindi grammatical structure — which would occur naturally in their conversation are not italicized.

10. MG stands for "minimum guarantee," which will be explained in the following chapter.

11. *Devdas* is an actual film, and here the filmmakers are referring to the 2002 version, starring Shah Rukh Khan, Madhuri Dixit, and Aishwarya Rai, directed by Sanjay Leela Bhansali. Based on the 1917 Bengali novel by Saratchandra Chattopadhyay, the story of *Devdas* has been a favorite of Indian filmmakers since 1928, and there have been numerous filmed versions of the story in a number of Indian languages over the years.

Chapter Five

1. During my dissertation defense I was told that my chapter about the importance of kinship as a structuring organizational principle in the industry was not revealing of the production practices in the industry and why had I not defined all of the various occupational roles in the industry? For example, what does an executive producer do? At that time of my initial research, there was no executive producer category in the Hindi film industry.

2. I thank Faye Ginsburg for coining this phrase.

3. Sippy's first production was *Sazaa* (Punishment, 1951).

4. BIG pictures produced eight films, but as co-productions. UTV produced five films solo and two others as co-productions. Yashraj produced three films solo.

5. Both events were heavily covered by the Indian press. For more information about Gulshan Kumar's murder see Koppikar and Baweja (1997). About Bharat Shah's arrest, see Raval and Chopra (2001).

6. Chopra established his banner, B. R. Films in 1955, and his younger brother, Yash, started assisting him and then directed films for the banner from 1959, until he broke off and formed his own banner, Yashraj Films, in 1971. Though B. R. Chopra passed away in 2008, the banner continues to produce films with his son Ravi, who had started directing films from the 1970s, at the helm.

7. Even if a film's rights have been sold for all of the territories, a producer would still need finance to bridge the gap between the advance and the final payment.

8. These are: (1) Bombay; (2) Delhi/U.P.; (3) East Punjab; (4) West Bengal, or Eastern; (5) Bihar/Nepal; (6) Assam; (7) Orissa; (8) C.P. (Central Province)/Berar; (9) C.I. (Central India); (10) Rajasthan; (11) Nizam; (12) Mysore; (13) Andhra; (14) South, or Tamil Nadu/Kerala.

9. Very little research has been done about how the distribution system came into being and who the earliest distributors were. Distributors were not very sure about the history of the system. I hazard a guess that the divisions arise from older regional commercial centers. There needs to be historical work done on how these distribution territories arose and who went into film distribution in India.

10. Pakistan and Bangladesh are not included in this distribution network, since each country has banned the import of Indian films since 1952 (Pakistan) and 1962 (East Pakistan, which became Bangladesh in 1971), although a thriving pirated-film culture exists, especially in Pakistan. In 2006, Pakistan relaxed the ban and allowed the import of three Hindi films; in 2008, a Pakistani Senate committee recommended lifting the ban on Indian films and importing them on a reciprocal basis, after which a select number of Hindi films began to be screened in Pakistan ("Race a Hit" 2008).

11. Before the advent of video and its concomitant, piracy, Hindi films were not re-leased in all of the major cities simultaneously. Films would first be released in Bombay or Delhi and then open a few weeks later in other cities. The simultaneous release of films in A-class centers began in the 1990s to thwart the problems of video and cable piracy in the higher revenue centers.

12. Traditionally, distributors bid for and bought the exclusive rights to distribute a film theatrically for five to ten years in their particular territory. Each subsequent innovation in audiovisual technology has chipped away at distributors' monopoly over the circulation of films, however. The entry of video in the early 1980s made a significant impact on the theatrical business in B- and C-class centers due to the time lag between a film's release in Bombay and its eventual appearance in the smaller towns, by which time the pirated videos of the films were easily available. The entry of satellite television in the early 1990s reduced the theatrical life of a film so that the terms of theatrical distribution have shrunk over the years from five years, to one year, to six months and, as of this writing, to three months. Cur-rently, the film industry has even invested in digital delivery systems as a measure to fight piracy.

13. During the course of my research, I have calculated those chances, based on fig-ures from the trade press, to range from 10 to 15 percent.

14. For example, Yash Chopra opened up distribution offices in London and New York in the late 1990s in order to distribute his and others' films.

15. I thank Vipul Agrawal for introducing me to this concept and pointing out this particular phenomenon.

16. There are remarkably very few "people" along the lines of "have my people call your people."

17. In terms of other members of the industry, they—directors, producers, choreographers, art directors, music directors, editors, and others—have assistants who help them on the specific film project at hand, but do not have personal assistants necessarily, nor do they have secretaries like stars. Writers do not have agents. There just is not the same layer of mediators as exists in the United States.

18. Bhagnani's first film was *Coolie No. 1*, starring Govinda and directed by David Dhawan. He continued to work with Dhawan and Govinda for two more films—*Hero No. 1* and *Bade Miyan Chote Miyan*, and Dhawan in *Biwi No. 1*. With his first four films being box-office successes, Bhagnani gained standing in the industry as an A-list producer.

19. Shabana Azmi is an award-winning actress who has also garnered a great deal of international recognition for her films and her social activism.

20. The fact that I had met Tanuja in Philadelphia is a result of social networks—specifically of graduate students from India among the Penn, Temple, and Drexel campuses. Even though I grew up in the United States, when I started graduate school at Penn, my apartment mates and their friends had all come from India to the United States for graduate studies. Chandra was attending film school at Temple the same time that I was at Penn, and we met through mutual friends.

21. How did I meet Chopra's mother? Also through social networks—a tenant of my friend's parents knew Mrs. Chopra well and arranged the introduction.

22. My second stint as an assistant on the film *Ghulam* was the result of having become good friends with the director Vikram Bhatt, who then asked me if I would like to assist him.

23. The ability of unconnected women to get a break has been a longstanding feature of Hindi film production. For example, I came across a published interview with producer/director Subhash Ghai from April 1983 where the interviewer was remarking that Ghai, by introducing a completely unknown actor, Jackie Shroff, as the lead in his film *Hero*, was doing something extraordinary. The writer's introduction to the interview states: "In the existing setup of our film world, it is only girls who get breaks in A-class projects. The reason is simple. A new girl in an A-class project does not make much of a difference in the film's selling ratio. But a new boy in an A-class project can make all the difference. As such, over the years we've always had names in leading men's roles in big films, or else we've had star sons, who are as good as established names . . . As such, Jackie Shroff getting a break in *Hero* is nothing short of a miracle" (Kathuria 2008 [1983]: 11).

24. I am not trying to underestimate the significance of female stars, but just accounting for the greater number of outsider women as compared to men.

25. Kumar is referring to actor Abhishek Bachchan and director Rohan Sippy, who are good friends, having grown up together in the industry; their fathers, Amitabh Bachchan and Ramesh Sippy, worked together.

26. The other means of trying to enter the industry include the advertising world, modeling, beauty pageants, and professional training institutions such as the National School of Drama or the Film and Television Institute of India (FTII), the latter which provides a pool of technical skill for the industry.

27. For example, Dadasaheb Phalke, who made the first feature film in India and earned the appellation the "Father of Indian Cinema," did not create any sort of directing or producing lineage; he died a forgotten and penniless man; his birth-date started being commemorated in 1970.

28. For example in the pre-Independence/colonial era—some of the directors and technicians working in Bombay—at Bombay Talkies—were from Germany; one of the top stars in the silent and early sound era was Mary Evans, known as Fearless Nadia.

29. Shah Rukh Khan and Akshay Kumar are the two actors who were complete outsiders to Bombay and the Hindi film industry.

30. Aamir Khan turned producer with film *Lagaan* (2001) and then he turned director for the film *Taare Zameen Par* (2007).

31. See Marcus and Hall (1992), Pedroso de Lima (2000), Rudner (1994), Yanagisako (2002), and Creed (2000).

32. I am grateful to David Ludden for making me aware of this point.

33. Hindi has three second-person pronouns—*tu*, *tum*, and *aap*—which have a corresponding verb conjugation and possessive pronouns that represent a continuum of most familiar (*tu*) to most respectful (*aap*). Unfortunately these differences in register are masked by writing the chapter four sketch in English.

34. Sanjay Dutt has had a very tumultuous personal and professional life, which has been covered by the Indian press in great detail as well. In his twenties he was troubled by drug addiction and was sent to the United States for rehab. In 1993 he was arrested for weapons possession under the Terrorist and Disruptive Activities Act (TADA) in conjunction with the bomb blasts that occurred in Bombay earlier that year. He spent sixteen months in jail until he was finally granted bail in late 1995. During my fieldwork in 1996, he returned to acting, and his first day of shooting, in March 1996, was marked by a great deal of ceremony and celebration. The studio was decked out with flowers; there was a band of *dhol* (a large drum) players welcoming him into the studio complex; there were young women showering him with flowers as he walked into the shooting floor; and the press photographers went berserk taking photos of him. In July 2007, Dutt was sentenced to six years of rigorous imprisonment for illegally possessing weapons while being cleared of charges of terrorism. After spending a few weeks in jail, Dutt's appeal for bail was granted by the Supreme Court of India. He has an appeal for acquittal pending before the Supreme Court.

35. Later in the day the bodyguard, in an attempt to save face with Akhtar, approached him, but instead of apologizing said that he remembered seeing him at some awards ceremony the previous year. I was watching this interaction, still incredulous about the man's lack of self-consciousness, when I caught the eye of the Indian crewmember who had intercepted the bodyguard—he looked at me, rolled his eyes, and shook his head in disbelief.

36. Therefore, an actor starting out in his or her career in leading roles will be referred to as a "newcomer," whereas actors past their prime are termed "veterans." Actors who play roles other than that of the male or female leads are called "character actors."

37. This feature of Hindi filmmaking has been commented upon even by Hollywood executives. For example, Michael Lynton, the chairman of Sony Pictures Entertainment, was quoted in an article about the star-driven nature of the Bombay film industry in the *New York Times*: "There is a variety of ways in which a picture

gets made in Hollywood, but I can say without qualification that in Hindi pictures stars are the determining factor much more than they are in Los Angeles" (Chopra 2008).

38. Since 2000, Roshan has only directed films starring his son Hrithik, who became an enormous box-office sensation after his debut film, *Kaho Na Pyaar Hai* (Say That it Is Love). In this respect, Roshan is still unique among his peers—he is the only producer/director who has a major bankable star in his immediate family.

39. For example, in his film *Pardes* (Foreign Land, 1997), Ghai introduced the actress Mahima Chaudhary, but for *Taal* (Rhythm, 1999) and *Yaadein* (Memories, 2001), the leading roles were played by actors already known and established—or becoming established—in the industry, such as Aishwarya Rai, Akshaye Khanna, and Anil Kapoor in *Taal*, and Hrithik Roshan, Kareena Kapoor, and Jackie Shroff in *Yaadein*. For *Kisna* (2005), Ghai introduced two new actresses—Isha Shervani and Antonia Bernath—but *Yuvraaj* (2008) featured stars such as Salman Khan, Anil Kapoor, and Katrina Kaif.

Chapter Six

1. The film was the directorial debut of Manish Acharya—originally from Bombay and a former IT industry professional working in the United States—who decided to go to film school and received an MFA degree in filmmaking from New York University's Tisch School of the Arts. Implicit in Jariwalla's remarks was that Acharya with his U.S. film school education brought a different approach and sensibility to filmmaking.

2. There have been a number of novels and films set against the backdrop of the Hindi film industry: Salman Rushdie's *Satanic Verses* (1989), Shashi Tharoor's *Show Business* (1993), Guru Dutt's *Kaagaz ke Phool* (Paper Flowers, 1959), Hrishikesh Mukherjee's *Guddi* (Doll, 1971), Ram Gopal Varma's *Rangeela* (Colorful, 1995) and *Mast* (Fun-loving, 1999), Farah Khan's *Om Shanti Om* (2007), and Punit Malhotra's *I Hate Luv Storys* (2010).

3. When I did set up appointments beforehand, they were mostly with members of the industry who would either not be present or spend much time at production sites: like screenwriters whose primary labor took place prior to a film's production; directors or actors who were not shooting a film at the moment; producers, directors, or actors who had retired from filmmaking; or those who dealt explicitly with the commercial aspect of filmmaking, such as distributors and exhibitors.

4. In fact my first interview of Subhash Ghai—a very successful and prominent producer/director—was very multi-sited—over the course of three days—the interview began in his home, continued in his car, then his editing studio, then his office, then a restaurant, then Filmistan studios, where he was shooting his film *Pardes*, and finally ended in one of the makeup rooms at Filmistan.

5. Radhika and Tarun are pseudonyms.

6. There is a clear division of labor between dance, music, and story, although with the examples of Vishal Bharadwaj—a music composer who is also a director—and Farah Khan (a choreographer turned director), those roles are also getting blurred.

7. He had also acted in a very small role in the previous year's box-office hit, DDLJ, in which he assisted his good friend, Aditya Chopra.

8. Sandeep is a pseudonym.

9. The action director used to be known as the fight master.

10. While choreography, music composition, and cinematography have tended to remain distinct occupational specializations, recently there have been some individuals who have combined those specializations with film direction as well: Farah Khan (choreographer and director); Vishal Bhardwaj (composer and director); Anil Mehta (cinematographer and director).

11. The main details that are worked upon during this phase are the screenplay and dialogues in terms of the script, the melodies and lyrics in terms of the music, and locations, sets, props, and costumes in terms of production details.

12. For example, Satyajit Ray was valorized as the auteur par excellence.

13. A particularly humorous instance of dubbing that I encountered was the actor kissing his own hand to simulate the sound of kissing the actresses's hand.

14. The amount of time that dubbing takes depends on the actor's experience and the length of the role; an experienced lead actor can finish dubbing for a film in a few days.

15. Of course, during the shooting, actors still have to be able to make the correct lip movements so that the dubbed speech appears synchronous.

16. Two cases that I am familiar with from my fieldwork—Rani Mukherji who was just beginning her career in *Ghulam* (Vassal, 1998) had her husky, throaty voice overdubbed by someone with a much higher-pitched voice; Aftab Shivdasani's voice in *Kasoor* (Fault, 2000) was not considered old and deep enough for the age he was playing in the film, so the director, Vikram Bhatt, dubbed for Shivdasani, which I was able to observe firsthand. More recently I read in the trade magazine *Film Information* ("Heard, Not Seen" 2008) that producer/director Subhash Ghai dubbed over actor Anil Kapoor's own dubbing for one scene in his film *Black & White*, because he thought he could do it even better.

17. *Lagaan* holds a very special place in the contemporary Hindi film industry, for it signifies for filmmakers the global success of the mainstream Hindi film form, winning awards in European film festivals and having been nominated for an Academy Award in the Best Foreign Language Film category in 2002—only the third time that a film from India had been nominated for an Oscar.

18. This style of working is itself a result of the undercapitalized nature of the film industry—a scenario that existed until about 2003. Since films are shot in a series of schedules, rather than being out of work while a particular film is not being shot, actors took on multiple assignments to be assured a steady stream of work and earnings.

19. At various points in the industry's history, producers have attempted to curtail the number of films that actors could work on simultaneously—imposing ceilings on the number of films actors could sign or limiting the number of shifts that an actor could work in at once.

20. I agreed to play the role, which involved two scenes, but since the film went through a lot of changes—including the original heroine being replaced—the scenes I acted in never saw the light of day.

21. In another instance during my fieldwork, on the shoot of *Dastak* (Knock), even after an actor had been hired to do a scene—that of a television journalist reporting from a special event—I was asked by an assistant director if I would like to play the part of the television reporter. I declined the offer.

22. I too learned my few lines of dialogue on the set. I was not given anything to read, but was tutored in my lines by an assistant director.

23. One reason for this was that both songs were love songs, involving two actors

on location, without any background dancers. The elaborate production numbers that "Bollywood" has become known for, involving a retinue of background dancers and lavish sets, would have more complicated choreography that would entail rehearsals and planning beforehand.

24. Films started being edited digitally on computerized editing systems only since 1998. While the means of visual production are relatively simple, sound is another matter. Filmmakers employ state-of-the-art sound recording and mixing technologies, and most Hindi films are presented in Dolby Digital sound. The postproduction phase is very high-tech.

25. Filmmakers are also quite efficient with other resources as well. For example, when a scene requires a smoky atmosphere, rather than using a dry ice machine, smoke is created by throwing water on hot coals in a shallow metal basket and having a crewmember walk through the set carrying the basket. Lumber to construct a set is rented and therefore reused continually, rather than discarded after one use; sometimes even sets are reused.

26. As budgets have increased the proportion of the budget devoted to raw stock has decreased, but the actual costs remain high. As of August 2009, the price for 400 feet of Fuji color positive was 12,000 rupees. An average Hindi film production shoots about 100,000 feet; thereby the raw stock cost would be 3 million rupees. I thank Vikram Bhatt for providing me this information.

27. One tin contains 400 feet of stock, so per Roshan's claims, he shoots from 40,000 to 52,800 feet of film, while his colleagues shoot anywhere from 160,000 to 200,000 feet of film.

28. For example, see Caldwell (2008), Ohmann (1996), and Zafirau (2009b).

29. In that sense Hindi filmmakers' loose use of the term "Hollywood" to refer to all English-language filmmaking in the West parallels the indiscriminate use of the term "Bollywood."

30. Since the late 2000s, casting directors are starting to be a recognizable job specialization in the Hindi film industry, which is represented by the press as a further sign of Bollywood's increasing "professionalization"—see Joshi (2010).

Chapter Seven

1. Gmelch's discussion of "baseball magic" (2003) is another instance where Malinowski's ideas of magic have been applied in a contemporary, modern context.

2. Although most Hindu producers did begin a new film project with a small *puja*— as a way of commencing the production auspiciously.

3. Malinowski's description of economic magic is the most relevant to my example: "In economic magic the growing of plants, the approach of animals, the arrival of fish in shoals are depicted" (1954 [1922]: 74).

4. *Sitaare* is a pseudonym.

5. The only established figures of the crew were the music directors (composers) who had come into some national prominence by virtue of their previous film, which was a huge commercial success. The editor was very respected within the industry and the screenwriter had recently tasted success with his previous film, but distributors do not buy the rights for a film based on the status or prestige of technicians like composers, editors, or writers; they base their decisions on the cast.

6. The film had a new actress; it was rumored to be because distributors did not like the original actress chosen for the role. Many of the portions that I had observed

being shot in 1996 were reshot. The film did not enjoy wide circulation. I have also been unable to obtain the film's DVD, since friends in India have not been able to find it in mainstream retail outlets.

7. Kunal Madhvani is a pseudonym.

8. *Tapori* is a Bombay Hindi slang term to refer to young street-smart men, coming from poor or working-class backgrounds, who occupy a significant presence in the urban landscape. They could be interchangeable with the category of "front-bencher" discussed in chapter two. See Mazumdar (2007) for a discussion of the cinematic representations of the *tapori*. The reference to "families upstairs" has to do with class-segregated viewing practices associated with the cinema hall and filmmakers' representations of their audiences, which will be discussed in chapters eight and nine.

9. Ooty is the shortened name of Ootacamund—a picturesque and popular hill resort town known as "hill stations" in India—in the southern state of Tamil Nadu. Such hill stations are a favorite locale to shoot song sequences.

10. Sound and music arrived in Indian cinema with the release of the Hindi film *Alam Ara* (Beauty of the World), on March 14, 1931, at the Majestic Theatre in Bombay. Advertised as an "all-talking, all-singing, all-dancing film," this production, by Ardeshir Irani, with its seven songs established music, song, and dance as staples of Indian cinema. Others sought to emulate its success and the number of songs proliferated in films during the early sound era—with as many as 70 in *Indrasabha* (Indra's Court, 1932). The presence of songs in Indian cinema has been explained in terms of cultural antecedents and the influence of indigenous performance traditions (Barnouw and Krishnaswamy 1980; Ganti 2000, 2002).

11. These songs circulate in a rich, complex aural economy, where they take on a life of their own, disassociated from any particular film (Ganti 2000; Gopal and Moorti 2008). Until the early 1980s, film music was the only form of popular music in India that was produced, distributed, and consumed on a mass scale, and even today film music accounts for the majority—nearly 70 percent—of music sales in India. Entering a music store in India, one is faced with a staggering selection of film music: categorized and packaged by films, music directors (composers), singers, actors, actresses, directors, decades, and themes, as well as the more recent phenomenon of remixes.

12. When Hindi filmmakers term a film a "musical," they are referring to a film that is explicitly about music, musicians, or performers in some way. The mere existence of songs does not automatically make a film a "musical" within the genre distinctions of popular Hindi cinema.

13. For example, in 1995 the music from the year's biggest hit, *Dilwale Dulhaniya Le Jayenge*, sold a 100 million units and this figure does not account for the sales of pirated versions of the soundtrack (Chaya 1996).

14. According to one news report, more than 200 films have been shot there since the 1980s (Hugo Miller 2006). In 2002, the Swiss government honored Hindi producer/director Yash Chopra, for whom Switzerland has been an especially favorite location for song sequences for two decades, with a special award for helping to raise awareness about and projecting Switzerland as an idyllic tourist destination.

15. The fact that the mise-en-scène of these sequences may be completely disjunctive with the rest of the film is not of concern to filmmakers, who are more interested in establishing that these sequences have been shot outside of India, which is one of the reasons that filmmakers tend to shoot in cities and areas that have land-

scapes and architectural styles distinct from those found in India. Thus Europe, North America, and Australia are preferred to other parts of Asia. When songs have been filmed in Singapore or Malaysia, the focus is always on a built part of the landscape like the PETRONAS Towers in Kuala Lumpur. Although more recently, entire films have been shot in Malaysia—*Don* (2006), Singapore—*Krrish* (2006), and South Korea—*Gangster* (2006), because the respective governments wooed filmmakers with a variety of incentives.

16. I have not been able to find the origins of this phrase, but it appears to have become very common parlance within the United Kindgom. The earliest reference I found was in a March 5, 2003, memorandum submitted to the U.K. Parliament's Select Committee on Culture, Media, and Sport, by Julia Toppin. It appears in a sentence describing the indirect financial contributions of filmmaking in the United Kingdom—"Income is also derived indirectly from product placement, location tourism, or a highlighted cultural aspect, i.e., the Bollywood Effect." http://www.publications.parliament.uk. The phrase has become part of the British Tourist Authority's official discourse and appears in its annual reports, "India: Market and Trade Profile," in the section detailing strategies of how to reach Indian consumers (British Tourist Authority 2007).

17. The impetus is to revive the Swiss tourism industry by drawing visitors from India as Swiss government data showed that, while overall tourism to Switzerland has reduced, the percentage of tourists arriving from India has been on the upsurge.

18. The screenwriter relayed his experience, but asked me to keep the details of the film in confidence, as he did not want the director to learn of his feelings, so the name of the film, director, and writer are pseudonyms.

19. Soon after the release of *Khalnayak* (The Villain, 1993), there were reports in the press about how often people were seeing the film, but only until the main hit number of the film—*Choli ke peeche kya hai?* (What Is Behind My Blouse?).

20. There have been a few films made without songs: *Kanoon* (Law, 1960), by B. R. Chopra, and *Ittefaq* (Chance, 1969), by Yash Chopra were the most notable ones. In more recent times, *Bhoot* (Ghost, 2003) was made as a song-less film, but the director decided to produce an album with songs in order to reap revenues from the sale of the soundtrack, shooting two music videos to promote the film on television. According to the director, Ram Gopal Varma, the music sales were disappointing and a failed experiment. The film went on to do quite well at the box-office, however; its success was heavily commented upon by the media in 2003, and Varma was touted as a renegade and a risk-taker who had shattered a prevailing myth of the industry. See Jha (2003).

21. This is the tag line that appears on all of the PNC (Pritish Nandy Communications) literature.

22. Unfortunately, in September 1997 Anand died from a heart attack, just a month before his 45th birthday.

23. For example, *Outlook*'s article on July 17, 1996, "There's No Business Like . . ." begins with the following assertion, "Call it an infusion of corporate culture in Tinseltown . . . but slowly and surely, in Bollywood, the loose-script-shuffling, cash-toting producers of yesteryear are giving way to staid, pin-striped business managers who are more comfortable spewing net profits and earnings per share than zoom, long shot, and cut" (Annuncio 1996). Needless to say, I never met examples of either type during my fieldwork.

24. To give an indication of Bachchan's star power, the news of ABCL's formation

made the front page of the *Times of India* on January 14, 1995, in a story that appeared right below the newspaper's masthead, "Amitabh firm set to create new trend" (Dalal 1995). Months later, *India Today* carried an eight-page special feature, "From Superstar to Tycoon" (Jain 1995) in its November 30 issue. ABCL initially raised capital from institutional investors in 1995 and then floated a public issue in early 1996. For more details see Banker (1999).

25. Prasar Bharati (Broadcasting Corporation of India) which is comprised of Doordarshan (TV) and All India Radio, filed a petition in the Bombay High Court in 1999, requesting that the company be "wound up"—Indian legal parlance for declaring bankruptcy, as it owed Doordarshan more than 220 million rupees (Chakravorty 1999). The company began its winding up process in April 2000, and was fully liquidated, with an auction of its movable assets and property, in February 2002.

26. For more on ABCL's and Bachchan's financial troubles, see Aiyar (1999); Annuncio (1997); Ghosh and Guha Ray (1999); Madhu Jain (1998); and Menezes (1997). Bachchan repaid his creditors and relaunched the company in 2003 as AB Corporation. A testament to Bachchan's charisma and exceptional status from the perspective of the Indian media is the way that this second chance has been represented—once again a great deal of press and much of it in hyperbolic tones, and the frequent use of cricket and cinema metaphors ("Amitabh Bachchan, Now Unlimited" 2003) and ("Time to Don the Mantle" 2003).

27. In November 2008, Cinema Capital Venture Fund (CCVF), India's first SEBI-approved (Securities and Exchange Board of India) venture capital fund focused on the film and entertainment industry, came into existence and invested close to 1 billion rupees in the industry within the year ("Your Ticket to Blockbuster Return" 2010).

28. Yashraj Films often has Pvt. Ltd. listed after its name, but it is not prominently displayed on their website or their promotional literature. A private limited company refers to a company that has private investors other than the founders, who are due some form of dividend from the company's profits.

29. Yashraj demonstrates the value assigned to the term "corporate." In their own promotional literature, they represent themselves as a "corporate" entity: they refer to a corporate office; they use language such as chairman and vice chairman to describe Yash Chopra and Aditya Chopra, respectively; and they have vice presidents of various divisions. See the "About Us" section of the Yash Raj Films website, http://www.yashrajfilms.com.

30. Bhatt pointed out, however, that for "independent" filmmakers—by which he meant individual producers—the problem of raising finance from one production schedule to the next still existed.

31. Co-branding enables what is referred to as "cross-promotions" where a consumer brand and a film are advertised simultaneously in one go—for example, *Kaante* (Thorns) (2002) tied up with Indian soft-drink brand Thums Up and advertisements depicting the film's characters drinking Thums Up were aired across a variety of Indian satellite channels during some key viewing periods, such as cricket matches (Tandon 2002).

32. For example, both of Manmohan Shetty's daughters work in Walkwater Media—one as joint managing director and the other as creative head of their film division—and previously worked in Adlabs; Pritish Nandy's two daughters occupy

the positions of creative director and vice president, creative services in PNC; Subhash Ghai has his brothers-in-law, daughter, and son-in-law in high positions at Mukta Arts. Shravan Shroff heads the exhibition division of Shringar, the distribution company started by his father and uncle.

33. In May 2006, when my interview with Shroff was conducted, the "big" actors he refers to would have been Shah Rukh Khan, Aamir Khan, Salman Khan, Hrithik Roshan, and Sanjay Dutt, who had consistently starred in the biggest commercial successes between 2000 and 2005. Among this group, Shah Rukh Khan had the most sustained record of success: five huge hits over five years. When I began my fieldwork in 1996, the most in-demand stars were Shah Rukh Khan, Aamir Khan, Salman Khan, Govinda, Sunny Deol, and Ajay Devgan. In 2010, the top stars continue to be the three Khans, plus Hrithik Roshan, Akshay Kumar, Ajay Devgan, and Ranbir Kapoor. Note the consistent presence of the three Khans since 1996.

34. There is a longstanding and prolific discourse about the unreasonable nature of star remuneration—referred to as star "prices"—within the trade press. The rates quoted in some stories seem somewhat sensationalist, in order to emphasize the unreasonable nature of stars. Many producers and directors during my fieldwork claimed that stars were never paid as much as they claimed to be—at least by "legitimate" producers. The discussion about star prices can be viewed as a part of the boundary-work engaged in by filmmakers: the illegitimate producers—the "proposal-makers"—are those who pay stars unreasonable fees.

35. For example, Rajjat Barjatya stated, "The sort of films being made today—the reason why they're flopping is because the foundation is so weak. Today, producers just, you know, they sign a good director; they sign a couple of good artistes; they launch the *mahurat*; collect money; and with the money they have collected from the distributors, they start making the film piece by piece. That's no way of making a film" (Barjatya, interview, April 1996).

36. For example, a distributor would enter into an MG agreement (chapter five) with a producer for a particular territory, and then he would sell off the subterritory rights within his territory to other distributors as a way of raising funds for the minimum guarantee that he promised to advance to the producer.

Chapter Eight

1. Bihar is a state located in northern India—lying southeast of New Delhi, northwest of Calcutta, and bordered by Nepal to the north.

2. This is a marked difference between the Hindi film industry and Hollywood, which has a vast market research and marketing apparatus that produces an immense amount of data and "surveillance" about film audiences (Miller et al. 2001). While marketing a film in terms of promotion and advertising across various media platforms has increased significantly since 2000, centralized market research of the sort carried out by the National Research Group in the United States—test screenings, tracking studies, focus-group studies—does not exist to this date in the Hindi film industry. Some filmmakers screen their films prerelease—referred to as "trials"—to friends, family, colleagues, distributors, journalists, and other members connected to the industry, while others are very proprietary and show their films to a select few. The system of paid previews began selectively in 2006 and gained greater momentum in 2008, but in these cases, films basically open to the public a day or two before their official release and serve

as a revenue generator (tickets are frequently higher priced) rather than as a test of content.

3. See Hughes (2006) for a related discussion about how film genres in South India in the 1920s enabled exhibitors to imagine the social reality of their audiences, which enables one to do a historiography of early cinema audiences.

4. I thank Faye Ginsburg for this phrase.

5. For example, in *Media Worlds*, Louisa Schein asserts, in her chapter about Hmong media practices, "The way people understand who they are and how they belong is never anterior to, is indeed inseparable from, the kinds of media they consume" (2002: 30). Other scholars who have theorized and examined the relationship between media consumption and subjectivity are Abu-Lughod (2005), Appadurai (1996), Hall (1990), Mankekar (1999), Yang (2002).

6. See Srinivas (2009) for a very cogent and incisive summary of spectatorship theory in film studies.

7. See Ganti (2002, 2009) for a further discussion of this issue in terms of adapting Hollywood films (2002) and state censorship (2009).

8. The most obvious example of this is a film of the *Twilight* series, where numbers of people were seeing the film to mock it or make fun of it, but this particular form of engagement does not get registered by aggregate box-office figures; instead such actions also add to the commercial success of the film, which then gets interpreted by its makers as approval and endorsement. While one can argue that the plethora of viewer-generated commentary about films that one finds online is a source of public opinion about films, such commentary, when it counters box-office figures, does not get registered as any sort of verifiable reality. Instead, box-office figures are used to trump any charges of negative response. Additionally, the multiplicity of distribution outlets for films—television, home video, Internet—means that film consumption takes place across a great variety of venues and sites, with much of it being unquantifiable. If one takes piracy into account, it is actually very hard to quantify how many people have watched a film and even harder to quantify how many people liked a film.

9. The film opened in India with only 29 prints, which was a comparatively tiny number, and included showing in only one theater in all of Bombay. The films' producer/distributors also tied the release with the upgrading of theaters to digital sound. As mentioned in chapter two—as a measure to combat the loss of revenue from piracy—since 1987 Hindi filmmakers had been releasing videocassettes simultaneously with a film's theatrical release. At the time of my fieldwork in 1996, the official video of HAHK had still not been released. The film's videocassettes were finally released several years later, in 1999. The measures that the film's makers instituted to check piracy involved coding the film prints so that pirated videos could be traced back to the source. Rajjat Barjatya informed me, "Each print of HAHK was marked so that even if an unauthorized video was circulating in the market, we could decode that video, and exactly find out which print it was made from. So we know which print it was made from, and we know where that print has been screening. Indirectly we know which cinema that it's come from" (Barjatya, interview, 29 April 1996).

10. There is still a burden on filmmakers insofar as they are expected to be aware of audience sensibilities, discussed later in the chapter.

11. There are parallels to the Hispanic marketing industry (Dàvila 2001), which organizes the Latino market in the United States regionally, where regions are asso-

12. Dharmendra is frequently referred to as "the Jat" and his elder son, Sunny, as "the junior Jat"—a powerful landed caste in northern India, specifically Punjab, Haryana, and western Uttar Pradesh.

13. *Film Information*, September 29, 2001, pp. 5–6.

14. The South, with the exception of the state of Andhra Pradesh, is not considered a very receptive market for Hindi films because of the longstanding historical antagonisms against the Hindi language, especially in Tamil Nadu; further, the existence of prolific film industries in the southern Indian states of Tamil Nadu and Andhra Pradesh is a hurdle. Andhra Pradesh, which includes the sub-territory of Nizam, is considered a more favorable market for Hindi films than the other southern Indian states because of the existence of a native Urdu-speaking population residing in the capital city of Hyderabad.

15. "Emotion" is used to denote kinship relations, an issue which is discussed in greater detail in Ganti (2002).

16. Movie theaters in India also operate on what is referred to as an advance booking system—people reserve and buy movie tickets beforehand for a specific day and time, sometimes a few weeks before a movie's release. Advance booking is one way for producers, distributors, and exhibitors to gauge the initial interest in a film as well as predict its opening weekend.

17. Deborah Matzner (2010), in her ethnography of Indian television producers, observed the same phenomenon.

18. Matunga is a central suburb of Bombay, with a heavily South Indian population; in Rajabali's statements, the "man from Matunga" represents non-elite viewers.

19. Rural bandits or outlaws—the Hindi word is *daaku*.

20. Rahul Agrawal is a pseudonym.

21. See Ganti (2002) for a discussion of Hollywood adaptations and the case of *Ghulam* specifically.

22. The review in *Film Information* predicted that its business would be better in Bombay, Maharashtra, and South. In the year-end analysis of box-office outcome, *Ghulam*'s overall business was categorized as an overflow earner, which meant that its distributors would have recovered their investment, earned their commission, and earned enough to share the overflow with the film's producer.

23. One could easily argue that Hindi films have always had a generic North Indianness, and from the late 1990s have been especially Punjab-centric.

24. This is a folk dance and musical form from Punjab.

25. While none of my informants ever raised the issue explicitly, explaining their judgments about the moral conservatism of audiences mainly through the medium of box-office outcome, another reason for filmmakers' perceptions of audiences as morally conservative would also be linked to the way that Hindi films periodically become embroiled in moral panics and controversies—often over sexually charged imagery—in the public sphere around issues of obscenity, vulgarity, and the constitution of "Indian-ness." For more on this issue see Ganti (2009). For an example of a particularly heated and documented moral panic around the 1993 Hindi film song "*Choli ke Peeche*" (What Is Behind My Blouse?) see Ghosh (1999).

26. Nargis was the lead character in *Mother India* (1957), a classic by Mehboob Khan that has been the focus of many a scholarly article about Indian cinema. See Ganti (2004) for a brief biography and filmography.

27. In our many conversations about filmmaking over the years, Rajabali has consistently exhibited a much more complex and generous understanding of audiences than his colleagues in the film industry.

Chapter Nine

The title of this chapter draws explicit inspiration from Arjun Appadurai's *The Fear of Small Numbers* (2006).

1. According to *Variety*, the film grossed $591,289 in three days from 44 screens across the United States, which was a very high per screen average of $13,438 ("Box Office" 1999; Chhabra 1999). Promotional trailers for the film, aired as commercials during community-produced Indian television shows in the United States, led with voice-overs and title cards: "Bollywood Beats Hollywood!"

2. This caricature of diasporic audiences has been remarkably persistent—I encountered it as recently as 2009: director Sudhir Mishra asserted at the panel discussion, "Reframing Cinema," being held at NYU in November 2009, as part of the MIAAC Film Festival, "With the rise of corporates, films are being made for the homesickness market in the U.S." Director Kabir Khan stated on a panel discussion in Bombay about the impact of multiplexes, "The diaspora is still ten years behind us" (Pillai 2009).

3. Bhagnani was speaking in Hindi and his exact sentence was, "*Unko chahiye ek* regular *wohi ghisi-piti* film, cliché, *jhagda, janwar panthi, khoon-kharaba*." The English translation doesn't communicate the full level of disdain expressed in the Hindi.

4. Bhatt's discussion is similar to what Zafirau (2009a) noted in his research about Hollywood producers who often relied on their own children to assess the appeal and potential popularity of films targeting children.

5. This binary was perhaps first articulated in the mid-1990s as "rural Bharat vs. urban India," by Sharad Joshi, leader of the farmer's movement in Maharashtra. For an articulate and insightful discussion of this issue see Gupta (1998).

6. Johar's previous success, *Kuch Kuch Hota Hai*, and the draw of the star cast of *Kabhi Khushi Kabhie Gham*—Shah Rukh Khan, Kajol, Amitabh Bachchan, Jaya Bachchan, Hrithik Roshan, and Kareena Kapoor—was what enabled him to be in such a commanding position. *Kabhi Khushi Kabhie Gham* was, until 2009, the most successful Hindi film in the United Kingdom and North America.

7. Even those who feel the right to enter can still have problems. For example, during my fieldwork in May 2006, the security guard at Fame Cinemas, Kandivali branch, stopped owner Shyam Shroff, who was giving me a tour of the chain of multiplexes, from entering the premises—because it was in between show times. The guard asked him in Hindi, "Who are you?" When Shroff said his name and it didn't register with the guard, Shroff finally said in Hindi, "I'm the owner [*Main malik hoon*]." Other examples—I was asked to stop taking photographs of the Raghuleela Mall in Kandivali; I was also asked to stop taking photographs of Fame Adlabs, until I informed them that I was a guest of Shroff, and then I was allowed to continue.

8. See the BIG Cinemas website, http://www.bigcinemas.com/in/advertise.asp.

9. Language from the BIG cinemas website describing their audience profile to potential advertisers interested in promoting their brands at the multiplex chain. See the BIG Cinemas website, http://www.bigcinemas.com/in/advertise.asp.

10. Official exchange rates for 2008 pegged the dollar to be equal to about 48 rupees. Exchange rates, however, do not accurately reflect the purchasing power or value

of a particular currency. Purchasing power parity (PPP) is a better indicator of currency value and in 2008, $1 = Rs. 13.42, which meant that $1 and Rs. 13.42 were able to purchase the same amount of goods and services (World Bank 2009); therefore, using the PPP rate to convert rupees into dollars, the cost of tickets at multiplexes ranged from $8.20–$9.69 in contrast to $1.49–$4.47. I thank Omkar Goswami for calculating the PPP conversion factor between the U.S. dollar and the Indian rupee.

11. PPP Rates: $13.04–$22.35 for multiplexes; $3.73–$8.20 for single screens in Bombay.

12. See Fame Cinemas website, http://www.famecinemas.com.

13. Nahta's exact statement was, "They've got different classes where the highest classes are so high priced that they are assured that these *jhopad-patti wallahs* [slum-dwellers] will not come and sit next to them."

14. See a related discussion of the idea of a "decent crowd" noted by Athique and Hill (2010).

15. For example, in 1996, Komal Nahta, editor of *Film Information*, discussing films that had become box-office successes that year, remarked about the film *Agnisakshi* (Fire-Witness), "I think five years back, it would be even suicidal to think that an *Agnisakshi* can run in Bombay. A woman gets married, she runs away and gets married again and all that. People are open even to such films" (Nahta, interview, September 1996).

16. I visited five different multiplexes in May 2006: Fame Adlabs, Fame Malad, Fame Raghuleela, Cinemax Versova, and PVR Cinemas, Juhu. Of the three chains that I visited, only Fame Cinemas had an offering of films in other Indian languages, namely Malayalam, Bengali, and Marathi, but these were only screened in one theater at off-peak times.

17. See Bamzai (2007); KPMG (2009, 2011); Pricewaterhouse Coopers (2006a, 2010).

18. BIG Cinemas' press release, March 17, 2009: "Major exhibitors come together to address film revenue share issues" asserted that in 2005–6, 45–50 percent of theatrical revenues came from multiplexes while in 2007–8, this figure rose to 65–70 percent. http://www.bigcinemas.com/IN/pressrelease_majorExhibitors.html.

19. Yet I could not come across consistent figures for the number of multiplex screens in India—they were all estimates—and the percentage of revenues multiplexes were purported to generate were also widely inconsistent across various information sources.

20. There seems to be an industry of generating reports about the film industry in India by Andersen Consulting, Yes Bank, KPMG, Pricewaterhouse Coopers, A.T. Kearney, Dodona Research, and Screen Digest. Even these various reports do not present consistent information about the film industry, filmmaking, or film-going in India—many figures are presented as estimates, and facts are referenced with respect to other prepared reports.

21. Mukesh Bhatt, whom I quoted discussing the two Indias trope, is not related to Vikram Bhatt, despite the shared last name. Both Bhatts are related in terms of work, however—Mukesh has produced many of Vikram's directorial ventures.

22. Of course the growing popularity and increasing commercial scale and profitability of Bhojpuri films (Bhojpuri is a language spoken in Bihar and eastern Uttar Pradesh), from about 2005 onward, belies the point made by Hindi filmmakers about the dearth of revenue from the "interiors" like Bihar and Uttar Pradesh.

23. Ashok Kumar (1911–2000) was one of the first stars of Hindi cinema who began his acting career in the 1930s.

24. Examples of such filmmakers include Anurag Kashyap, Vishal Bharadwaj, Dibakar Banerjee, and Sudhir Mishra.

25. Johar's own filmmaking career has been characterized by a desire to make a presence in the global media landscape. For example, he always sells his audio rights to Sony Music rather than an Indian music company; he was the first to use white European background dancers for his second film, flying them into Bombay; he sold the worldwide distribution rights for his film *My Name Is Khan* to 20th Century Fox. From his directorial debut, *Kuch Kuch Hota Hai* (Something Happens, 1998) to his magnum opus, *My Name Is Khan* (2010), Johar's films have always been associated with urban, metro, overseas, and "classes" audiences. His film, *Kabhi Khushi Kabhie Gham* (Sometimes Happiness, Sometimes Sorrow, 2001) was, until 2009, the most successful Hindi film in North America and the United Kingdom. His filmmaking typifies the gentrification of Hindi cinema and the transformation of the Hindi film industry into Bollywood.

26. See Fernandes (2006); Lukose (2009); Mankekar (1999); Mazzarella (2003); Rajagopal (2001).

Epilogue

1. Apropos of the nature of the Hindi film industry already discussed in the book, the exact figures of how much Fox paid for the distribution rights is never confirmed. *Film Information* (Nahta 2009a) first reported that the sum was 80 *crore* (800 million) and a subsequent issue (Bhatia 2010) stated the sum was 85 *crore* (850 million); a report in the *Business Standard* (Sinha 2009) pegged the figure at over 100 *crore* (1 billion rupees). At the exchange rates prevailing in August 2009, when the deal was announced, Fox's cost of acquisition was approximately between $16 and $17 million. The film was in the news once again around the time of its release in February 2010, because the Shiv Sena, an ethnic and Hindu chauvinist political party in Maharashtra, warned exhibitors across the state to boycott the film or face the ire of the party, on account of Khan's statements of regret about Pakistani cricketers not being drafted for the cricket teams comprising the Indian Premier League. Shiv Sena leader Bal Thackeray asserted that Khan was anti-national and anti-Mumbai and demanded an apology, in the absence of which, party members would protest and disrupt the screenings of MNIK—a pattern that always involved a great deal of vandalism and destruction of property. Khan refused to apologize for his statements. The film opened as scheduled in Bombay cinemas; under a great deal of police protection, including pre-emptive arrests of hundreds of Sena party workers, but some theaters were still vandalized by Sena members. The whole episode monopolized much of the news headlines in India for that week.

2. The review of MNIK in *The Hollywood Reporter*, however, portrays a slightly different picture of Fox's strategy, at least with respect to the United States and Europe, implying that the company either did not make an effort or was complacent in the way they tried to promote the film. It states, "The film is getting released in India, North America, and many other territories February 12, but its North American distributor, Fox Searchlight, adopted the puzzling strategy of playing the film out of competition here at the Berlinale, but refusing to screen it to U.S. press ahead of its release . . . it's a pity that the non-Indian press are discouraged from shouting out the news about a film that delves compellingly into Americans' anti-Muslim hysteria" (Honeycutt 2010).

3. *Film Information*'s review was pessimistic about the film's commercial prospects. It stated, "On the whole, *My Name Is Khan* is far from entertaining, and [it is] also too boring for the general masses. It will be liked, probably even loved, by the Muslim classes and by the audiences abroad. But for the heavy budget at which it has been sold, it will keep either its worldwide distributors (Fox Searchlight) or those to whom they have further sold the rights, in the red. Business in big cities, especially in South India, Muslim centres, and Overseas will be better, but it will be below the mark in North India as also in smaller centres and single-screen cinemas. It may be appreciated by the class audience, but a large chunk of the masses will reject the film. The controversy surrounding the film will definitely help boost its collections" (Nahta 2010b). The following week's issue of the trade magazine seemed to have its predictions confirmed when it reported, "The collections in the Overseas territory of MNIK are absolutely fantastic . . . but the response on home ground is definitely not up to mark, as is evident from the sharp decline in collections from Monday onwards" (Nahta 2010a).

4. For example, in the above-mentioned interview with *rediff.com*, Johar used the examples of the film's commercial performance in Indonesia and Poland as indicative of the film's cross-cultural appeal. About Indonesia he asserted, "If a Hindi language film grossed about $75,000 there, it is considered excellent, but our film struck a chord, and it became a sleeper hit grossing over $1.6 million." Regarding Poland, "It grossed about $75,000 in its first week, which is very good for a territory like Poland. I believe the second week is even stronger" (Pais 2010).

5. Sony co-produced *Saawariya* (Beloved, 2007) directed by Sanjay Leela Bhansali, and Warner Bros. co-produced *Chandni Chowk to China* (2009) directed by Nikhil Advani.

6. In July 2011, Disney made an offer to buy out UTV for $454 million in order to expand its filmmaking operations in India (Gokhale 2011).

7. Reliance ADA (Anil Dhirubhai Ambani Group) is one of India's largest conglomerates, with dealings in communications, financial services, power, and infrastructure. According to their website, they have a market capitalization of $81 billion, net assets exceeding $29 billion, and a net worth of $14 billion. The website also states that the group has a "business presence that extends to over 20,000 towns and 450,000 villages in India, and five continents across the world" (http://www.relianceadagroup.com/ada/overview.html).

8. Anil Ambani, the chair of Reliance ADA, the parent company of Reliance Big, was quoted in *Variety*, "Our partnership with Stacey and Steven is the cornerstone of our Hollywood strategy as we grow our film interests across the globe" (McClintock 2009).

9. In 2011, Johar won the award for best director for MNIK in three out of four annual awards ceremonies that felicitate Hindi filmmaking: the Filmfare Awards; the Zee Cine Awards; and the Apsara Awards. MNIK was also awarded the "Best Marketed Film" title—the first award of its kind—at the Zee Cine Awards function.

10. I was not present at the ceremony, but watched it on television in New York City on the Indian satellite channel, Star Plus, that is available as part of Verizon's Fios Networks' South Asian Package. Ramnath Goenka was the founder of the newspaper *Indian Express*, and the Ramnath Goenka Memorial Foundation and Trust was established in his memory in 1992, to encourage and promote high-quality journalism. The Indian Express Group publishes *Screen*, a weekly newspaper that

focuses on the entertainment industries in India, primarily the Hindi film and television industries centered in Bombay. The Ramnath Goenka Memorial Award is a special award that "recognizes excellence in cinema" and is awarded to a "film-maker who dares to make a difference in society with his work" (http://in.movies .yahoo.com).

11. Footage of this entire sequence can be viewed on YouTube (http://www.youtube .com/watch?v=9ePKl76LbhY).

12. In the February 20, 2010, issue of *Film Information*, an article about MNIK asserted, "Though MNIK will probably prove, according to trade pundits, a losing proposition for worldwide distributor Fox due to the huge price it paid for it, there is no denying that MNIK has been wonderful for the Hindi film industry." The reason being that MNIK was the "most widely exploited Hindi film in recent times. The Shah Rukh Khan starrer is the first Hindi film to be dubbed in German and Turkish languages; while it is too early to say how the dubbed versions will fare, they may create fresh markets for our industry. Also very significantly, Fox will be releasing a shortened 'Americanised' version of MNIK in the United States and related markets. That too may generate curiosity in those markets and the Bollywood idiom and songs may enchant foreigners" (Bhatia 2010: 22).

13. One could also argue that the film's own distributors had not anticipated the film's success. Warner Bros., the film's original studio backer, was skeptical of the film's commercial viability and had plans to release it directly on DVD, forgoing a theatrical release, after its small-budget film division, Warner Independent, shut down in May 2008. Fox Searchlight bought the rights for theatrical distribution from Warner (Walker 2009).

14. Prominent examples include *Om Shanti Om, Once Upon a Time in Mumbai, Action Replayy*.

15. *Dabangg* won the Best Film category at the *Filmfare* Awards, Zee Cine Awards, the Apsara Awards, and the IIFA Awards.

16. Such regimes are especially evident in sites such as international film festivals: Cannes; Toronto; Venice; Berlin, where unofficial quotas exist for films that are marked as representing a national cinema in the case of non–Euro-American contexts, but not for films from the United States, France, Britain, etc., which serve as the unmarked representatives of "cinema" or "world/international" cinema.

BIBLIOGRAPHY

"Aamir Khan Denies Re-Shooting 'Lagaan.'" 2001. *Times of India*, January 22.

Abraham, Itty. 1998. *The Making of the Indian Atomic Bomb: Science, Secrecy and the Postcolonial State*. London: Zed Books.

Abu-Lughod, Lila. 2005. *Dramas of Nationhood: The Politics of Television in Egypt*. Chicago: University of Chicago Press.

Aiyar, V. Shankar. 1999. "Badshah in the Red." *India Today*, April 26.

Aiyar, V. Shankar, and Anupama Chopra. 1998. "Waiting for Action." *India Today*, May 25.

Allor, Martin. 1996. "The Politics of Producing Audiences." *The Audience and Its Landscape*, edited by James Hay, Lawrence Grossberg, and Ella Wartella, 209–47. Boulder, Colo.: Westview Press.

Amin, Tushar A. 2007. "Marching to a Different Beat." *Filmfare*, November 1.

"Amitabh Bachchan, Now Unlimited." 2003. *Financial Express*, June 14.

Anderson, Benedict. 1983. *Imagined Communities: Reflections on the Origin and Spread of Nationalism*. London: Verso.

Anderson, James A. 1996. "The Pragmatics of Audience in Research and Theory." *The Audience and Its Landscape*, edited by James Hay, Lawrence Grossberg, and Ella Wartella, 75–93. Boulder, Colo.: Westview Press.

Ang, Ien. 1991. *Desperately Seeking the Audience*. London: Routledge.

Annuncio, Charubala. 1997. "Bankruptcy Blues." *Outlook*, April 23.

———. 1996. "There's No Business Like . . ." *Outlook*, July 17.

"A Plus Film, Minus the Madness?" 1996. *Screen* (Bombay), May 17.

Appadurai, Arjun. 1996. *Modernity at Large: Cultural Dimensions of Globalization*. Minneapolis: University of Minnesota Press.

———. 1986. "Introduction: Commodities and the Politics of Value." *The Social Life of Things: Commodities in Cultural Perspective*, edited by Arjun Appadurai, 3–63. Cambridge: Cambridge University Press.

Arthur Andersen. 2000. *The Indian Entertainment Industry: Strategy & Vision*. New Delhi: Federation of Indian Chambers of Commerce and Industry (FICCI).

Assayag, Jackie, and Chris Fuller, eds. 2006. *Globalizing India: Perspectives from Below*. London: Anthem Press.

"A Tale of Akshay and Akshaye." 2008. *Film Information*, March 29.

Athique, Adrian, and Douglas Hill. 2010. *The Multiplex in India: A Cultural Economy of Urban Leisure*. London: Routledge.

Bajaj, Vikas. 2011. "Disney Offers to Buy Out Partners in Indian Media Company." *New York Times (Deal Book)*, July 26.

Bakhle, Janaki. 2005. *Two Men and Music: Nationalism in the Making of an Indian Classical Tradition*. New York: Oxford University Press.

Bamzai, Kaveree. 2007. "How India Watches Movies." *India Today*, December 6.

Bandyopadhyay, Samik, ed. 1993. *Indian Cinema: Contemporary Perceptions from the Thirties*. Jamshedpur: Celluloid Chapter.

Banker, Ashok. 1999. "What went wrong with ABCL." *rediff.com*, June 22.

Bannerjee, Sumanta.1998. *The Parlour and the Streets: Elite and Popular Culture in Nineteenth Century Calcutta*. Calcutta: Seagull Books.

Barnouw, Eric, and Subrahmanyam Krishnaswamy. 1980. *Indian Film*. New York: Oxford University Press.

Benegal, Shyam. 2007. "The Audience Is No More a Grey Mass." *Indian Express*, July 4.

Bennett, Tony. 1996. "Figuring Audiences and Readers." *The Audience and Its Landscape*, edited by James Hay, Lawrence Grossberg, and Ella Wartella, 145–60. Boulder, Colo.: Westview Press.

Bhaskar, Ira, and Richard Allen. 2009. *Islamicate Cultures of Bombay Cinema*. New Delhi: Tulika Books.

Bhatia, Surindra. 2010. "Here & There: Spiralling Collections." *Film Information*, February 20.

Bhatkal, Satyajit. 2002. *The Spirit of Lagaan*. Bombay: Popular Prakashan.

Bhatt, S. C. 1996. *Satellite Invasion of India*. New Delhi: Gyan Publishing.

BIG Cinemas. 2010. "The Power of BIG Cinemas." January 27.

Binford, Mira Reym. 1989. Introduction to *Quarterly Review of Film and Video* 11, no. 3, 1–9.

———. 1987. "The Two Cinemas of India." *Film and Politics in the Third World*, edited by John D. H. Downing, 145–66. New York: Praeger.

———. 1983. "The New Cinema of India." *Quarterly Review of Film Studies* 8, no. 4 (Fall), 47–61.

Blumler, Jay G. 1996. "Recasting the Audience in the New Television Marketplace?" *The Audience and Its Landscape*, edited by James Hay, Lawrence Grossberg, and Ella Wartella, 97–112. Boulder, Colo.: Westview Press.

"Bollywood 101." 2005. ABC *News Nightline*, aired January 14.

"Bollywood Out of the Red for Second Consecutive Year." 2008. *Film Information*, January 12.

"Bollywood's Attempt to Escape Murky Past Falters after Box-Office Flops." 2005. Agence France-Presse (AFP), April 28.

"Boost for Bollywood." 1998. *Times of India*, May 12.

Booth, Gregory D. 2008. *Behind the Curtain: Making Music in Mumbai's Film Studios*. New York: Oxford University Press.

Bourdieu, Pierre. 1993. *The Field of Cultural Production*. Edited and introduced by Randal Johnson. New York: Columbia University Press.

———. 1984. *Distinction: A Social Critique of the Judgment of Taste*. Translated by Richard Nice. Cambridge, Mass.: Harvard University Press.

———. 1977. *Outline of a Theory of Practice*. Translated by Richard Nice. Cambridge: Cambridge University Press.

"Box Office." 1999. *Variety*, August 23–29.

British Tourist Authority. 2007. *India: Market and Trade Profile*. London: VisitBritain.

Caldarola, Victor J. 1992. "Reading the Television Text in Outer Indonesia." *Howard Journal of Communications* 4, nos. 1/2, 28–49.

Caldwell, John Thornton. 2008. *Production Culture: Industrial Reflexivity and Critical Practice in Film and Television*. Durham: Duke University Press.

"Call for Ban Against Shakti Kapoor." 2005. Press Trust of India (PTI), March 14.

"Calling Us Bollywood Is Derogatory: Naseerudin, Om." 2007. PTI, July 3.

Cantor, Muriel G. 1988. *The Hollywood TV Producer: His Work and His Audience*. New Brunswick, N.J.: Transaction Books.

Cassidy, John. 1997. "Chaos in Hollywood: Can Science Explain Why a Movie Is a Hit or a Flop?" *New Yorker*, March 31.

"Cast and Credits of 1995 Releases." 1996. *Film Information*, January 6.

"Cast and Credits of 1996 Releases." 1997. *Film Information*, January 4.

"Cast and Credits of 1997 Releases." 1998. *Film Information*, January 3.

"Cast and Credits of 1998 Releases." 1999. *Film Information*, January 2.

"Cast and Credits of 1999 Releases." 2000. *Film Information*, January 1.

"Cast and Credits of 2000 Releases." 2001. *Film Information*, January 6.

"Cast and Credits of 2001 Releases." 2002. *Film Information*, January 5.

"Cast and Credits of 2005 Releases." 2006. *Film Information*, January 7.

"Cast and Credits of 2006 Releases." 2007. *Film Information*, January 6.

"Cast and Credits of 2007 Releases." 2008. *Film Information*, January 5.

"Cast and Credits of 2008 Releases." 2009. *Film Information*, January 3.

"Cast and Credits of 2009 Releases." 2010. *Film Information*, January 2.

"Cast and Credits of 2010 Releases." 2011. *Film Information*, January 7.

"Centenary Fete Lacks Glitz." 1996. *Indian Express*, July 8.

Chakrabarty, Dipesh. 2000. *Provincializing Europe: Postcolonial Thought and Historical Difference*. Princeton: Princeton University Press.

Chakravarty, Sumita S. 1993. *National Identity in Indian Popular Cinema, 1947–1987*. Austin: University of Texas Press.

Chakravorty, Aruna. 1999. "High Court Directs Plus Channel to Pay Rs 4 Cr. or Shut Shop." *Indian Express*, November 17.

Chandra, Anupama. 1995. "Goodbye to Formula?" *India Today*, November 30.

Chandran, Rina. 2003. "20th Century Gets Formula Right for Jhankaar Beats." *Financial Times*, July 2.

Chatterjee, Partha. 1993. *Nation and Its Fragments: Colonial and Postcolonial Histories*. Princeton: Princeton University Press.

———. 1989. "Colonialism, Nationalism, and Colonialized Women: The Contest in India." *American Ethnologist* 16, no. 3, 622–33.

Chatterjee, Saibal. 2006. "Multiplexes Roll, Boutique Films Don't." *Financial Express*, July 16.

———. 1996. "Back to the Movies." *Outlook*, January 17.

Chaudhury, Shoma. 2007. "I Wish I Could Call Myself Karan Saxena, not Karan Johar." *Tehelka*, October 6.

———. 2005. "Sex, Tape, Truth." *Tehelka*, March 26.

Chaware, Dilip. 1996. "Thespians and Vintage Cars Will Mark Movie Centenary." *Times of India*, June 30.

Chaya, R. B. 1996. "Discordant Notes." *Screen* (Bombay), November 15.

Chhabra, Aseem. 1999. "Taal Dances to Record Numbers." *rediff.com*, August 18.

Chhabria, Suresh. 1996. "Celebrating the Hundredth Year of the Arrival of Cinema in Mumbai July 7–14." Bombay: Prabhat Chitra Mandal.

Chopra, Anupama. 2008. "Flush with Cash: Bollywood Glows." *New York Times*, August 24.

————. 2007. *King of Bollywood: Shah Rukh Khan and the Seductive World of Indian Cinema*. New York: Warner Books.

————. 2005. "Suits Stumble at B.O." *Variety*, March 28–April 3.

Chopra, Yash. 1998. "Taxation Issues Related to the Film Industry." National Conference on Challenges before Indian Cinema, FICCI and Film Federation of India (FFI), May 10.

"Classification: 1995." 1996. *Film Information*, January 6.

"Classification: 1996." 1997. *Film Information*, January 4.

"Classification: 1997." 1998. *Film Information*, January 3.

"Classification: 1998." 1999. *Film Information*, January 2.

"Classification: 1999." 2000. *Film Information*, January 1.

"Classification: 2000." 2001. *Film Information*, January 6.

"Classification: 2001." 2002. *Film Information*, January 5.

"Classification: 2005." 2006. *Film Information*, January 7.

"Classification: 2006." 2007. *Film Information*, January 6.

"Classification: 2007." 2008. *Film Information*, January 5.

"Classification: 2008." 2009. *Film Information*, January 3.

"Classification: 2009." 2010. *Film Information*, January 2.

"Classification: 2010." 2011. *Film Information*, January 7.

Clifford, James. 1988. *The Predicament of Culture*. Cambridge, Mass.: Harvard University Press.

Condry, Ian. 2006. *Hip-Hop Japan: Rap and the Paths of Cultural Globalization*. Durham: Duke University Press.

Crawford, Peter I., and Sigurjon Baldur Hafsteinsson, eds. 1993. *The Construction of the Viewer*. Aarhus: Intervention Press.

Creed, Gerald W. 2000. "'Family Values' and Domestic Economies." *Annual Review of Anthropology* 29, 329–55.

Dalal, Sucheta. 1995. "Amitabh Firm Set to Create New Trend." *Times of India*, January 14.

Das Gupta, Chidananda. 1991. *The Painted Face: Studies in India's Popular Cinema*. New Delhi: Roli Books.

————. 1986. "Indian Cinema: Dynamics of Old and New." *India 2000: The Next Fifteen Years*, edited by James R. Roach, 81–95. Riverdale, Colo: Riverdale.

————. 1981. *Talking About Films*. New Delhi: Orient Longman.

Das Sharma, Biren. 1993. "Indian Cinema and National Leadership." *Indian Cinema: Contemporary Perceptions from the Thirties*, edited by Samik Bandyopadhyay, 135–40. Jamshedpur: Celluloid Chapter.

Dàvila, Arlene. 2001. *Latinos, Inc.: The Marketing and Making of a People*. Berkeley: University of California Press.

Dayal, John. 1983. "The Role of the Government: Story of an Uneasy Truce." *Indian Cinema Superbazaar*, edited by Aruna Vasudev and Phillippe Lenglet, 53–61. New Delhi: Vikas.

Deger, Jennifer. 2006. *Shimmering Screens: Making Media in an Aboriginal Community*. Minneapolis: University of Minnesota Press.

Derne, Steve. 2008. *Globalization on the Ground: Media and the Transformation of Culture, Class, and Gender in India*. New Delhi: Sage.

Desai, S. M. 1998. "Bollywood Celebrates 'Independence Day.'" *Indian Express*, May 12.

Deshpande, Satish. 2003. *Contemporary India: A Sociological View*. New Delhi: Penguin.

———. 1993. "Imagined Economies: Styles of Nation-building in Twentieth Century India." *Journal of Arts and Ideas*, nos. 25/26, 5–35.

Deshpande, Sudhanva. 2005. "The Consumable Hero of Globalised India." *Bollyworld: Popular Indian Cinema through a Transnational Lens*, edited by Raminder Kaur and Ajay J. Sinha, 186–203. New Delhi: Sage.

Dey, Sudipto. 2004. "Silicon Valley Techies Target B'wood." *Economic Times*, April 20.

Dickey, Sara. 1993. *Cinema and the Urban Poor in South India*. Cambridge: Cambridge University Press.

Dornfeld, Barry. 1998. *Producing Public Television, Producing Public Culture*. Princeton: Princeton University Press.

Dua, Aarti. 2006. "Scripting a Screen Success." *Telegraph* (Calcutta), January 14.

Dutta, Sudipt. 1997. *Family Business in India*. New Delhi: Response Books.

Dwyer, Rachel. 2000. *All You Want Is Money, All You Need Is Love: Sex and Romance in Modern India*. London: Cassell.

Dwyer, Rachel, and Divia Patel. 2002. *Cinema India: The Visual Culture of Hindi Film*. New Brunswick, N.J.: Rutgers University Press.

Elliott, Michael. 2006. "India Awakens." *Time*, June 26.

Espinosa, Paul. 1982. "The Audience in the Text: Ethnographic Observations of a Hollywood Story Conference." *Media, Culture and Society* 4, no. 1, 77–86.

Ettema, James S., and D. Charles Whitney, eds. 1994. *Audiencemaking: How the Media Create the Audience*. Thousand Oaks, Calif.: Sage.

Fabian, Johannes. 2002. *Time and the Other: How Anthropology Makes Its Object*. Reprint edition. New York: Columbia University Press.

Ferguson, James, and Akhil Gupta. 2002. "Spatializing States: Toward an Ethnography of Neoliberal Governmentality." *American Ethnologist* 29, no. 4, 981–1002.

Fernandes, Leela. 2006. *India's New Middle Class: Democratic Politics in an Era of Economic Reform*. Minneapolis: University of Minnesota Press.

———. 2004. "The Politics of Forgetting: Class Politics, State Power and the Restructuring of Urban Space in India." *Urban Studies* 41, no. 12, 2415–30.

Film Federation of India (FFI). 1956. *Indian Talkie 1931–56: Silver Jubilee Souvenir*.

"Film Information's Best of 2007." 2008. *Film Information*, January 5.

"Finally an Industry." 1998. *Indian Express*, May 12.

Fuller, Chris J., and Haripriya Narasimhan. 2007. "Information Technology Professionals and the New-Rich Middle Class in Chennai (Madras)." *Modern Asian Studies* 41, no. 1, 121–50.

Ganguly-Scrase, Ruchira, and Timothy J. Scrase. 2009. *Globalisation and the Middle Classes in India: The Social and Cultural Impact of Neoliberal Reforms*. London: Routledge.

Gans, Herbert J. 1957. "The Creator-Audience Relationship in the Mass Media: An Analysis of Movie-Making." *Mass Culture: The Popular Arts in America*, edited by B. Rosenberg and D. M. White, 315–24. New York: Free Press.

Ganti, Tejaswini. 2009. "The Limits of Decency and the Decency of Limits: Censorship and the Bombay Film Industry." *Censorship in South Asia*, edited by Raminder Kaur and William Mazzarella, 87–122. Indianapolis: Indiana University Press.

———. 2004. *Bollywood: A Guidebook to Popular Hindi Cinema*. London: Routledge.

———. 2002. "And Yet My Heart Is Still Indian: The Bombay Film Industry and the (H)Indianization of Hollywood." *Media Worlds: Anthropology on New Terrain*, edited by Faye D. Ginsburg, Lila Abu-Lughod, and Brian Larkin, 281–300. Berkeley: University of California Press.

———. 2000. "Casting Culture: The Social Life of Hindi Film Production in Contemporary India." PhD diss. New York University.

———. 1998. "Centenary Commemorations or Centenary Contestations? Celebrating a Hundred Years of Cinema in Bombay." *Visual Anthropology* 11, no. 4, 399–419.

———. 1994. "The Good, the Bad, and the Ugly: Discourse about Hindi Cinema." MA thesis. University of Pennsylvania.

Garga, B. D. 1996. *So Many Cinemas*. Bombay: Eminence Designs.

Geertz, Clifford. 1973. *The Interpretation of Cultures*. New York: Basic Books.

Ghelani, Sailesh. 2007. "Loin Queen." *Filmfare*, November 1.

Ghosh, Shekhar, and Shantanu Guha Ray. 1999. "From Big B to IOU." *Outlook*, April 26.

Ghosh, Shohini. 1999. "The Troubled Existence of Sex and Sexuality: Feminists Engaged with Censorship." *Image Journeys: Audio-Visual Media & Cultural Change in India*, edited by Christiane Brosius and Melissa Butcher, 233–60. New Delhi: Sage.

Gieryn, Thomas F. 1983. "Boundary-Work and the Demarcation of Science from Non-Science: Strains and Interests in Professional Ideologies of Scientists." *American Sociological Review* 48, no. 6, 781–95.

Gillespie, Marie. 1995. *Television, Ethnicity and Cultural Change*. London: Routledge.

Ginsburg, Faye. 1995. "The Parallax Effect: The Impact of Aboriginal Media on Ethnographic Film." *Visual Anthropology Review* 11, no. 2, 64–76.

———. 1994. "Culture/media: A (mild) Polemic." *Anthropology Today* 10, no. 2, 5–15.

———. 1993. "Aboriginal Media and the Australian Imaginary." *Public Culture* 5, no. 3, 557–78.

Ginsburg, Faye D., Lila Abu-Lughod, and Brian Larkin, eds. 2002. *Media Worlds: Anthropology on New Terrain*. Berkeley: University of California Press.

Gmelch, George. 2003. "Baseball Magic." *Conformity and Conflict*, edited by James Spradley and David W. McCurdy, 348–57. Boston: Allyn and Bacon.

Goffman, Erving. 1963. *Stigma: Notes on the Management of Spoiled Identity*. New York: Simon and Schuster.

———. 1955. "On Face-Work: An Analysis of Ritual Elements in Social Interaction." *Psychiatry* 18, no. 3, 213–38.

Gokhale, Ketaki. 2011. "Disney Offers to Buy Out UTV Software for $454 Million to Expand in India." *bloomberg.com*, July 26.

Gopal, Sangita, and Sujata Moorti, eds. 2008. *Global Bollywood: Travels of Hindi Song and Dance*. Minneapolis: University of Minnesota Press.

Gopalan, Lalitha. 2002. *Cinema of Interruptions: Action Genres in Contemporary Indian Cinema*. London: British Film Institute.

Gupta, Akhil. 1998. *Postcolonial Developments: Agriculture in the Making of Modern India*. Durham: Duke University Press.

———. 1995. "Blurred Boundaries: The Discourse of Corruption, the Culture of Politics, and the Imagined State." *American Ethnologist* 22, no. 2, 375–402.

Hall, Stuart. 1990. "Cultural Identity and Diaspora." *Identity: Community, Culture, Difference*, edited by Jonathan Rutherford, 222–37. London: Lawrence and Wishart.

Hannerz, Ulf. 2004. *Foreign News: Exploring the World of Foreign Correspondents*. Chicago: University of Chicago Press.

Hansen, Kathryn. 1992. *Grounds for Play: The Nautanki Theatre of North India*. Berkeley: University of California Press.

Hansen, Miriam. 1991. *Babel and Babylon: Spectatorship in American Silent Film*. Cambridge, Mass.: Harvard University Press.

Hansen, Thomas Blom. 2001. *Wages of Violence: Naming and Identity in Postcolonial Bombay*. Princeton: Princeton University Press.

———. 1999. *The Saffron Wave: Democracy and Hindu Nationalism in Modern India*. Princeton: Princeton University Press.

Hartley, John. 1992. *Tele-ology: Studies in Television*. London: Routledge.

———. 1987. "Invisible Fictions: Television Audiences, Paedocracy, Pleasure." *Textual Practice* 1, no. 2, 121–38.

Harvey, David. 2005. *A Brief History of Neoliberalism*. Oxford: Oxford University Press.

———. 1990. *The Condition of Postmodernity*. Cambridge: Blackwell.

"Heard Not Seen." 2008. *Film Information*, March 9.

Himpele, Jeff. 2008. *Circuits of Culture: Media, Politics, and Indigenous Identity in the Andes*. Minneapolis: University of Minnesota Press.

———. 1996. "Film Distribution as Media: Mapping Difference in the Bolivian Cinemascape." *Visual Anthropology Review* 12, no. 1, 47–66.

Hjort, Mette, and Duncan Petrie, eds. 2007. *The Cinema of Small Nations*. Bloomington: Indiana University Press.

Holland, Dorothy, and Kevin Leander. 2004. "Ethnographic Studies of Positioning and Subjectivity: An Introduction." *Ethos* 32, no. 2, 127–39.

Honeycutt, Kirk. 2010. Review of "My Name Is Khan." *Hollywood Reporter*. February 12.

Hughes, Stephen. 2006. "House Full: Silent Film Genre, Exhibition and Audiences in South India." *Indian Economic and Social History Review* 43, no. 1, 31–62.

Inden, Ronald. 1999. "Transnational Class, Erotic Arcadia and Commercial Utopia in Hindi Films." *Image Journeys: Audio-visual Media and Cultural Change in India*, edited by Christiane Brosius and Melissa Butcher, 41–66. New Delhi: Sage.

"India Battles Invasion by Satellite TV." 1993. *New Strait Times*, July 10.

Indian Institute of Mass Communication and Directorate of Film Festivals. 1979. "Symposium on Cinema in Developing Countries." New Delhi: Ministry of Information and Broadcasting.

"Industry Status Granted to Films." 1998. *Times of India*, May 11.

"International Film Festival Opened." 1995. *Times of India*, January 1.

"Is the Film Industry Y2K OK?" 2000. *Film Information*, January 1.

Jacob, Preminda. 2009. *Celluloid Deities: The Visual Culture of Cinema and Politics in South India*. Lanham, Md.: Lexington Books.

Jain, Kajri. 2007. *Gods in the Bazaar: The Economies of Indian Calendar Art*. Durham: Duke University Press.

Jain, Madhu. 1998. "Acting for Survival." *India Today*, May 18.

———. 1995. "From Superstar to Tycoon." *India Today*, November 30.

———. 1991. "Cinema Turns Sexy." *India Today*, November 15.

Jeffrey, Robin. 2006. "The Mahatma Didn't Like the Movies and Why It Matters: Indian Broadcasting Policy 1920s–1990s." *Global Media and Communication* 2, no. 2, 204–24.

Jha, Subhash K. 2005. "The 'Bollywood' Man." *Telegraph* (Calcutta), April 1.

———. 2003. "Bhoot Will Make Audiences Uneasy." *rediff.com*, May 27.

Jhamkandikar, Shilpa. 2009. "Just a Minute With: Amit Khanna on Reliance-DreamWorks Deal." Reuters India, July 16.

Johar, Karan. 2007. "In Conversation with Richard Allen." Department of Cinema Studies, New York University, February 17.

Joseph, Manu. 2000a. "Bodies to Nobodies." *Outlook*, January 24.

———. 2000b. "Riverdale Sonata." *Outlook*, November 6.

Joshi, Namrata. 2010. "The Role Call." *Outlook*, April 12.

Joshi, Sanjay. 2001. *Fractured Modernity: Making of a Middle Class in Colonial North India*. New Delhi: Oxford University Press.

Kapsis, Robert. 1986. "Hollywood Filmmaking and Audience Image." *Media, Audience, and Social Structure*, edited by Sandra J. Ball-Rokeach and Muriel G. Cantor, 161–73. London: Sage.

Kapur, Jyotsna, and Manjunath Pendakur. 2007. "The Strange Disappearance of Bombay from its Own Cinema." *Democratic Communique* 21, no. 1, 43–59.

Karanth, K. S., ed. 1980. *Report of the Working Group on National Film Policy*. New Delhi: Ministry of Information and Broadcasting.

Kathuria, Harmeet. 2008 [1983]. "It Takes Guts to Cast a Newcomer in a Crore-Plus Project." *Film Information*. March 29.

———. 2007 [1982]. "Rakesh Roshan Has Excelled in Kaamchor." *Film Information*, June 30.

Kaul, Gautam. 1998. *Cinema and the Indian Freedom Struggle*. New Delhi: Sterling.

Kaur, Raminder, and Ajay J. Sinha, eds. 2005. *Bollyworld: Popular Indian Cinema through a Transnational Lens*. New Delhi: Sage.

Kavoori, Anandam P., and Aswin Punathambekar, eds. 2008. *Global Bollywood*. New York: New York University Press.

Kazmi, Fareed. 1999. *The Politics of India's Conventional Cinema*. New Delhi: Sage.

Keating, H. R. F. 1976. *Filmi, Filmi, Inspector Ghote*. Chicago: Academy Chicago Publishers.

Khanna, Aditya. 2007. "But Cinema Is a Community Experience." *Indian Express*, July 5.

Khanna, Amit. 1998. "Industry Status for Film Industry." National Conference on Challenges before Indian Cinema, FICCI and FFI, May 10.

Khanna, Namita, and Devina Dutt. 1992. "The Goonda as Hero." *Sunday*, February 16–22.

Khatib, Salma. 1997. "A New Approach to Music Marketing." *Screen* (Bombay), September 19.

Kheterpal, Sunir. 2005. *Bollywood: Emerging Business Trends and Growth Drivers*. Bombay: The Film and Television Producers Guild of India and YES BANK Ltd.

Khote, Durga. 2006. *I, Durga Khote: An Autobiography*. Translated by Shanta Gokhale. New Delhi: Oxford University Press.

"Kites Satellite Deal Renegotiated." 2010. *Film Information*, June 19.

Kondo, Dorinne K. 1990. *Crafting Selves: Power, Gender, and Discourses of Identity in a Japanese Workplace*. Chicago: University of Chicago Press.

Kopikar, Smruti, and Harinder Baweja. 1997. "Murder in Mumbai." *India Today*, August 25.

KPMG. 2011. *Hitting the High Notes: FICCI-KPMG Indian Media and Entertainment Industry Report*. New Delhi: FICCI.

———. 2009. *Media and Entertainment Industry Report: In the Interval, but Ready for the Next Act*. New Delhi: FICCI.

Krishna, Sankaran. 1999. *Postcolonial Insecurities: India, Sri Lanka, and the Question of Nationhood*. Minneapolis: University of Minnesota Press.

Kumar, Arun. 2005. "India's Black Economy: The Macroeconomic Implications." *South Asia: Journal of South Asian Studies* 28, no. 2, 249–63.

Lakshman, Nandin, and Ron Grover. 2008. "Why India's Reliance Is Going Hollywood." *BusinessWeek*, June 18.

Larkin, Brian. 2008. *Signal and Noise: Media, Infrastructure, and Urban Culture in Nigeria*. Durham: Duke University Press.

———. 2002. "The Materiality of Cinema Theaters in Northern Nigeria." *Media Worlds: Anthropology on New Terrain*, edited by Faye D. Ginsburg, Lila Abu-Lughod, and Brian Larkin, 319–36. Berkeley: University of California Press.

"Latest Position." 2010. *Film Information*, May 22.

"Latest Position." 2010. *Film Information*, June 19.

Lavin, Carl. 2009. "Bachchan on Davos, Escapism and the Power of the Dark Theater." *Forbes.com*, February 2.

Liechty, Mark. 2003. *Suitably Modern: Making Middle-Class Culture in a New Consumer Society*. Princeton: Princeton University Press.

"Looking for a Job in a Film Corporate?" 2010. *Film Information*, June 19.

Lukose, Ritty. 2009. *Liberalization's Children: Gender, Youth, and Consumer Citizenship in Globalizing India*. Durham: Duke University Press.

Mahindra Indo-American Arts Council Film Festival (MIAAC). 2009a. "FilmIndia—The Industry Panels." HBO Headquarters, New York, November 14.

———. 2009b. "Reframing Indian Cinema" Panel discussion, New York University, November 13.

Majumdar, Neepa. 2009. *Wanted Cultured Ladies Only! Female Stardom and Cinema in India, 1930s–1950*. Urbana: University of Illinois Press.

Malinowski, Bronislaw. 1972. "The Role of Magic and Religion." *Reader in Comparative Religion: An Anthropological Approach*, edited by William A. Less and Evon Z. Vogt, 63–71. New York: Harper and Row.

———. 1954 [1922]. *Magic, Science, and Religion and Other Essays*. New York: Doubleday Anchor Books.

Mankekar, Purnima. 1999. *Screening Culture, Viewing Politics: An Ethnography of Television, Womanhood, and Nation in Postcolonial India*. Durham: Duke University Press.

Marcus, George, and Peter D. Hall. 1992. *Lives in Trust: The Fortunes of Dynastic Families in Late Twentieth-Century America*. Boulder, Colo.: Westview Press.

Martin, Sylvia J. 2009. "Fantasy at Work: The Culture of Production in the Hollywood and Hong Kong Media Industries." PhD diss. University of California, Irvine.

Mathur, Arti. 2002. "Official pic funding fights crime." *Variety*, April 1.

Matzner, Deborah. 2010. "Mediating Women: Producing Commercial Satellite Television Programming and Documentary Film in Mumbai." PhD diss. New York University.

Mayer, Vicki, Miranda J. Banks, and John Thornton Caldwell. 2009. *Production Studies: Cultural Studies of Media Industries*. New York: Routledge.

Mayne, Judith. 1993. *Cinema and Spectatorship*. London: Routledge.

Mayo, Katherine. 1927. *Mother India*. New York: Harcourt Brace.

Mazumdar, Ranjani. 2007. *Bombay Cinema: An Archive of the City*. Minneapolis: University of Minnesota Press.

Mazzarella, William. 2005. "Middle Class." *South Asia Keywords* [an online encyclopedia], edited by Rachel Dwyer. School of Oriental and African Studies.

———. 2003. *Shoveling Smoke: Advertising and Globalization in Contemporary India*. Durham: Duke University Press.

McClintock, Pamela. 2009. "Reliance, DreamWorks Close Deal." *Variety*, August 17.

McQuail, Denis. 1997. *Audience Analysis*. Thousand Oaks, Calif.: Sage.

Mead, George Herbert. 1934. *Mind, Self, and Society*. Edited by and with an introduction from Charles W. Morris. Chicago: University of Chicago Press.

Meduri, Avanthi. 1988. "Bharatha Natyam—What Are You?" *Asian Theatre Journal* 5, no. 1, 1–22.

Menezes, Saira. 1997. "The Last Rites?" *Outlook*, June 18.

Miller, Daniel, and Heather Horst. 2006. *The Cell Phone: An Anthropology of Communication*. London: Berg.

Miller, Daniel, and Don Slater. 2000. *The Internet: An Ethnographic Approach*. London: Berg.

Miller, Hugo. 2006. "Bern Woos Bollywood, and India: Switzerland Counts on Films to Revive its Tourism Industry." *International Herald Tribune*, October 4.

Miller, Toby. 1998. "Hollywood and the World." *The Oxford Guide to Film Studies*, edited by John Hill and Pamela Church Gibson, 371–81. Oxford: Oxford University Press.

Miller, Toby, Nitin Govil, John McMurria, and Richard Maxwell. 2001. *Global Hollywood*. London: British Film Institute.

Mishra, Vijay. 2002. *Bollywood Cinema: Temples of Desire*. London: Routledge.

Mittal, Ashok. 1995. *Cinema Industry in India: Pricing and Taxation*. New Delhi: Indus.

Moore, Robert L. 2004. "We're Cool, Mom and Dad Are Swell: Basic Slang and Generational Shifts in Values." *American Speech* 79, no. 1, 59–86.

Mosse, George. 1985. *Nationalism and Sexuality: Middle-Class Morality and Sexual Norms in Modern Europe*. Madison: University of Wisconsin Press.

Mukherjee, Pradipta. 2009. "Multiplexes May Invest Rs. 400 Crore in 2010." *Business Standard* (Calcutta), December 23.

"The Multiplex Effect." 2003. *Indian Express*, February 2.

Myers, Fred R. 2002. *Painting Culture: The Making of an Aboriginal High Art*. Durham: Duke University Press.

———. 2001. Introduction to *The Empire of Things: Regimes of Value and Material Culture*, edited by Fred R. Myers, 3–61. Santa Fe, N.M.: School of American Research Press.

N, Patcy. 2009. "My Film is not like Chandni Chowk." *rediff.com*, June 24.

Nahta, Komal. 2010a. "'MNIK' Versus '3 Idiots.'" *Film Information*, February 20.

———. 2010b. Review of "My Name Is Khan." *Film Information*, February 13.

———. 2009a. "'My Name Is Khan' For Rs. 80 Crore!! Don't Be Foxed—It's Actually a Steal!" *Film Information*, August 8.

———. 2009b. Review of "Wanted." *Film Information*, September 19.

———. 2007. "Are Corporates Helping the Film Industry or Harming It?" *Film Information*, November 19.

———. 2001. Review of "Chandni Bar." *Film Information*, September 29.

———. 2000a. Review of "Mela." *Film Information*, January 7.

————. 2000b. "Millennium Exclusive: 'I want to return to my childhood. Yes, that's my millennium resolution . . .'" *Film Information*, January 1.

————. 1999. Review of "Taal." *Film Information*, August 14.

————. 1996. Review of "Raja Hindustani." *Film Information*, November 16.

Nancarrow, Clive, Pamela Nancarrow, and Julie Page. 2002. "An Analysis of the Concept of *Cool* and its Marketing Implications." *Journal of Consumer Behavior* 1, no. 4, 311–22.

Nandy, Ashis. 1998. "Indian Popular Cinema as a Slum's Eye View of Politics." *The Secret Politics of Our Desires: Innocence, Culpability and Indian Popular Cinema*, edited by Ashis Nandy, 1–18. New Delhi: Oxford University Press.

————. 1995. "An Intelligent Critic's Guide to Indian Cinema." *The Savage Freud*, 196–236. Princeton: Princeton University Press.

————. 1987. "An Intelligent Critic's Guide to Indian Cinema: The Cultural Matrix of the Popular Film." *Deep Focus* 1, no. 1, 68–72.

————. 1981. "The Popular Hindi Film: Ideology and First Principles." *India International Centre Quarterly* 8, no. 1, 89–96.

National Association of Theatre Owners (NATO). 2009. Number of Movie Screens. http://www.natoonline.org/.

"NFDC's Tribute to First Film Venue." 1995. *Times of India*, January 13.

Ohmann, Richard. 1996a. "Knowing/Creating Wants." *Making and Selling Culture*, edited by Richard Ohmann, 224–38. Hanover, N.H.: Wesleyan University Press.

————, ed. 1996b. *Making and Selling Culture*. Hanover, N.H.: Wesleyan University Press.

Oldenburg, Veena Talwar. 1991. "Lifestyle as Resistance." *Contesting Power: Resistance and Everyday Social Relations in South Asia* edited by Douglas Haynes and Gyan Prakash, 23–61. Berkeley: University of California Press.

Olsberg-SPI. 2007. "Stately Attraction: How Film and Television Programmes Promote Tourism in the U.K." London. http://www.ukfilmcouncil.org.uk.

"Overseas Market: Is Its Bigness Eclipsing Home Market?" 1999. *Film Information*, August 21.

Oza, Rupal. 2006. *The Making of Neoliberal India*. New York: Routledge.

Pais, Arthur J. 2010. "MNIK is highest-grossing Hindi film outside India." *rediff.com*. May 12.

Patil, S. K., ed. 1951. *Report of the Film Enquiry Committee*. New Delhi: Government of India Press.

Pedroso de Lima, Antonia. 2000. "Is Blood Thicker than Economic Interest in Familial Entreprises?" *Dividends of Kinship: Meanings and Uses of Social Relatedness*, edited by Peter P. Schweitzer, 153–78. New York: Routledge.

Pendakur, Manjunath. 1989. "New Cultural Technologies and the Fading Glitter of Indian Cinema." *Quarterly Review of Film and Video* 11, no. 3, 69–78.

Peters, John Durham. 1997. "Seeing Bifocally: Media, Place, and Culture." *Culture, Power, Place: Explorations in Critical Anthropology*, edited by Akhil Gupta and James Ferguson, 75–92. Durham: Duke University Press.

Pherwani, Seema. 2005. "Just wait and watch there are more in the pipeline." *Indiantelevision.com*, March 17.

Pillai, Pooja. 2009. "Riding the Multiplex Wave." *Indian Express*, September 17.

Pinney, Christopher. 1997. *Camera Indica: The Social Life of Indian Photographs*. Chicago: University of Chicago Press.

Pinney, Christopher, and Nicholas Peterson, eds. 2003. *Photography's Other Histories*. Durham: Duke University Press.

Pountain, Dick, and David Robins. 2000. *Cool Rules: Anatomy of an Attitude*. London: Reaktion.

Prakash, Om. 1998. "Institutional Financing of Film Industry." National Conference on Challenges before Indian Cinema, FICCI and FFI, May 10.

Prakash, Sanjeev. 1983. "Music, Dance and the Popular Films: Indian Fantasies, Indian Repressions." *Indian Cinema Superbazaar*, edited by Aruna Vasudev and Phillipe Lenglet, 114–18. New Delhi: Vikas.

Prasad, Madhava. 2003. "This Thing Called Bollywood." In "Unsettling Cinema: A Symposium on the Place of Cinema in India," *Seminar* 525 (May). http://www.india-seminar.com.

———. 1998. *Ideology of the Hindi Film: A Historical Construction*. Delhi: Oxford University Press.

Pricewaterhouse Coopers. 2010. *Indian Entertainment and Media Outlook*. New Delhi: FICCI.

———. 2006a. *The Indian Entertainment and Media Industry: Unravelling the Potential*. New Delhi: FICCI.

———. 2006b. *Entertainment and Media*. Gurgaon, Haryana: India Brand Equity Foundation (IBEF).

"Race a Hit, Now Taare Zameen Par Heads for Pakistani Screens." 2008. *Indian Express*, March 26.

Rai, Amit S. 2009. *Untimely Bollywood: Globalization and India's New Media Assemblage*. Durham: Duke University Press.

Rajadhyaksha, Ashish. 2009. *Indian Cinema in the Time of Celluloid: From Bollywood to the Emergency*. New Delhi: Tulika Books.

———. 2003. "The 'Bollywoodization' of the Indian Cinema: Cultural Nationalism in a Global Arena." *Inter-Asia Cultural Studies* 4, no. 1, 25–39.

———. 1993. "The Epic Melodrama: Themes of Nationality in Indian Cinema." *Journal of Arts and Ideas*, nos. 25/26, 55–70.

———. 1992. "Buying Times." *Sight and Sound* 2, no. 3, 6.

———. 1986. "Neo-Traditionalism: Film as Popular Art in India." *Framework* 32/33, 20–67.

Rajagopal, Arvind. 2001. *Politics After Television: Hindu Nationalism and the Reshaping of the Public in India*. Cambridge: Cambridge University Press.

Rajagopalan, Sudha. 2008. *Indian Films in Soviet Cinema: The Culture of Movie-Going After Stalin*. Bloomington: Indiana University Press.

Ramachandran, T. M., ed. 1985. *70 Years of Indian Cinema (1913–1983)*. Bombay: CINEMA India-International.

———, ed. 1981. *50 Years of Indian Talkies (1931–1981)*. Bombay: Indian Academy of Motion Pictures Arts and Sciences.

Rangoonwalla, Firoze. 1995a. *A Hundred Years of Cinema in India: A Conspectus*. New Delhi: Ministry of Information and Broadcasting, Directorate of Advertising and Visual Publicity.

———. 1995b. *Bharat mein Cinema ke 100 Varsh: Ek Pariprekshya*. New Delhi: Ministry of Information and Broadcasting, Directorate of Advertising and Visual Publicity.

———. 1983. *Indian Cinema, Past and Present*. New Delhi: Clarion Books.

Raval, Sheela, and Anupama Chopra. 2001. "Body Blow." *India Today*, January 22.

"The Real Stab!" 2007 [1982]. *Film Information*, April 7.

Rofel, Lisa B. 1994. "Yearnings: Televisual Love and Melodramatic Politics in Contemporary China." *American Ethnologist* 21, no. 4, 700–722.

Roy, R. M., ed. 1956. *Sangeet Natak Akademi Film Seminar Report: 1955*. New Delhi: Sangeet Natak Akademi.

Rudner, David. 1994. *Caste and Capitalism in Colonial India*. Berkeley: University of California Press.

Saari, Anil. 1985. "A Critic's Notes." *The Hindi Film: Agent and Re-Agent of Cultural Change*, edited by Beatrix Pfleiderer and Lothar Lutze, 46–57. New Delhi: Manohar.

Sangari, Kumkum, and Sudesh Vaid. 1989. *Recasting Women:Essays in Colonial History*. New Delhi: Kali for Women.

Sanghvi, Vir. 2005. "Of Bites and Stings." *Mid-Day*, March 20.

Sarkar, Kobita. 1975. *Indian Cinema Today*. New Delhi: Sterling.

Sarkar, Sumit, and Tanika Sarkar. 2008. *Women and Social Reform in India*. Bloomington: Indiana University Press.

Schein, Louisa. 2002. "Mapping Hmong Media in Diasporic Space." *Media Worlds: Anthropology on New Terrain*, edited by Faye Ginsburg, Lila Abu-Lughod, and Brian Larkin, 229–44. Berkeley: University of California Press.

Seizer, Susan. 2005. *Stigmas of the Tamil Stage: An Ethnography of Special Drama Artists in South India*. Durham: Duke University Press.

Shah, Anand, and Shweta Boob. 2009. "Multiplex Sector Update." Angel Broking, April 16.

Sharma, Aradhana. 2008. *Logics of Empowerment: Development, Gender, and Governance in Neoliberal India*. Minneapolis: University of Minnesota Press.

Shetty-Saha, Shubha. 2009. "Karan Johar and SRK Sign Deal with Fox Star." *DNA* (Daily News and Analysis), August 6.

Shoesmith, Brian. 1988. "Swadeshi Cinema: Cinema, Politics and Culture: The Writings of D.G. Phalke." *Continuum* 2, no. 1, 44–73.

———. 1987. "From Monopoly to Commodity: The Bombay Studios in the 1930s." *History On/And/In Film*, edited by Tom O' Regan and Brian Shoesmith, 68–75. Perth: History and Film Association of Australia.

Shringar Cinemas Limited. 2005. "Red Herring Prospectus." March 18.

Singh, Khushwant. 1976. "We Sell Them Dreams." *New York Times Magazine*, October 30.

Sinha, Ashish. 2009. "Fox Bags Rights for My Name Is Khan in Rs. 100 Crore Deal." *Business Standard*, July 28.

Sinha, Mrinalini. 2006. *Specters of Mother India: The Global Restructuring of an Empire*. Durham: Duke University Press.

Skeggs, Beverly. 1997. *Formations of Class and Gender*. London: Sage.

Someshwar, Savera R., and Saisuresh Sivaswamy. 2007. "I Wish to Always Be Remembered." *rediff.com*, February 15.

Spitulnik, Debra. 2002. "Mobile Machines and Fluid Audiences: Rethinking Reception through Zambian Radio Culture." *Media Worlds: Anthropology on New Terrain*, edited by Faye D. Ginsburg, Lila Abu-Lughod, and Brian Larkin, 337–54. Berkeley: University of California Press.

Srinivas, S. V. 2009. *Megastar: Chiranjeevi and Telugu Cinema after N.T. Rama Rao*. New Delhi: Oxford University Press.

Strassler, Karen. 2010. *Refracted Visions: Popular Photography and National Modernity in Java*. Durham: Duke University Press.

Strathern, Marilyn. 1992. *After Nature: English Kinship in the Late 20th Century*. Cambridge: Cambridge University Press.

Tandon, Tina. 2002. "Cool aur Kaante." *Economic Times*, June 4.

Taylor, Charles. 1992. "The Politics of Recognition." *Multiculturalism and the Politics of Recognition*, edited by Amy Guttman, 25–73. Princeton: Princeton University Press.

Taylor, Charles. 2007. "Star of India. Review of King of Bollywood: Shah Rukh Khan and the Seductive World of Indian Cinema." *New York Times Book Review*, October 7.

Thomas, Rosie. 1995. "Melodrama and the Negotiation of Morality in Mainstream Hindi Film." *Consuming Modernity: Public Culture in a South Asian World*, edited by Carol A. Breckenridge, 157–82. Minneapolis: University of Minnesota Press.

———. 1985. "Indian Cinema, Pleasures and Popularity." *Screen* 26, nos. 3/4, 116–31.

Tidwell, Blair. 2010. "Manhattan Masala: Indian dance classes get kids grooving to Bollywood beats." *Time Out New York: Kids*, March.

"Time to Don the Mantle." 2003. *Financial Express*, October 21.

Timmons, Heather. 2008. "Bollywood Goes to Hollywood, Seeking Bargains." *New York Times*, June 23.

"Top Billing for Veterans in Bollywood Procession." 1996. *Indian Express*, July 1.

Traube, Elizabeth. 1996. Introduction to *Making and Selling Culture*, edited by Richard Ohmann, xi–xxiii. Hanover, N.H.: Wesleyan University Press.

Uberoi, Patricia. 2001. "Imagining the Family: An Ethnography of Viewing *Hum Aapke Hain Koun . . . !*" *Pleasure and the Nation: The History, Politics and Consumption of Public Culture in India*, edited by Rachel Dwyer and Christopher Pinney, 309–51. Delhi: Oxford University Press.

Upala, KBR. 2009. "Amitabh Gets World Economic Forum's Crystal Award." *Mid-Day*, January 30.

Upala, KBR, and Zahra Khan. 2005. "Shakti's journey from fame to shame." *Mid-Day*, March 14.

Valicha, Kishore. 1988. *The Moving Image: A Study of Indian Cinema*. Bombay: Orient Longman.

Vasudev, Aruna. 1986. *The New Indian Cinema*. Delhi: Macmillan India.

Vasudev, Aruna, and Phillippe Lenglet, eds. 1983. *Indian Cinema Superbazaar*. Delhi: Vikas.

Vasudevan, Ravi. 2010. *The Melodramatic Public: Film Form and Spectatorship in Indian Cinema*. New Delhi: Permanent Black.

———. 2008. "The Meanings of 'Bollywood.'" *Journal of the Moving Image* 7 (December).

———. 2000, ed. *Making Meaning in Indian Cinema*. New Delhi: Oxford University Press.

———. 1995. "Addressing the Spectator of a 'Third World' National Cinema: The Bombay 'Social' Film of the 1940s and 1950s." *Screen* 36, no. 4, 305–34.

———. 1990. "Indian Commercial Cinema." *Screen* 31, no. 4, 446–53.

———. 1989. "The Melodramatic Mode and the Commercial Hindi Cinema: Notes on Film History, Narrative and Performance." *Screen* 30, no. 3, 29–50.

Venkatesan, V. 2005. "Public Interest vs. Privacy" *Frontline*, April 23–May 6.

Verma, Suparn. 1997. "The Hit Squad." *rediff.com*, July 18.

Vicziany, Marika. 2005. "The Indian Economy in the Twenty-First Century: The Tough Questions That Just Won't Go Away." *South Asia: Journal of South Asian Studies* 28, no. 2, 211–32.

Virdi, Jyotika. 2003. *The Cinematic Imagination: Indian Popular Films as Social History.* New Brunswick, N.J.: Rutgers University Press.

Vitali, Valentina. 2008. *Hindi Action Cinema: Industries, Narratives, Bodies.* New Delhi: Oxford University Press.

Walker, Tim. 2009. "All You Need to Know About Slumdog Millionaire." *Independent*, January 21.

Weber, Max. 1947. *The Theory of Social and Economic Organization.* Edited with an introduction by Talcott Parsons. New York: Free Press.

Weidman, Amanda J. 2006. *Singing the Classical, Voicing the Modern: The Postcolonial Politics of Music in South India.* Durham: Duke University Press.

"Why no Universally Appealing Film?" 2009. *Film Information*, October 10.

Wilkinson-Weber, Clare. 2006. "The Dressman's Line: Transforming the Work of Costumers in Popular Hindi Film." *Anthropological Quarterly* 79, no. 4, 581–608.

———. 2005. "Behind the Seams: Designers and Tailors in Popular Hindi Cinema." *Visual Anthropology Review* 20, no. 2, 3–21.

Willemen, Paul. 1994. *Looks and Frictions: Essays in Cultural Studies and Film Theory.* London: British Film Institute.

Williams, Raymond. 1983. *Keywords: A Vocabulary of Culture and Society.* Revised edition. New York: Oxford University Press.

World Bank. 2009. "PPP and Exchange Rates." International Comparison Program, World Bank. http://web.worldbank.org.

Wyatt, Andrew. 2005. "Building the Temples of Postmodern India: Economic Constructions of National Identity." *Contemporary South Asia* 14, no. 4, 465–80.

Wyatt, Kristen. 2009. "Bollywood-style dance classes drawing big crowds." Associated Press, February 19.

Yanagisako, Sylvia. 2002. *Producing Culture and Capital: Family Firms in Italy.* Princeton: Princeton University Press.

Yang, Mayfair Mei. 1994. "Film Discussion Groups in China: State Discourse or a Plebian Public Sphere?" *Visual Anthropology Review* 10, no. 1, 112–25.

Yang, Mayfair Mei-hui. 2002. "Mass Media and Transnational Subjectivity in Shanghai: Notes on (Re)Cosmopolitanism in a Chinese Metropolis." *Media Worlds: Anthropology on New Terrain*, edited by Faye D. Ginsburg, Lila Abu-Lughod, and Brian Larkin, 189–210. Berkeley: University of California Press.

"Your Ticket to Blockbuster Return." 2010. Cinema Capital Venture Fund Quarterly Newsletter, March (http://www.cinemacapitalindia.com).

Zafirau, Stephen. 2009a. "Audience Knowledge and the Everyday Lives of Cultural Producers in Hollywood." *Production Studies: Cultural Studies of Media Industries*, edited by Vicki Mayer, Miranda J. Banks, and John Thornton Caldwell, 190–202. New York: Routledge.

———. 2009b. "Imagined Audiences: Intuitive and Technical Knowledge in Hollywood." PhD diss. University of Southern California.

Interviews by Author

Adarsh, Taran. 1996. September 29: Bombay.
Akhtar, Javed. 1996. November 25: Bombay.
Anand, Mukul. 1996. June 22: Bombay.
Bajaj, Raj Kumar. 2006. May 12: Bombay.
Barjatya, Rajjat. 1996. April 29: Bombay.
Bhagnani, Vashu 2000. October 29: Bombay.
Bhatt, Mukesh 2000. October 18: Bombay.
———. 1996. October 10: Bombay.
Bhatt, Vikram. 2006. January 5: New York.
———. 1999. March 7: Email.
Bhaumick, Sachin. 1996. October 15: Bombay.
Chaubey, Abhishek. 2010. September 22: New York.
Chopra, Aditya. 1996. April 2: Bombay.
Chopra, B. R. 1996. August 7, 12, 14: Bombay.
Chopra, Pamela. 1996, February 28; March 26: Bombay.
Damani, Lala. 2000. October 20: Bombay.
Dixit, Madhuri. 1996. November 25, 26: Bombay.
D'Souza, Nester. 2006. May 12: Bombay.
———. 1996. June 14: Bombay.
Dutt, Sanjay. 1996. May 6: Bombay.
Ghai, Subhash. 2000. October 25: Bombay.
———. 1996. December 7, 10: Bombay.
Ghai-Puri, Meghna. 2006. May 10: Bombay.
Gupta, Sutanu. 1996. November 2, 18: Bombay.
Irani, Honey. 1996. May 5: Bombay.
Iyer, Meena. 1996. August 11: Bombay.
Jaffery, Rumi. 1996. November 22: Bombay.
Jhulka, Ayesha. 1996. May 28, 29: Bombay.
Kanakia, Rashesh. 2006. May 15: Bombay.
Kapoor, Shashi. 1996. August 6, 8: Bombay.
Khan, Aamir. 1996. March 23: Bombay.
Khan, Mansoor. 1996. April 1, 4: Bombay.
Khan, Shah Rukh. 1996. March 15, 20, 21: Bombay.
Khanna, Amit. 1996. June 28: Bombay.
Kharabanda, Punkej. 1996. April 17, 22: Bombay.
Koirala, Manisha. 1996. May 23, 24: Bombay.
Mohan, R. 1996. May 20: Bombay.
Nadiadwala, Firoz. 2000. October 20: Bombay.
Nahta, Komal. 1996. September 30: Bombay.
Nihalani, Govind. 2006. May 12: Bombay.
Rajabali, Anjum. 2006. May 11: Bombay.
———. 2005. January 12: Bombay.
———. 2000. October 20: Bombay.
———. 1996. September 14: Bombay.
Roshan, Rakesh. 1996. May 21: Bombay.
Roy, Sharmishta. 2000. October 26: Bombay.

Shroff, Shravan. 2006. May 9: Bombay.

Shroff, Shyam. 2006. May 9: Bombay.

———. 2005. January 14: Bombay.

———. 2000. October 22: Bombay.

———. 1996. April 13: Bombay.

Sippy, G. P. 1996. September 22, October 14, December 9: Bombay.

Sippy, Ramesh. 1996. April 25, June 25, July 8: Bombay.

Subramaniam, Chitra. 2006. May 11: Bombay.

box-office outcomes, 86–87, 342; of *Lamhe*
(Moments), 9–11, 343; multiplexes' impact on, 349–50; ticket prices' impact
on, 345–46, 369 n. 17. *See also* commercial outcomes

cable television. *See* television
casting couch, 119–24, 140
celebrity, 208. *See also* stardom; stars
Central Board of Film Certification, 13, 31,
370 n. 35
Chakrabarty, Dipesh, 318
Chopra, Aditya, 95, 106–8, 143–47, 266,
285–86, 296, 303, 310–14, 366, 382
n. 28. See also *Dilwale Dulhaniya Le
Jayenge*
Chopra, Pamela, 132–33, 147–48, 199–200,
219, 224–25, 237, 284–85
cinema: as economic activity, 63–73; economic imaginary and, 75; as national
heritage, 59–63; perception as non-
Indian, 57; as social problem, 58; state
commemoration of, 60–61; state perceptions of, 56–58; state policies supporting, 65; as vice in India, 53. *See also*
Bollywood; Hindi cinema; Hindi film
industry; multiplex theaters; single-
screen theaters
cinema hall, 73, 112–15, 319, 376 n. 43;
absence of elite viewers in, 90; spatial hierarchies inside, 10, 97, 390 n. 8;
ticket prices, 10, 336. *See also* multiplex
theaters; single-screen theaters
cinema history: in India, 50, 59–60
circulation. *See* film circulation
class: in the cinema hall, 97, 319, 336; representations of, 98–100
commercial outcomes, 40, 23, 87, 183–89;
determined by distributors, 286–91;
measures of, 114–15, 190–91, 270, 283,
302–3, 351–53; as social barometer,
282–90. *See also* box office; proposal-
makers; universal hit
corporatization, 11, 35, 70–73, 224–25,
246–48; critiques of, 273–78; as disciplinary mechanism, 262; failures of,
262–65, 273–75, 392 nn. 25–26; as mode
of distinction, 259–70
courtesans, 16, 121–26, 318 n. 11; as property owners, 318 n. 12

cultural capital, 33, 200
culture. *See* production culture; work
culture

Dabangg, 363–64, 400 n. 15
diasporic audiences, 10–12, 100–101,
321–25
diasporic film markets, 186–90, 291–95,
319–28, 341, 350–55, 396 n. 2. *See also*
Overseas Territory
Dilwale Dulhaniya Le Jayenge (The Braveheart Will Take the Bride), 90–93,
101–2, 289–93, 301; box-office outcome
interpretations, 303, 341; commercial
success of, 93. *See also* Khan, Shah Rukh
disdain: toward audiences, 7–9, 86, 117–
21; distinction through, 301–6, 345;
Hindi film industry target of, 7–9,
14–16, 77–79, 90, 240–41; proposal-
makers target of, 182
distinction, 88–89, 185, 216; through the
"bound script," 215–16, 223; through
"coolness," 33, 79–80, 117–18, 316, 364
n. 22; through corporatization, 259–70;
through film stock usage, 234–35; of
Hindi filmmakers, 240–41; multiplex
cinema production of, 113–17; practices
of, 70; through sentiments of disdain,
301–6, 345; through technology, 50,
217, 233–39
distributors: as creative constraint, 354;
decreasing power of, 327–28; as determinant of commercial success, 27,
190–91, 376; expectations of commercial outcome by, 286–88, 313; as funding source for film industry, 186; and
territories, 290–92, 317–23. *See also*
Overseas Territory; winner's curse
Dixit, Madhuri, 91, 123, 135–45, 209, 382
n. 27

economic liberalization, 18, 43, 58, 202
elites, 78; of Hindi film industry, 27; perceptions of, 88
ethnicity, 106–8
ethnography, 22–24, 382 n. 1

facework, 122, 138, 144, 145
family: filmic representations of, 99–100,
306, 319–20; and respectability, 121, 125

Hindi film industry (*continued*)
production culture of, 21–22, 229–33; respectability of, 16–17, 34–35, 70–75, 121–33; social networks in, 31, 191–97; social norms in, 21, 203–5; social relations in, 155; state ambivalence about, 49–50; state policies toward, 17–18, 33, 42–55, 64; state support of, 51; state taxation of, 52, 54–55; stigma attached to, 124; structures in, 213; success in, 114–15, 302–3, 350–51; symbolic significance of, 62, 69; technological fetishization in, 235–36, 239; uncertainty in, 9–12, 244–47; understandings of consumption, 286–89, 291; use of technology in, 235–36; video technology impact on, 72, 94; work culture of, 156, 215–16, 225–27. *See also* corporatization

Hindi filmmakers, 4, 368 n. 6, 368 n. 9; social status of, 148–50, 185; social worlds of, 103–9

Hindi film set, 27–28, 202–8; ethnographic sketch of, 156–74; and hierarchy, 123, 202–5; as quasi-public space, 29, 217–21

hits/flops, 191, 276, 285, 313. *See also* box-office outcome; commercial outcome

Hollywood: contrasts with Bollywood, 236–41; film production norms in, 176; Hindi filmmakers understanding of, 237–39, 311; in Indian mediascape, 62–63, 377 n. 2; interactions with Bollywood, 216, 359–63

Hum Aapke Hain Koun! (What Do I Mean to You!), 90–98, 100, 257–58, 378 nn. 17–18; box-office outcome interpretations, 114–15, 287–301, 325, 341; commercial success of, 20, 93; distribution strategy of, 287–88, 379 n. 20, 389 n. 9; as first Hindi film with four-track optical stereo sound, 236. *See also* Barjatya, Sooraj

Indian state. *See* state

industry status: announcement of, 41–43, 65–67; impact of, 69–74, 121, 225, 265, 357

intersubjectivity, 33, 79, 117

Johar, Karan, 81–82, 103–8, 203–4, 220–23, 352–357, 359–62. *See also Kuch Kuch Hota Hai; My Name is Khan*

Khan, Aamir, 81, 143–47, 199, 218–19, 229–30, 238, 286, 365, 386 n. 30. *See also Lagaan*

Khan, Shah Rukh, 1–2, 88–92, 101–5, 116, 141–45, 194–95, 239–40, 286, 359–65. *See also Dilwale Dulhaniya Le Jayenge; My Name is Khan*

Khanna, Amit, 63, 84, 140, 261–63

kin networks: in Hindi film industry, 194–202

knowledge: as industry ideology, 245, 347–49

Koirala, Manisha, 138–39, 145–46

Kuch Kuch Hota Hai (Something Happens), 104–5, 396 n. 6, 398 n. 25. *See also* Johar, Karan; Khan, Shah Rukh

Lagaan (Land Tax), 81, 227–29, 328, 386 n. 30; as first Hindi film shot in synchronous sound, 236; global success of, 388 n. 17. *See also* Khan, Aamir

Lamhe (Moments), 84–85, 94–96, 301–13; commercial outcome of, 86, 300; interpretations of, 284–85, 306–8, 342

liberalization, economic, 18, 43, 58, 202, 368 n. 7

Love Sex aur Dhokha (Love, Sex, and Betrayal), 364–65

love story, 92–93, 306; filmic representations of, 99; perceptions of, 159, 162. *See also Hum Aapke Hain Koun!; Lamhe*

Luimère Brothers, 59–61

mahurat: as magical rite, 248–50

Malinowski, Bronislaw, 247–48, 250–51, 389 n. 3

mass audience, 7–8, 95–96, 296, 300, 314, 355–58

mass media: role in state projects, 42–43; state policies toward, 17–18

media anthropology, 21–23; Hindi film industry as research site for, 25–27

mediascape, 18, 62–63; Bollywood's distinctiveness in, 252–53; in India, 96, 106, 324–25; transformations of, 2–3,

single-screen theaters (*continued*)
at, 345; sizes of, 9–10; spatial hierarchy in, 295; taxation of, 71–73, 376 n. 45; ticket prices, 336–37; viewing experience at, 338–40

social respectability. *See* respectability

songs: commercial significance of, 246, 253–55, 326–28; as distinctive feature of Bollywood, 251–59; as production fiction, 257–59

spatial politics, 217

spectatorship, 283–85

stardom, 200; definition of, 208; gendered dimensions of, 159, 209

stars, 207–13, 261–62; as central to the production process, 34–35, 208–9, 223; cost of, 393 n. 34; gendered dimension of, 210–11; as mode or risk management, 271–73; production of, 26, 212

state: cultural policies of, 52, 58, 67; developmentalist policies of, 48; filmmaking policies of, 41–43, 56; industry status granted by, 41–43, 65–67, 69–74, 265; taxation of film industry by, 54; television policies of, 372 n. 2

studios: and demise of the studio system, 5; as gendered space, 125–26; only as production facilities, 6

success-talk, 250–51

symbolic capital, 2–4, 15, 27, 31, 88, 316, 355; of stars, 200–202

synchronized sound: in Hindi cinema, 227–28

television, 256, 371 nn. 3–4; competition for audiences, 83, 94–95, 113–17, 289; as revenue source for film industry, 84, 263; as untaxed by the state, 55

theaters. *See* cinema hall; multiplex theaters; single-screen theaters

uncertainty: of film finances, 189–90; as key process in production culture, 9–12, 244–47

universal hit, 283, 358; diminished significance of, 351–55

video, 82; impact on film industry, 72, 189, 379 n. 20, 384 n. 11

video piracy, 24–25, 82, 93–94, 384 nn. 11–12

viewing experience, 110–17; at video parlors, 82–83. *See also* cinema hall; multiplex theaters

winner's curse, 191

women, 130; in Hindi cinema, 120–25. *See also* actresses; gender

work culture, 22, 240–45; of the Hindi film industry, 156, 215–16, 225–27, 59; as oral, 222–25

Working Group on National Film Policy, 56–60, 74, 178–84, 372 n. 4

Tejaswini Ganti is an associate professor of anthropology at New York University. She is the author of *Bollywood: A Guidebook to Popular Hindi Cinema* (Routledge, 2004).

Library of Congress Cataloging-in-Publication Data
Ganti, Tejaswini.
Producing Bollywood : inside the contemporary Hindi film industry /
Tejaswini Ganti.
p. cm.
Includes bibliographical references and index.
ISBN 978-0-8223-5202-0 (cloth : alk. paper)
ISBN 978-0-8223-5213-6 (pbk. : alk. paper)
1. Includes index. 2. Motion picture industry — India — Bombay.
3. Motion pictures, Hindi — India — Bombay. I. Title.
PN1993.5.I8G27 2012
791.430954'792 — dc23   2011035964